The Motet in the Age of Du Fay

During the lifetime of Guillaume Du Fay (*c.* 1400–1474) the motet underwent a profound transformation. Because of the protean nature of the motet during this period, problems of definition have always stood in the way of a full understanding of this crucial shift. Through a comprehensive survey of the surviving repertory, Julie Cumming shows that the motet is best understood on the level of the subgenre. She employs new ideas about categories taken from cognitive psychology and evolutionary theory to illuminate the process by which the subgenres of the motet arose and evolved. One important finding is the nature and extent of the crucial role that English music played in the genre's transformation. Cumming provides a close reading of many little-known pieces; she also shows how Du Fay's motets were the product of sophisticated experimentation with generic boundaries.

JULIE E. CUMMING is Associate Professor of Music at McGill University, Montreal.

The Motet in the Age of Du Fay

Julie E. Cumming

CAMBRIDGE
UNIVERSITY PRESS

PUBLISHED BY THE PRESS SYNDICATE OF THE UNIVERSITY OF CAMBRIDGE
The Pitt Building, Trumpington Street, Cambridge, United Kingdom

CAMBRIDGE UNIVERSITY PRESS
The Edinburgh Building, Cambridge CB2 2RU, UK   http://www.cup.cam.ac.uk
40 West 20th Street, New York, NY 10011–4211, USA   http://www.cup.org
10 Stamford Road, Oakleigh, Melbourne 3166, Australia

First published 1999

Printed in the United Kingdom at the University Press, Cambridge

Typeset in Monotype Janson 11/14 pt. in QuarkXPress®   [SE]

A catalogue record for this book is available from the British Library

Library of Congress cataloguing in publication data

Cumming, Julie Emelyn.
    The motet in the age of Du Fay / Julie E. Cumming.
      p.   cm.
    Includes bibliographical references and index.
    ISBN 0 521 47377 2 (hardback)
      1. Motet – 15th century.   2. Dufay, Guillaume, d. 1474.   Motets.
    I. Title.
    ML3275.C86 1999
    782.2′6′09031–dc21   98–44114   CIP   MN

ISBN 0 521 47377 2 hardback

Contents

v

Contents

Tables

Musical examples

List of music examples

x

Acknowledgments

My initial debt is to my teachers – Richard Taruskin, Richard Crocker, Daniel Heartz, Anthony Newcomb, and Joseph Kerman. Something from each of them is in this book. Thanks to Laurence Dreyfus, who helped me start thinking about genre and told me to read Alastair Fowler. Some of the ideas in chapter 3 were first developed in a seminar with James Haar at Berkeley in 1983. Early drafts of material in the book were presented at National Meetings of the American Musicological Society (Oakland 1990, Pittsburgh 1992, and New York 1995); at Wellesley College, June 1993; and at the 27th International Congress on Medieval Studies, Kalamazoo, Michigan, May 1992. I have received helpful comments on early versions of portions of this book from Michael Allsen, Margaret Bent, David Fallows, Richard Taruskin, and Rob Wegman. Michael Allsen graciously sent me a copy of his dissertation, an invaluable aid to my research. Joshua Rifkin and Margaret Bent sent me copies of unpublished articles. Many thanks to the staffs of the Wellesley College Music Library and the Marvin Duchow Music Library at McGill University; special thanks to David Curtis and Cynthia Leive at McGill. My "motet seminar" at McGill forced me to refine and clarify many of my ideas, and I am also grateful to my students for their help in data collection. Thanks to my former student and Montreal friend Miriam Tees for collating my many bibliographies. My sister Susanna Cumming gave me some helpful references from linguistics. Anthony Newcomb and Jeffrey Kallberg invited me to submit my initial proposal to Cambridge, for which I am very grateful; Penny Souster, my Cambridge editor, has been understanding about my many delays. Ann Lewis, my copy-editor, and Caroline Murray, my Production controller, were both a pleasure to work with.

Acknowledgments

Thanks to my friend and colleague Peter Schubert for many stimulating conversations about Renaissance music over the years and for a crucial reading of the antepenultimate draft that eliminated many *longeurs*. Thanks to Thomas Brothers, a fellow enthusiast of the fifteenth century and friend since graduate school, who read the penultimate draft of the book and made many helpful suggestions. Thanks to Lars T. Lih for help with Latin translations, discussions about Darwinian evolution, careful reading of the book at many stages, unstinting help with child care, and unwavering moral support.

Any faults that remain despite all this help are my own. The book is dedicated to my family: Lars, Emelyn, and Ariadne Lih.

Notes to the reader

Pitch notation

Where the octave is relevant, specific pitches are indicated in the text according to the terminology of the Guidonian gamut:

[DD EE FF] GG A B C D E F G a b **c** d e f g aa bb cc dd ee [ff gg]
                              *

* = middle C

Musical examples

Musical examples for which manuscript and folios are given are new transcriptions that I made from microfilm or facsimile of that manuscript. Musical examples for which a modern edition is given are derived from that edition. I have regularized the transcriptions in all the musical examples without comment, according to the following principles:

- The final long is transcribed as a breve in all examples.
- Most examples in Part II (chapters 4–6) use a 4:1 reduction ratio of note values (semibreve = quarter note in the transcription).
- Most examples in Part III (chapters 9–12) use a 2:1 reduction ratio of note values (semibreve = half note in the transcription).
- Where the reduction ratios are different from those given above, the note value equivalencies are shown.
- In complete pieces original clefs, mensuration signs, ligatures, and coloration are indicated. In excerpts these signs are usually omitted, except when they have some relevance to the discussion.

Abbreviations for modern editions and manuscripts in the captions are those used in the Index of works and are listed in Modern editions of music and Sources and sigla.

Index of works

This index gives the sources, modern editions, and subgenre assignments of all the motets listed by name in the book, as well as related Masses and chansons that receive some discussion.

Bibliographical abbreviations (see also Modern editions of music)

AH	Guido Maria Dreves and Clemens Blume, eds. *Analecta Hymnica Medii Aevi.* 52 vols. Leipzig, 1886–1909. *Register*, ed. Max Lütolf. 2 vols. Berne and Munich: Francke, 1978.
DTÖ	Denkmäler der Tonkunst in Österreich. Vienna: Artaria.
EDM	Das Erbe deutscher Musik. Leipzig: Breitkopf & Härtel.
EECM	Early English Church Music. London: Stainer and Bell.
MGG	Friedrich Blume, ed. *Die Musik in Geschichte und Gegenwart.* 17 vols. Kassel: Bärenreiter, 1949–86.
NG	Stanley Sadie, ed. *The New Grove Dictionary of Music and Musicians.* 20 vols. London: Macmillan, 1980.
REM	Reinhard Strohm. *The Rise of European Music, 1380–1500.* Cambridge: Cambridge University Press, 1993.

Abbreviations for music manuscripts and prints: see Sources and sigla

Abbreviations for musical terms

A	antiphon
B	bassus
cpf	*cantus prius factus*
Ct.	contratenor
D	discantus
Mot.	motetus
N	new text
R	responsory
SoS	*Song of Songs*
S	sequence
T	tenor
Trip.	triplum

Spelling of composers' names

I have chosen in several cases to use spellings different from those found in most dictionaries and library catalogues. The scholars who have worked on these composers believe that the standard spellings are not true to the documents. My decision to follow their lead was made in recognition of these scholars' research.

Du Fay (not Dufay), as advocated by Alejandro Planchart
Dunstaple (not Dunstable), as advocated by Margaret Bent
Busnoys (not Busnois), as advocated by Richard Taruskin
Puyllois (not Pullois), as advocated by Pamela Starr

Introduction

The age of Du Fay (*c.* 1400–1474) was a time of transition. Viewed both as the late Middle Ages and the early Renaissance, the fifteenth century saw the continuation of the fourteenth-century chanson in the *formes fixes* and the birth of the new genre of the Mass Ordinary cycle. In the motet – the genre that occupies a middle position between the chanson and the Mass both in terms of size and place in the genre hierarchy – we see both continuity and change: while the fifteenth-century motet had strong roots in the fourteenth-century motet, it also underwent a radical transformation of style, text types, and texture over the course of the century. Study of the motet provides a unique view into the musical world of the fifteenth century.

Two related problems make study of the fifteenth-century motet difficult. The first is the radical transformation of the genre: from the late medieval motet to the motet of the Josquin generation – from a motet in which several new texts are sung simultaneously over a slow-moving tenor, to a motet in which a single pre-existent liturgical text is sung by all voices in a homogeneous contrapuntal texture.[1] This transformation is not well understood. For the crucial decades around the middle of the century most of the surviving motets are anonymous, and many are not yet available in modern edition. Du Fay seems to have focused his compositional energies in this period on liturgical chant settings, especially Mass Proper cycles, and then on the new four-voice tenor Mass. There is thus a gaping hole in our history of the genre: the question of how we got from early Du Fay to Josquin has gone unanswered.[2]

The second problem is one of definition. How do we decide which fifteenth-century compositions are motets? Contemporary definitions of the term are extremely vague and there is little scholarly consensus in the twentieth century on the nature and function of the fifteenth-century motet: the boundary with liturgical music is especially problematic.[3] At one end of the spectrum are the scholars who use "motet" loosely as a catch-all term for the many kinds of Latin-texted polyphonic music other than the Mass; on the other end are the scholars who treat the "motet" as a residual category, containing only pieces without pre-existent liturgical texts (i.e. with new texts, or pre-existent texts whose original genre or function is difficult to identify).[4] The closest thing to a definition of the motet in terms of shared characteristics – a through-composed composition with a sacred Latin text – is both too broad and too narrow: many pieces answering to this definition are not motets (such as Mass movements or Vespers antiphon settings), while some fifteenth-century motets have secular or vernacular texts. Even when we limit ourselves to pieces in motet sections of generically organized manuscripts such as Bologna Q15 we find a bewildering variety of styles, textures, and text types. The problem is compounded by the transformation of the genre: a definition that applies to one decade may not apply to the next.

If we try to define the motet in terms of function the problems are just as great.[5] The little evidence we have suggests that motets were used in numerous contexts, almost none of them liturgically prescribed: as filler during Mass or at Vespers; for special devotional services for the Virgin Mary; during processions or while welcoming visiting dignitaries; or as recreational music for voices and instruments to be performed in the home. In the sixteenth century, and surely before, motets were performed during dinner in the papal chambers.[6] Part of the genre's *raison d'être* seems to have been a kind of functional indeterminism which makes clear definition almost impossible.

The transformation of the motet and the difficulty of defining it lead to other problems. The failure to understand the changes in the motet is a failure to understand central issues of music history in the fifteenth century such as the role of English music, the development of homogeneous four-voice textures, and the expanding role of polyphony. The lack of a coherent definition of the genre makes it almost impossible to interpret individual works: without a basis for comparison, extensive knowledge of repertory, and a set of generic expectations we cannot tell if a work is normal or unusual, innovative or traditional, central or peripheral. Nor can we identify its field of reference – to the history of the genre, to other genres and to specific compositions.

In attempting to solve these problems I have drawn on ideas from a variety of disciplines; my basic methodology is laid out in Part I (chapters 1–3). In thinking about problems of definition I have turned to category theory in the fields of cognitive psychology and linguistics (chapter 1). In thinking about change and transformation over time I have turned to concepts deriving from Darwinian evolution, especially the ideas of descent with modification and of selection pressures (chapter 1). In thinking about genre and interpretation I have turned to literary criticism (chapters 1 and 2). I have also considered evidence about the motet from fifteenth-century sources: treatises, archival documents, and music manuscripts (chapter 3). My approach centers on the idea of the subgenre. While a coherent definition of the genre as a whole is impossible, it is possible to sort the genre into identifiable subgenres (see Table C.1 and "Notes on the index of works" for a complete list). The subgenres are categories that can be structured in different ways. Tracing the origins, extinctions, and evolution of the subgenres allows us to track the transformation of the genre as a whole over the course of the century. At the same time, the subgenre provides a set of generic expectations and a field of reference for the individual work, allowing us to identify its generic references, interpret its meaning and tone, and position it in the genre hierarchy.

The bulk of the book, therefore, is devoted to establishing and discussing the various subgenres of the motet. I discuss many individual works in some detail, both as examples of their subgenres and as subjects for interpretation. Many of these works are little known, and some have never before been published in reliable modern editions; when space allows, I include complete transcriptions. In Part II (chapters 4–7) I deal with the first third of the fifteenth century, and focus on the contents of the motet section of Bologna Q15 (*c.* 1420–1435). In Part III (chapters 8–12) I treat the second and third quarters of the century, and focus on the major mid-century sources for the motet: the Trent Codices (*c.* 1429–1477) and Modena X.1.11 (*c.* 1448). I have compared these repertories with the motets in the other major contemporary manuscripts. I have therefore considered virtually the complete surviving repertory of motets copied during the first three-quarters of the fifteenth century, for a total of over four hundred compositions (those mentioned by name in the book are listed in the "Index of Works").[7] The result is a detailed portrait of the evolution and transformation of the motet over Du Fay's lifetime. The portrait includes an account of some of the internal and external forces that may have influenced the transformation of the motet and of fifteenth-century music more generally. At the same time, the book provides a method for the interpretation of individual works and some of the background knowledge required to apply it.

Part I:

Models and methods

1 Approaches and analogies

The motet in the fifteenth century poses problems of categorization, genre and history. What kind of a category is the motet in the fifteenth century? How can a genre have any communicative function when it is so amorphous? How can we explain its transformation over the course of the century? While searching for an approach or methodology that would allow me to deal with these problems, I read Alastair Fowler's useful discussion of literary genre theory, *Kinds of Literature* (1982). I was struck in particular by one passage:

Just as "lyric" has assimilated other short poetic kinds, making them all subgenres of lyric, so "the novel" has assimilated other kinds of prose fiction. A genre so comprehensive can have but a weak unitary force. Indeed the novel has largely ceased to function as a kind [genre] in the ordinary way.[1]

"Yes!" I said – "that's just like the motet" – and I immediately adapted Fowler's passage to make it apply:

The motet in the fifteenth century assimilated many of the kinds of Latin-texted polyphony. A genre so comprehensive can have but a weak unitary force. Indeed the motet largely ceased to function as a genre in the ordinary way.

Fowler's quotation continues:

Its minimal specification has even been stated as "an extended piece of prose fiction" – a specification in which external form appears, but only as "extended" and "prose." Within this enormous field, the novel in a stronger sense – the verisimilar novel of Austen and Thackeray, which many would consider the central tradition – is now only one of several equipollent forms.

This could be adapted as well:

In its minimal specification, as stated by Tinctoris – "a composition of moderate length, to which words of any kind are set, but more often those of a sacred nature" – external form

7

appears, but only as "moderate length" and "often sacred." Within this enormous field, the motet in a stronger sense – the motet with long-note cantus firmus, as in Vitry, Du Fay, and even Josquin, which many would consider the central tradition – became only one of several equipollent forms.

In such a situation, says Fowler, "we find the status of subgenres . . . enhanced."[2] He goes on to discuss the origins of the novel:

For the novel has ramifying roots in earlier fiction and nonfiction: epic, romance, picaresque, biography, history, journal, letter, exemplary tale, novella, to name only the most obvious. These filiations have persisted in the developed novel, giving rise in some instances to distinct subgenres. But the subgenres have only very gradually been acknowledged by critical thought.[3]

Once again this can be transformed into a description of the fifteenth-century motet:

It has ramifying roots in earlier motet types and in other genres: in the French isorhythmic motet, in English and Italian motet types, in liturgical chant settings, Mass Ordinary movements, the English cantilena, even the chanson. These filiations persisted in the later fifteenth-century motet, giving rise in some instances to distinct subgenres. But the subgenres have barely been acknowledged by critical thought.

The analogy with the novel tells us that the status of the subgenre is enhanced in the motet, and takes on some of the normal characteristics of genre, such as recognizable external form and a complex of associations and expectations.[4] In order to make generic sense of the motet we must first identify its subgenres, and subgenre identification will be the center of this study. It is at the level of the subgenre that identification and interpretation of the "genre" become possible; as we learn to recognize the different types of motet, we will also develop associations and expectations to bring to individual works.

Fowler implies that one way to sort out subgenres is to trace their "ramifying roots" or "filiations." The roots of a subgenre can also be understood as its ancestors or forebears; this image in turn suggests analogies with a family, or, more generally, with biology and the "descent of species." In thinking about the historical processes that genres undergo, Fowler finds biological analogies illuminating, as do I. Many literary critics emphasize the role of generic mixture in generic change; we could compare this process to marriage and procreation, or to hybridization.[5]

Biological and evolutionary analogies for generic change have frequently been attacked in the field of literary criticism.[6] Fowler was almost alone in defending them until recently, when David Fishelov came out with a spirited defense of both family and biological analogies for genre in his *Metaphors of Genre: The Role of Analogies in Genre Theory* (1993). Fishelov begins with a defense of analogy and metaphor in theoretical or scientific discourse in general; he stresses the fact that metaphor is fundamental to all cognitive activity.[7] He then treats four different metaphors for genre: biological, family, institutional, and speech-act. He advocates a "pluralistic approach" to genre studies, in which different metaphors or analogies are applied to different aspects of genre theory.[8] The family analogy can help in the recognition of "the plural nature" of categories and genres, and in the idea of a generic heritage passing from parents to children.[9] The biological analogy is particularly appropriate to "questions of generic evolution and interrelationship, the complex process of the emergence of new genres on the literary scene, and the decline of old ones."[10]

Categories have structure

Another path also leads us to biological or evolutionary analogies: new approaches to the problem of categorization. When we look at a mass of data (such as motets), and try to make sense of them by sorting them into subgenres, we tend to group them into traditional categories defined by a list of necessary and sufficient features. This classical or Aristotelian approach to categorization is deeply ingrained in our culture, not only as an essential feature of logical operations such as the syllogism, but also as a folk concept of what a category is. The classical category is like a box: it has a clear boundary, so objects belong either inside or outside, and there is no opportunity for gradation within the box. Features are binary: an entity either possesses the feature, or it does not. The classical category has no internal structure: there is no best example of the category, since every object satisfying the list of features is an equally good example.[11] For some kinds of things this kind of category works very well: even and odd numbers, for example, or chemical elements. But for many kinds of things it does not, including the motet and its subgenres.

Over the past few decades scholars in a variety of disciplines (including cognitive psychology, linguistics, and genre theory) have begun to search for a new approach to classification. They are concerned both with the structure of categories (such as words in a language) and the way categories are created, perceived, or processed by the human mind.

For many terms or categories there is no list of necessary and sufficient features that covers all the objects understood by most people to be in that category. Take "tall" for example, or "boot": these are categories with fuzzy boundaries, that merge into other categories such as "medium sized" or "shoe."[12] Wittgenstein recognized this problem in his famous discussion of "games" and proposed a type of category characterized by "family resemblance":

> For if you look at them you will not see something that is common to *all*, but similarities, relationships, and a whole series of them at that.... I can think of no better expression to characterize these similarities than "family resemblances"; for the various resemblances between members of a family: build, features, colour of eyes, gait, temperament, etc., etc., overlap and criss-cross in the same way.[13]

This passage has sometimes been treated rather uncritically, for if the concept is carried too far, then anything can be said to resemble anything.[14] If classical categories are too limiting, Wittgenstein's family resemblance categories are too loose. Nevertheless, the concept of a set of features, not all of which are required for category membership, is very stimulating. The term "family resemblance" also suggests a source for the similarities among the members of a category: actual genetic relationships.[15] This implies that one of the conditions of membership in a category would be relationship, and in particular common parents or ancestors. Works that appear quite different (with few attributes in common) could then be understood as members of the same genre (or subgenre) if one could demonstrate common parentage or ancestry.[16] A work could also be descended from two different "families" with features derived from both. This brings us back to what Fowler calls "ramifying roots": genre history usually consists of tracing the "lineage" or "ancestry" of a work, genre, or subgenre to earlier precedents and models. From now on my usage of the term "family resemblance category" (unlike Wittgenstein's) will involve this conception of relationship or descent.

It also appears that there is a human tendency to structure categories into typical and less typical members. The pioneer in this area is the cognitive psychologist Eleanor Rosch, who showed that for many people a robin is a more typical bird than an ostrich is, or a chair is a better example of furniture than a magazine rack or a television.[17] The best examples of any particular category are known as prototypes. Rosch proved this with a series of different experiments on the structure of categories. She asked her subjects to rank to what extent entities were good examples of a category on a scale of one to seven; she also gave a category, listed an object, and timed the response time; and she requested examples for certain categories. In every case there was clear correlation: prototypical examples of a category were ranked first, the response time was shortest for prototypical examples, and they were the first objects listed for the category. Even classical categories such as "even numbers" demonstrate this "prototype effect": the number 2 is perceived as "more even" than 10, 1,000 as "more even" than 1,008.[18] Rosch's work provides a new model of human cognition in which categories in the mind are internally structured, moving out from central prototypical members toward marginal and less typical members. She combines prototype theory with Wittgenstein's idea of family resemblance as follows:

Members of a category come to be viewed as prototypical of the category as a whole in proportion to the extent to which they bear a family resemblance to (have attributes which overlap those of) other members of the category. Conversely, items viewed as most prototypical of one category will be those with least family resemblance to or membership in other categories.[19]

Scholars concerned with category and genre theory have found this combination of family resemblance and prototype theory very powerful.[20] Fishelov points out that it leads to

the perception of genres neither as rigid and unified categories, nor as conglomerations of texts, randomly collected, sharing merely a loose network of similarities. Rather, literary genres would be perceived as structured categories, with a "hard core" consisting of prototypical members, characterized by their relatively high degree of resemblance to each other.[21]

Marie-Laure Ryan uses another metaphor:

This approach invites us to think of genres as clubs imposing a certain number of conditions for membership, but tolerating as quasi-members those individuals who can fulfill only some of the requirements, and who do not seem to fit into any other club. As these quasi-members become more numerous, the conditions for admission may be modified, so that they, too, will become full members. Once admitted to the club, however, a member remains a member, even if he cannot satisfy the new rules of admission.[22]

This is an especially appealing formation, because it allows us to talk about the history of a genre: admission of enough "quasi-members" can fundamentally change the rules for admission, and thus the basic characteristics of the genre. Some aspects of the transformation of the fifteenth-century motet can be described in exactly these terms: English cantilenas (such as the three-voice English antiphon settings in the motet section of Modena X.1.11) were first admitted as "quasi-members" to the "motet" club; as they became more and more numerous, they were admitted as full members, and some of their

11

characteristics (a single top voice, use of a single devotional text) became features of the genre as a whole.

Another kind of prototype/family resemblance category has one or more prestigious works (e.g. Virgil's *Aeneid*) that serve as exemplars or prototypes.[23] Additional members of the category may imitate different aspects of the prototype and thus bear little resemblance to each other; they will all be related, however, since they "descend" from the same exemplar.

Category theory thus tells us that we need not be limited to one kind of category: different genres can be structured in different ways.[24] Some genres will be classical categories; some will be organized on the basis of "family relationship"; prototype categories can have single or multiple prototypical members, clear or fuzzy boundaries, or any combination of the above. A single work may sit on the boundary between two categories with fuzzy boundaries, or combine features from two categories normally viewed as distinct.

So what is the status of these categories? Are they inherent in the data (the motets)? Are they simply imposed by category makers (composers, audiences, or modern scholars)? My answer is that categories function in the space between the data and the categorizers – creators and audience, then and now.[25] People are category makers: there is so much data out there that unless we classify things we will be drowned in detail. Categories help us decide what to attend to and what to ignore; they articulate the relationships among different things; they allow us to use our past experience of members of a category in dealing with any new member.[26] The features of an object leading a category maker to recognize or classify an object one way rather than another are real. Features might be observable physical properties, similarity to another object or objects, or facts about the history of the object or its function; but unless they have some real connection to the object, the category assignment will fail to be useful. In this sense, then, the category is inherent in the object, though this is not to say that the object could not be categorized differently by another person, or the same person under different circumstances.

Let us turn to a more concrete example of how this could work. A listener turns on the radio and hears a piece of music; immediately she recognizes it as being a Classical piano sonata that she has never heard before. This process of "recognition" is an act of classification. How might that classification take place? First of all she recognizes the sound of the piano. This is so obvious to us that we don't really realize that it is an act of classification. Is "piano sound" represented in her mind by a single exemplar, a single piano? It might be, if she had only heard one piano before. But probably she has a more abstract construct of piano sound, one that can encompass the sounds of all the pianos (uprights, grands, in tune, out of tune) played by all the pianists (beginners, virtuosos, bangers, etc.) she has ever heard. If this piano sounds significantly different from any piano she has heard previously, then she might alter the abstract representation a bit to include this new sound possibility.

Having recognized the sound of the piano, and that she is hearing music (rather than, say, a piano being tuned), she has narrowed the field to the category "piano music." Features of the piece – Alberti bass, regularity of phrase lengths, and so forth – indicate to her that this is a Classical work. Again, if she rarely listened to classical music, or had never taken a music history class, she might have a single exemplar or prototype, and think "that sounds like that piece I heard on the radio last week." If our listener is knowledgable about classical music, she will compare this piece in her mind to some kind of abstract representation of the category classical music, a representation that might be structured in a variety of different ways.[27] That representation might have been acquired unconsciously, and would probably be difficult to articulate (our ability to explain how we recognize things, even everyday things like faces, is poor). She might be a music student, or teacher, and be able to describe in part what about it sounds Classical. Still, even for professionals, it is often difficult to articulate exactly what it is that leads us to a particular identification or classification, even if we are absolutely certain we are correct.

On hearing an unfamiliar work the listener works her way down through a set of gradually more specific categories. A novice will stop near the top, a specialist will go on to determine that she is hearing (say) the development section from a first movement of a sonata by Clementi probably written in the 1790s. In either case, category membership is determined by comparison of the work to some kind of mental representation or representations: either the memory of individual work(s) or abstractions ("piano," "Classical") derived from numerous past experiences.

Now let us assume the work on the radio was peculiar in some way – a fantasy, not a sonata; or borderline Romantic; or an unusual slow movement. Then instead of "that sounds like" she could say "that sounds sort of like"; or she could say "that sounds like both x and y" (where x and y are different

13

categories: fantasy and sonata, Classical and Romantic). "Sort of like" is what is known in linguistics as a "hedge": a word or phrase that is used to express a degree of category membership.[28] "Both x and y" indicates that a piece sits on the fuzzy boundary between two categories (Classical and Romantic) or that it has features characteristic of two different genres (fantasy and sonata).[29] She might then wait for the radio announcer to tell her what it is, and adjust and expand her set of categories accordingly;[30] or she might listen to the work with two sets of generic expectations in mind.

The act of classification is the first way the listener interacts with the piece. Having made a genre identification the listener now knows what to listen for: the transition and second theme, the repeat of the exposition, the drama of the development. The genre identification serves an important function, and guides the subsequent experience of the work. The category/genre "Classical piano sonata" is a real category that exists outside the mind of the listener (in part because composers intended the works to belong to the category); it has clear, even if fuzzy, boundaries, and more and less typical members. There are marginal cases that sometimes belong to more than one category: pieces composed at the boundaries of a time period (Galant? early Romantic?), or pieces that don't fit the sonata mold very well. Thus it is a graded prototype category, in which some members are more central than others.

How does this work for the composer? Let us take Du Fay as an example, since he will figure largely below. Du Fay sits down to write a piece. He would have begun with several of the parameters in mind: an occasion, or a text, or a moment in a church service, or a particular group of performers. When he wrote *Ecclesie militantis* he was probably asked to write an especially grand piece in honor of Eugenius IV, to be performed by the papal chapel on a certain date.[31] Under those circumstances Du Fay would think about grand occasional pieces he had heard (and written himself); most of them belonged to the subgenre of the motet now known as the isorhythmic motet. Some highly admired works might be central, or prototypical, leading him to say to himself "I want to write a piece sort of like X" or "like X & Y" where X & Y are other motets. Or he might have a more abstract internal representation of isorhythmic motet that included both specific features he could articulate to himself and some less-easily expressible qualities of melodic style, harmony, and counterpoint. Thus part of the process of composing is imitation, making sure that the piece meets the conditions for membership in the club. But in most cases there is also an opposing force: the drive to write a work that differs

14

in various ways from previous works. In this case Du Fay wanted to express Eugenius's claim to the tradition of papal power. He therefore wanted to write a bigger, grander piece than ever before; he also wanted to write a piece that referred to its own generic traditions. By writing a piece that looked backward towards its own history, Du Fay suggested that Eugenius had similar ties to the history and tradition of the papacy. Du Fay did this in *Ecclesie militantis* by taking traditional features of the isorhythmic motet, such as polytextuality and isorhythm, and exaggerating them: the work has three different texts instead of two, two tenors instead of one, five voices instead of four, plus an exceptionally complex rhythmic organization. This is not, then, a typical isorhythmic motet: it is in fact extremely unusual. But it is clearly "related" to the isorhythmic motet – all of its features can be understood as related to (or descended from) features of the traditional model. One way of expressing that relationship is to describe the structure of the category "isorhythmic motet" as a prototype or family resemblance category. The features of this unusual motet then become part of the ongoing definition of the category.

These examples have brought out a number of important points. Recognition and classification are essentially the same activity. Recognition often involves phrases such as "it sounds like" or "it sounds sort of like." These phrases have to do with similarity. Similarity does not lend itself to the binary either/or choices of classical categories: it is better represented by graded prototype or family resemblance categories. The category or mental representation that we compare things to in the process of recognition consists of an abstraction that includes features derived from one or many different works. Both listener and composer work with essentially the same kind of mental representation of a category or genre: the listener says "that sounds like a [genre]"; the composer says "I'm going to write a [genre]" or "I'm going to write a piece like [those English pieces I heard last week]" or "like [specific piece]."

When a composer sits down to write a piece belonging to a particular genre, he may not have a conscious list of generic features (or not a very long one), but that doesn't mean that a list could not be made. In fact, making such a list (for listeners or beginning composers) is a good way of speeding up the process of genre acquisition.[32] We are all beginners when it comes to the fifteenth-century motet; while lists of features are never the whole story, since they cannot hope to match the expert's complex internal category representation and graded similarity judgments, they will assist our genre (and subgenre) acquisition.

15

Listeners and composers thus have mental representations of genres which are invoked (often unconsciously) as part of the process of recognition and of creation. Mental representations (i.e. categories) are often organized in a hierarchy, and we can work down the hierarchy towards more and more specific identifications. These mental representations can also be internally structured in a variety of ways. Sometimes a work shares a list of necessary and sufficient features with an abstraction derived from multiple examples (classical category). In other cases a work's membership in a genre is measured by its similarity to a central or prototypical member (prototype category). A work may share some, but not all, attributes with a mental representation, and be related to or descended from the genre as a whole, or specific works within it (family resemblance category). A work may also belong to more than one category. We need to be alive to all these possibilities in our investigation of the motet and its many subgenres.

Generic evolution

What does it mean "to be descended from" a genre or category? Every new work is necessarily descended from previous works in the same genre (or, in the case of generic mixture, from more than one genre), in as much as every work is created in relation to past works, on the one hand, and every work is perceived or recognized in relation to past works, on the other. This is almost a tautology or a truism. It does, however, point to the engine behind generic change: the pressure for novelty within a tradition. The concepts of relationship and descent also lead directly to our next analogy: evolution and natural selection. In thinking about categories, and their role in creation and recognition, we have been concentrating on the function of the genre inside the mind. With Darwin we look as well at the fate of the work once it has left its creator, and the way in which that fate affects the origin, development, and change of the genre or subgenre as a whole.

In defending evolutionary analogies for genre Fishelov points out that their critics often mix models and refer to the life span of the individual organism or to Lamarckian adaptation rather than to true Darwinian evolution and natural selection. He finds the careful application of the Darwinian selection model to be much more fruitful for genre studies than the mixed models.[33] In order to understand the analogy between generic change and Darwinian evolution, it is thus essential to have a clear understanding of Darwin's basic

theory, which is all too often misunderstood. Because eloquent recent explica-
tions of evolution (by Richard Dawkins, for example) are necessarily
informed by knowledge of genetics, they are not directly relevant to my
analogy with the motet.[34] I have chosen Darwin's own presentation of evolution and natural selection because of its power and authority, and because the
actual mechanisms of inheritance were still unknown to Darwin, making his
version peculiarly suitable to our problem.[35]

Darwin's use of the word "species" also differed from the technical biological definition used today. Modern biologists define species as a reproductive
community: all the members of a species can mate and produce fertile
offspring.[36] For Darwin species meant no more than "a set of individuals
closely resembling each other . . . it does not essentially differ from the term
variety, which is given to less distinct and more fluctuating forms."[37] His per-
sistent claim was that forms of life "can be classed in groups under groups,"
although the boundaries of these groups were essentially arbitrary.[38] The
arbitrariness of Darwin's presentation is especially applicable to genre, since
there are no necessary limitations on generic mixture or interbreeding.

Darwin's theory of evolution was first fully presented in *The Origin of
Species* published in 1859. The problem that Darwin posed himself was one of
categorization and classification: what is the relationship between species and
varieties, and are species fixed? He first had to free himself of the Aristotelian
habit of seeing species as classical categories; he had to demonstrate that
change is continuous. Darwin's concern thus speaks very directly to our
problem of generic formation and change.

In *The Origin of Species* Darwin first set out to show that species were not
fixed, "immutable productions . . . separately created," but that they
"descended, like varieties, from other species."[39] Having demonstrated this,
largely by means of a "careful study of domesticated animals and of cultivated plants," he then went on to show "how the innumerable species of the
world have been modified, so as to acquire that perfection of structure and
coadaptation which most justly excites our imagination."[40] Modification is
achieved by means of "Natural Selection": given the "Struggle for Existence
among all organic beings,"[41] "individuals having any advantage . . . over others,
would have the best chance of surviving and of procreating their kind," and
"variation in the least degree injurious would be rigidly destroyed."[42] The
organisms which are selected – i.e. survive to reproduce – are those better
adapted to their specific conditions of life. A change in conditions will lead to

17

the selection (survival and reproduction) of different organisms.[43] Natural selection will thus lead, on the one hand, to extinction of some species and varieties, and on the other to "divergence of character."[44] "Thus the small differences distinguishing varieties of the same species, will steadily tend to increase till they come to equal the greater differences between species of the same genus, or even of distinct genera."[45] Darwin concludes his chapter on natural selection with an extended analogy.

The affinities of all the beings of the same class have sometimes been represented by a great tree. . . . The green and budding twigs may represent existing species; and those produced during each former year may represent the long succession of extinct species. . . . The limbs divided into great branches, and these into lesser and lesser branches, were themselves once, when the tree was small, budding twigs; and this connexion of the former and present buds by ramifying branches may well represent the classification of all extinct and living species in groups subordinate to groups. . . . So by generation I believe it has been with the great Tree of Life, which fills with its dead and broken branches the crust of the earth, and covers the surface with its ever branching and beautiful ramifications.[46]

The "ramifications" of Darwin's Tree of Life recall Fowler's "ramifying roots": in both natural and generic evolution, the "former and present" are linked by means of constant descent with variation. Darwin's formulation makes clear that there is a powerful connection between variations in the environment and those ramifications that survive.

Analogies with genre

Darwin's basic idea has been extremely productive in a wide variety of fields. It can also serve as a stimulating model for generic change and for the problems of categorization and classification of the motet.[47] The analogy goes like this.

The motet is the organism; the genre is the species; the subgenre is the variety. The natural environment is equivalent to the cultural environment. New motets are "generated" from earlier ones in ways that guarantee both similarity and variety. Motets vary, as organisms do: no two organisms are the same, and each new composition is different from its predecessors. The new motets that are received favorably by the cultural environment – by performers, patrons, audiences – survive and reproduce; those that fail to thrive and are poorly received are not copied into repertory manuscripts or imitated by other composers (most of these works are probably lost to us today). The offspring of a motet can be either copies or imitations. Copies are literal reproductions: a single work is copied into multiple manuscripts. Imitations are new works that resemble the first work (this kind of reproduction is more analogous to biological reproduction). A work will be reproduced if the original motet is perceived as successful: if there is a good fit between the work and its cultural environment.[48] A new subgenre (variety) results from the production of a work markedly different from previous works that serves in turn as a model for other works like it, or possibly from the interbreeding of two different subgenres.

But where does the composer belong in this schema? If we take as our model the subset of natural selection known as artificial selection – conscious manipulation of the environment by humans in order to create varieties according to desired specifications – then the composer is the breeder. "Variation under domestication," as Darwin called it, involves selecting plants or animals with certain characteristics and allowing them to reproduce, while "weeding out" any without the desired characteristics. In the first chapter of *The Origin of Species* Darwin uses the breeding of domestic animals to demonstrate variation, and he spends pages and pages documenting the extremes to which such variation can go: "Breeders habitually speak of an animal's organization as something quite plastic, which they can model as they please."[49] Composers, like breeders, select the features that they wish to propagate from the available options, reproducing some traits, introducing new varieties, and forming new hybrids. Like a breeder, the composer takes over some of nature's role, manipulating the environment in order to select for specific features. As Darwin comments, "one of the most remarkable features in our domesticated races is that we see in them adaptation, not indeed to the animal's or plant's own good, but to man's use or fancy."[50] The works of the composer/breeder are, however, subject to a subsequent selection process as well: that of the external world, the "market" or the cultural environment. Some of the works will be well received, others will not; as the composer/breeder becomes aware of this it will influence his future works.

Analogy need not mean identity, however; and there are important differences between biological and cultural evolution. In culture, unlike biology, there are few rigid limitations on breeding: it is possible to combine features from any two different genres (to combine, through breeding, features from two different species, even from different genera) and to take as "parent" a work from several generations back.[51] Composers are not limited to the chance combinations of hereditary traits appearing in the offspring of two parents; they can pick and choose their traits from a wide range of "parents." The offspring of a work can be either physical copies or imitations, and we will explore the extent to which these two kinds of reproduction are inter-related.

Nevertheless, the analogy is productive and leads to some fruitful and unexpected implications. Geographical isolation, for example, is likely to lead to "divergence of character" and the development of new species or varieties (genres or subgenres). In Darwin's travels in the Beagle, he studied the flora and fauna of the Galapagos Islands. He discovered that while the finches on all the islands resembled each other and resembled finches on the Latin American mainland, they had developed different kinds of beaks on each of the different islands. The beaks were an adaptation to the kinds of food avail-able on each island.[52] Motets could evolve in just the same way to fit the cul-tural "niches" available to them in different regions. The coming together of previously separated varieties is likely to lead to new hybrids. New varieties can be developed to suit the desires and cultural practices of patrons and audience.

The evolutionary analogy thus accounts for the variety of kinds of motet in a way that is responsive to cultural and political developments. Subgenres can be explained by their antecedents or ancestors; new subgenres are formed by the coming together of previously separated or distinct varieties and genres; subgenres that survive are those that are able to respond to the changing tastes and needs of patrons and audiences. To tell the story of the motet in the fif-teenth century is to tell the story of the creation, evolution, and extinction of the various subgenres.

The evolution of the medieval motet

Before we turn to the fifteenth-century motet, let us see how the analogy works for a genre whose history is relatively well known: the medieval motet. The facts I present are uncontroversial; only my manner of presentation is unusual.

We begin with the aboriginal motet: the thirteenth-century motet in France. It generally had three voices: triplum and motetus over a slower-moving pre-existing tenor. Triplum and motetus each had its own text, in Latin or in French. Imagine that the motet was a species of bird on an island, called France. (I will call the different regions islands, to emphasize their cultural separation.) We could call it a finch, after Darwin's finches. But we want a bird that is bred by humans and that undergoes "variation under domestication." One of Darwin's prime examples was the pigeon, which like the motet developed an astonishing variety of forms and was put to many different uses. In the nineteenth century different strains of pigeon were developed for eating (the squab), for communication (the carrier pigeon) and for aesthetic enjoyment (the pouter, the Jacobin, the fantail).[53]

So let us think of our motet as a kind of pigeon, cultivated by pigeon breeders (composers and performers), and consumed, used and admired by pigeon fanciers (other musicians, patrons, audience). It first emerged as a distinct species in France in the early thirteenth century, and it flourished there: breeders put some effort into developing different varieties, and there was consistent demand from fanciers. Visitors from other islands sailed to France, liked the pigeons and brought some home to their own islands, England and Italy.[54] The climates and native flora in France, England and Italy were all a little different; the fanciers used the pigeons in different ways and valued different features in a good pigeon, so the breeders selected for the desired qualities. On each island only the pigeons with the appropriate qualities were allowed to reproduce, and only those that flourished in the native habitat did well. For a while contacts between France, England and Italy were rather limited; gradually the varieties of pigeon on the three islands grew different from each other, helped along by the breeding efforts of the French, English and Italians.

Having set up the analogy, let us continue the narrative by calling a motet a motet. It was during the fourteenth century that the different national varieties of motet developed in different directions. In France many features of the aboriginal motet continued into the fourteenth century. The pre-existent, rhythmically patterned tenor part persisted, but slowed down, while the triplum and motetus (still with their own texts) sped up. The motets also got bigger and more complex with the addition of a contratenor and the development of isorhythm. French-texted motets gradually died out, as a new French-texted species, the chanson, made its appearance, and took over the ecological niche formerly held by the French-texted motet; the new larger Latin-texted motet took on a life of its own. The motet fanciers – university-trained clerics and cathedral officials who admired and discussed motets at private gatherings – liked a learned, acerbic flavor. The motets they enjoyed

21

were characterized by complex isorhythmic schemes and Latin texts often filled with sardonic commentary on government and society.[55]

English motets developed many distinctive features during the first half of the fourteenth century. The French-texted motets did poorly in England, while the Latin-texted motets, especially those with sacred subjects, flourished. (Motet fanciers on every island spoke Latin, but French-texted motets were valued highly only in France.) While the rhythmic layering of the French motet persisted, the use of cantus firmus was not an essential feature of the English motets. The motet fanciers seem to have been monks, who preferred a devotional flavor and bred their motets (and most other polyphony) for use in church: English motets generally had multi-purpose sacred texts, with no political or social allusions.[56] The importation of isorhythmic French motets in the second half of the century virtually wiped out the new English strain. Certain sub-breeds or varieties of French motet were preferred in England, however, and a certain amount of interbreeding went on.[57]

Motets (or any other kind of written polyphony) do not seem to have been cultivated in Italy in the thirteenth century, and climatic conditions were such that there are few fossil remains of fourteenth-century Italian motets. From what we can see, however, Italian motets (like English ones) did not have preexistent cantus firmi, but they retained the slow tenor and faster upper voices of the thirteenth-century motet. Isorhythm did not develop, but some motets were characterized by repetition of the rhythms of all the voices for the second half of the piece. Texts were usually laudatory, about doges, princes, bishops, or saints. Italians bred their motets for use at court or in church, usually in the context of some civic ceremony.[58]

At the beginning of the fifteenth century conditions changed. England won a significant battle with France (the Battle of Agincourt, 1415) and occupied large portions of the country; English lords who took up residence in France brought music and musicians (motets and motet breeders) with them.[59] The urgent need to end the papal schism brought religious and political leaders from all over Europe together at the Council of Constance (1414–18); they also brought their musicians along.[60] Suddenly motet breeders (composers and performers) were brought together from all over. This brings us to the situation in the early fifteenth century, the starting place for this book.

The evolutionary analogy thus clarifies the motet's historical development. By the early fifteenth century there were many different varieties (subgenres) of the motet, many of them developed to suit the different tastes of the

French, English, and Italians. Although the various subgenres or varieties were different from each other, they all descended ultimately from the aboriginal thirteenth-century French motet. This makes the motet a good example of a family resemblance category: we can recognize the different national traditions of motet composition as belonging to the same genre or family because we know their history. Different features are prominent in different subgenres, varieties, or branches of the family. The ways in which these different subgenres interacted with each other and with other evolving genres, along with the pressures brought to bear on those interactions by subsequent political and cultural events, determined the history of the motet in the fifteenth century.

2 Subgenre, interpretation, and the generic repertory

Our look at category theory has provided us with tools for dealing with the problematic category of the motet and its many subgenres, while the evolutionary model can serve as a way of conceptualizing and explaining the massive changes in the motet over the course of the fifteenth century. But how does this framework help us to understand individual fifteenth-century motets? In this chapter I will suggest how knowledge of the motet's subgenres and history can help us to interpret individual works. I will also list some of the different kinds of generic features to be considered in classification and interpretation.

Genre, subgenre, and interpretation

As many critics have pointed out, genre and generic conventions make possible communication between the author and the reader or listener. Communication is only possible within a context in which the basic rules and guidelines are understood: these tell us what to pay attention to, what to ignore, and how to assemble the data as we progress through the work. Generic conventions provide such guidelines.[1] A witty demonstration of this is provided by Heather Dubrow, who provides a hypothetical opening paragraph that could belong to either a mystery novel or a *Bildungsroman:* our reading strategies and interpretation of important details in this passage are very different depending on which we believe it is.[2] In order to understand an individual work we need to develop a "horizon of expectation" (as Hans Robert Jauss puts it), against which to position the work. Jauss explains that:

24

The reconstruction of the horizon of expectations, in the face of which a work was created and received in the past, enables one . . . to pose questions that the text gave an answer to, and thereby to discover how the contemporary reader could have viewed and understood the work.[3]

He points out that this is especially useful for repertories distant in time:

The method of historical reception is indispensable for the understanding of literature from the distant past. When the author of a work is unknown, his intent undeclared, and his relationship to sources and models only indirectly accessible, the philological question of how the text is "properly" – that is, "from its intention and time" – to be understood can best be answered if one foregrounds it against those works that the author explicitly or implicitly presupposed his contemporary audience to know.[4]

It has been difficult to develop a horizon of expectation for the motet because of its multiple varieties and constant evolution. A set of historically and geographically grounded subgenres will allow us to develop an appropriate horizon of expectation for each individual work.[5] There is no need to limit ourselves to this kind of "historical reception," of course, but it provides a good starting place for unfamiliar repertories.

To put it another way, the ability to recognize the various subgenres of the motet will allow us to approach what Peter Rabinowitz calls the "authorial reading." Rabinowitz points out that the author of a work imagines an audience with certain kinds of experiences, assumptions, skills, and knowledge of conventions; an authorial reader is thus one equipped with roughly the same skills, tools, and knowledge. This equipment allows the reader to decode the work, interpret it, or understand its meaning.[6] Likewise, composers of motets wrote for listeners equipped with some basic knowledge of the music and the compositional conventions of the fifteenth century who could give to the work a "composer's hearing." Recognition of the principal subgenres of the motet (whether conscious or unconscious), I argue, would have been a basic part of a listener's equipment; a composer would have assumed this knowledge as he set out to write a new piece. Most twentieth-century readers or listeners lack the knowledge of fifteenth-century repertory that would allow us to recognize subgenres; only by recovering that knowledge can we approach a "composer's hearing" of a work. This in turn will enable us to understand and interpret the work in terms the composer's original audience would understand. That original audience is the one that determined the success or failure of a work, and thus its ultimate role in the evolution or transformation of the genre as a whole.

The "composer's hearing" is only one of the many possible hearings of a work, and modern listeners will never achieve it completely; in attempting to acquire the skills of the composer's original audience, however, we will develop our own ways of making sense of this music.[7] I can suggest two ways in which those skills can contribute to our understanding of the motet: one has to do with musical associations, the other with the intersection of text and music.

As we will see in chapter 3, the motet occupied a middling place in the genre hierarchy, with close ties to each of the other genres: Mass, chanson, and liturgical service music. Individual works, and in fact whole subgenres, could make reference to these other genres by means of specific musical features. Thus a short three-voice treble-dominated motet resembles a chanson, a large four-voice motet in two sections with foreign cantus firmus resembles a Mass movement, and a piece with simple chant paraphrase in the top voice recalls liturgical service music. These musical resemblances carry with them a whole set of extra-musical associations. A motet that resembles a chanson evokes the intimate, courtly, amorous world of chanson poetry and of the contexts in which chansons were performed. A motet that resembles a Mass movement evokes the solemn, grandiose, hieratic world of the feasts of highest rank, those performed with complex polyphonic Masses. A motet that resembles liturgical service music evokes the humbler context of daily or weekly devotions and improvised polyphony. These resemblances or musical references affect a work's position in the genre hierarchy, its position on a scale of cultural values, and its tone (intimate, grandiose, simple, complex, informal, formal). Musical references to genres outside the motet can also be mixed: a piece may (and many do) combine the chant paraphrase of liturgical service music with the two-section structure of the Mass movement or the three voices of the chanson, resulting in a more complex blend of associations and resonances. Some motets also make reference to the genre's history by using "archaic" musical devices (such as isorhythm) that are no longer generally in use.[8] As we come to recognize the different subgenres we can recognize their references to genres outside the motet, to the genre's history, and to each other. Each of these musical references carries with it a whole complex of associations that generate meaning.

Motets, however, do not consist of music alone: they also have texts. The style, tone, and meaning of the text mixes with the associations generated by the musical setting, a rich convergence that results in a meaning that is greater and more nuanced than that of the text alone. The texts of the motet belong to many different literary genres, each with its own traditions and associations. Genres of text and musical subgenres are conjoined in complex ways. Some text types, such as the laudatory political text, tend to be set in one particular way: as large-scale isorhythmic motets in the early fifteenth century,[9] or later as four- and five-voice tenor motets. Others, such as the four main Marian antiphons, are set in every conceivable way, from the most intimate song motet to the largest tenor motet. Each of these different kinds of setting casts a new light on the text, reinterprets it, changes its meaning. Preferred text types and musical types change radically over the course of the century. New conjunctions of text type and musical type can give rise to new subgenres.

Once we are in command of the various subgenres, their histories, and their relationships among themselves and with other genres, we can begin to recognize a motet's tone, style height, associations, and conservative or experimental qualities. Composers made many choices in the course of writing a motet; only if we have a sense of the possibilities can we evaluate their effect. Knowledge of the various subgenres of the motet and the complex of associations generated by text and music will provide us with Jauss's horizon of expectation, as well as the knowledge and skills for Rabinowitz's authorial reading (or composer's hearing). These in turn will enable us to interpret individual works.

A generic repertory for the motet

Alastair Fowler, in his discussion of historical genres, or "kinds," as he calls them, finds it useful to provide a "generic repertoire": "the whole range of potential points of resemblance that a genre may exhibit."[10] He points out that "every genre has a unique repertoire, from which its representatives select characteristics." He goes on to stress that genres are best characterized in terms of both "external" features of form and structure, and "internal" features of content or subject matter.[11] These are very roughly comparable to music and text in the motet. Some of the features of Fowler's literary repertory apply equally well to ours: "external structure" (division into chapters or acts: in music, division into sections or *partes*); "metrical structure" (poetic

27

meter, for the text of a motet; in music, mensuration); "size"; "subject"; "mood"; "occasion" (where and when was it performed, at least initially); and "style," or style height.[12] In music, as in poetic literary genres, "external" form and structure are especially important, but the "internal" subject matter of the text and the affect of the melody and harmony also play a role. "Almost any feature, it seems, can become genre-linked."[13] But "every characteristic feature, as a means of communication, must be recognizable, and this limits the relevant possibilities at any particular time. . . . We may find that a few striking traits effectively characterize a genre."[14] Even "absent features," features normally excluded from a genre or subgenre, can help us recognize a genre.[15] Many other features of the generic repertory of the motet also deserve discussion. I have divided my list of generic features into three kinds: musical, textual, and those resulting from the interaction of text and music.

Musical features of the generic repertory

TEXTURE

My subgenres are determined primarily by musical features, and only secondarily by text. The most important musical feature – and the least understood – is texture: the ways in which the voices are woven together, and how they interact. In genre and subgenre identification texture was for the fifteenth century what orchestration is for us today. In the repertory that has received the most analytical attention (music of the eighteenth and nineteenth centuries), texture is rarely discussed,[16] while orchestration is studied in some detail. Genre, period, and composer identification almost always begin with orchestration (as we saw in our hypothetical example of the piano sonata on the radio). Because instrumental music is central to our study of the common practice period, and because orchestration determines texture to a great extent, it is possible to ignore texture in favor of orchestration.

In contrast, virtually all the surviving music from the fifteenth century is vocal music, much of it for a small group (three to twenty) of male singers (men, or men and boys), with a total range of well under three octaves.[17] This was a fairly limited palette of tone color, and orchestration played no part in genre or composer recognition. This is not to say that there wasn't a rich variety of instrumental colors in the fifteenth century; there was, but most of the music played on instruments was not written down, or, if it was, it started off as vocal music and was then adapted for instruments. Orchestration, in fact, was the performer's job, not the composer's. Any piece could potentially be played on almost any workable combination of instruments (solo or ensemble) or instruments and voices.

There was, however, a great deal of textural variety in vocal writing. In much fifteenth-century polyphonic music two voices are in the same range most of the time. Whether these voices are high, middle or low makes a substantial difference in the sound of a work. There was also a great deal of variety in rhythmic and melodic motion of the individual voices. Texture is the most important element in our generic repertory for the fifteenth-century motet: let us therefore consider its major components.

NUMBER OF VOICES

Most fifteenth-century motets are for three or four voices. Three-voice pieces are usually fairly short and song-like, while most four-voice pieces are longer and more ambitious in terms of form and structure. There are, however, many exceptions to this statement, including short simple four-voice pieces and long complex three-voice ones.[18] The situation is also complicated by the practice of adding a fourth voice to three-voice pieces. Over the course of the century the amount of three-voice writing decreases, while music for four voices becomes the norm.

VOICE RANGES

There are several variables here: the range of each individual voice, the range for the piece as a whole, and the extent to which voices overlap or coincide in range. All have effects on the texture of the work, but the last variable, concerning relative ranges and voice crossing, is especially important. The most typical combinations have strong associations with genres outside the motet; they also change radically over the course of the century.[19] I list the most common motet textures in Table 2.1, providing labels in most cases to indicate the generic associations of the texture. The label does not indicate that the texture is restricted to that genre, just that it is strongly associated with it.

29

Table 2.1. *Relative voice ranges for the motet and their generic associations*

Early in the century (1410–45)			
Medieval motet	*chanson/cantilena*		
2 high	1 high		
1 or 2 low	2 low		

Mid-century (1445–75)			
4-v. Tenor Mass		*chanson/cantilena*	
1 high	1 high	1 high	1 high
2 middle	1 middle	2 low or	1 middle
1 low	2 low		1 low

The terms "high," "middle," and "low" in the Table refer to the relative ranges of the voices.

MELODIC BEHAVIOR (LEAPS, STEPS)

The extent to which voices are differentiated in melodic style affects texture profoundly. Beginning in the sixteenth century there was a strong sense of melodic decorum that applied to all voices. There were some things voices just did not do (such as leap up or down a seventh, or have two large leaps in the same direction). Palestrina's style is perhaps the extreme example, but we can see the attention to melodic decorum for all voices beginning even in Josquin. For most of the fifteenth century, however, different voice functions were often associated with extremely different styles of melody. The upper discantus voices were melodic, with relatively restrained use of leaps and predominantly stepwise melodies. Tenor voices were somewhat freer, but consisted primarily of conjunct motion. Freest of all were contratenor voices, with large leaps of dissonant intervals, motion through a twelfth in the space of two or three beats, and so forth. They also generally had the widest range. Different skills were required for singing tenor and contratenor parts, even when they were in the same range: singers were known as "tenorista" and "contratenorista," and if one or the other was missing the piece could not be sung.[20] The lack of melodic decorum in the contratenor is one of the most characteristic features of early fifteenth-century music.

RELATIVE SPEED OF VOICES

Faster motion in one voice makes it dominate the texture; slower motion suggests a supporting role, but also often indicates use of pre-existent material. Generally if one voice is faster than the others it is the top voice; if one is slower than the others it is on the bottom or middle. Two voices in the same range (two discantus parts, for example, or tenor and contratenor) often have the same kind of rhythmic motion (unless the tenor is a long-note cantus firmus). In some pieces all voices move at about the same speed, and in others each voice moves at a different speed. Differentiation of rhythmic motion is typical of the medieval motet and its closest fifteenth-century descendants.

COORDINATION OF RHYTHM: HOMORHYTHM, POLYPHONY

Even when all voices had the same type and speed of rhythmic motion, they could be coordinated in a variety of different ways: all voices could have the same rhythm at the same time, resulting in a completely homorhythmic or homophonic texture, or voices could retain rhythmic independence to varying degrees, resulting in a polyphonic texture. A completely homo-rhythmic texture recalls techniques of simple polyphony improvised on a chant such as English discant or fauxbourdon.

COORDINATION OF PHRASES

No matter what the nature of the rhythmic and melodic motion, in some pieces phrases end together with a clear cadence in all voices, while in others continuity is emphasized with overlapping phrases. Clear phrase structure in all voices is associated especially with the chanson; overlapping phrase structure with the medieval motet.

REDUCED SCORING, OR USE OF RESTS

Within a three- or four-voice piece there is opportunity for variety of texture if one or more voices rest or drop out, resulting in duets and trios for the remaining voices. Some subgenres of the motet and Mass movements, for example, often begin with extended duets, while duet sections are often found in the middle of English cantilenas. Chansons and chant settings, on the other hand, usually keep all the voices singing throughout.

CONSTRUCTION AND COUNTERPOINT

Less immediately audible than the features listed above, but still an essential determinant of texture, is the compositional construction of the work and the resultant contrapuntal constraints. In what Reinhard Strohm calls "chanson format" the discantus and tenor are contrapuntally complete, and the contratenor is inessential.[21] Contrapuntal completeness means that fourths between the discantus and tenor are not treated as consonances, since fourths require another voice to sing a third or a fifth below to make them consonant; it also implies that the cantus and tenor voices participate together in all the cadences, defining them by contrary motion to the octave (or, less often, the unison or fifth). An inessential voice (usually a contratenor) is one that is not needed to make fourths consonant between cantus and tenor (or any other pair of voices), nor is it required at cadences. In addition, an inessential voice should not participate in any sections with reduced scoring for two voices, because if it were removed a solo section would result. Chanson format is used most often for three-voice pieces, but can also be found in four-voice pieces with two contratenors. It began in the fourteenth century (if not before) and extended into the sixteenth; it is one way of writing pieces, but never the only way. Chanson format is virtually always used in chansons, hence the name; it is also used in some subgenres of the motet.

Pieces that are not in chanson format are much more flexible: they can have cadences defined by any pair of voices, and sections of reduced scoring can involve or omit any of the voices. There are many different kinds of piece that are not in chanson format, extending well back into the fourteenth century.[22] In these pieces the tenor can have a fourth below the upper voice, or it can have the fifth above the lowest note of a simultaneity. One kind of texture that becomes more and more common towards the end of the fifteenth century has an essential contratenor voice, the range of which is significantly below that of the tenor.[23] The preference for this new low contratenor may have resulted from the desire to expand the total range of a composition, or from a dawning interest in separation of ranges for individual voices. There is no need to associate it with any kind of proto-tonality or functional harmony.

HIERARCHIC VS. INTEGRATED OR HOMOGENEOUS

Hierarchic textures are those in which some voices are clearly differentiated from the others, by some of the means discussed above: the faster-moving top voice, the long-note cantus firmus, the slow tenor/contratenor pair, or the leapy contratenor. Integrated or homogeneous textures are those in which the melodic and rhythmic style of all the voices is very similar. The various parameters discussed above are combined into numerous different textures in the fifteenth century, many of which come to define individual subgenres, as we shall see. There is a general movement over the course of the century from predominantly hierarchic textures to predominantly integrated or homogeneous ones, though both can be found throughout the century.

Other musical features of the generic repertory

There are other musical features that are not directly associated with texture and that can vary independently from it.

LENGTH

Individual subgenres tend to have a characteristic length, though there is a great deal of leeway here. In general short pieces are simpler, long pieces more complex and ambitious formally; thus length is one indicator of style height.

NUMBER OF SECTIONS OR *PARTES*

Sections can be defined in many different ways: by talea or color in isorhythmic motets, by extended passages in reduced scoring, by change of meter, and/or by strong cadences in all voices followed by double bars. This feature of external form is important in the definition of some subgenres, less important in others.

MENSURATION(S)

Mensural usage changes over time and varies geographically. Some subgenres are characterized by the use of certain mensurations or combinations of mensurations: these include the "cut-circle" motet of the first part of the

33

century, or the large motet with two *partes* in O and ₵ of the second half of the century. Mensurations also often go together with the style of rhythmic motion. In general the fluid almost non-metrical rhythms often found in combination with perfect tempus (O: 3/2) are associated with a high style, while simpler, more metrical rhythms suggest a lower, more popular style.

LARGE-SCALE RHYTHMIC ORGANIZATION

The most well-known example of this kind of structure is isorhythm.[24] However, rhythmic organization on the level of the long, as in perfect modus, or cantus firmi that are repeated according to some scheme of strict proportions (as in Busnoys's *In hydraulis*), also result in large-scale rhythmic organization. Works demonstrating this kind of rhythmic organization tend to be ambitious, formal, and backward-looking: these works are at the top of the genre hierarchy, and they are often occasional or dedicatory.

COMPLEXITY

The complexity of a work's construction also affects its style height. Complexity can be achieved in many ways: through arcane canons, difficult or conflicting rhythms, lack of congruence in phrase structures among the parts, and pitch materials. Complexity indicates learnedness, and is thus an indicator of a high position on the style hierarchy; it is sometimes used as a special effect, and seems to have been valued more early in the century.

USE OF PRE-EXISTENT MUSICAL MATERIAL (*CPF*)

I put this last because I think it is less important than modern scholarship would suggest. Most of the research into the fifteenth-century motet until now has been focused on pre-existent material: tracking it down and describing how it is used. This is important work, and I have learned a great deal from its practitioners, especially Sparks and Stephan.[25] Sometimes, however, the concentration on pre-existent material causes scholars to assume it is there even if they cannot find it, and leads them to ignore other features of the motet.

I am concerned with re-creating the level of expertise of an intelligent musical patron of the fifteenth century, not an expert on chant and its dialects. This means being on the alert for the use of well-known tunes (such as the

Marian antiphons), and for obvious surface indicators of the use of pre-existent material such as chant incipits, long notes, or contrasting text. As we shall
see, other features of texture and style also often go along with use of chant,
and one can often make an educated guess about its presence based on knowledge of subgeneric conventions. If a composer wants you to know that he is
using chant, he finds ways of letting you know. If a well-educated twentieth-
century musicologist cannot tell if there is pre-existent material after con-
sulting the standard references, odds are most of the fifteenth-century
audience could not tell either. And if it is not recognizable, it is not a major
element in genre identification (though it might have symbolic or musical
importance for those in the know). Obvious use of pre-existent material is
thus an important element in the generic repertory; hidden use of obscure
chants is less important.[26]

Textual features of the repertory

The texts of fifteenth-century motets fall into many different genres, and
these, of course, are subject to the same difficulties of categorization as the
motet, or as any literary production. Many motets, especially early in the
century, have multiple texts. Study of the various genres of motet texts could
be a book in itself and we cannot go into the matter in depth here. There are,
however, some elements of the generic repertory of motet texts that especially demand to be taken into consideration.

NEW VS. PRE-EXISTENT TEXTS

A motet composer could set either a new text, written close to the time of the
composition, often for the motet; or he could choose a pre-existent text; or
some combination of the two. The preference for these strategies changed
radically over the course of the fifteenth century. In 1400 motets generally
had new texts, written for the composition. By the 1470s composers usually
chose pre-existent texts and set them to music. This change reflected a fundamental transformation in both the form and meaning of the motet.

The genre of a new text was essentially the genre "motet text," since the
text had no pre-existent generic affiliations. New texts were written in many
different styles, however, and sometimes resembled pre-existent texts with
identifiable genres. Some motet texts outlived their settings, to be circulated

35

as literature or set to new music much later.[27] Features relevant to all motet texts are as follows.

PROSE OR POETRY

Depending on the musical setting, this distinction can have a great impact on the musical work's form and structure; it also affects the tone of the work a great deal. There are also of course numerous finer distinctions: what kind of prose? and especially, what kind of poetry – quantitative or accentual meter, rhyming, stanzaic, lyric, heroic? Each of these has its own traditions and associations.

LENGTH

A long motet can have a short text, but there are limits on how short a piece with a long text can be. Long and short texts also have very different rhetorical impacts.

SUBJECT MATTER

Motet texts can be divided into sacred and secular, though sometimes the distinction is difficult to make. Sacred texts include those in honor of the Virgin, of Christ, and the saints. Secular texts include admonitory texts about the evils of the world or of the church and laudatory political texts about rulers (and church leaders), sometimes with reference to specific occasions.[28]

TONE AND ASPECT

Is the text intimate and personal, or formal and hieratic? Is it in first person, singular or plural, or second? Is it a prayer, a narrative, a celebration, or an admonition? Or some combination of these?

LITERARY REFERENCES

To what extent is the text self-consciously literary or learned? What literary traditions does it refer to? Does it contain specific textual allusions or quotations? Is it susceptible to more than one reading?

Pre-existent texts can be divided many different ways. Important questions to ask about a pre-existent text are as follows.

WAS THE TEXT WELL KNOWN OR RARE?

If well known, then the recognition factor would have played a role in the "composer's hearing" of the motet; if extremely rare the distinction between it and a new text disappears.

DOES THE MOTET USE THE COMPLETE TEXT? IS THE TEXT COMPOSITE OR A CENTO?

It was fairly normal to use selected stanzas of a strophic text, or simply excerpts or fragments of longer texts. Late in the fifteenth century the compilation of motet texts out of fragments of other texts became common. In this case we have a text newly created for the motet, but assembled from pre-existent material.[29]

WAS THE TEXT ASSOCIATED WITH MUSIC OR NOT?

Texts associated with music include chant texts of all kinds (especially the various kinds of antiphons and sequences) and the various kinds of Latin songs (Central European *cantiones* and *Leisen*, or Italian laude). These texts have their own textual/musical/liturgical generic traditions. Texts without musical associations include devotional poetry (sometimes found in books of hours), saints' lives, and prayers. There is a middle group which consists of texts that were recited to a tone of some kind, but were not associated with a real melody: this group includes psalms and lessons.

WHAT WAS THE FUNCTION OR LITURGICAL POSITION OF THE TEXT IN ITS ORIGINAL FORM?

Did it have a narrowly prescribed liturgical position? Or was it used for special endowments and devotions, group or private? If the original context (textual or liturgical) of the text was well known, this might have a significant impact on the meaning of the motet.

Text and music together

The ways in which text and music are combined also plays a role in the generic repertory. The extent to which text is foregrounded or backgrounded has a major effect on the work. Some of the issues to consider in the combination follow.

NUMBER OF TEXTS

Polytextuality was a standard feature of the medieval motet, and it persisted in the fifteenth century, especially in more retrospective works. Isorhythmic motets are among those most associated with multiple texts, but non-isorhythmic works with two upper voices in the same range were also often polytextual. After 1450 polytextuality is rare, except in the case of the tenor motet with a foreign tenor, in which the pre-existent tenor voice carries its own text, different from the text in the other voices.[30]

NUMBER OF TEXTED VOICES

In most manuscripts of the fifteenth century not all voices are texted. This remains a dilemma for performance practice: should we add the text found in the discantus part, for example, to the other voices? Should singers of untexted voices vocalize on a syllable or syllables? Or should untexted voices be played on instruments?[31] Whatever the performance decision, there are standard patterns for texting. If only one voice is texted it will be the discantus; upper voices are texted more than lower voices, and long-note tenors and contratenors are rarely texted. We may infer that there must be text in the upper voices, where it will project most clearly; the presence of text in the lower voices may be optional. Texting and texture are closely tied.

NUMBER OF NOTES PER SYLLABLE

When a piece is syllabic the text is foregrounded, and becomes a generator of rhythm and phrase structure (as in Dunstaple's *Quam pulchra es*, for example). Here the difference between prose and poetry is very marked, and can lead to different approaches to phrase structure and form. When a piece is highly melismatic, with many notes per syllable, the text recedes into the background, since phrase lengths and rhythm are governed primarily by musical considerations, and the form of the text is obscured. Most pieces are somewhere in between, and the prominence of the text varies over the course of the piece. Texting can combine with texture to produce some special effects: when syllabic text setting is combined with declamation, for example (as in *Quam pulchra*), or when polytextuality reinforces the independence of individual voices in an isorhythmic motet.

STRUCTURAL CORRESPONDENCES BETWEEN TEXT AND MUSIC

Most motets demonstrate correspondences between text and music: a clause or line of the text receives a phrase of music, or each stanza corresponds to a section of the piece. The tightness of the connection varies greatly, however, and some pieces are provided with additional or contrafact texts, where the connections are usually weakened.

Clusters of features

Each subgenre of the motet is characterized by clusters of features. While any one feature is found in many different subgenres, it is combined with a different combination of additional features. Thus in the mid-fifteenth century four-voice motets with two *partes* in contrasting mensurations (O₵) become fairly common. These two features are shared by three different subgenres, each in turn characterized by other distinguishing features. Some are tenor motets with occasional texts and long-note foreign tenors; these have extensive duet sections beginning each *pars*. Some paraphrase chants in the upper voice; these have no sections in reduced scoring and tend to use votive antiphon texts. Some freely composed motets have sections in reduced scoring, like the tenor motets, but lack the long-note tenor. These three subgenres also recall genres outside the motet: the tenor motet resembles the cyclic Mass movement, the chant paraphrase motets recall liturgical service music, and the freely composed pieces recall both the three-voice cantilena and the *sine nomine* Mass cycle. The specific features of an individual work will serve to refine its meaning in this larger context of allusion and association.

The features of the generic repertory listed here will play a large role in our identification of the different subgenres of the motet. Identification of the subgenres will allow us to develop a horizon of expectation for any individual

39

work. The horizon of expectation will enable us to recognize the ways in which a work negotiates the conflicting claims of tradition and innovation. Is it typical of its subgenre? If not, does it exhibit features that lead to new subgenres? Does it employ generic (or subgeneric) mixture? Recognition of the associations and references to the history of the motet, to other genres, and to other subgenres invoked by specific features will enable us to locate individual works and whole subgenres on the genre hierarchy and detail the ways in which text and music work together for expressive effect.

3 Fifteenth-century uses of the term "motet"

Before turning to a study of the repertory, we should consider what the term "motet" meant to people in the fifteenth century.[1] The word "motet" is used in three different kinds of sources in the fifteenth century: treatises, archival documents, and music manuscripts. The treatises and archival documents virtually never mention fifteenth-century works that we can identify, and thus it is difficult to know exactly what kinds of pieces are meant by their use of the term "motet." They do, however, help us to develop some sense of the term's associations and its relationship to other generic labels of the period. I know of two music manuscripts that use the term "motet"; they allow us to associate surviving compositions with the term, and to contrast the "motets" with works belonging to other genres. Manuscript usage of the term can also be supplemented with evidence from manuscripts that are organized by genre. Although the meaning of the term "motet" evades precise definition, the combined evidence from these three kinds of source allows us to make a fundamental distinction between the motet and the prescribed liturgical genres, and to establish a repertory of motets.

Treatises

The motet is frequently discussed in the music treatises of fourteenth-century France, where contemporary examples are often cited.[2] These discussions are primarily concerned with the construction and rhythmic notation of what we now call the French isorhythmic motet. Early fifteenth-century music theorists (such as Prosdocimus de Beldemandis and Ugolino of Orvieto) made little attempt to modify their discussions of the motet in response to changes in the genre or in musical style: their treatises are essentially glosses on fourteenth-century French treatises, especially the *Libellus cantus mensurabilis* of Jean de Muris, where the term "motet" refers only to the French-style isorhythmic motet.[3] (One treatise from early fourteenth-century Italy does discuss the independent tradition of the Italian motet in relation to the caccia, but it is not taken up in fifteenth-century writings.[4]) Only toward the end of the fifteenth century do we find theoretical definitions in which the term "motet" refers to more than the French isorhythmic motet of the fourteenth century. We will begin with the first of these new definitions.

Johannes Tinctoris

The most famous definition of the motet in the fifteenth century is by the theorist Johannes Tinctoris in his music dictionary of 1476. His definition of the motet (*motetum*) must be understood in the context of his definitions of chanson (*cantilena*) and Mass (*missa*).

A *cantilena* is a small piece which is set to a text on any kind of subject, but more often to an amatory one.

A motet is a composition of moderate length, to which words of any kind are set, but more often those of a sacred nature.

The Mass is a large composition for which the texts Kyrie, Et in terra, Patrem, Sanctus, and Agnus, and sometimes other parts, are set for singing by several voices. It is called the Office by some.[5]

These definitions are echoed in the discussion of the necessity for variety in musical works found in Tinctoris's *Liber de arte contrapuncti*:

There is not as much variety in a chanson as in a motet, nor is there as much variety in a motet as in a Mass. Every composed work, therefore, must be made diverse according to its quality and quantity.[6] [My translation.]

These definitions help us very little in establishing boundaries for the category motet. The vagueness of the phrase "words of any kind" suggests that fifteenth-century people were not too clear about what a motet was either.

There is still much to be learned from Tinctoris's definition. His division into small, medium, and large (*cantus parvus*, *cantus mediocris*, and *cantus magnus*) correlates with the relative length of each genre: chansons are the shortest, motets are middle-sized, Masses are longest. It also corresponds to the medieval generic hierarchy known as the "Rota Virgiliana," in which the works of Virgil, and by extension all literary works, could be divided into three style heights: the "humilis stilus" (pastoral: the *Eclogues*), the "mediocris stilus" (farming: the *Georgics*) and the "gravis stilus" (epic: the *Aeneid*).[7] Tinctoris's aim was as much to align the music of his day with classical literature as it was to define genres in any detailed way. His reference to a genre hierarchy does show that one of the functions of generic classification is to establish style height and tone. The motet's intermediate position in the hierarchy suggests that it might have a range of lengths and style heights: from the humble intimacy of the three-voice chanson up to the grandeur and solemnity of the lengthy four-voice Mass (or Mass movement). This potential flexibility of style height corresponds to the flexibility of text type and subject matter.

Paolo Cortese

Tinctoris's generic hierarchy was recalled almost thirty-five years later in Paolo Cortese's *De Cardinalatu libri tres* (1510), a humanist treatise on correct behavior for cardinals.[8] In the final section of his chapter on "How passions should be avoided, and music used after meals,"[9] Cortese discusses the role of music in promoting pleasure, knowledge, and morals, and goes into some detail discussing different types of instrumental and vocal music. Toward the end of this section he discusses three types of song. Cortese invents new classicizing Latin terms for the different genres; the marginal glosses, however, make his meaning clear by using Tinctoris's triad of "misse, moteti and cantilene." The new terms are "litatoria" (Masses: sacrificial or propitiatory songs), "praecentoria" (motets: precentorial songs for the precentors or leaders of the choir), and "carmina" (songs: settings of vernacular poetry).[10] The *litatoria*, as in Tinctoris, seem to be characterized by their variety, since they use the most learned devices ("omnia pthongorum [modes] / prosodiarum [mensurations] analogicarumque mensionum [imitations] genera" – Cortese himself may not have known what he meant by these very learned-sounding neologisms); they are also at the top of the genre hierarchy, since "no one should be included in the number of the most eminent musicians, who is not very conversant with the making of the propitiatory [*litatorius*] mode."[11] He identifies Josquin as the pre-eminent composer because of his excellence in writing Masses.

The *praecentoria* (identified as "moteti" in the margin) are those which "although mixed with the propitiatory singing, can be seen to be supernumerary [*ascriptitia*] and ingrafted [*insititia*], since for them there is free option of choice." This can only mean that motets are inserted into the Mass service as extra, optional additions; the text of the motets and perhaps their location in the service are also flexible. Thus Cortese stresses the motet's flexibility of function and its optional character, characteristics that correlate with the vagueness of Tinctoris's definition and with modern scholars' confusion about the motet's liturgical function. Cortese goes on to suggest that this flexibility of function also leads to flexibility of style: "for this reason it happens, they say, that those modes all of one kind [*uniusmodi modi*: perhaps "ways of preserving unity"] on which the propitiatory songs [Masses] unremittingly insist, are not preserved by them [motets]."[12] This probably means that movements of a cyclic Mass are all bound to use the same cantus firmus (or other "modi" of unification), but that motets are not so bound. The discussion of the motet ends with a detailed assessment of the achievement of several different composers from the late fifteenth and early sixteenth centuries (Obrecht, Isaac, Agricola, Brumel, Compère, and the theorist Spataro), all of whom "have expertly practiced in this precentorial genre."[13] Cortese writes as an experienced listener, with opinions about the strengths and weaknesses of each composer.

The term for Cortese's third type of vocal music, *carmina* or songs (identified as "cantilene" in the margin), refers to the singing of vernacular Italian poetry to the lute. The *carmina* are at the bottom of the genre hierarchy, but they are also the most moving: "it can rightly be said that the motions of the souls are usually appeased and excited with more vehemence by the *carmina* in this genre." The only specific figures he mentions here are Petrarch and the poet/performer Serafino Aquilano. It was evidently in the motet that Cortese felt most at home evaluating the relative merits and styles of individual composers of his day.

Both Tinctoris and Cortese, different as they are in their aims, intellectual frameworks, and period, project a similar image of the motet: it lies in the middle of the genre hierarchy; it can have a broad range of tone and style height; it is textually and functionally flexible, with no fixed subject matter and no prescribed liturgical position; and it is a genre in which composers can display their individuality by means of variety.

44

Archival references

The term "motetum" is used in some fifteenth-century documents. In *Music in Late Medieval Bruges* Reinhard Strohm records quite a few, extracted primarily from the archives of the collegiate church of St. Donatian in Bruges, but also from some of the other churches in the city. Strohm's material can be supplemented with the findings of Barbara Haagh, Paula Higgins, Maria Carmen Gómez Muntané, and others. The word "motetum" comes up in several different contexts, including documentary references to physical copies of motets, and endowments for the performance of motets.[14]

Libri motetorum and motet singing

There are archival references to motet books extending from the late fourteenth century until about 1460. None of these "libri motetorum" have been identified with surviving manuscripts, so we do not know what they contained. There is evidence that they included not only motets but also chansons (especially in the fourteenth century) and Mass movements. In 1379 the Duke of Gerona, for example, requested his ambassador in Avignon to send "a book where there are many motets, rondeaux, ballades, and virelais."[15] Such a book would resemble the surviving Chantilly and Cypriot codices, which contain motets and chansons.[16] In Bruges there is a reference to the copying of "quibusdam motetis, scilicet Patrem, Et in terra, ac Sanctus" ("several motets, that is to say [the Mass movements] Credo, Gloria, and Sanctus") into the *Libri puerorum choralium* (the choirboys' books) in 1427.[17] This may be a reference to Mass movements in motet texture or style (with cantus firmus and two upper parts). When the Duke of Bedford, English regent in France, died in 1435, a "livre de motetz en la maniere de France" was found among his possessions.[18] And as late as 1455 in Bruges a *Missa de gratiarum actione* was copied into the "magnus liber motetorum."[19] "Motet," then, can mean polyphony in general; "Liber motetorum" seems to mean a book of polyphony, including motets and/or Mass movements. Such motet books correspond to surviving manuscripts of Masses and motets such as Bologna Q15 or the Trent Codices.

Still, while "motet" could have a general meaning of "polyphony" (perhaps "Latin-texted polyphony" in the fifteenth century), it also clearly had a more

specific meaning. In 1408 the chapter of the Sainte-Chapelle in Bourges pur-
chased a "book of motets and Patrems [i.e. Credos]" for the choirboys.[20] Here
motets are clearly distinguished from Mass movements. In 1420 Johannes
Coutreman received a raise for instructing the boys in "motet singing" and in
1452 singers at St. Donatian in Bruges were reprimanded for refusing to assist
the succentor in motet-singing on the eve of Epiphany.[21] These could be
references to actual motets, rather than to polyphony in general, since singing
motets may have been more difficult than singing other genres. The term
"liber motetorum" seems to fall out of usage after *c.* 1460, at least in Bruges;
from then on books of polyphony are called "libri discantu." In 1479/80
Strohm finds a reference to a "liber missarum et motetarum": here Masses are
clearly distinguished from motets in the title of the manuscript.[22] Barbara
Haagh has found records for copying music at St. Niklaas in Brussels: in
1485/6 payment is made to Abertijne "for 30 sexterns with motets and Salve
Reginas"; these motets are not Mass movements, for later in the same document there is a payment for the copying of "22 Masses." The next year
Abertijne was still at it, receiving another payment for "22 Masses and various
motets."[23]

Endowments

An endowment was a gift of money to a church to pay for the performance of
devotions to a patron saint, in honor of a deceased relative, or both.[24] Often
such endowments described in some detail the desired devotions, sometimes
stipulating the performance of polyphony. Quite a few of the Bruges endowments specify the performance of motets, usually at processions at Vespers
services for certain saints, as a way of stepping up the formality and rank of
these services. Thus in 1415 an endowment provided for the performance of
two motets by the succentor and the choirboys at the end of first and second
Vespers of the feast of the Exaltation of the Cross (14 September) and in
1417 a motet was performed during the procession on the octave of the feast
of Corpus Christi.[25] An endowment of 1432 stipulated a motet to be sung
during the procession to the altar of the saints during Vespers at the parish
church of St. James; another such endowment is found from 1454.[26] In the
1470s and 1480s at the parish church of St. Saviour there was a series of
endowments for the performance of motets at Vespers processions.[27] Douglas
Salokar has found many references to the performance of motets at Vespers

in the Church of Our Lady in Bruges during the last quarter of the fifteenth century.[28] There is evidence that motets were sung also at Mass: in an endowment of 1451 Philip the Good specified a polyphonic Mass "with a motet afterwards" to be sung annually just after the feast of the Assumption,[29] and in 1460 a motet by Charles the Bold was sung after Mass at Cambrai Cathedral.[30]

It is fairly clear in all these cases that "motet" does not mean a Mass movement; what it does mean exactly remains a mystery. For in addition to endowments specifying motets there are endowments for more specific liturgical items: Masses and *Magnificat* settings, but also votive Marian antiphons such as *Salve regina* and *Alma redemptoris mater*, and sequences such as *Inviolata integra et casta*. For example, Strohm finds endowments for the performance of the four great Marian antiphons in polyphony beginning in 1434,[31] while in 1461 the Fraternity of Notre Dame de la Treille in Lille endowed the solemn performance of the prose *Inviolata* daily after Vespers between Christmas and Candlemas.[32] Salokar's endowed Vespers services generally list specific antiphons to be sung (perhaps in chant?) and then add an unspecified motet (perhaps *ad libitum* polyphony?).[33] Endowments for polyphonic settings of specific Marian chants are commonplace in England.[34] Do these pieces count as motets? Barbara Haagh's reference to a manuscript of "motets and *Salve reginas*" in Brussels suggests that there is some distinction between the two; on the other hand, the fact that they are found in the same manuscript might also suggest that they had similar uses. We can be sure that there was a great deal of regional and temporal variation in liturgical practice and generic classification.

Archival references to *libri motetorum* and to motet singing suggest that the term "motet" had both a general meaning and a specific one in the first half of the century. As stated above, in its general usage, motet could refer to any vocal polyphony, and a *liber motetorum* was a manuscript of polyphonic music. The specific meaning refers to polyphony other than the chanson and the Mass. Later in the century the general meaning is dropped, and motets are even more clearly contrasted with Masses. Endowments allow us to refine the specific meaning: a motet is a polyphonic work used to adorn devotions, especially Vespers, but also Mass. Motets also appear outside the service proper: during processions or after the service (whether Mass or Vespers). They thus lack a specific, prescribed liturgical function. Polyphonic settings of sequences or Marian antiphon texts could also have been considered motets.

47

Music manuscripts

The literary critic Gary Saul Morson points out that the aims of the classifier often determine the articulation of genre.[35] Scribes and compilers of music manuscripts are fifteenth-century classifiers, and in music manuscripts, unlike treatises and archival documents, it is finally possible to associate known, surviving compositions with the term "motet." Only two fifteenth-century manuscripts use the term "motet" in their indices: Modena X.1.11 (*c.* 1448), and Berlin 40021 (*c.* 1485–1500). Careful study of Modena X.1.11 proves very instructive. The Berlin manuscript falls outside the time frame of this study, so I will consider it only briefly here. After examining how the word "motet" is used in these two sources we will consider the representation of the motet in the whole range of fifteenth-century sources.

Modena X.1.11

A collection of polyphonic music for Vespers, Modena X.1.11 is clearly organized by genre into four sections containing hymns, *Magnificat* settings, Vespers antiphons, and motets (the motets are further subdivided into continental and English groups).[36] In the index or table of contents, listing the pieces in manuscript order, the scribe indicated the beginning of the motet section with the phrase "Hic incipiunt motteti." Most of the eighteen motets in the continental group are by Du Fay, and most of the fifty-two motets in the English group are by Dunstaple; nevertheless, the motet section in Modena X.1.11 has a miscellaneous character, including a variety of text types and musical types. The motet texts include antiphons of all kinds, devotional poems, and new occasional texts. Some pieces have one text, some have two, some have three; some have three voices, some have four; some use isorhythm, some do not.

   The motets in this manuscript are thus clearly distinguished, by means of the organization of the manuscript, from three genres of liturgical service music: polyphonic settings of hymns, *Magnificat* settings, and Vespers antiphons. There is little chance of confusion between motets and *Magnificat* settings: like the Mass Ordinary, the *Magnificat* text is well known, and the genre has a clear place in the Vespers liturgy. Polyphonic hymn settings have occasionally been considered motets, but Tom Ward's catalogue of fifteenth-century polyphonic Office hymns has, as he says, removed "755 works from that vague category 'motet'."[37] None of the pieces in the motet section uses a hymn text in any case.

Many of the pieces in the motet section do set antiphon texts. What led the scribe of Modena X.1.11 to put some antiphon settings in the antiphon section of the manuscript, and others in the motet section? The answer to this question will help to straighten out a long-standing confusion between the motet and the polyphonic antiphon.

ANTIPHON SETTINGS IN THE ANTIPHON SECTION (SEE TABLE 3.1)

There are sixteen antiphons in this section: seven by Du Fay, five by Binchois, and a few each by Fede and Benoit, composers associated with Ferrara.[38] Half are *Magnificat* antiphons, plus some psalm and processional antiphons.[39] Most are for saints, and some are provided with rubrics identifying the feast on which the antiphon is to be sung. There is only one antiphon to the Virgin.[40] Although there is a range of styles and approaches, almost all use chant in a fairly obvious way (with a monophonic intonation to begin the piece, light paraphrase of the chant in one voice, or statement of the chant in equal values). Almost half use fauxbourdon, found primarily in other simple liturgical service music such as the hymns and *Magnificat* settings in this manuscript.[41] In other words, these antiphons are like the hymns in the hymn section: they are liturgically equivalent to prescribed chant. This is indicated musically by the clear presentation of the chant in the musical setting and the use of fauxbourdon, and in the manuscript by rubrics and the fact that the antiphons are grouped in a special section along with other pieces of the same type and function.[42] Looking at the figures in Table 3.1 and choosing as prototypical those features found in a majority of the antiphons, we would say that the prototypical antiphon in the antiphon section is a *Magnificat* antiphon for a saint, which uses chant and begins with a chant intonation, is one page long, and has three voices. Less essential features are the use of fauxbourdon and rubrics identifying its feast day.

ANTIPHON SETTINGS IN THE MOTET SECTION

The motet section of Modena X.1.11 is divided into two subsections: the first is devoted to continental motets, while the second, larger subsection is

Table 3.1. *Settings of antiphon texts in Modena X.1.11*

Section:	Antiphon	Cont. motet	Eng. motet
Total As/total in section	16/18	6/18	39/52
Antiphon types:			
Magnificat As	8	1	1
Other As	5 (2 Ps. As)	4	30
Other genres, not found (=?)	3 (?)	1 (?)	7 (3 S, 4?)
Subject matter:			
Saints	15	1	2
Virgin/+Cross	1	5	34/+2
Rubrics	5	—	—
Musical features:			
Use chant (with intonation)	15 (11)	3 (1 1/2)	8 (1)
Freely composed	1	3	31
Fauxbourdon	7	—	—
3 vv.	16	4	38
4 vv.	—	2	—
Length in MS pages:			
1/2	6	—	—
1	9	3	6
2	1	3	28
3	—	—	2
4	—	—	2

devoted to English repertory.[43] I will consider them both, but keep them separate (see Table 3.1). I include as an antiphon setting any piece using an antiphon text, unless the antiphon appears only in the cantus firmus of an iso-rhythmic motet. I also include in Table 3.1 pieces with antiphon-like texts that have not been identified (marked as ?), and sequence texts that could be used as votive antiphon texts (shown as S).[44] Under "use chant" I include any kind of cantus firmus usage, including extremely free paraphrase, or tenor cantus firmi distinct from the antiphon text found in the other voices.

The distinctions between the pieces in the antiphon and motet sections are clearest where we find low and high numbers in the same row of Table 3.1. Thus while the antiphon texts in the antiphon section are mostly for the *Magnificat*, few of the motet-section pieces are. The antiphon-section pieces are for saints, while all but four of the motet-section pieces are settings of texts in honor of the Virgin, chiefly votive and processional antiphons – texts whose association with the liturgy is flexible and highly variable, rather than the prescribed *Magnificat* antiphons of the antiphon section.[45] The antiphon-section pieces use chant, the motet-section pieces do not (at least the English ones do not). The prototypical English antiphon setting is a processional or votive antiphon for the Virgin, freely composed for three voices and two pages (one opening) long. This prototype is different from the antiphon-section prototype in every way, except for the number of voices. The continental antiphon settings in the motet section fall somewhere in between the two prototypes: although they basically line up with the English prototype, they are as likely to use chant as not, and as likely to be one page as two. Unlike either prototype, the continental motet-antiphons can have four voices.[46]

While some of the pieces in the motet section have individual features typical of the antiphon-section pieces, when all their features are considered together they are significantly different from the pieces in the antiphon section, and the scribe's categorization makes sense. Du Fay's and Dunstaple's settings of the Marian antiphon *Ave regina celorum* are a case in point. Both are found in the motet section. Like the pieces in the antiphon section they have chant intonations and paraphrase the chant in the discantus. Unlike the antiphon-section pieces, their chant paraphrase is quite free, they use Marian antiphon texts, and they have contrasting sections in different mensurations, much more typical of the motet-section pieces.

LESSONS FROM MODENA X.1.11

Polyphonic settings of Latin texts can be divided up and categorized in many different ways. One common twentieth-century musicological method of classification divides the pieces into "liturgical" and "non-liturgical": "liturgical" pieces have texts associated with chant melodies, "non-liturgical" pieces have texts for which no music is known (devotional poetry with no known music, or new texts for occasional, political, and dedicatory works). Settings of "liturgical" texts, whether or not they use the melody that goes with the chant text, are often assumed to substitute for the chant at its prescribed place in the liturgy. The "non-liturgical" category is often equated with the motet.

The Modena scribe, however, makes a different distinction: between settings of chants (both text and melody) with prescribed positions in the liturgy

(*Magnificat* settings, hymns, Vespers antiphons for saints), and settings of all the other kinds of sacred Latin texts, which he lumps together as motets. He includes under motets both pieces with "non-liturgical" texts and settings of "liturgical" texts (and sometimes melodies) for which the liturgical function or position is optional or movable, especially settings of texts addressed to the Virgin. The distinction can be diagrammed as follows:

	associated with chant melodies			texts without music
texts:	prescribed	|	optional	sacred, non-liturgical; secular
twentieth-century:	liturgical polyphony		|	motets ⟶
Mod X.1.11:	service music	|	motets ⟶	

The generic distinction between the prescribed service music (hymns, *Magnificat* settings, and Vespers antiphons for the *Magnificat*) and the motets is made explicit in Modena X.1.11 both by means of organization and by differentiation in musical style. Each genre of service music has its own section, devoted to texts of a single type; liturgical function is often indicated by means of rubrics, calendrical ordering (the hymns), or both; and the pieces are composed in such a way as to display the chant clearly and concisely. In the motet section, on the other hand, text types are mixed; chant melodies are used sparingly, and often concealed rather than displayed; and there are no rubrics. The different kinds of text used for the motet will be important in identifying its different subgenres, but text type alone is not enough to determine whether a piece is a motet or a piece of service music: manuscript context, musical style, and treatment of chant must also come into play.

How does the usage of the term "motet" in Modena X.1.11 correspond to the usage in the later manuscript Berlin 40021? The music in the Berlin manuscript is not clearly organized, but it does have a table of contents organized by genre, with four categories: "Offitia" (Mass music); "*Magnificat*"; "Cantica. hymni. sequentiae"; and "Muteti et alia."[47] Genres of prescribed liturgical music – Mass Ordinary and Propers, *Magnificat* settings or other canticles (*Nunc dimittis* and *Te deum*), sequences, and hymns – are clearly distinguished from motets. This finding corresponds to the organization of Modena X.1.11.

The Marian antiphons *Salve regina* and *Regina celi* are included under "Cantica," and thus are considered liturgical service music, not motets. This treatment of the Marian antiphons contrasts with the situation in Modena X.1.11, but it may reflect regional variations and changing liturgical and compositional practice. One *Salve regina* that uses a borrowed cantus firmus rather than the Marian antiphon melody was added to the index later and in the wrong place; this suggests some confusion about how to classify it.

Settings of other antiphon texts and melodies are included in both "Cantica" and "Muteti et alia." Those listed under "Cantica" tend to be simple chant settings, while those listed with "Muteti et alia" are more complex. One piece in this second category, *Stabat virgo/T: In exitu*, is labeled a "mutete de compassione marie." This suggests that pieces in which the cantus firmus is a foreign tenor, with a text different from that of the other voices, are definitely considered motets. Such works descend from the isorhythmic motets with cantus firmus found in Modena X.1.11.

Study of these two manuscripts has shown that the boundary between the motet and the genres of prescribed liturgical service music is permeable: there are always pieces that seem to sit on the fence. Liturgical practices vary over space and time as well, and the fence moves with them. The main difficulty lies in the borderland between the motet and settings of antiphons and sequences, especially those in honor of the Virgin. These are the genres of chant whose position in the liturgy is variable, optional, flexible; they therefore make ideal material for the variable, optional, flexible motet.

The way the term "motet" is used in these two manuscripts accords with our findings about the meanings of the term "motet" in fifteenth-century theoretical and archival sources. Together they suggest that "motet" was commonly understood as follows. It excluded prescribed liturgical service music, but it included polyphonic settings of many chant texts and/or melodies for which the liturgical usage is optional or flexible, as well as settings of many other kinds of texts with no associated melodies.

Such a statement does not get us very far toward a concrete description of the motet. As we shall see, description must be done at the level of the sub-genre. It does, however, point toward a method for identifying motets and excluding non-motets in other manuscripts. In generically organized sources, pieces found in the same section belong to the same genre (excluding page fillers and later additions). While few manuscripts label their sections, many have distinct motet sections comparable to the motet section in Modena X.1.11. We can safely assume, then, that a piece found in a motet section is a motet, at least according to the compiler of that manuscript. Other manuscripts are assembled piecemeal, and lack any overarching generic organization. Once we exclude the non-motets in these sources – prescribed liturgical service music, Masses, and chansons – what we are left with should be motets. Comparison of the pieces in this residual class with the kinds of pieces found in distinct motet sections will enable us to confirm or disconfirm our identification of the pieces as motets.

Motets in other fifteenth-century sources

There are no fifteenth-century sources containing only motets (the first Renaissance collection devoted to motets comes immediately after the turn of the century: Petrucci's *Motetti A* of 1502). There are sources devoted to each of the other genres (chansons, Masses, and prescribed liturgical service music).[48] The sources containing motets can thus be classified according to the principal genres they include along with the motets: all-purpose collections (with and without secular music); Masses; Vespers music; and secular music (see Table 3.2). Some of the source types can be associated with specific regions and time periods, as different types of contents were assembled for different purposes. The fact that motets can be found in conjunction with all the other genres, and in manuscripts compiled for so many different purposes, points again to its functional flexibility and its position in the middle of the genre hierarchy. Motets could mix with everything: with the aristocratic Mass cycles, the hardworking liturgical service music, and fun-loving secular songs.

Knowledge of the various types of motet source for our period can therefore help us to recognize the different subgenres and functions of the motet, and their position in the genre hierarchy.[49] In Table 3.2 I have listed all the fifteenth-century motet sources copied on the Continent containing more than five motets, in approximate chronological order, but grouped by provenance.[50] I have omitted sources copied in the fifteenth century but containing primarily fourteenth-century repertory. The number of sources copied *c.* 1500 increases greatly; I chose to include a few of each type, without trying for complete coverage. I end with the first collection devoted to motets, also the first printed book of motets, *Motetti A.*

Manuscripts with small numbers of motets (fewer than ten, but more than five) are in parentheses; manuscripts with clear motet sections are shown in bold-face type. The x's indicate the contents of the sources in addition to motets; when the x's are spaced out it means that there are not very many examples of that category in the source, relative to the total contents. By "Masses" I mean Mass Ordinary movements, individual, paired, and in cycles.

By "service" I mean prescribed liturgical service music with clear presentation of the chant: this category includes Mass Propers, alternatim sequences, and especially Vespers music (*Magnificat* settings, hymns, psalms, and Vespers antiphons). By "secular" I mean primarily French chansons, but also Italian and German songs, and pieces without text (some of which, at least, were instrumental).[51] Each type of source reveals something about the function of the motet in the fifteenth century.

ALL-PURPOSE COLLECTIONS (WITH AND WITHOUT SECULAR MUSIC)

The most common type of source containing motets is the all-purpose collection, including a little bit of everything. These can be divided into two groups: the early Italian sources that include secular music, and the many Central and Eastern European sources that include Latin-texted music of all kinds (secular music, in these sources, usually has Latin contrafact texts). The Italian group consists of the early manuscripts from the Veneto: Oxford 213, Bologna 2216, and Bologna Q15, all of which include some secular music. None of these manuscripts has yet been associated with any particular institution, but it seems likely that they functioned as repertory manuscripts for princely chapels of some kind. Oxford 213, our main source for Du Fay's early chansons, looks back in some ways to the sources of fourteenth-century repertory devoted to chansons and motets such as the Chantilly Codex, and in fact includes some fourteenth-century repertory.[52] It adds to this mix a substantial number of Mass movements, but avoids the more utilitarian liturgical service music. Bologna 2216 has a similar profile, with a final section devoted to Italian and French songs; it also includes a few *Magnificat* settings, a hymn, and some *Benedicamus Domino* settings. Bologna Q15 is a complex manuscript compiled by a scribe with idiosyncratic and changing tastes. It includes all the polyphony required by a functioning chapel, including Masses and hymns and *Magnificat* settings for Vespers. Laude and chansons are added as page fillers. We will return to this manuscript at more length below.[53]

The second group comes primarily from Central and Eastern Europe: the Council of Basel group, the mid-century Trent Codices, to which we shall return below, and the later German and Eastern European sources, including Berlin 40021. All of these sources are devoted primarily to Latin-texted music

55

Table 3.2. *Fifteenth-century manuscripts containing more than five motets*

Date	MS	Masses	Service	Secular	
Veneto					
1420–36	**Bologna Q15**	xxxxxxxxxx	xxxxxxxxxx	x x x x	Early 15th C.
c. 1440	**B2216**	xxxxxxxxxx	x x x x	xxxxxxxxxx	
1430–6	Ox 213	xxxxxxxxxx	xxxxxxxxxx	xxxxxxxxxx	
Austrian/Swiss (Council of Basel)					
1429–40	Trent 92	xxxxxxxxxx	xxxxxxxxxx	x x x x	
1430–45	Trent 87	xxxxxxxxxx	xxxxxxxxxx	x x x x	
1434–42	Aosta	xxxxxxxxxx	xxxxxxxxxx		
1435–43	MuEm	xxxxxxxxxx	xxxxxxxxxx	x x x	
Ferrara					
c. 1448	**Modena X.1.11**		xxxxxxxxxx		
Trent					
1452–9	Trent 90	xxxxxxxxxx	xxxxxxxxxx	x x x x	
1456–62	Trent 88	xxxxxxxxxx	xxxxxxxxxx	x x x x	
1460–6	Trent 89	xxxxxxxxxx	xxxxxxxxxx	x x x x	
1472–7	Trent 91	xxxxxxxxxx	xxxxxxxxxx	x x x x	
German					
1461–7	Schedel			xxxxxxxxxx	
1478–80	Glogauer		xxxxxxxxxx	xxxxxxxxxx	
Italian					Mid-15th C.
1460–70	F112bis	xxxxxxxxxx	xxxxxxxxxx		
1463–75	(SP B80)	xxxxxxxxxx	xxxxxxxxxx		
Netherlands					
1462–80	(Br 5557)	xxxxxxxxxx	(2 *Magnificat* settings, 1 hymn)		
1467–72	Lucca	xxxxxxxxxx	(2 *Magnificat* settings)		

German			
1466–1511	**Mu 3154**	xxxxxxxxx	x x x x
German			
1485–1500	Berlin 40021	xxxxxxxxx	xxxxxxxxx	x x x x
1490–1504	Apel Codex	xxxxxxxxx	xxxxxxxxx	x x x x
c. 1500	Breslau 2016	xxxxxxxxx	xxxxxxxxx	x x x x
Eastern European			
1475–80	Strahov	xxxxxxxxx	xxxxxxxxx	x x x x
1480–1540	Speciálník	xxxxxxxxx	xxxxxxxxx	x x x x
Netherlands			
1493–1503	Chigi	xxxxxxxxx	xxxxxxxxx	
c. 1505	**Brussels 9126**	xxxxxxxxx	(3 *Magnificat* settings)	Late 15th C.
Italian			
1480–1500	(MC)		xxxxxxxxx	xxxxxxxxx
1481 (?)	Siena		xxxxxxxxx	xxxxxxxxx
1484–90	**Milan 1**			xxxxxxxxx
1490–1500	(Milan 2)		xxxxxxxxx	(4 *Magnificat* settings)
c. 1500	**Milan 3**		xxxxxxxxx	(6 *Magnificat* settings)
1500–1510	Milan 4		xxxxxxxxx	
c. 1490	(Verona 755)	xxxxxxxxx		
c. 1500	**Verona 758**			xxxxxxxxx
c. 1492	(CS 35)	xxxxxxxxx		
1495–7	**CS 15**			xxxxxxxxx
1495–1507	CS 63		x x x x	x x x x
1502	**Motetti A**			

of all kinds. Aosta stands slightly outside this tradition since it lacks any secular music and has an exceptionally large concentration of English music; Strohm suggests that it belonged to successive institutions associated with the royal/Imperial Habsburg court and that of Duke Frederick of Tyrol.[54] All the others include secular music as well (including German songs, both sacred and secular). More often than not chansons have contrafact Latin texts or no text at all. Reinhard Strohm associates these manuscripts with the *Kantorei*, choir schools associated with churches and universities, whose schoolmasters and students provided much of the occasional polyphony and public music for towns in Central Europe, inside and outside of church.

> Common features [of such manuscripts] are a rather miscellaneous nature and yet an unmistakable link with liturgical practice. The users had to perform in church every day, but many of the pieces served only for teaching purposes or for fun between school hours. Typically the manuscripts display many scribal hands, rounding out the work of one dominating scribe. This pattern of scribal collaboration is almost a portrait of the *Kantorei*. The assistants learned music and musical notation by filling the master's book.[55]

These all-purpose manuscripts contain the whole range of motet composition, from brief three-voice works resembling songs or liturgical service music, to the large multi-partite works for four or sometimes even five voices, from local traditions of composition to an international repertory of broadly disseminated works.

MASSES

Manuscripts containing Masses and motets (plus a few *Magnificat* settings). There are five such manuscripts with substantial numbers of motets: Lucca 238, Milan Librone 3, Milan Librone 4, Chigi, and Brussels 9126. Four more manuscripts seem to follow the same basic pattern, but include fewer than ten motets: Brussels 5557, Milan Librone 2, Verona 755, and CS 35. Most of them have a large section devoted to Masses at the beginning of the manuscript, followed by a shorter motet section at the end.[56] All of them come from the second half of the century, after the rise of the cyclic Mass. They can be divided into two different groups: repertory manuscripts for a cathedral or chapel of some importance (the Milan, Verona, and Cappella Sistina sources) or deluxe presentation manuscripts (Lucca 238, Brussels 5557, Chigi, and Brussels 9126). (Lucca 238 was a presentation manuscript that became a chapel manuscript; some of the other presentation manuscripts may have had similar functions.) The Mass Ordinary cycle was the largest musical genre of the fifteenth century and stood at the top of the genre hierarchy: it was therefore the ideal genre for inclusion in a presentation manuscript. By the middle of the century musical establishments that wanted to demonstrate their status and importance required such Mass cycles for regular performance; collections such as these (and others containing only Masses) were thus essential parts of the chapels' repertories. The fact that motets were included in some of the Mass manuscripts may indicate that motets were performed as an optional adjunct to Mass and that they approached the Mass cycle in prestige value. Endowments for the performance of polyphonic Masses and motets had become an important way of demonstrating both piety and prestige; these manuscripts would have provided the music to be performed for such endowed services. Motets in these manuscripts aspire toward the form and grandeur of the cyclic Mass, with four or more voices, two or more *partes*, and long-note tenor cantus firmi.

VESPERS MUSIC

Manuscripts with motets and liturgical service music (other than the Mass). These are Modena X.1.11; Florence 112bis; Milan Librone 1; Verona 758; and CS 15.[57] All the liturgical service music in this group of manuscripts is for Vespers, and includes in every case hymns and *Magnificat* settings, and in some cases psalm and antiphon settings as well. Most of the manuscripts begin with hymns, then *Magnificat* settings, and end with motets.[58] All have a clear section devoted to motets (like that of Modena X.1.11), which are thus set apart from and distinguished from the genres of prescribed liturgical service music. All are chapel manuscripts, compiled to suit the needs for polyphonic Vespers music for specific institutions. In Milan, Verona, and Rome the Vespers music manuscripts complement manuscripts devoted primarily to music for Mass.[59] In these institutions the choirs might well have sung from the Mass book at Mass, the Vespers book for Vespers (in conjunction, perhaps, with the appropriate chant books, the Graduale for Mass and the Antiphonale for Vespers). The fact that motets are found in both Mass and Vespers manuscripts suggests again that they were a common, if optional, adornment to both services.

SECULAR MUSIC

Most manuscripts containing substantial amounts of secular music lack motets and thus are not included in Table 3.2.[60] The most important exceptions to this rule from the mid-fifteenth century are the Schedel and Glogauer *Liederbücher*.[61] Both sources seem to have been personal collections compiled by well-educated intellectuals, presumably for performance by their circle of acquaintances, on voices or instruments or some combination. Both sources concentrate on short pieces for three voices, with only occasional four-voice pieces: chansons (generally lacking their French texts), German songs, and motets. Glogauer – probably compiled by an Augustinian canon – also contains many settings of chants in equal breves, presumably for liturgical use.[62] Like the Central European all-purpose manuscripts they contain a mix of local and international repertories. The motets found in these sources are thus primarily recreational music and equivalent to vernacular songs, and could have been used in the same courtly and household entertainment contexts.

Conclusion

Happily, there is little or no contradiction among these different kinds of sources about the meaning of the word "motet." The theorists Tinctoris and Cortese portray a genre that is textually and functionally flexible, with no fixed subject matter and no prescribed liturgical position, that lies in the middle of the genre hierarchy, and thus has a broad range of tone and style height: "to which words of any kind are set" (Tinctoris), "supernumerary and ingrafted, since for them there is free option of choice" (Cortese). Archival references suggest that "motet" can mean simply "polyphony" in some contexts, but it also has a more specific meaning: a genre without a prescribed liturgical function that was used to adorn devotions, especially Vespers, but also Mass. The use of the word "motet" in Modena X.1.11 reveals that there was a distinction between the motet and various types of prescribed liturgical service music set to polyphony. Survey of the sources reveals that the motet is found in association with all the other genres, and thus runs the gamut in terms of position in the genre hierarchy and function. In the deluxe presentation manuscripts the motet aspires to the heights of the Mass and may have been performed at Mass. The inclusion of motets in Vespers music manuscripts suggests that motets were also used at Vespers; their relegation in these sources to a separate section, often at the end of the manuscript, implies that the motets served as an optional adornment, not a prescribed part of the liturgy. Motets also mingle with secular music, especially in Central Europe; genre distinctions matter little when it is a question of recreational or instructional music. Essential to the identity of the genre is the idea of functional flexibility. Motets, like the optional chants that provide so many of their texts, can be used in many different contexts, within the liturgy and outside it.

But we still do not know what a motet is – or rather, we know that there are many different kinds of motets, found in many different kinds of sources. In the past three chapters I have laid out the basic assumptions and methodologies that I bring to my study of the motet in the early and mid-fifteenth century. In the following chapters I will put them to work in detailed study of the motet repertory as a whole. In Part II I will focus on the contents of the largest early fifteenth-century collection of motets: the pieces in the motet section of Bologna Q15 (*c.* 1420–1436). In Part III I will move on to the mid-century source complex known as the Trent Codices (*c.* 1429–1477), in which the motets are scattered throughout. Here the problem of distinguishing motets from non-motets is much more complex, and will be discussed in some detail. The generically organized Bologna Q15 and Modena X.1.11 will serve as check or comparison manuscripts for the Trent repertory.

Having established a repertory of motets found in these sources, the central task will be to identify the different kinds of motet and to establish the different subgenres. Subgenres are categories, and different subgenres will be characterized by clusters of features of different kinds. Subgenres may also be structured in a variety of ways, and some pieces may be found in more than one subgenre, or on the edge between two.

In establishing the subgenres of the fifteenth century motet we will also be concerned with tracing their origins and evolution. We begin with the situation as presented at the end of chapter 1, with the local varieties of motet as they had evolved during the fourteenth century. Patrons, composers, and performers of these different motet types (subgenres) met each other in France and in Constance in the second decade of the fifteenth century; evidence of this meeting is found in the substantial manuscripts copied in northern Italy beginning in 1420, especially in Bologna Q15. In Part II (chapters 4–7) we will trace the continuing histories of the fourteenth-century local traditions. In Part III (chapters 8–12) we will go on to trace the extinction and/or evolution

61

of the Q15 subgenres, and the origins of others in the Trent Codices and Modena X.1.11, ending in the early 1470s, just before the emergence of the Milan style and the first compositions in this new style by members of the Josquin generation. In the conclusion we will revisit all the various subgenres of the motet in the age of Du Fay, their evolution and relationships (see Table C.1 for a complete list).

Along the way we will stop from time to time to examine and interpret individual works. Some pieces will illustrate their subgenres by their position near the prototypical center, others by their position near the subgenre boundaries. These works use subgeneric ambiguity or mixture for expressive purposes. Much of the music we will be looking at is anonymous, or by little-known composers; much of it is also extremely good, well worthy of revival and performance today. The hero of this book is a genre, not a person, but Guillaume Du Fay emerges as the master of generic manipulation. His constant experimentation, ability to integrate foreign musical traditions into his own music, and sensitivity to the expressive potential of genre associations were unsurpassed.

Part II

Motets in the early fifteenth century: the case of Bologna Q15

4 The motet section of Bologna Q15 and its ramifying roots

As we have seen, an important source of evidence for genre in the case of the fifteenth-century motet is the practice of organizing manuscripts by genre. The principal early fifteenth-century manuscripts with distinct motet sections are Bologna Q15, Bologna 2216, and Modena X.1.11 (as was shown in Table 3.2).[1] All have similar organizational schemes, with the two Bologna manuscripts including Mass movements, and Modena X.1.11 concentrating on music for Vespers, with *Magnificat* settings and Vespers antiphons. Bologna Q15 provides music for both Mass and Vespers.

B2216:	Mass movements	motets	"recreational music"	
Q15:	Mass movements	motets	hymns *Magnificat* settings	
Mod:			hymns *Magnificat* settings	antiphons motets

Although the motet sections of the two Bologna manuscripts are not identified as such, the Modena motet section is labeled, as we have seen. It includes a broad range of kinds of pieces, as do the motet sections of Q15 and Bologna 2216, and some motets appear in all three.

The largest motet section from the period (with more than one hundred pieces) is the one in Bologna Q15. Margaret Bent has shown that the manuscript was copied by a single scribe over a period that extended from the early 1420s to the late 1430s, while the music was composed over a much longer period (from the 1370s to the late 1430s).[2] Composers whose motets are found in the manuscript come from all over Europe: from France (Carmen, Cesaris, Tapissier), from the Netherlands (Brassart, Ciconia, Du Fay, Grenon, Hugh and Arnold de Lantins), from Italy (Antonius Romanus, Cristoforus de Monte), and from England (Dunstaple, Power, and Forest). Knowledge of the

65

motets in Bologna Q15 will enable us to understand almost the whole range of motet types from the early fifteenth century.[3]

The identity of the scribe of Bologna Q15, the institution where it was used, and its exact provenance remain a mystery. Bent has established, however, that the manuscript is from the Veneto, with connections to Padua and Vicenza.[4] How did this pan-European repertory come to be collected in a single manuscript in northern Italy? We don't know, but we can make a few observations. Northern Italy, especially the Veneto, seems to have been a center for music manuscript production in the early fifteenth century. Much of the late fourteenth-century French repertory survives in early fifteenth-century Italian manuscripts, and newer repertory from all over Europe continued to find its way to Italy.[5] The 1410s saw two events that would bring together important figures from all over Europe, with their musicians: the English victory over the French in 1415, resulting in a major English presence on the Continent for the next two decades, and the Council of Constance (1414–18), during which church leaders and representatives of all the great powers worked to heal the papal schism and return the papacy to Rome. The first major surviving manuscript to be copied after these events is Bologna Q15: its enormous repertorial range bears witness to the new mobility of musicians and musical styles that resulted from these political upheavals.[6]

The motet section of Bologna Q15: compilation, chronology, and contents

Bologna Q15 has thirty fascicles, 343 folios, and 322 compositions. Bent has established three main layers or stages of copying, with stage I in the early 1420s and stages II and III in the early 1430s. Sometime during the hiatus between stages I and II the scribe disassembled the manuscript and discarded at least one hundred folios, saving the colored capitals to paste on to newly copied music. Many of the discarded pieces, however, were recopied in the later stages (Bent deduced this from the bits of music found on the back of the pasted-on capitals). She suggests that one reason for discarding and recopying had to do with the scribe's desire to rearrange the manuscript; another had to do with a change in taste, from an earlier francophile stage to a greater interest in things Italian.[7]

The motet section of Bologna Q15 begins in the middle of fascicle 18 with Q15.168, Du Fay's *Supremum est mortalibus bonum* (which also begins the motet section of Bologna 2216).[8] It continues to the middle of fascicle 27. The 106 motets in the manuscript were added in all three stages of copying.[9]

Fascicle(s)	initiated in	no. of motets
22–5	stage I (*c.* 1420–25)	45
18–19, 21 & 26–7	stage II (*c.* 1430–33)	51
20	stage III (*c.* 1433–35)	10

The section includes some pieces, mostly page fillers, that belong to other genres: a hymn, rondeaux, and laude. These genres are recognizably different from motets.[10] The hymn uses the fauxbourdon and chant paraphrase typical of hymn settings.[11] The rondeaux have French texts, clear medial cadences, and additional stanzas of text written below or around the music. French-texted rondeaux appear as page fillers in the stage I fascicles in both Mass and motet sections of the manuscript; their presence in the motet section therefore does not make them motets.

The laude are somewhat more problematic, and may have been added to the motet section because of some generic affinity to motets. Like the majority of the pieces in the motet section, most have Latin texts (one has an Italian text). Like chansons, however, laude are strophic or use some other fixed form. They are easily recognizable (and thus distinguishable from motets) because of the additional stanzas of text written below and around the music.[12] Laude are found as page fillers only in the later fascicles of the motet section; Bent has suggested that as the Q15 scribe's interest shifted from French to Italian music he switched to laude as page fillers instead of chansons.[13]

Searching for subgenres

Accepting the guidance of the scribe, as indicated by his organization of the manuscript, and excluding the page fillers and later additions belonging to other genres allows us to establish a substantial repertory of works considered to be motets in the fifteenth century. The problem now is to identify the different subgenres of the motet found in the manuscript.

My search for subgenres works from several directions at once. I begin by looking at texture, and dividing the works into groups of similar textures; I then refine and further subdivide those groups into subgenres characterized by different elements from the generic repertory. At the same time I allow an evolutionary outlook to guide my search. The local varieties of motet (French, Italian, English), which evolved to conform to the tastes and practices of different regions in the fourteenth century, became important subgenres of the fifteenth-century motet. The English presence in France and the Council of Constance provided the conditions for a musical melting pot, and other genres entered the mix, resulting in new hybrid subgenres that combine features from different genres and from earlier local traditions. The "filiations" and "ramifying roots" aid me in the identification of various subgenres; they also provide evidence as to the origins of the many different kinds of motet in the early fifteenth century.

Modifications to my basic scheme are certainly possible, but debates about individual works will not seriously affect the overall structure presented here.[14] No classification can express the whole range of relationships and influences among and within works, but I hope to convey the reality, flexibility, and usefulness of this system in the discussion of the individual subgenres and in the interpretation of individual works.

Examination of the motets of Bologna Q15 with an eye to texture reveals two basic approaches (see Table 4.1). One texture is the one we would expect looking forward from the fourteenth-century motet. These pieces have two texted voices in the same range above a slower-moving tenor, or tenor–contratenor pair; I call them motet-style motets. The other approach to texture is more surprising: it is that of the French chanson or the English cantilena (a three-voice setting of a votive Marian text). These pieces have three voices, with a single cantus voice above the tenor and contratenor; I call them cantilena-style motets.[15]

My use of the term "cantilena-style" differs from that of scholars who do not use texture as a criterion for dividing up the repertory. In *Bourdon und Fauxbourdon* Besseler distinguishes "Motettensatz" and "Liedsatz"; the "Mottetensatz" is defined by isorhythm, and "Liedsatz" includes pieces with two texted upper parts; in the introduction to the motet volume of his Du Fay edition he calls the non-isorhythmic motets "cantilena-type motets."[16] Besseler does not consider pieces using antiphon texts as motets at all: they are found in the volume devoted to liturgical music (V: *Compositiones liturgicae minores*). In other words, for Besseler "cantilena-type" motets are those which are not isorhythmic and do not use chant or set Marian antiphon texts; they include motets from my "motet-style" and "cantilena-style" categories.

Fallows follows Besseler's division in his book on Du Fay, but does include the Marian antiphon settings in his chapter on "Cantilenas and Related

Table 4.1. *Subgenres of the motet in Bologna Q15*

4.1.1: Grouped according to texture

Motet-style motets (56)
Italian	20
no isorhythm (14)	
double-statement structure (6)	
French isorhythmic	19
English isorhythmic	1
Retrospective double-discantus	6
Devotional double-discantus	7
Other double-discantus	3

Cantilena-style motets (41)
English cantilena	10
Cut-circle motet (Ø)	23
Declamation motet	5
Continental cantilena	3

Other (9)
Unus–chorus motet	3
Borderline cases	6
2 voices (3)	
Total	106

4.1.2: Grouped according to history

Ramifying roots (50)
Italian	20
no isorhythm (14)	
double-statement structure (6)	
French isorhythmic	19
English isorhythmic	1
English cantilena	10

New hybrid subgenres (56)
Retrospective double-discantus	6
Devotional double-discantus	7
Other double-discantus	3
Cut-circle motet (Ø)	23
Declamation motet	5
Continental cantilena	3
Unus–chorus motet	3
Borderline cases	6
2 voices (3)	
Total	106

Works." Alejandro Planchart defines the term "cantilena" primarily on the basis of the origin of the text: he uses it to refer to continental settings of sacred texts that are not associated with chant (including both "motet-style" and "cantilena-style" pieces).[17] In reference to some pieces by Du Fay, Brassart, and Sarto, Peter Wright defines the "cantilena motet" chiefly by the lack of pre-existent material: "a freely conceived setting, usually of a Marian text, which follows no particular formal scheme and does not depend on borrowed material."[18]

While the presence or absence of isorhythm, the use of chant, and the origins of the text can all play an important role in category membership, my primary division of the repertory into "motet-style" and "cantilena-style" on the basis of texture makes more sense out of the repertory for a number of reasons.[19] It corresponds to the history of the genre, since it allows the non-isorhythmic motet-style motets to be seen in relation to the medieval motet tradition, and the cantilena-style motets to be seen in relation to the English cantilena, the new arrival on the Continent. It largely coincides with another important distinction: between new texts and pre-existent (usually liturgical) texts. New texts are almost exclusively associated with the motet style, pre-existent texts with the cantilena style.[20] This correlation between text types and musical types makes sense historically: the traditional medieval motet always had a new text (sometimes written to fit the music), while the English cantilena was generally a setting of a pre-existent text.[21] The exceptions to this statement correspond to new hybrid subgenres of the motet, as we will see below. The motet/cantilena distinction also corresponds to the copying history of the manuscript. Almost two-thirds of the motet-style motets – the older, more traditional motet type – are copied in stage I (*c.* 1420–25), while more than three-quarters of the cantilena-style motets are copied in stages II and III (*c.* 1430–35).

After the basic division by texture, the actual subgenres are revealed by their "ramifying roots," or connections to earlier local traditions: French iso-rhythmic motets, Italian motets, and English cantilenas (the only English motet-style work is from the fourteenth century; see Table 4.1). Listing the pieces in the manuscript by Italian and English composers revealed subgenres that also have musical cohesiveness, and that conform fairly closely to the fourteenth-century precedents.[22] The isorhythmic motets by French and Netherlandish composers can also be seen as a continuation of a fourteenth-century genre, but the variety and influence from other subgenres is greater than in the case of the English and Italian motets. I categorized the rest of the pieces (primarily by northern composers) first according to musical characteristics (such as texture, structure, and mensurations), and then according to source and type of text. These subgenres are what I call the new hybrid subgenres, different in various ways from the earlier local traditions. I will discuss first the "ramifying roots," the continuations of local traditions, with reference to the ways in which they perpetuate fourteenth-century genres and the ways in which they evolve in the early fifteenth century. I will then go on to address the new hybrids in the next chapter.

Italian motets

I have included here all the motets by Italian composers, plus those by Ciconia (see Table 4.2).[23] The motets in this subgenre can be seen as a clear continuation of the fourteenth-century Italian motet as described by Margaret Bent.[24] In order to acquaint ourselves with the style, we shall examine Cristoforus de Monte's *Dominicus a dono* (Ex. 4.1).[25] Monte is an Italian composer believed by Suzanne Clercx to be the Cristoforus who worked in Padua from 1402 to 1426; if this is true, he would have known Ciconia, and certainly there are many similarities between the music of the two composers. More recently this identification has been questioned, and Robert Nosow has suggested that he is the Christophorus de Feltro who visited Udine in 1432.[26] In any case he was from the Veneto, and his motet will serve to exemplify the Italian motet tradition.

Texture, cadences and construction

The texture of the Italian motet consists of two texted upper parts in the same range (we will call them discantus 1 and 2, or D1 and D2), and a generally slower tenor (T) without text. This texture thus resembles that of the thirteenth-century French motet, although unlike most French motets the tenor is usually freely composed, as in Example 4.1. Bent has found evidence that the caccia also had an influence on the trecento Italian motet, which may partially explain the lack of *cantus prius factus* (*cpf*).[27] *Dominicus a dono* (Ex. 4.1) also has a contratenor part, like most late fourteenth- and early fifteenth-century French motets.

The two discantus parts are equally important. They have the same kind of

Table 4.2. *Italian motets in Q15 (20) (stage I unless otherwise noted)*

MS no.	Composer	Title (source or subject of text)	vv.-texts	Contratenor	Opening
NO ISORHYTHM (14)					
saints					
254	Ciconia	O virum omnimoda/O lux et decus T: O beatae Nicolae (St. Nicholas of Trani)	4–3	problematic (Bent)	Echo im.
242	Civitato	Pie pater Dominice/O Petre martir inclite T (S): O Thoma lux ecclesie (Dominican saints)	4–3	**added** layer III	D1&2 im.
274	Civitato	Sanctus itaque patriarcha Leuncius (II) (St. Leuncius of Brindisi and Trani)	4–1	okay (inessential)	tutti
sacred					
221	Brixia	Jhesus postquam monstraverat (processional H)	4–1	problematic (Nosow)	Echo im.
200	Rubeus	Missus est Gabriel angelus/Missus (4 As for Mary)	3–2	–	Echo im.
262	Rubeus	Caro mea vere est cibus (All. V, Corpus Christi) (II)	3–1	–	Echo im.
laudatory: ecclesiastics					
216	Ciconia	O felix templum jubila (Stefano da Carrara, Bishop of Padua, 1402–6)	4–1	**added** layer II	Echo im.
220	Monte-	Dominicus a dono (Dominicans)	4–1	problematic (Nosow, Cumming)	D1&2 im.
208	Civitato	O felix flos Florentia/Gaude felix Dominice (II) (Florence and Leonardi Dati, elected superior general of the Dominicans in 1414)	3–2	–	3vv. im.
laudatory: secular rulers and cities					
256	Ciconia	O Padua sidus preclarum (city of Padua)	3–1	–	tutti
257	Ciconia	Venecie mundi splendor/Michael qui Stena domus (city of Venice and Doge Michele Steno, 1406?)	3–2	–	tutti

243	Romanus	Ducalis sedes inclita/Stirps Mocinico (Tommaso Mocenigo, Doge 1413–23)	4–2	**added**; 3vv. in B 2216	Echo im.
219	Romanus	Aurea flamigeri iam excedis (Francesco Gonzaga, 1414?)	4–1	**added** layer II	Echo im.
215	Monte	Plaude decus mundi (Doge Francesco Foscari, *c.* 1423)	4–1	problematic? (Cumming)	Echo im.

DOUBLE-STATEMENT RHYTHMIC STRUCTURE (6)

Marian

227	Anon.	O Maria virgo davitica/O Maria maris stella (Solus tenor) (Old motet text: Mo, Ba, etc., there with T Veritatem)	3–2	4 *vv.* in PadD, essential Ct.	tutti

laudatory: ecclesiastics

273	Ciconia	Albane misse celitus/Albane doctor maxime (II) (Albane Michele, Venetian bishop of Padua 1406–9)	4–2	problematic (Bent)	D1&2
245	Ciconia	Petrum Marcello venerum/O Petre antistes inclite (Pietro Marcello, Venetian bishop of Padua 1409–) (diminution)	4–2	okay (inessential)	D1&2, Ct.
259	Ciconia	Ut te per omnes celitus/Ingens alumnus Padue (St. Francis and Francesco Zabarella)	3–2	Ct. **added** in Ox. 213	tutti
272	Ciconia	Doctorum principem/Melodia suavissima/T: Vir mitis (II) (Francesco Zabarella) (more complex isorhythm)	4–2	problematic (Bent)	tutti

laudatory: secular rulers and cities

206	Romanus	Carminibus festos/O requies populi (II) (Doge Francesco Foscari, *c.* 1423)	4–2	essential (Cumming)	tutti

Example 4.1 Cristoforus de Monte, *Dominicus a dono* (Q15.220, 227'–228)

Example 4.1 (*cont.*)

Example 4.2 Cadence types in three and four voices

rhythmic motion, with a fair amount of trading of motifs and imitative effects. Either voice can take the lead: in *Dominicus a dono* discantus 1 is the first to begin the new phrase at the beginning and mm. 24 and 30, but discantus 2 leads in 39 and 48. Both voices are also contrapuntally essential. The tenor can be involved in imitation with either of the discantus parts (see mm. 33–4, D1 & T, and mm. 59–60, D2 & T), and either discantus can move to the octave with the tenor at cadences.

Recognition of different cadence types is vital to the understanding of the construction of all fifteenth-century music. It is worth going into detail on the topic here, since it will inform our discussion for the rest of the book. Most cadences in the fifteenth century have contrary motion by step from sixth to octave between two voices, generally the tenor and an upper voice (see Ex. 4.2a).[28] There is often a suspension (as in Ex. 4.2a) and/or some other cadential figuration in the upper voice. In chansons and cantilena-style pieces this cadential motion to the octave is virtually always found between the single discantus voice and the tenor, and the whole piece is thus controlled by a two-voice discantus–tenor framework that is contrapuntally complete. Contratenors can be and sometimes are discarded or replaced.

In motet-style pieces with equal discantus parts, on the other hand, the discantus parts both make cadences with the tenor. Thus in Example 4.1, at the cadence on A at m. 24, discantus 1 moves to the octave above the tenor, while in the cadence on F at m. 30 discantus 2 moves to the octave. All three voices are thus implicated in the contrapuntal texture, and none can be easily discarded.

The two-voice cadential progression to the octave can be harmonized in several different ways. In the three-voice cadence most common in French music the third voice (contratenor or second discantus) moves from third to fifth above the tenor, with parallel fourths between the top two parts (6/3–8/5: see Ex. 4.2b, but ignore the bottom part for now).[29] This cadence also occurs in Italian motets; see *Dominicus*, mm. 23–4 and 72–3; I will call it the 6/3–8/5 cadence.

Another harmonization of the two-voice framework puts the third voice (a discantus voice) above the voice moving to the octave with the tenor, resulting in parallel fifths between the upper parts (10/6–12/8: Ex. 4.2c, top three voices, and Ex. 4.1, mm. 12, 18, 38, 47, 65, 69, and the final cadence). This cadence is typical of Italian caccias and motets, and the brilliant arrival on the resonant octave and twelfth contribute to the characteristic sound of the Italian motet; I will call it the Italian cadence.[30]

A third harmonization of the two-voice framework, just beginning in the 1420s, is known as the leaping-contratenor cadence (Ex. 4.2d, all three voices): here the contratenor goes below the tenor and then leaps an octave to the fifth above the cadential note (10/5–8/5). In related forms the contratenor leaps to the tenor note or to the octave below (Ex. 4.2e, without Ct.1); I call this a 5–1 cadence. Use of Arabic numerals with reference to the scale degrees of the contratenor in relation to the tenor note at the cadence is meant to contrast with the triadic implications of the roman-numeral V–I. (Neither of these cadence forms is used in three-voice Italian motets, since they involve a fairly low contratenor rather than a second discantus part.) The 5–1 cadence lends itself well to four-voice cadences, as can be seen in Example 4.2e.

Occasionally we find the 6/3–8/5 cadence combined with the leaping contratenor or 5–1 cadence (see Ex. 4.2f). I call this the 4/5 cadence, since it results in the simultaneous sounding of the fourth degree in the higher contratenor with the fifth degree in the low contratenor. This dissonant cadence form presumably resulted from the addition of a lower voice to a pre-existent three-voice work; it persisted into the 1460s, however, even in pieces that were conceived originally for four voices.

CONTRATENOR

While most fourteenth-century Italian motets are for three voices, most (fifteen out of twenty) of the Italian motets in Bologna Q15 have a fourth voice in at least one source: a contratenor in the same range as the tenor. Bent has shown that many of the contratenors in Q15 are later additions, probably by the Q15 scribe, possibly to make the pieces more modern or more "French" in style.[31] There are two kinds of evidence about added voices: external (chiefly the existence of multiple sources for a piece with and without the added voice) and internal (based on an assessment of the voice's role in the piece in terms of counterpoint and structure). External evidence indicates that contratenors were added to five of the fifteen four-voice pieces (shown on Table 4.2 by the word "added"). This is certainly a high enough proportion to make us want to check on the authenticity of the contratenors of the other ten, and internal evidence reveals that the contratenor is contrapuntally essential in only two of the pieces and free of problems in only two others.

When external evidence is lacking, decisions about the status of the contratenor are often difficult to make. What constitutes a problematic part? What kind of counterpoint rules apply in this context? Examination of four-voice music of this period reveals that many of our usual assumptions about dissonance and avoidance of parallel perfect intervals do not apply. This is the case especially when adding a fourth voice to the 6/3–8/5 and Italian cadences (at least if it is desired to keep all voices in the texture and arrive at an octave and fifth at the cadence).

The most common solutions involve parallel octaves and fifths (Exx. 4.2b and 4.2c, all four voices). Different figuration in the two parts in parallel often creates additional dissonance (see *Dominicus*, Ex. 4.1, mm. 17–18, 29–30, 37–8, 46–7, 64–5, final cadence). The same kind of parallelism and dissonance occurs in pieces in which the contratenor is essential or clearly belongs to the original conception of the work, such as Dunstaple's four-voice motets, the Italian motets *Carminibus festos* by Romanus (m. 25), *Petrum Marcello* by Ciconia (m. 46), or Du Fay's *Vassilissa* (m. 30), and *Balsamus* (final cadence).[32] Example 4.2b (with all voices), rare in the four-voice Italian motets, is found repeatedly in *Vassilissa*. This kind of parallelism and dissonance at cadences, odd though it seems to us, is not enough to prove that a contratenor part is a later addition (though unrelenting clumsy dissonance is suggestive). There must be evidence about texture and counterpoint at other places in the piece as well.

Less problematic solutions to the problem of writing cadences in four voices involve the insertion of rests in the contratenor, movement to the third of the chord, avoidance of standard cadence forms, or use of the leaping-contratenor or 5–1 cadences. These techniques tend to be used in the big isorhythmic motets with long-note tenor and contratenor parts, and in some of

the later four-voice pieces, as we shall see. In Du Fay's *Balsamus* the final
cadence is an Italian cadence in four voices with parallel fifths and octaves
(like Ex. 4.2c); for the rest of the piece, however, Du Fay avoids these parallels
by the means listed here. Parallelism and dissonance treatment remain problems in the four-voice cadence, however, well into the fifteenth century.

Is the contratenor of *Dominicus a dono* a later addition? I think so: it is not
essential to the counterpoint, the amount of dissonance created by the part is
excessive, and it clutters the texture.[33] For dissonance or parallel octaves near
cadences see mm. 17, 23, 27, 29, 37, 46; for other dissonances see m. 13 (gra-
tuitous E against F in two other voices), 63 (C against D in two other voices),
79 (A–G against G–A). In the two passages of three-voice echo imitation
(mm. 47–50 and 73–6) the contratenor clutters the texture with its unison
doublings (mm. 47–9) and dissonance (73). I have therefore notated the
contratenor in smaller print in Example 4.1 to indicate its dubious status.

Italian motets in Bologna Q15 such as *Dominicus a dono*, then, have a slow
tenor and two active discantus parts of equal importance. All three voices are
contrapuntally essential. Contratenor parts, when present, are usually
inessential, and in most cases are later additions. In construction and style the
Q15 Italian motets are very similar to fourteenth-century Italian motets, and
the lively trading off among the discantus voices and the brilliant "Italian"
cadences with their parallel fifths contribute to an exciting, even triumphant,
character.

Form

Six of the twenty Italian motets use some kind of rhythmic patterning in one
or more voices. Of these, four use a double-statement rhythmic structure, in
which the second half of the piece is a rhythmic duplication of the first half
in all voices.[34] Two of Ciconia's motets (*Doctorum principem* and *Petrum
Marcello*) use somewhat more complex rhythmic structures, perhaps due to
the composer's northern origins or as an attempt to write learned works for
learned patrons.[35] The fourteen other Italian motets are freely composed,
with no use of strict rhythmic repetitions or proportions, mensural reinterpretation, patterning, pre-existent material, or other techniques that we associate with the term isorhythm.

Lack of strict construction or "isorhythm" does not mean that these works
have no form. All but three of the non-isorhythmic Italian motets (those
marked "tutti" in the last column of Table 4.2) have an introductory section in

a reduced texture, known as an "introitus," usually involving imitation.[36] (See the last column of Table 4.2 for the various types of opening textures.) The introitus leads the listener into the piece and allows clear presentation of text, which serves to announce the subject matter of the motet. *Dominicus a dono* begins with a two-voice imitative opening that may recall the Italian caccia. Even more common at the beginning of an Italian motet is "echo imitation," where the first voice rests while the second voice repeats its opening material.[37] Monte uses echo imitation later in the piece (mm. 48–50 and 74–6; see also the beginning of Ex. 6.2, *Ihesu salvator seculi* by Salinis).

After the introitus, Italian motets can generally be divided into several distinct sections, often of similar lengths, that respond to the structure of the text. *Dominicus a dono* is through composed, but it can be divided into the introitus plus two halves almost equal in length (36 and 34 mm., plus the final long which would bring it to 35), each of which cadences on F. The two halves are clearly differentiated: the second half eliminates the florid melismas found throughout the first half, and it is framed by the echo-imitation passages.

Imitation is used in this motet to signal the beginning, middle, and end of the piece. The introitus is imitative, and the first passage of echo imitation (mm. 48–50) comes just after midpoint of the piece (once you subtract the introitus) serving to introduce the second half. The final imitative passage (mm. 74–6, in which the imitation is more rhythmic than melodic) announces the end of the piece; its rhythmic motif is heard again in m. 79, leading into a repeated cadence on F.

Imitative introitus	3vv.	Echo imitation	Echo imitation	End
1–11	12	48–50	74–6	82
D1, D2		D2, T, D1	T, D2, D1	

Imitative material of a more casual kind is traded among the upper voices during the rest of the piece: in the first part there are numerous eighth-note melismas (minims in the original), with a mixture of scales and falling-third figures (see especially mm. 22–30). There is also a hocket-like figure that is introduced at the end of the introitus (m. 10) and returns in mm. 25–6 and in discantus II just before the final passage of echo imitation (m. 72). The tenor is usually very much in the background, moving in longs and breves, and frequently leaping fourths and fifths, very unlike chant. Occasionally, however, it speeds up, sometimes in order to enter into imitation with one of the discantus parts (see mm. 32–3, D1–T; 59–60, D2–T; 63–4, T–D1).

Table 4.3. *Subjects of motet texts from fourteenth-century Italy (before Ciconia)*

(1) Sacred		11	58 per cent
(A) BVM	(3; 16 per cent)		
(B) Other	(3; 16 per cent)		
(C) Saints	(5; 26 per cent)		
(2) Laudatory		8	42 per cent
(A) Doges	(3; 16 per cent)		
(B) Luchino Visconti	(2; 10 per cent)		
(C) Other (ecclesiastics)	(3; 16 per cent)		
Total		19	100 per cent

Text

Dominicus a dono has one text in the two discantus voices. The text honors St. Dominic and the Dominicans,[38] by whom the composer was educated in his youth. At the end of the motet we learn of the composer's origins:

in Feltro natus / Cristoforus et educatus / modice peritus cantu / in montibusque nutritus.

Cristoforus was born and educated in Feltre, and skilled in the ways of song he was nourished in the mountains.

This kind of self-reference on the part of composers (and/or poets) in motet texts is typical of the Italian motet; it is found as far back as the fourteenth-century *Principum nobilissime* in honor of Andrea Contarini, Doge of Venice 1368–81, and Ciconia refers to himself at the end of no fewer than five motets.[39] Use of one text rather than two was an option in Italy, unlike in France. Almost all Italian motets use new poetic texts; the text of *Dominicus a dono* is exceptionally shapeless, with seemingly haphazard line lengths and use of rhyme.[40] When there are two texts in an Italian motet, they are generally the same length (the motetus text is generally shorter in French motets).[41] Most Italian motet texts are occasional, and all are laudatory: they praise secular and ecclesiastical leaders, or God and the saints (compare Table 4.2 with Table 4.3).

Dominicus a dono can thus be seen as a fairly typical example of an Italian motet, and part of a tradition that extends from the fourteenth century well into the 1420s (the last securely datable pieces on the list are those in honor of the installation of Francesco Foscari as Doge of Venice in 1423).[42]

The Italian motet descended from the thirteenth-century French motet, with some influence from the trecento secular song, especially the caccia; it also demonstrates distinct differences from the motet as it developed in France.

French isorhythmic motets

This is the most studied and best understood of all the subgenres of the motet in the early fifteenth century (see Table 4.4).[43] It has the most impressive pedigree, for it is directly descended from the original thirteenth-century motet via that great monument of medieval rationalism, the fourteenth-century French isorhythmic motet.[44] Fifteenth-century isorhythmic motets are sometimes considered a decadent hangover from the Middle Ages. Michael Allsen has shown, however, that there are more surviving isorhythmic motets from the first half of the fifteenth century than there are from the entire fourteenth century, and the greatest composers of the day continued to give it their best efforts.[45] The subgenre exploited and developed techniques and features derived from Italian and English traditions of motet composition, as well as other subgenres and genres. Because it has been so thoroughly studied elsewhere we will discuss it only briefly here.[46]

"Isorhythm" is a modern term with a variety of possible meanings; different scholars use it in different ways. Excessive emphasis on the distinction between "isorhythmic" and "non-isorhythmic" limits our understanding of different kinds of rhythmic structures, and the relationships among "isorhythmic" and other works, as Margaret Bent points out.[47] Nevertheless the term isorhythm has a long tradition, and I will continue to use it, defining it loosely to mean systematic rhythmic organization of the tenor voice, generally by means of rhythmic repetition or reinterpretation (mensural or proportional) of a rhythmic pattern in the tenor (known as a talea). In fifteenth-century isorhythmic motets rhythmic organization often extends beyond the tenor, and rhythmic organization is normally combined with repetition of the pitch material, or color, of the tenor voice.

In this subgenre of the French isorhythmic motet (Table 4.4) I have included all the isorhythmic motets by composers from France and the Netherlands (I will refer to them all as "French" for the sake of convenience) found in Bologna Q15, and there is little doubt that they continue in the French tradition of complex and sophisticated musical and textual manipula-

82

Table 4.4. *French isorhythmic motets in Q15 (19) (stage I unless otherwise noted)*

Marian (3)

	231: Anon.	Cuius fructus ventris Ihesus/Te Maria rogitassem (4–2)
	229: Brassart	Ave Maria gracia plena/O Maria gracia plena (New tropes to pre-existent Marian texts) (4–2)
	236: Franchois	Ave virgo lux Maria (4–1)

sacred (not Marian) (6)

	217: Carmen	Venite adoremus dominum/Salve sancta eterna trinitas (God, Trinity, schism) (4–2)
	246: Carmen	Salve pater creator omnium/Felix et beata deo (Trinity and Virgin) (4–2)
	251: Rondelly	Verbum tuum/In cruce (Easter) (3–2)
	223: Grenon	Plasmatoris humani generis/Verbigine mater ecclesia (Easter) (4–2)
II	209: Grenon	Ad honorem sancte trinitatis/Celorum regnum supernum (All Saints, Trinity) (4–2)
II	176: Grenon	Nova vobis gaudia refero (Christmas; Noel refrain) (3–1)

saints (5)

	253: Loqueville	O flos in divo/Sacris pignoribus (St. Yvo) (3–2)
	211: Du Fay	O sancte Sebastiane/O martir Sebastiane/O quam mira (St. Sebastian; discantus 1 and 2 one poem, Ct. another, found in poetic sources) (4–3)
	263: Du Fay	O gemma lux et speculum/Sacer pastor Barensium (T: Beatus Nicolaus) (St. Nicholas of Bari) (4–2)
II	174: Du Fay	Rite maiorem Iacobum canimus/Artibus summis miseri (T: Ora pro nobis dominum qui te vocabit Iacobum) (St. James the Apostle, with an acrostic mentioning the curate Robertus Auclou; *c.* 1427?) (4–2)
III	195: Benoit	Gaude tu baptista Christi (Sequence, St. John) (4–1)

laudatory (5)

	252: Brassart	Magne decus potencie/Genus regale esperie (For a pope?) (4–2)
	244: Du Fay	Vasilissa ergo gaude (Marriage of Cleofe Malatesta, 1420) (4–1)
	237: Du Fay	Apostolo glorioso/Cum tua doctrina (T: Andreas Christi) (5 vcs: 2 Ct.'s, each of which has one of the upper Italian texts) (Rededication of church of St. Andrew in Patras, Pandolfo Malatesta, bishop, 1426) (5–2)

Table 4.4. (*cont.*)

II 169: Du Fay	Balsamus et munda cera cum crismatis unda	
	(Blessing of wax Agnus Dei figures, 1431) (4–1)	
II 168: Du Fay	Supremum est mortalibus bonum	
	(Pope Eugenius IV and Emperor Sigismund, 1433) (3–1)	
English isorhythmic motet		
218: Alanus	Sub Arturo/Fons citharizancium (T: In omnem terram)	
	(14th-c. English musicians' motet) (3–2)	

tions.[48] I also list here one English motet from the fourteenth century (218: *Sub Arturo plebs / Fons citharizancium / T: In omnem terram*, by J. Alanus), which fits clearly into the fourteenth-century French tradition of isorhythmic motets with texts about music and musicians.[49]

Many of the composers of these motets worked in Italy for part of their lives, and some pieces show Italian musical traits such as cadence types, iso-rhythmic schemes reminiscent of Italian double-statement structure, or lack of pre-existent cantus firmus. Comparison of the text types of the motets in Table 4.4 to fourteenth-century French and Italian text types (Tables 4.3 and 4.5) reveals that the French advisory, condemnatory, and *admonitio* texts have disappeared, and that Italian-style laudatory political texts have assumed greater importance. Six of the nineteen motets have only one text, an Italian feature, and one (237: Du Fay's *Apostolo glorioso / Cum tua doctrina*) has two Italian texts.

While each of these motets is different – the approaches to form and texture vary much more than in the Italian motets – Du Fay emerges as the most energetic experimenter: each one of his motets features a different combination of text types, textures, and individual features derived from different national traditions. Du Fay uses one text, two texts, and a single pre-existent text divided among the two discantus parts. His textures range from three to five voices – and the five-voice texture of *Apostolo glorioso* is very unusual, with two contratenors whose rate of rhythmic motion is equal to that of the discantus voices.[50] In *Vasilissa ergo gaude* Du Fay deliberately imitates the Italian style, with a single laudatory text, double-statement rhythmic structure (though with a *cantus prius factus* and four original voices); he even uses Italian-style cadences with parallel fifths, but reserves them for the final cadence of each half of the piece, as if to make a deliberate gesture in the

Table 4.5. *Subjects of Latin-texted motets from fourteenth-century France*

Sacred		10	24 per cent
To the BVM	(4; 10 per cent)		
Other	(2; 4 per cent)		
To Saints	(4; 10 per cent)		
Laudatory		7	17 per cent
Advisory and Condemnatory		9	21 per cent
Evils of the world: complaint, *admonitio*		10	24 per cent
Music, musicians, aesthetics		5	12 per cent
Secular love		1	2 per cent
Total		42	100 per cent

direction of Italian style.[51] We will return below to one of his most radical experiments, *Supremum est mortalibus bonum.*

English cantilenas

All but two of the English pieces in the motet section of Bologna Q15 are in chanson format, with a single top voice and tenor and contratenor in the same range (see Table 4.6).[52] I call these works English cantilenas, and their antecedents can be traced to an English genre that was quite distinct from the motet in the fourteenth century.

"Cantilena" is a medieval Latin term meaning "song," with all the ambiguity of the modern English usage of that term (sometimes extending to all music).[53] It has been appropriated by several modern scholars to refer to genres (or subgenres) of polyphony that lacked identifying labels in the late Middle Ages. Each scholar uses the term in a slightly different way; inspired by them I propose yet another meaning. A review of the usage of the term and the history of the genre I call the English cantilena will clarify the issues.

Terminology and history

The majority of surviving English polyphony from the fourteenth century was copied in a score format in which three voices are positioned above one another, with the text under the bottom voice (alignment is approximate). This format was used for all the different kinds of pieces in which three voices sing a

Table 4.6.1. *English cantilenas in Q15 (10) (stage II unless otherwise noted)*

I	238:	Anon., Regina celi (chant incipit) (A) (1 MS)
		[C] ‖ Ø . (Brief two-voice passages throughout.)
I	240:	Power, Salve regina/Tro:Virgo mater (A) (1 MS)
		(chant paraphrase, Alma redemptoris)
		Ø (discantus)‖ O ‖ ‖ Ɛ ‖ ‖ C —> Ɛ ‖ ‖
		Ɛ (T & Ct.) unus unus unus
		Passages marked "unus" are duos, setting trope text.
	164:	[Forest], Alma redemptoris (A) (4 MSS)
		C; duo in middle.
	184:	Anon., Spes nostra salus nostra (Trinity A) (1 MS)
		[O] ‖ ‖. Short and simple, no duets.
	185:	De Anglia, Benedicta es caelorum (S) (4 MSS, 1E)
		[O] ‖ unus ‖ C "Ave" with fermatas ‖ unus ‖
		Passages marked "unus" are duos. Uses chant.
	280:	Dunstaple, Regina celi (chant incipit) (A) (4 MSS)
		[O] ‖ ‖ Ȼ ‖. No duets.
	289:	Binchois [Dunstaple], Beata dei genitrix (A) (5 MSS)
		O ‖ C ‖ O. Lower v. duo in middle section.
	290:	Dunstaple, Sub tuam protectionem (A) (duo) (5 MSS: 4+2Bux)
		C ‖ Duo ad lib. ‖ O ‖. Duo has optional contratenor.
	291:	Dunstaple, Quam pulchra es et quam decora (A) (7 MSS, 1E)
		O; breve rest before "Veni" with fermatas; Ɛ. No duets.
III	192:	Power/Binchois/[Dunstaple], Alma redemptoris (A) (5 MSS)
		O ‖ duo ‖ Ȼ. Very free use of chant, mostly in discantus.

Table 4.6.2. *Mensurations of the cantilenas*

Begin perfect tempus		Begin imperfect tempus	
O	184	C	164
OC	185	CO	290
OȻ	280	CØ	238
OȻ	192		
OƐ	291		
OCO	289		
ØOƐCƐ Ɛ	240		

single text at the same time: Mass Ordinary movements, Mass Propers, hymns, and new settings of poetic texts. Pieces in which the rhythmic motion in the different voices is markedly different, or in which there are multiple texts, were copied in choirbook format, with each part copied separately on a different region of the page or opening. Pieces copied in choirbook format are mainly motets or pieces written in motet texture, including some Mass movements.

Pieces in score format can be divided into those that set a pre-existent chant melody (*cantus prius factus* or *cpf*) and those that do not. The ones that do not use a *cpf* have been labeled "cantilenas" by Ernest Sanders, "free set-tings" by William Summers.[54] The pieces that do use a *cpf* are often known as English discant (or descant) settings. English discant is a method described in some English treatises for composing or improvising one or more additional voices around a chant melody (*cpf*) in a primarily note-against-note texture.[55] Many of the simpler pieces in score format with *cpf* resemble the kind of pieces that would result from the application of English discant to a chant melody; they are thus considered to be written examples of the technique of English discant, and labeled accordingly. Used in this fashion, "cantilena" or "free setting" and "English discant" are terms associated with style and compositional technique, rather than genre, since the techniques are found in a variety of genres. Most of the surviving English settings of the shorter movements of the Mass Ordinary (especially the Sanctus and Agnus) are in English discant, as are some Glorias and Credos and many settings of chants for the Mass Proper and the Office.[56] These need not concern us.

"Cantilenas" or "free settings" in score format also include settings of rhyming Marian texts in double-versicle sequence form (aa bb cc, etc.) that resemble short polyphonic sequences (and indeed, they are sometimes called sequences).[57] But unlike chant sequences, used at Mass on almost all of the major feasts of the Church year, these pieces almost all have Marian texts. While most settings of this kind were freely composed, a few use a *cpf*. Peter Lefferts uses the term "cantilena" for these fourteenth-century settings of Marian sequence-like texts for three voices copied in score format, whether or not they use a *cpf*.[58]

The "cantilena" became the primary genre of Marian polyphony in four-teenth-century England (most English motets of the period did not have Marian texts).[59] Lefferts has shown that it was developed in response to the desire for polyphonic music for the newer Marian devotions, especially the daily Lady Masses and, later, the evening devotions following Compline known as Salve services. "Cantilenas" were used originally as sequences and as offertory substitutes, but also as hymn substitutes, and, later, as processional and votive antiphons for the Salve services, where they joined the predominantly prose antiphon texts in honor of the Virgin (including the four famous Marian antiphons, plus other votive and processional antiphons including excerpts from the *Song of Songs*). According to Sanders cantilenas may also have served as a kind of "clerical chamber music."[60]

Toward the end of the fourteenth and at the beginning of the fifteenth century the number of polyphonic settings of the prose antiphon texts increased, while the number of Lefferts's "cantilenas" (settings of the poetic sequence-like texts) declined.[61] While "cantilenas" were generally freely composed, some polyphonic settings of antiphon texts also used the antiphon melody as a *cpf*.[62] In terms of musical style, however, cantilenas and antiphons, with and without *cpf*, are almost impossible to distinguish: by 1420 both have a more florid upper voice over two lower voices in more or less the same range, a texture that resembles the French chanson rather than the older parallel layered texture of English discant.[63] In the largest surviving English source of the early fifteenth century, the Old Hall Manuscript, settings of both kinds of text are found mixed together in their own section of the manuscript (see Table 4.7). Functionally and musically the polyphonic cantilenas and antiphon settings are identical: they belong to a single genre which encompasses two different kinds of liturgically flexible texts for the Virgin.

We lack a general generic label for this English repertory of three-voice Marian polyphony. Focus on text type or use of *cpf* has caused scholars to artificially divide the repertory into antiphon settings vs. sequence settings or "cantilenas." My solution is to extend Lefferts's term "cantilena" to include the polyphonic antiphon settings.[64] I prefer the term "cantilena" to "antiphon" because "antiphon" already has too many meanings (psalm, *Magnificat*, processional, votive, monophonic and polyphonic, simple liturgical chant settings, free settings of antiphon texts, etc). The early fifteenth-century cantilena, as I use the term, is an English polyphonic setting for three voices of a Marian text.[65] The text can be prose (a biblical or antiphon text) or poetry (often sequence-like), and it can be freely composed or use a *cpf*.[66]

In England the cantilena was a genre distinct in style, manuscript format, and subject matter from the motet.[67] In English sources cantilenas were mostly copied in score format, with a single Marian text under the bottom voice; motets were copied in choirbook format, with multiple texts about

Table 4.7. *Motets and cantilenas in the Old Hall Manuscript*

Cantilenas

15 cantilenas copied in score format between the Glorias and Credos

   8 are antiphons to the BVM, six of which use *cpf*

   7 are settings of poetic sequence-like texts, without *cpf*

2 cantilenas copied in choirbook format, in the middle of the Credos

   both are antiphons to the BVM (one uses a different antiphon in the Tenor voice)

—

17 cantilenas to the BVM

Isorhythmic motets copied in choirbook format

1 Pentecost (copied with the 2 cantilenas in choirbook format)

2 to BVM

2 to BVM and St. George

2 to saints: Catherine of Alexandria and Thomas of Canterbury

2 Deo Gratias substitutes

—

9 isorhythmic motets

With the exception of the Pentecost motet, the isorhythmic motets are copied in two groups: three are found in the middle of the Sanctus section, and five are at the very end of the manuscript, following the Agnus section (the last two are the *Deo gratias* substitutes).

saints or major feasts in the Temporale (see Table 4.7: all but two of the cantilenas in Old Hall are copied in score format). After the Old Hall Manuscript, however, most English cantilenas are found in continental manuscripts, where they are always copied in choirbook format.[68] When cantilenas appear in generically organized manuscripts, such as Bologna Q15 or Modena X.1.11, they are found mixed with motet-style motets in the motet section – not in their own section, and not with the prescribed antiphon settings for Vespers (in Modena X.1.11), or the polyphonic alternatim sequences (in Q15). The English cantilena, while distinct from the motet at home in England, was treated as a subgenre of the motet on the Continent. Why was this the case? I propose the following scenario.

There was no polyphonic genre like the cantilena on the Continent in the fourteenth and early fifteenth centuries. Marian devotions were not as elaborate (witness the fact that Lady chapels, ubiquitous in England, are not a regular feature of church architecture on the Continent), and monophony or improvised polyphony sufficed. When the English cantilenas arrived on the

Continent in the early fifteenth century, therefore, they fit no existing generic category. The closest fit was that of the motet, a genre that was also Latin-texted and functionally flexible. Furthermore, the motet genre was itself expanding to absorb all the different local varieties of motet composition. For want of a better category, cantilenas were regarded as, and thus became, motets.[69]

The English cantilenas in Bologna Q15

I will continue to call these English three-voice Marian works in chanson format cantilenas, recognizing their distinct generic status and function in their place of origin (England); but I consider them one of the subgenres of the motet on the Continent. The English cantilenas in Bologna Q15 are listed in Table 4.6.1.[70] Charles Hamm, Margaret Bent, Reinhard Strohm, and others, have discussed typical features of English music and the cantilena in particular.[71] The style is quite distinctive, and no early fifteenth-century piece with an undisputed attribution to a continental composer has been mistaken for English.[72] The ten English cantilenas in Bologna Q15 conform to the English style although none of the pieces has all the features considered typically English.

All ten use versatile Marian texts: nine use processional or votive antiphon texts, one a poetic sequence-like text (*Benedicta es celorum regina*) of the type described by Lefferts.[73] These text types can be compared to the cantilena texts in the Old Hall Manuscript (Table 4.7). Half of the Q15 cantilenas use chant, half do not.[74]

There is a considerable range of complexity, from the short and simple *Spes nostra*, to the more elaborate and expansive Dunstaple works such as *Beata dei genitrix* or *Alma redemptoris*. Dunstaple's *Quam pulchra es* is a special case, to which we will return later.[75] Almost all of the pieces divide into two or more sections, by means of a double bar, change in mensuration, change in texture, or (usually) by some combination of those. All but three have duets of some kind for the discantus and one of the lower voices; the normal position for the duet is in the middle of the work. Some of the duets are marked as "unus" with the implication that they were sung by soloists. Power's *Salve regina* uses this "unus" duo texture for the three phrases of the trope inserted between the final invocations of the *Salve regina* text.

The mensural practice of these pieces is also typical of English music (see

Table 4.6.2). All but two have at least one change of mensuration, and all but three begin in perfect tempus (O: triple meter). Just over half begin in perfect tempus and change to some kind of imperfect tempus (duple meter: C, ₵, or ₵).[76] Particularly striking in these English cantilenas, especially in contrast with continental music of the period, is the flexible rhythmic writing, in both perfect and imperfect time, leading to an almost "ametrical" flow at times.[77] In my view this characteristic of English music should be considered a major component of the famous "contenance angloise," since it distinguishes English music from contemporary continental genres, especially in the 1420s and 1430s.

FOREST'S ALMA REDEMPTORIS MATER

As an example of an English cantilena, let us examine Forest's *Alma redemptoris mater* (Ex. 4.3). Power's and Dunstaple's music has been much discussed, and has long been available in good modern editions; Forest's music deserves more attention. Little is known about Forest: he is believed to be an Englishman who lived from *c.* 1370 to 1446, and Alejandro Planchart has recently located an archival document attesting to the presence of a composer named John Forest at the Council of Constance with the Bishop of Lichfield.[78] The piece is incomplete in Q15, but it appears in three later continental sources.[79] It is unusual in its use of duple mensuration throughout, its lack of internal double bars marking off sections, and its highly irregular phrase lengths. Every piece is atypical in some way or another, however, and this is an interesting piece that illustrates in an extreme form some of the traits of the English cantilena.

One way of understanding this piece is to see it as a deliberate exaggeration of traits common in English music. The choice of a Marian antiphon text is typical; although *Alma redemptoris* was not particularly common in the English cantilena repertory, it seems to have been a special favorite of Forest.[80] The composer chose not to use the chant melody, but he does begin the piece in the F modality associated with the chant: while the first sonority is on C, it moves immediately to F, and the first cadence is on F as well (as is the next major cadence, m. 14). Other cadences on F and C seem to confirm F as the tonal center (C: mm. 9, 20, 28, 50; F: mm. 38, 52, 54). The piece as a whole ends on G; this comes as something of a surprise (although G is established as a cadential goal in mm. 24, 36, and 42). Playing with our expectations concerning the

Example 4.3 John Forest, *Alma redemptoris mater* (Trent 90.1052, 341′–342, alternate ending to the contratenor)

Example 4.3 (*cont.*)

final is quite common in English music, and is found in two other *Alma* settings: one in Q15 (Q15.192, believed to be by Dunstaple, but attributed in Q15 to Power and Binchois), and Power's *Missa Alma redemptoris mater*.[81] The Dunstaple cantilena makes periodic references to the chant (transposed to C), but the piece as a whole ends on G; the tenor of Power's Mass is a segment of the chant that begins on F but ends on G. Forest may have been referring to this tradition without actually using the chant melody.

Typical of the English cantilena is the central duet for discantus and tenor featuring more lively rhythms, especially in the lower voice (see especially mm. 33–6, the most active passage for the tenor voice in the whole piece). Unlike most English cantilenas of this period, however, the boundaries between the three- and two-voice sections are blurred, which serves to reinforce the tonal ambiguity. In mm. 24–5 the duet emerges gradually from the sustained cadential sonority (so that only in hindsight do we realize that this G cadence was the end of the first section of the piece). The end of the discantus/tenor duet comes at m. 36 (also a cadence on G), but ambiguity is created by the two-measure duet for the lower voices leading to a cadence on F (m. 39). Which is the real ending of the duet?

93

The melodic writing in *Alma redemptoris* is typical in its long phrases and leisurely progress toward cadential goals with melodic motion primarily of steps and thirds. Note the hovering quality of the gradual descent in the first phrase (mm. 1–6) from the cc to the cadence on f: first cc down to aa, with neighbor motion to g; then the leap up again to cc's upper neighbor, and the descent to g; motion up to dd again, and then stepwise descent to f – but the f is on a weak beat, the final eighth note, and we must leap up again to bb-flat before the final descent to the arrival on f.[82]

Most English cantilenas have sections in imperfect tempus (C); Forest chose to limit himself here entirely to imperfect tempus (exceptionally, the mensuration sign is shown at the beginning of the piece in the sources, perhaps because the mensuration is so unclear). This did not mean, however, that Forest limited himself to duple-meter rhythms; he may have chosen imperfect tempus in part to avoid the notational ambiguities of triple mensurations while still being free to write rhythms appropriate to both. Forest's rhythms often sound more like triple meter than duple. I have, in fact, barred the whole last line in triple meter, which works well in all voices, but especially the tenor: this may be a deliberate reference on Forest's part to the common return to triple at the end of a piece. A tendency towards asymmetry and a deliberate blurring of metrical groupings is typical of English music.

Exceptional in this piece, however, is the *degree* of what I call "ametricality." In all of the other English cantilenas in Q15, and most others, the number of beats in the piece is a multiple of the mensuration: a multiple of three in perfect tempus, a multiple of two in imperfect tempus. Major cadences also always arrive at the beginning of a breve unit. This is not the case here. The number of beats (semibreves) in the piece before the final long is 221, a multiple of neither two nor three (it is in fact a multiple of two prime numbers, 13 and 17). The individual phrase lengths show a dazzling asymmetry as well, especially in the first half of the piece. The count for each phrase is the number of semibreves up to, but not including, the cadence notes; numbers followed by a semicolon cadence on a long in the tenor voice:

3 vv. (89 sbs):	19; 11, 19; 24, 16;
2 vv. (57 sbs):	17, 32; 8;
3 vv. (75 sbs):	14, 12; 20; 8, 6, 15 (or 19, incl. final long)

I have barred the piece primarily by the duple long (whole note), with occasional irregular measures at the end of a phrase, so that long notes in the tenor concord with the barring, ties are minimized, and major cadences come on the beat. Often, however, the individual voices seem to change meter at different points; no system of barring can do justice to the complexity of the rhythmic counterpoint.

Take the opening phrase once again. In the first two measures the tenor and contratenor articulate clear duple rhythms. The discantus, meanwhile, achieves a free-floating ametrical effect after its first note by interspersing odd numbers of eighth notes among the quarter and half notes – half, three-eighths, quarter, one-eighth, half, one-eighth, half, one-eighth, quarter – with the result that the voice is rhythmically suspended over each attack in the tenor part. In m. 3 the tenor breaks loose from its metrical moorings, with a sequence of three dotted-quarter notes in a row. Many other pieces have phrases with a stable opening, a metrically ambiguous middle section with a rhythmic crescendo towards the end, and a satisfying final cadence. But in most pieces the cadence arrives on the first beat of the prevailing mensural grouping: here the first major cadence comes after nineteen beats, a multiple of neither two nor three. I had to create a three-beat measure so that the cadence (and the tenor's whole note, or long) would come on a downbeat. Other passages, with their alternation of quarter and half notes, suggest the "six-eight" style rhythms common in triple meter – but here there is always an extra note somewhere to make the pattern irregular (see mm. 7–8, 10–11, etc.).

The "ametricality" of this piece is unusual, but not unique. Power, especially, is known for his "calculated disregard of regular mensuration," and his "predilection for asymmetry," resulting in "fluctuating bar lengths in modern transcription."[83] Dunstaple, in contrast, seems to have preferred greater rhythmic regularity and symmetry.[84]

The rhythmic and melodic writing in this piece are carefully calculated to keep us guessing – where will the next arrival (rhythmic and melodic) be? F or G for the final? Where does the duet begin and end? What is the appropriate metrical grouping here? Forest has taken features present to a limited extent in most English cantilenas and exaggerated them. The effect is not unlike the most elaborate Gregorian graduals, imparting a sense of mysterious suspension very much removed from the everyday world. This is the English style with a vengeance, and continental composers would never adopt it completely. Some of its features would, however, become influential on continental composers such as Du Fay, especially in the 1440s and 1450s.

The dissemination and transmission of English cantilenas

In spite, or because, of their difference from continental music in generic antecedents and style, English cantilenas were extremely popular on the Continent. The numbers of sources are indicated in Table 4.6.1 in parentheses after the identification of the text: seven out of the ten are found in four or more sources (counting Q15).[85] Only five continental motets from the early fifteenth century were this broadly disseminated, while fourteen early fifteenth-century English cantilenas have four or more sources (see Appendix, "Widely Disseminated Motets"). This suggests that English music, and especially English cantilenas, had a certain prestige value: every choir and copyist wanted some for their repertory. The fact that people wanted English cantilenas also accounts for the repertory's relatively high number of composer attributions (and conflicting attributions), and the rather unusual "De Anglia" or "Anglicanus" attributions indicating provenance (I know of no other pieces in which a country, city, or region of origin is indicated in the manuscript for an anonymous work).

When did English music, and the English cantilena in particular, first come to the Continent? This is an important question, since the answer affects our sense of the extent and timing of English influence on continental composers. Strohm argues that only at the Council of Basel (1431–49) did significant quantities of English music became known. He points out that most English music is found in manuscripts with connections to Basel compiled in the 1430s and later.[86] The fact is, however, that the first layer of Q15 (copied in the 1420s) contains two English cantilenas and eight English Mass movements (including two pairs),[87] while many of the English pieces in Q15 copied in the early 1430s must have been circulating in the 1420s as well. Some English music at least was available on the Continent well before the Council of Basel.

The mechanisms for the transmission of English music, especially at this early stage, are poorly understood. It has long been believed that the Council of Constance (1414–18) was central to the diffusion and transmission of music from all over the Continent and England (as Forest's presence would attest). Strohm, however, finds that much of the music associated with Constance was conservative: the great Ars Nova motets and Italian music from the first decade of the century. He finds no evidence of any English music there (though there may have been some continental influence on English musicians).[88] Nevertheless, there were many other opportunities for

English music and musicians to cross the channel. Following the Battle of Agincourt in 1415 some English musicians (including the royal chapel and Dunstaple) spent time in France. In Bruges the connections to England reached back far into the fourteenth century, English musicians were employed, and English-style devotional Lady Masses were instituted in the early 1420s. Other cities in the Netherlands had similar connections to England. Strohm suggests that the many composers from Liège whose music is found in Q15 may have provided a conduit for the transmission of English music to northern Italy.[89] It is certainly possible that composers such as Du Fay, the Lantins, and Lymburgia heard and sang English music in the 1420s.

Ramifying roots reviewed

Three of the subgenres of the motet found in the motet section of Bologna Q15 have clear ties to earlier local traditions. Two (Italian and French isorhythmic) can trace their ancestry back to the aboriginal thirteenth-century motet, and use the texture of the medieval motet, with two upper texted voices over a slower tenor. The Italian motets found in Bologna Q15 can be seen as a clear continuation of the fourteenth-century Italian motet tradition. The French isorhythmic motets similarly can be seen as a continuation of the fourteenth-century French tradition, but with a difference: many of the northern composers of the isorhythmic motets worked in Italy, for Italian patrons, and incorporated Italian elements (such as laudatory texts, imitative openings, and Italian cadences) into their motets. In the evolutionary history of the medieval motet presented at the end of chapter 2 we found that distinct varieties of motet evolved and were developed by composers in fourteenth-century France and Italy. As cultural relations between the two regions increased in the early fifteenth century the two varieties were brought into contact once more. French composers brought their motets to Italy: because of their patrons' preferences, local conditions, and the eternal search for novelty, they found themselves developing motets that resembled Italian motets. These new Italo-French isorhythmic motets could be considered hybrids of the two local varieties.

The third subgenre began life in England as a genre distinct from the motet in texture, text type, and style. Its incorporation into the motet on the Continent was a radical departure for the genre as a whole, which would have far-reaching consequences. In terms of the evolutionary analogy we can imagine that on their island of origin (England), motets (pigeons) and can-tilenas (let us call them quails) were perceived and treated as different species of bird. Quails did not exist on the Continent, however, so that when they arrived from England, continental breeders and fanciers did not quite know what to make of them. Since the quails resembled pigeons more than anything else, the quails were put into the same pens as the pigeons and were treated as a kind of pigeon. Continental taste for this imported novelty grew (as the number of concordances shows), with important implications for the pigeons. More quails were imported, continental breeders tried to develop pigeons that resembled quails, and the two species began to interbreed. Many of the cantilena's (quail's) features proved to be dominant: by the end of the fifteenth century most motets had a single top voice and a pre-existent sacred text. But even in the 1420s and 1430s continental composers went right to work writing pieces in cantilena texture. The various kinds of continental "cantilena-style motet" in Bologna Q15 can be seen as new hybrids of the older motet and the cantilena. One variety of cantilena-style motet became particularly popular in the 1420s and 1430s in Italy. This subgenre, which I call the cut-circle motet because of its usual mensuration, will be the subject of the next chapter.

5 A new hybrid subgenre: the cut-circle motet

Many of the motets in Bologna Q15 (especially motets by northern composers working in Italy) are recognizably different from earlier local traditions. I
call these new varieties of motet "new hybrid subgenres" – hybrids of the
various older local traditions. Some of these new hybrid subgenres retain the
texture of the medieval motet; others adopt the English cantilena texture.
Although composers drew on their experience of other treble-dominated
genres (such as the French chanson, the Italian lauda, or the Mass Ordinary
movement), I believe that it was the popularity of the English cantilena and
its absorption into the continental motet that spurred continental composers
to embrace so enthusiastically the new texture for the motet. The result was
an abundance of wonderful new music, as we shall see.[1]

Most of the non-English cantilena-style motets in Bologna Q15 can be
grouped into a subgenre that I call the "cut-circle motet" because of its use of
a rhythmic style associated with the mensuration known as cut-circle (Ø) or
tempus perfectum diminutum, although they do not all use this mensuration sign
(see Table 5.1, pp. 110–11). Many of the cut-circle motets are also characterized by other features, such as melodic figures, florid melismas, fermata sections, and repeated-note figures in imitation.[2] None of these features can be
associated with every one of the cut-circle motets, making this a good case of
a family resemblance category, in which the members are related in a variety
of ways, and features occur in various combinations. Ø (cut-circle) is probably the most controversial mensuration sign of the early fifteenth century; a
brief look at some of these controversies is in order before I discuss the subgenre in more detail.

The origins and meaning of the cut-circle mensuration sign (Ø)

The mensuration sign known informally as cut-circle – perfect tempus, minor prolation, with a stroke or virgule bisecting it (Ø) – has long been associated with certain kinds of rhythmic motion: Besseler discussed the new "tempus notation" that went along with "kantable Melodik" and "neue Strom-rhythmus";[3] Reynolds discussed features that can be associated with imperfect modus organization, such as hemiola-type coloration of longs and breves, and remote imperfection of the long;[4] Cox stressed the ease of writing strings of minims, and the availability of the semiminim.[5] These kinds of rhythmic treatment are central to the subgenre I call the "cut-circle motet": they are found, however, in motets with other explicit mensuration signs (both O and C), and in many motets and sections of motets with no mensuration sign at all. Cut-circle rhythmic style is also found in genres other than the motet. In order to understand this situation, we must review some features of early fifteenth-century mensural practice and twentieth-century understanding of that practice.

Cut-circle has long been believed to be a sign of diminution: its Latin name is "tempus perfectum diminutum," diminished perfect tempus, though the sign is only discussed in theoretical writings from after 1450.[6] The stroke became a sign of diminution during the fifteenth century (it remains so today: witness "cut time"), and cut-circle is sometimes found in conjunction with C-dot (C) in another voice. In such cases the note values are in a 2:1 ratio, so that two breves of cut-circle are equivalent to one breve of C-dot:

```
     L                        B
 Ø   B      B     =    C   S         S
     SSS    SSS            MMM    MMM
```

This relationship indicates that the values under Ø should be diminished, or sung twice as fast. It could also indicate that the C values are augmented; the ambiguity has led Hamm and Cox to call the relationship "pseudo-augmentation."[7] Another possibility is that the tempo of pieces in "pseudo-augmentation" settles somewhere in between normal tempos for O and C (if such "normal" tempos existed).

In other cases Ø is found in pieces with two or more sections with contrasting mensuration signs, most often ØOC. Unlike the simultaneous proportion with C discussed above, there is no sure way to know what the

100

proportional or tempo relationship between sections should be. The 2:1 proportion often does not seem to work musically; the kind of music written in adjacent sections in Ø and O is similar enough that doubling the tempo seems ridiculous. Most scholarship suggests that cut-circle must indicate a faster tempo than O, but exactly what degree faster has been much debated.[8]

Margaret Bent has recently suggested that in its earliest usage the stroke through the circle in Ø was not a sign of diminution or tempo: it indicated a new section, a change of scoring, or a repeat, in the manner of a "signum congruentiae" or "dal segno" mark. Her evidence is entirely convincing for the examples she discusses (mostly Mass movements), especially those in which the same music is to be sung twice, once in O and once in Ø. It leads her to suggest that successive sections in O and Ø can be sung at the same tempo.[9]

As Bent remarks, however, the same sign can have different meanings in different contexts.[10] I suggest that another meaning of Ø, closely related to the "pseudo-augmentation" discussed above, was a new kind of perfect tempus derived from the renotation of ₵ pieces up one mensural level and characterized by marked imperfect modus organization. This new kind of perfect tempus shows up in pieces with no mensuration sign at all, and with the plain old O mensuration sign, but it is most closely associated with Ø.

Renotation was common in the late fourteenth and early fifteenth centuries. Italian pieces were renotated from *brevis* to *longa* notation; French pieces were renotated in Italian notation, and vice versa; peculiarities of English notation were translated on the Continent.[11] In some cases we have explicit cases of renotation, where the same piece is found notated differently in different manuscripts. Many other cases of such renotation must have been lost, but we can often infer renotation based on notational peculiarities. Two Q15 motets are explicit examples of renotation: they are notated in perfect tempus (with no mensuration sign) in Q15, but in major prolation in Bologna 2216, with a 2:1 breve ratio. Romanus's *Ducalis/Stirps* is a case of "pseudo-augmentation": in Bologna 2216 it has ₵ for all voices; in Q15 ₵ is retained for the tenor (and added contratenor), but the upper voices are renotated in perfect tempus. Hugh de Lantins's *O lux et decus* (Q15) is a reworking of the earlier *Christus vincit* (Bologna 2216): in the process of reworking it and changing the text the original major prolation was changed to perfect tempus in all voices.[12] In none of the cases of explicit renotation do the renotated voices in perfect tempus have a mensuration sign. The singers of these parts without mensuration sign presumably worked out the mensural organization of their parts, that of plain old perfect tempus (O), and that was all they needed to know. Some of the pieces for which we can infer renotation, however, and more than half of the examples of pseudo-augmentation use the cut-circle sign for the voices in perfect tempus.[13] There is thus some evidence that Ø was often used for pieces renotated from ₵, though no mensuration sign was necessary (and O remained a possibility).

The kinds of rhythms resulting from the renotation of major prolation as perfect tempus are somewhat different from normal perfect tempus. ₵'s major prolation, imperfect tempus, becomes perfect tempus, imperfect modus. All the characteristic rhythmic patterns of ₵ are imported into Ø (or O). Just as the imperfect tempus of ₵ is usually fairly strongly marked metrically (think, for example of Du Fay's ₵ chansons *Ce jour de l'an*, or *J'attendray tant*), the imperfect modus of these renotated pieces is strongly marked, much more so than in normal perfect tempus, where modus organization is often not present at all. Other patterns typical of ₵, such as coloration producing hemiola, remote imperfection, and a pickup following paired rests would also appear. This marked imperfect modus can be seen easily in modern editions barred by the long, rather than the breve: using the usual reduction of 4:1, this results in measures of 6/4 rather than 3/4. There are few ties over the barline, coloration groupings and longs (imperfected and otherwise) tend to line up with the barlines, and major cadences come on the first beat of the measure.

Why renotate? The new "tempus notation," often indicated by Ø, had advantages over the older ₵, especially in passages with extensive figuration. It was easier to write minims than semiminims (void, colored, or flagged); there was more opportunity for ligatures in melismas, since c.o.p. ligatures could be used for semibreves; and the music had a more modern appearance, since major prolation was going out of style around 1430.[14] As scribes, singers, and composers became accustomed to renotating, and to singing from such renotated pieces, they must have come to like and recognize this special variety of perfect tempus with a strongly marked imperfect modus organization. Composers then of course began to write new pieces using the new style of "tempus" notation and the associated rhythms. New advantages then revealed themselves: declamation on the minim was now possible (declamation on the semiminim in ₵ was rare), and a new smaller note value, the semiminim, became available.

```
        L                                      B
[Ø]     B              B            =    Ҫ     S          S
        SSS            SSS                     MMM        MMM
        MMMMMM         MMMMMM                  ss ss ss   ss ss ss
        ss ss ss ss ss ss   ss ss ss ss ss ss
```

Pieces taking full advantage of this new "cut-circle" notation could use an exceptionally large range of note values. Longs are normally reserved for final cadences (if we exclude long-note tenors); here, however, the breves of Ҫ become longs, and are found in some voices at almost every cadence. At the same time declamation could occur at almost every level, and semiminims were available for the most detailed ornamental flourishes.[15] As the kind of music formerly notated in Ҫ began to be notated in perfect tempus, the musical habits associated with perfect tempus would have asserted themselves as well. A rhythmic style drawing from the characteristic rhythms of both Ҫ and O developed. This was a new rhythmic language of great expressive potential.

Reynolds, Nosow, and others, have examined the characteristic rhythms of pieces (and sections of pieces) with explicit O and Ø signs, and have found exactly these differences. Cut-circle (Ø) pieces use more longs (perfect, imperfected, and colored), more hemiola coloration, and all the other rhythmic patterns derived from Ҫ discussed above. They also often have long melismatic strings of minims, with very occasional semiminims.[16] Circle (O) pieces tend to stick to breves, semibreves, and minims, and use relatively little hemiola-type coloration of longs and breves. Circle (O) pieces are also more likely to have declamation on the minim, and minim triplets; they are less likely to have long melismatic passages of minims, or to use semiminims.[17] There are thus distinct differences between the two mensurations. On the other hand, there is also influence from one to the other, especially in the hands of the same composer, or composers writing in similar styles and subgenres. Individual works using one mensuration sign may use features associated with the other; pieces with no sign may combine both kinds of rhythmic motion.[18]

Do these findings have tempo implications? No; or rather, they suggest that the connections between mensuration and tempo are very loose indeed. Simultaneous proportions, such as pseudo-augmentation, cannot provide

103

conclusive evidence for tempo, because any conventional tempo usage, if different from the proportion, would have to be overridden by the necessity for vertical alignment. Likewise, renotation would seem to indicate that the minim in Ø is exactly twice as fast as the minim in ₵; and if we believe in minim equivalence between the primary mensurations, then it would go twice as fast as the minim in O as well. On the other hand, renotation is most likely to occur during a period of tempo change. Renotation is necessary because of the increase in small values in ₵. That increase in small values caused ₵ to slow down, which in turn may have disturbed the minim equivalence between ₵ and O. If this is the case, then the semibreve of a piece in Ø will be somewhat slower than the usual minim in ₵, and faster than the normal semibreve in O, but there will be no exact proportion.

The primary function of mensural signs is to indicate mensural organization so that the performer knows which notes should be altered and imperfected. Mensural signs are often omitted at the beginnings of pieces, since before starting the performer has time to work out the mensural organization; they always appear when there is a change of mensuration, since there is not time to work it out on the fly, while singing. Tempo indications are of secondary importance.

Why then, in pieces with alternating sections in O and Ø, do you need a new mensural sign, when the basic mensural organization does not change? I can think of several reasons.

- Music written in Ø does generally use more longs: the stroke indicates that the longs are imperfect, and alerts the performer to the likelihood of remote imperfection and coloration.
- The change of sign indicates a new section, as in Bent's hypothesis.
- [₵]O₵ was a common mensural pattern for tripartite pieces; when this pattern was renotated or newly composed as [Ø]OØ the tradition of indicating the subsequent mensurations may have persisted.
- The change of sign may also indicate a new tempo – not proportionally derived, but appropriate to the kind of music written in the new mensuration. Thus, when we change from Ø to O, it works best to slow down slightly for the new section, allowing minim triplets or declamation on the minim not to feel hurried. The return to Ø for the end of the piece will speed up again, or the beat might switch to the breve (analogous to a beat on the semibreve in ₵).

104

Let us summarize our conclusions so far. If we are concerned with the meaning of the sign Ø, then we can say that it has multiple meanings: one is Bent's use as a section marker or *signum congruentiae*; another is as an indicator of a special kind of perfect tempus with imperfect modus organization and rhythmic patterns derived from ₵. Either may be combined with a change of tempo. There may be additional meanings as well, yet to be discovered. Performers should choose whatever tempo works well for them when encountering a piece with a single section; when encountering a piece in multiple sections, with some mensuration signs, they should consider all the possibilities listed above before making a decision about relative tempos.

On the other hand, if we are concerned with identifying the approach to rhythm found in most pieces or sections of pieces that begin with the cut-circle mensuration sign (Ø), we can find it under other mensuration signs as well: ₵, O, and no sign at all. This characteristic rhythmic style, with duple grouping at the lowest and highest level, and triple division in the middle, is found in conjunction with pseudo-augmentation, renotation, and new composition with and without explicit signs. The fact that the same kind of music can appear with several different mensuration signs severely weakens any claims for strict proportional tempo relationships between mensurations.

As a concrete example of some of these issues let us consider Johannes de Sarto's *Ave mater, O Maria* (Q15.182; Ex. 5.1).[19] The piece is found in both Q15 and Trent 92, and the same mensuration signs are provided in both. The motet begins in O (explicitly shown in both sources) and changes to Ø two-thirds of the way through (mm. 37 or 38). The first section, though marked as O, looks quite a lot like Ø: it begins with a long with remote imperfection by two minims, and also has a few passages of coloration with imperfect longs (mm. 19, 30, and 32). Barring according to imperfect modus, as I have done here, works very well: the only cadence (and the only long) in the O section that does not fall on the first beat of a measure is the first (m. 4: a phrygian cadence on A); but that cadence may have been given a relatively weak metrical position so as not to impede the forward motion so near the beginning of the piece. Like pieces in Ø, this section uses very occasional semiminims (mm. 25, 32, 33); it also, however, has the minim triplets more typical of O, including an extensive passage in m. 17.

The final section marked Ø is also a peculiar mix of features associated with Ø and O. The main Ø feature is the extensive use of the characteristic

Example 5.1 Johannes de Sarto, *Ave mater, O Maria* (Q15.182, 203′–204; Trent 92.1529, 175′–176)

Example 5.1 (*cont.*)

hemiola coloration groups; it also lacks minim triplets (and semiminims). These features might suggest a slightly faster tempo. Unlike the first section, however, and more typical of O, this section has declamation on the minim (mm. 48–50): the text, "Cum transmigravero," is a mouthful, and is heard in imitation in all three voices. This would certainly limit the possible speed of the section, so any substantial tempo difference between sections seems improbable. Imperfect modus works less well here, also, as can be seen by my insertion of measures of 3/4 and 9/4 in order to keep the coloration groups within the barlines. Motivic connections between the sections also suggest similar tempos: the "-migravero" motif is first heard in the discantus in m. 24 (without text), and the homophonic repeated-note motif heard twice in the

107

first section (mm. 15 and 18) is treated in imitation in the last section (mm. 46–7: "Memor esto," "remember": could this be word painting?).

The change to Ø is in a different place in the two manuscripts, indicating a fuzzy boundary between the two sections. The text has three stanzas. The first ends in m. 14, with a major cadence on F. The second ends in m. 34, with a cadence on A arrived at by means of a climactic melismatic flurry. The third stanza begins with an acclamation to the Virgin, "Salve virgo," set with the fermatas typical of cut-circle motets. The fermata section has three phrases, ending with a solid cadence on C. Unlike the first two, however, the third phrase is cut off abruptly to allow the next phrase to enter with its pickup and hurry things on. Trent 92 lacks fermatas in m. 37, and begins the Ø there, after a rest. This ignores the connection of m. 37 to the preceding fermata passage, however. Q15 has fermatas in m. 37, and changes to Ø at m. 38, in the middle of the cadence to C. This makes some sense, since it comes at the end of the fermata section and at the end of a word, but it might have seemed odd to a scribe accustomed to more definite section endings for changes of mensuration sign. The fact that the mensuration sign occurs in different places also argues for near equivalence of tempo in the two sections.

So what is the function of the mensuration signs in this piece, and what do they mean? The first sign is superfluous according to normal practice in the first decades of the century. It was a period during which mensuration signs were more and more often provided at the beginning of a piece, however, and a certain amount of redundancy is normal in music notation in any case. It is possible that the O sign is a warning not to sing this first section too fast, given the minim triplets and semiminims to come, especially given the opening imperfected long, normally associated with Ø. The Ø signature signals, as in Bent's theory, a change of some kind: in this case a change of rhythmic style, especially the extended passages in hemiola coloration. It might also suggest a slight acceleration of the tempo, though any exact whole-number proportion (either 2:1 or 3:2) seems to me excessive.

Features of the cut-circle motet

Ave mater, O Maria can also serve as a representative example of the subgenre I call the cut-circle motet: a freely composed cantilena-style motet featuring the kind of rhythmic organization associated with the sign Ø. The subgenre also has a number of other characteristic features which I will discuss before returning to the issue of mensurations. Table 5.1 lists twenty-six cut-circle motets. The music of two of them (Lymburgia's *O baptista mirabilis* and *Gaude felix Padua*) is illegible; from what I could make out they resemble cut-circle motets, but in most cases I will not include them in the discussion, since individual features are not discernible. Thus there are a total of twenty-four motets to be considered.

Composers

The seven main composers of the cut-circle motets have similar biographies.[20] All are northerners (from Liège or Cambrai) and most worked in Italy, where the Ø motets were probably written. Du Fay and the two Lantins worked for the Malatestas; Du Fay, Brassart, and Arnold de Lantins all worked for the Papal chapel; Lymburgia and Feragut both worked in Vicenza; Sarto, Brassart, and Lymburgia all had connections to St. Jean l'Evangéliste in Liège, and Sarto and Brassart both worked for Albrecht II of Germany.[21] Lymburgia's works dominate (eleven out of twenty-six, two of which are illegible), but Lymburgia has a disproportionate representation in Q15 as a whole, leading some scholars to suggest that he had a hand in the compilation of the manuscript.[22] These composers must have known each other, and each other's work, for we see them ringing changes on the same theme.

Final and characteristic opening

Eleven of the twenty-six pieces have an F final with one flat in the lower voices. The two C-final pieces are in the same tonal world as the F-final pieces, with a b-flat in the lower voices and similar cadences. Twelve of these pieces (F-final and C-final) begin with the same characteristic opening, with a long on C imperfected by a semibreve in the discantus over an F in the tenor; some also go on in a similar fashion (Ex. 5.2).[23] There is thus a one-to-one correspondence between these two finals and the characteristic opening (a few of the pieces with other finals have variants of this characteristic opening, indicated in Table 5.1 in parentheses). The F- and C-final pieces should perhaps be considered a very cohesive subset of the subgenre as a whole.[24] The imperfected long is typical for Ø, but it is found here also in two pieces that begin in O: Arnold de Lantins's *Tota pulchra* (Ex. 6.1; Ex. 5.2c) and Sarto's *Ave mater* (Ex. 5.1; Ex. 5.2f); and in one piece in ₵, Arnold de Lantins's *O pulcherrima* (Ex. 5.2h).

109

Table 5.1. *Cut-circle motets in Q15 (26) (stage II unless otherwise noted)*

MS no.	Composer	Title (source of text)	final/sig.	opening	florid	fermatas	mensuration	repeated-note imitation
MARIAN								
264	Brassart	O flos fragrans (N)	F/♭	X	X	M	[Ø]	(X)
234	Du Fay	Flos florum (pre-existent) (I)	F/♭	X	X	E	[Ø]	
201	Du Fay	Vergene bella (Petrarch) [I]	D		X		[Ø]OƆ	X
202	A. de Lantins	Tota pulchra (SoS: A)	F/♭	X			O	
177	Lymburgia	Pulchra es amica (SoS: A + Bible)	G/♭				[Ø]OƆ	
204	Lymburgia	Surge propera (SoS; not A)	F/♭	up			[Ø]	
183	Lymburgia	Descendi in ortum (SoS: A)	G			E	[Ø]	X
265	Lymburgia	Ave mater nostri (N)	F/♭	X			[Ø]	(X)
284	Lymburgia	O Maria maris stella (old mot.)	G/♭	(in Ct.)			[Ø]	(X)
182	Sarto	Ave mater, O Maria (Lauda + N)	F/♭	X	X	M	OƆ	X
276	Sarto	O quam mirabilis (N)	F/♭	X			[Ø]	X
178	A. de Lantins	O pulcherrima mulierum (SoS: A)	F/♭	X		E	Ȼ OƆ	X
233	Anon.	Ave mater pietatis (N) (I)	D	(on D)		M	[Ȼ]OƆ	
GOD								
203	Grossin	Imera dat hodierno (N? Holy spirit)	G				[Ȼ]OƆ	(X)
222	H. de Lantins	Ave verum corpus natum (4–1) (I)	F/♭	(up on F)	X	E	[Ø]	
167	Lymburgia	Ostendit mihi angelus (R; Rev. 22)	G	(in Ct.)			[Ø]O	
SAINTS								
267	Brassart	Te dignitas presularis (N)	G/♮/♭			M	[Ø]O	
292	Du Fay	O beate Sebastiane (prayer)	C/♭	X	X	M	Ø	
181	H. de Lantins	O lux et decus Hispanie (A)	F/♭	X			[Ø]C	X
189	Lymburgia	In hac die celebri (N) (III)	F/♭♭				[Ø]	(X)

				sig.				[Ø]	(X)
186	Lymburgia	Martires dei incliti (N)		G					
286	Lymburgia	O baptista mirabilis (N) illegible		D					
288	Lymburgia	Gaude felix Padua (A) illegible		F/♭					
LAUDATORY									
271	Feragut	Excelsa civitas Vincencia (N)		C/♭	X	X	M/E	Ø	X
187	Lymburgia	Congruit mortalibus (N)	(III)	F/♭	X		M	Ø OØ	X
188	Anon.	Salve vere gracialis (N)	(III)	D/♭/♮	(up on A)		M/E	[O]ØO	X

Key:

sig. = key signature of bottom two voices;

opening = C long in cantus over F in tenor, imperfected by semibreve (see Ex. 5.2)

A = Antiphon; N = New text (or not yet found); E = End of piece; M = Middle of piece;

( ) = in final column indicate that the repeated-note figure is not much in evidence, and/or is not imitated

Example 5.2 Characteristic opening for cut-circle motets with F and C finals

(a) 264: Brassart, *O flos fragrans* (Brassart, vol. II, 3)

(b) 234: Du Fay, *Flos florum* (DufayB, vol. I, 6)

(c) 202: Arnold de Lantins, *Tota pulchra* – see Ex. 6.1, p. 128

(d) 204: Lymburgia, *Surge propera* (Lewis, 10)

(e) 265: Lymburgia, *Ave mater nostri* (Etheridge, vol. II, 291)

(f) 182: Sarto, *Ave mater* – see Ex. 5.1, p. 106

(g) 276: Sarto, *O quam mirabilis* (Cox, vol. II, 670)

(h) 178: Arnold de Lantins, *O pulcherrima* (*PS*, 269)

Example 5.2 (*cont.*)

(i) 292: Du Fay, *O beate Sebastiane* (DufayB, vol. I, 10)

(j) 181: Hugh de Lantins, *O lux et decus* (AllsenInt, 196)

(k) 271: Feragut, *Excelsa civitas* (Reaney, vol. VII, 90)

(l) 187: Lymburgia, *Congruit mortalibus* (Cox, vol. II, 101)

Floridity

Seven of the twenty-four pieces have florid melismas consisting of two or more breves' worth of minims (Ex. 5.3).[25] The best-known examples of this style are Du Fay's *Flos florum* (Q15.234) and *Vergene bella* (Q15.201), and Brassart's *O flos fragrans* (Q15.264) (note the possible word painting in conjunction with the two "flower" motets).[26] Most of the melismas in Example 5.3 share a sequential six-minim figure I call melisma x (bracketed in Ex. 5.3); closely related versions of this figure are labeled as x'.[27] All use a fluid style combining motion by step and by third. The melismatic writing recalls the florid Italian style of Ciconia's *Una panthera* or some of his motets, which can be seen also in de Monte's *Dominicus a dono* (Ex. 4.1). It also resembles figuration in the more florid of the late Franco-Italian Ars subtilior pieces.[28]

Example 5.3 Florid melismas in cut-circle motets (one melisma from each of the florid works listed in Table 5.1, plus melismas from related chansons)

(a) 264: Brassart, *O flos fragrans*, mm. 31–6 (Brassart, vol. II, 3)

(b) 234: Du Fay, *Flos florum*, mm. 51–3 (DufayB, vol. I, 6)

(c) 234: Du Fay, *Vergene bella*, mm. 81–4, 86 (DufayB, vol. VI, 9)

(d) 182: Sarto, *Ave mater* – see Ex. 5.1, pp. 106–7, mm. 16, 20, 24–5, 32–3

(e) 222: Hugh de Lantins, *Ave verum corpus*, mm. 56–8 (Nosow, 355)

(f) 292: Du Fay, *O beate Sebastiane*, mm. 6–8 (DufayB, vol. I, 10)

(g) 271: Feragut, *Excelsa civitas*, mm. 11–13 (Reaney, vol. VII, 90)

(h) Du Fay, *Resvellies vous*, mm. 5–6 (DufayB, vol. VI, 25)

(i) Melisma y: Du Fay, *Mon chier amy*, mm. 10 and 35 (DufayB, vol. VI, 30) and 234: *Vergene bella*, m. 17 (DufayB, vol. VI, 7)

Q15.234, Du Fay's *Flos florum*, copied in stage I, is one of the first of the florid motets; it may have been a prototype or exemplar for later pieces.[29]

Fermatas

Twelve of the twenty-four pieces have fermata sections, either in the middle of the piece or at the end. In these sections the individual syllables of a few words or phrases – usually the name or some attribute of the subject of the text – are marked by fermatas or coronas in all voices. Generally all voices are texted in these sections, even if they are not texted elsewhere in the piece.[30] In *Ave mater* (Ex. 5.1) the fermatas highlight the acclamation to the Virgin that begins the third stanza, "Salve virgo" (mm. 35–7). Fermata sections are known in other kinds of pieces as well: in some chansons, in Du Fay's isorhythmic motet *Supremum est* (Q15.168), and in Mass movements. But they seem to be more typical of the cut-circle motet.

Repeated-note figure in imitation

Another rhythmic/melodic figure typical of Ø, but also fairly common in O, is three semibreves (transcribed as quarter notes) on the same pitch, best known in the opening of Du Fay's *Vergene bella*. Lymburgia uses this repeated-note figure so often that it has been associated with his personal style, but it is used by other composers as well.[31] Often the figure is treated in imitation between cantus and tenor, sometimes among all three voices (see Ex. 5.4). Fourteen out of the twenty-four pieces use this kind of imitation, to varying degrees. In *Ave mater* (Ex. 5.1) Sarto uses the repeated-note figure in discantus and tenor to introduce phrases in mm. 15 and 18, and in imitation in all three voices in m. 46.

Text types

Half (thirteen) of the texts are Marian, but not the votive and processional antiphon texts typical of the English cantilena. Here the text sources are much more varied. Most are non-liturgical poetic texts, some pre-existent, some new. Du Fay's *Vergene bella* is a stanza from a canzona by Petrarch; *Flos florum*, in Leonine hexameters, is known from several collections of devotional poetry; *O Maria maris stella* is a thirteenth-century motet text;[32] *Ave mater* starts

Example 5.4 Repeated-note figure in imitation in cut-circle motets (selected examples from among those listed in Table 5.1)

(a) 183: Lymburgia, *Descendi in ortum*, mm. 54–60 (Lewis, 8)

(b) 182: Sarto, *Ave mater* – see Ex. 5.1, p. 107, m. 46

(c) 181: Hugh de Lantins, *O lux et decus*, mm. 17–23 (AllsenInt, 198–9)

(d) 188: Anon., *Salve vere gracialis*, mm. 12–16 (Cox, vol. II, 111)

with two stanzas from a lauda but ends with a new third stanza.[33] The only antiphon texts (and the only texts set by English composers) are from the *Song of Songs*; of the five *Song* texts two of the Lymburgia texts seem to be taken directly from the Bible, rather than from the liturgy.[34] The cut-circle motets resemble English cantilenas because so many are Marian cantilena-style motets, but their largely new rhyming stanzaic texts are closer to the traditional poetic texts of the motet-style motet.

Seven of the texts are in honor of saints. As in the case of the Marian motets, few (two) use pre-existent antiphon texts, while the rest appear to be new.[35] The subject matter of the cantilena-style motet is thus expanded by applying the personal devotional tone usually associated with the Virgin to other holy figures.

Three of the motets have laudatory texts for ecclesiastics in the Venetian orbit. These are the only laudatory texts with cantilena-type settings in the manuscript; such texts belong especially to the Italian motet tradition (see Table 4.3). But once the cantilena has been expanded to include new texts for saints, it is only a small leap to honor distinguished ecclesiastics.[36] Thus the new subjects of many of the cut-circle motets show once more affinities with the motet-style motets.

Borderline cases

Three of the pieces listed as cut-circle motets have four voices rather than three: Q15.202, Arnold de Lantins's *Tota pulchra*, Q15.204, Lymburgia's *Surge propera*, and Q15.222, Hugh de Lantins's *Ave verum corpus*. This last motet, unlike the other two, has a single upper voice, and several of the typical features of the cut-circle subgenre (the rhythm of the typical opening figure, florid melismas, and fermatas).[37] I therefore admit it to the club of cut-circle cantilena-style motets.

Tota pulchra and *Surge propera* appear in Q15 as motet-style motets, with two discantus voices over the tenor and contratenor. *Tota pulchra*, however, appears in several sources (including Bologna 2216, which often seems to preserve an earlier notational stage) with only three parts (it is discussed in the next chapter: see Ex. 6.1).[38] The fourth part is the second discantus, and its status as a later addition is confirmed by the fact that it never moves to the octave with the tenor voice at cadences, unlike "real" motet-style motets (such as Ex. 4.1, *Dominicus a dono*), where both discantus voices make cadences with the tenor. *Surge propera* is found in only one source (Q15), but its second discantus acts just like that of *Tota pulchra*, and must also have been a later addition.[39] These two works, then, began their lives as cantilena-style motets and were transformed into motet-style motets by the addition of another voice. I therefore include them in two categories: here and with the double-discantus motet-style motets. The adapter may have been the scribe of Q15, already known for adding and subtracting contratenor parts.

Tota pulchra (Ex. 6.1) is a borderline case for other reasons as well: it is the only piece included in the cut-circle subgenre with an explicit mensuration sign of O throughout, and it is more declamatory and syllabic than the others. Like *Ave mater* (Ex. 5.1), however, *Tota pulchra* exhibits signs of combining elements of O and Ø style. Typical of O are the minimal use of hemiola-type coloration, declamation on the minim, and occasional use of minim triplets.[40]

117

Typical of Ø are the opening, the frequent longs (cadential and imperfected), and the modest melismas in the first twenty measures. The declamatory quality of *Tota pulchra* aligns it with another subgenre to be discussed below called the declamation motet. This motet can thus be seen as belonging to three different subgenres.

Mensurations and multiple sections

Thirteen of the cut-circle motets have only one section. Four have two sections: one is Q15.182, Sarto's *Ave mater*, discussed above (Ex. 5.1), and another is Q15.181, Hugh de Lantins' *O lux et decus*, the only work to include a section in C, imperfect tempus minor prolation. This work was mentioned above as an example of renotation: its first section, without a sign here, was originally in ℭ. In the other two (Q15.284, Lymburgia's *O Maria*, and Q15.267, Brassart's *Te dignitas*) the change to O comes near the end of the piece, and as in *Ave mater* there is no major break between sections.

Seven of the cut-circle motets have three sections. Three of these are in ØOØ: Q15.201, Du Fay's *Vergene bella*, and nos. 177 and 187, Lymburgia's *Pulchra es* and *Congruit mortalibus* (the mensuration sign of the first section is explicit in only one). Three are in ℭOℭ: Q15.178, Arnold de Lantins's *O pulcherrima*, Q15.233, *Ave mater pietatis*, and Q15.203, Grossin's *Imera dat hodierno*. One reverses the usual pattern by beginning in perfect tempus (OØO): Q15.188, *Salve vere gracialis*. Given the fact that Ø can be understood as a renotation of ℭ, ØOØ and ℭOℭ should perhaps be understood as two versions of essentially the same mensural plan. Both patterns were fairly common for tripartite pieces in all genres (motets, Masses, and chansons). A group of related works from other genres by the composers who wrote the tripartite cut-circle motets can shed light on the relationship between these two mensural schemes: the early cyclic Masses by Lymburgia and Arnold de Lantins, and two of Du Fay's ballades, *Mon chier amy* and *Resvellies vous*. These works also shed light on the use of Ø-style music in other genres.

Related music in other genres

RELATED MASSES

In Lymburgia's only complete Mass Ordinary cycle the discantus voice has the pattern ØOØ in all the movements of the Mass except the Sanctus (which

is troped and uses a more complex "unus/chorus" alternation).[41] The tenor
and contratenor move from ℂ to Ø over the course of the Mass:

	Kyrie	Gloria	Credo and Agnus
D	ØOØ	ØOØ	ØOØ
T	ℂOℂ	ØOØ	ØOØ
Ct.	ℂOℂ	ℂOℂ	ØOØ

The Gloria and Credo are the most closely linked musically, with similar
headmotifs. The contratenor thus sings almost the same music at two different
mensural levels in successive movements. It almost seems that in the course of
composing (or copying) this Mass, Lymburgia (or the scribe) was gradually
abandoning the older ℂOℂ in favor of the more modern ØOØ. Certainly the
implication is that the two were equivalent at some point in time.

All the movements in Lymburgia's Mass except the Kyrie use the standard
Ø opening figure (long imperfected by semibreve) in the discantus, supported
here, however, by C rather than F in the tenor. Kyrie, Gloria, and Credo have
an F final, while Sanctus and Agnus have a C final (all have one flat in tenor
and contratenor), further supporting our sense that C and F are almost inter-
changeable finals in this kind of music.

Arnold de Lantins's Mass, dubbed "Missa Verbum incarnatum" by Van den
Borren in *Polyphonia sacra* because of its Kyrie trope, has been renamed "Missa
O pulcherrima" by Reinhard Strohm because of its similarity to the motet by
that name, one of the works I have included among the cut-circle motets.[42]
The mensural scheme of this Mass is as follows:

Motet & Gloria	Kyrie & Credo	Sanctus	Agnus
ℂOℂ	ℂOℂℂ	ØOØ	ØOC

Here again we see the composer moving toward modern tempus notation over
the course of the Mass.[43] All the movements have an F final, and begin with
the standard cut-circle opening. The Mass, like the motet (and many of the
other cut-circle motets), also has fermata sections in every movement.

RELATED CHANSONS

Du Fay's ballades, *Resvellies vous* and *Mon chier amy*, use the mensuration plan
ℂOℂ. They also resemble some of the florid cut-circle motets, with especially close ties to *Vergene bella*. *Resvellies vous* was written in connection with
the marriage of Carlo Malatesta da Pesaro and Vittoria Colonna in 1423.

Table 5.2. *Three related works by Du Fay*

First section:				
Resvellies vous.	[C]	15+21=36+L	(B)	mel. x
Vergene bella.	[Ø]	38+L	(L)	mel. y
Mon chier amy.	[C]	9+13=22+L	(B)	mel. y

Middle section:				
Resvellies vous.	O	27+4L=35 (B) BBB opening; m. decl.; mel. x;	6/8 im.; triplets
Vergene bella.	O	35 (B) BBB opening; m. decl.;	6/8 im.; triplets; m. decl.
Mon chier amy.	O	13+L= 15 (B) BBB opening;	6/8 im.; triplets

Final section:		
Resvellies vous.	C 13+L (B) mel. with triplets, including mel. x′	Final: G with B-flat
Vergene bella.	Ø 12+L (L) mel. x, x′	Final: D
Mon chier amy.	C 10+L (B) mel. y	Final: D

Key: mel. x = melisma x; m. decl. = minim declamation

For each section I have provided first the mensuration sign, then the length. After the count I indicate the mensural value being counted (B = breve, L = long). For the ballades the length of the first section includes the repeat up to the sign. I have not counted the final longs of the first sections (where they are followed by a double bar) and at the ends of the pieces, but indicate them; for the end of the middle section, where there is less of a break, I include them in the count.

Fallows argues that *Mon chier amy*, a condolence to a friend who is mourning the death of another, was written in connection with the death of Pandolfo Malatesta da Rimini in 1427, but it may have been earlier.[44] *Vergene bella* may also have been written during the Malatesta years.[45] Its status as a motet is confirmed by its presence in the motet sections of Q15 and Bologna 2216, and by its sacred subject, but its use of Italian also ties it to the world of the secular song.[46] The three works share a great deal of material, as can be seen in Table 5.2.

In all three of these works, as in most of the tripartite motets, the first section is the longest and the final section is significantly shorter than the others. All use approximately the same tonal type, as well: the G final with a flat in the lower voices of *Resvellies vous* can be seen as a transposed version of the others' D final without signature. The dimensions of *Resvellies vous* and *Vergene bella* are astonishingly close, if we assume that the breve of C and the long of Ø are equivalent. They also both use the figure found in so many of the florid cut-circle motets (see Ex. 5.3c and h). *Mon chier amy* is like a smaller, less elaborate version of the other two pieces. While it shares its genre and mensuration scheme with *Resvellies vous*, it shares final and melodic material (melisma y: Ex. 5.3i) with *Vergene bella*.

The B sections of all three works, now in the same mensuration (O), are especially similar. All three begin with three breves: in *Vergene bella* and *Mon chier amy* all three are on the same pitch, in *Resvellies vous* the first two are. After a calm beginning, all three intensify: *Resvellies vous* and *Vergene bella* introduce declamation at the level of the minim ("m. decl."; *Vergene bella* treats it in imitation), *Resvellies vous* inserts a melismatic passage, and all three pieces have a passage with a kind of rhythmic canon of alternating quarter and eighth notes off by one beat (*Resvellies vous* mm. 39–43; *Vergene bella* mm. 50–52; *Mon chier amy* mm. 18–20). All also have passages with minim triplets: *Vergene bella* and *Mon chier amy* start the same, *Vergene bella* and *Mon chier amy* share material later on, with the same gasping inserted rests. *Resvellies vous* ends with a fermata passage, like so many cut-circle motets. In the final section both *Vergene bella* and *Resvellies vous* refer to melisma x, while as a rhymed ballade *Mon chier amy* brings back melisma y.

The similarity in style, dimensions, and musical material between *Vergene bella* and the two ballades provides more evidence that Ȼ and Ø are two ways of notating the same kind of music. This is further supported by a notational feature of the ballades, where the semiminims in Ȼ are replaced by the minims with the proportional cipher "2." This means that the florid melismas in Ȼ (including melisma x) are written in the same values as they are in *Vergene bella* under Ø: here we have renotation at the local level.

Quite a few other chansons by Du Fay share this same musical language. Another tripartite dedicatory ballade from the 1430s, *C'est bien raison*, for Niccolò III d'Este, Marquis of Ferrara, uses the mensuration signs [Ø]OØ.[47] While the proportions are rather different, it does use a variant of melisma y (mm. 3–4) and minim declamation in the B section. It also uses pre-cadential A-flats like the one in the tenor in *Ave mater* (though without the simultaneous cross-relation).[48]

The ballade was the most serious of the *formes fixes*, at the top of the chanson value hierarchy. In Du Fay's day it was already going out of date, and it was reserved for dedicatory pieces and laments. It could be said to aspire to the generic height of the motet – and indeed, with a Latin text and no repeat of the A section *Resvellies vous* or *C'est bien raison* would be almost indistinguishable from the cut-circle motets.[49] Conversely, Grossin's tripartite cut-circle motet *Imera dat hodierno* (Q15.203) recalls the form of the rhymed ballade, since the final Ȼ section is a literal restatement of the end of the first Ȼ section. Influence was traveling in both directions: the borders between genres were an especially fruitful breeding ground.

Cut-circle style is also found in chanson forms other than the ballade. Rondeaux generally remain in the same mensuration throughout, but then so do half of the cut-circle motets. All the rondeaux in Besseler's edition that he includes under "Tempus perfectum diminutum (vetustioris stili)" (nos. 47–60) and "Tempus perfectum diminutum (recentioris stili)" (nos. 61–6) have a claim to our attention.[50] I find the following rondeaux especially close to the style of the cut-circle motets. *Belle, veuillies vostre mercy* (Besseler's no. 47) uses "melisma y" (m. 13), as does no. 49, *Hé compaignons* (m. 21, transposed). No. 48, *Pour l'amour de ma doulce amye,* uses "melisma x" (m. 3), while no. 54, *Mon cuer me fait,* begins with a version of the Ø opening. These chansons demonstrate that Du Fay was experimenting with the "cut-circle" musical language in many different genres.

Concluding thoughts on the cut-circle motet

How much does the cut-circle motet owe to the English cantilena? And what are its roots, or forebears? The differences between cut-circle motets and English cantilenas are numerous. The range of text types in the cut-circle motet is much larger, and the texts are less likely to be associated with chant; this may account in part for the fact that the cut-circle motet rarely uses pre-existent material, while about half of the English cantilenas do. It is the differences in musical style, however, that are most striking. Cut-circle motets almost never use contrasting duet sections (the only one with such sections is Q15.234, Du Fay's *Flos florum*). They almost never use imperfect tempus, minor prolation (C; the only example is Q15.181, Hugh de Lantins' *O lux et decus*). The melodic language is also very different. English cantilenas rarely use repeated notes, and almost never three in a row, a basic vocabulary item in cut-circle motets; English cantilenas often begin with ascending triadic figures, and avoid remote imperfection of longs, while cut-circle motets usually begin with a high imperfected long and move down; and English cantilenas almost never use the extended strings of minims found in the more florid cut-circle motets. English cantilenas, as we have seen, also have a tendency toward "ametricality" (seen in an extreme form in Forest's *Alma*

Example 5.5 240: Power, *Salve regina*, opening, mm. 1–21 (Power, 13)

redemtoris*), while cut-circle motets generally have a clear metrical framework, against which they impose hemiola patterns at various levels. These differences become clear even when comparing cut-circle motets with English cantilenas found with the Ø mensuration sign: see Sarto's *Ave mater* (Ex. 5.1) and the first eleven measures of Power's *Salve regina* (Ex. 5.5), which begins with pseudo-augmentation (Ø in the discantus and [C] in the tenor and contratenor).[51] While hemiola coloration is found in both the Power and Sarto pieces, Sarto generally uses it in all three voices or in rhythmic harmony between the discantus and tenor, while Power uses it to create rhythmic opposition between the discantus and tenor.

The musical language of the cut-circle motet stems from the chanson and the three-voice Mass as much as it does from the English cantilena. Still, the cut-circle composers sometimes aimed for the kind of rhythmic variety and even ametricality characteristic of English music: this is true, for example, in *Ave mater* (Ex. 5.1, mm. 5–9), where a rhythmic sequence of dotted-quarter –eighth contradicts the meter, and is itself interrupted, in English fashion, by insertions that destroy its symmetry (the cc in m. 7, or the f quarter note in m. 8). The attempt to make the rhythms of each breve or long grouping (measure in modern transcription) different from the surrounding ones, the incessant search for variety typical of the cut-circle motets, may derive from English style.[52]

Cut-circle motets, like English cantilenas, are cantilena-style pieces predominantly devoted to the Virgin Mary. Like English cantilenas, they some-

times use fermata sections to highlight important words,[53] and they sometimes have multiple sections with contrasting mensuration signs. Both use
texts derived from the *Song of Songs*, though the English texts tend to be
derived from the liturgy, the continental ones directly from the Bible.

The cut-circle motet, then, is a true hybrid that fuses elements deriving
from many different genres. English music probably provided the model for a
Marian devotional piece in a three-voice song texture. The musical style was
taken over from pieces much closer to home: the dedicatory ballades and the
more elaborate rondeaux composed at the same period by the same composers. This style may have been partly derived in turn from Italian music. The
continental three-voice Mass provided another model for a sacred genre in
chanson format. Text types were drawn from the liturgical genres of the
English cantilena, poetic biblical prose such as the *Song of Songs*, and the Latin
strophic poetry of the traditional motet, both devotional and dedicatory. The
result was one of the most attractive products of this period of rich cross-fertilization.

6 Other new hybrid subgenres

New hybrid subgenres in Q15 other than the cut-circle motet are smaller, represented by only a few examples in some cases. The two cantilena-style subgenres seem to imitate specific features of the English cantilena: I call them the declamation motet and the continental cantilena. Another subgenre, the unus–chorus motet, makes references to both motet and cantilena textures, though it probably derives originally from unus–chorus Mass movements.

The three new motet-style subgenres use the double-discantus texture of the Italian and French continuations of fourteenth-century local traditions discussed in chapter 4, but they are composed by northern composers, not Italians, and lack the isorhythm typical of French motets.[1] I call them the retrospective, devotional, and other double-discantus motets. I will end with a brief look at the pieces that are borderline cases for the motet genre as a whole.

Declamation motets

Although the number of declamation motets is not large, they are among the most popular pieces of the period, judging by the number of sources in which they are found (see Table 6.1). At least one of these pieces is found in every major manuscript of the period. With the exception of Du Fay's *Supremum est* and Salinis's *Ihesu salvator*, the only other works with comparable dissemination from the first half of the century are English (see the Appendix).

The declamation motet is characterized by chiefly syllabic text setting and homorhythmic texture (some sources for some pieces provide text for all

125

Table 6.1. *Declamation motets in Q15 (5) (stage II unless otherwise noted)*

Qp	291:	Dunstaple, Quam pulchra es (A) (7 MSS; 1 English) O ¢
Tp	202:	A. de Lantins, Tota pulchra (A) (4 vv.; but D2 added) (6 MSS) O, one section
Id	203:	Grossin, Imera dat hodierno (N?: Holy Spirit) (6 MSS) ¢ O ¢
Arc	225:	Du Fay, Ave regina celorum (A) (5 MSS) (stage I) O, one section
Vd	279:	Lymburgia [Du Fay], Veni dilecte my (SoS; not A) (3 MSS) O, one section
Ip	249:	Anon., In Pharaonis atrio (N: Joseph in Egypt) (2 MSS) (stage I) O, one section

Distribution in continental manuscripts (all, of course, are also in Q15)

B2216	MuEm	Ox 213	Par 4379	92	Str	87	Ven	Aosta	Mod
Qp	Qp			Qp				Qp	Qp
Tp	Tp	Tp	Tp		Tp				
Id	Id	Id	Id	Id					
		Arc	Arc				Arc	Arc	
						Vd		Vd	
	Ip								

three voices).[2] It is often hard to draw the line between declamation motets and those which alternate syllabic sections with more melismatic passages; I limit this subgenre to the most extreme examples of a declamatory style, though even these have the occasional melisma.[3] Within these limits the pieces show a range of styles, and in fact I have included three of them in other subgenres as well. The most famous and widely disseminated piece of the group is an English cantilena, Dunstaple's *Quam pulchra*, whose homo-rhythmic style, atypical of Dunstaple, recalls the simple score-format cantilenas of the Old Hall Manuscript. Arnold de Lantins's *Tota pulchra* and Grossin's *Imera dat hodierno* are also included among the cut-circle motets. These two pieces, plus *Veni dilecte my*, may have been inspired in part by Dunstaple's *Quam pulchra*. The two stage I pieces (Du Fay's *Ave regina celorum I* and the anonymous *In Pharaonis atrio*) are among the simplest, and may derive in part from the simple polyphonic Italian lauda.[4]

The proposed origins of the declamation motet in the lauda and/or the English score-format cantilenas point to roots in simple polyphony and devotional song, genres open to participation by unskilled singers and lay people as well as to professionals.[5] The homorhythmic texture and text-generated rhythms of the declamation motets sound simple, and thus evoke the intimacy of private devotions or the communality of devotional choral singing. This, no doubt, is the desired effect, and it must account to some extent for their popularity. On closer examination, however, these pieces reveal themselves as extremely sophisticated.

Look, for example, at *Tota pulchra es* (Ex. 6.1). I present here the three-voice version in Bologna 2216, where both discantus and tenor are fully texted, revealing the declamatory quality of the piece most clearly. (The contratenor could easily be texted in coordination with the tenor with the division of some of the longer note values, but it is not texted in any surviving source.[6]) The text is concerned in the first half with the beauty of the beloved, with especial attention to her sublime taste and smell. The second half (beginning with "Jam enim hiems transiit," m. 21) is largely concerned with the arrival of spring and its accompanying sensations; parallelism or even identification of spring with the beloved is suggested by the return of "odor" as a prominent feature of spring. The final phrase returns to address the beloved once again, urging her to come from Lebanon to be crowned.

Tota pulchra es, amica mea,	Thou art all fair, O my love,
et macula non est in te.	and there is not a spot in thee.
Favus distillans labia tua,	Thy lips are as a dropping honeycomb,
mel et lac sub lingua tua.	honey and milk are under thy tongue.
Odor unguentorum tuorum	The sweet smell of thy ointments
super omnia aromata.	is above all aromatical spices.
Jam enim hiems transiit;	For winter is now past,
imber abiit, et recessit.	the rain is over and gone.
Flores apparuerunt,	The flowers have appeared,
vineae florentes	the vines in flower
odorem dederunt.	yield their sweet smell.
Et vox turturis	And the voice of the turtle
audita est in terra nostra.	is heard in our land.
Surge, propera, amica mea;	Arise, make haste, my love
veni de Libano,	Come from Libanus,
veni coronaberis.	come, thou shalt be crowned.[7]

The antiphon text is a cento from *Song of Songs* 4 and 2 structured like a psalm text, with each line consisting of a sentence that divides into two

Example 6.1 Arnold de Lantins, *Tota pulchra* (B2216, no. 48, pp. 66–7)

Example 6.1 (*cont.*)

half-lines. Lantins's setting responds carefully to the form of the text. Each sentence corresponds to a phrase of music ending with a cadence and (in most cases) a rest or fermata. The first and last sentences receive longer phrases (ten measures). All the other phrases are four or five measures long (each one receives a system in the transcription), and begin with the same long–short (breve–semibreve) rhythmic figure (all but m. 21 with a repeated note). Within each phrase the end of the first half-line is marked by a rest in the discantus voice, and usually a cadence as well. At the central cadences, however, there is less of a pause (an imperfect breve, rather than a perfect one) and sometimes one of the voices keeps moving through the cadence (as at mm. 13 and 36).

The pacing of the text declamation and the coordination of the voices are carefully controlled for expressive effect. For the opening acclamation (mm. 1–10) Lantins permits himself an expansive, melismatic style approaching that of the more florid cut-circle motets: this may be an example of word painting, as the florid melismas depict the beauty of the beloved. Within this opening salvo, however, Lantins also introduces the declamatory techniques that will dominate in the rest of the piece: the long–short (two beat–one beat) alternation for successive syllables at "macula non est in te" (mm. 7–8); declamation on every semibreve ("Amica" in the tenor, mm. 5–6); and the special effect of minim declamation on "Amica mea" in the discantus (m. 5).

Lantins exploits these three effects with care. For the description of the beloved's taste and smell (mm. 11–20, "Favus distillans" to "aromata"), the tenor part generally sticks to a relaxed long–short alternation of syllables, with a slight relaxation at the ends of some phrases (three beats for "tua" m. 15, and "-mata," m. 20). While the outer parts declaim the text simultaneously for the most part, the discantus part subtly varies its rhythms, now pushing ahead ("labia tua," m. 12), now lagging ("omnia aromata," m. 20). Most phrases also include some kind of internal rhythmic intensification, either by the introduction of shorter values in the discantus ("labia tua," m. 12, or "transiit," m. 22), or by faster declamation ("unguentorum," m. 16).

The second half of the piece ("Jam enim hiems," m. 21) begins with the long–short pattern as before; the transition to a faster, more urgent declamatory style is announced with the surprising rhythms at "transiit" (m. 22) leading (after a minim rest and a leap of a minor seventh) to minim declamation on "imber abiit" (m. 23). "Imber abiit" is reminiscent of "ibi dabo tibi" from Dunstaple's *Quam pulchra*, with its heavy emphasis on the letters "i" and "b" and its identical metrical position; but here, rather than being low in the range of the discantus, it is at the very top, and the effect is triumphant rather than sensual, as appropriate for the words announcing that "the rain is over and gone." An urgent semibreve declamation is retained for the next phrase, "Flores apparuerunt," but it relaxes a bit in the tenor for the voice of the turtle dove. For the final address to the beloved ("Surge propera," m. 34 to the end) the tenor retains the long–short declamation pattern, but the discantus varies this to achieve a more urgent declamation on every semibreve. The two come together for minim declamation at "veni de Libano," leading into the crowning final phrase, in which the repeated text, eighth-note pickups, semibreve declamation in the discantus, and predominantly ascending lines keep up the urgency until just before the final cadence.

The piece as a whole has an erotic shape worthy of the text. The florid contemplation of the beloved gives way to a relaxed enjoyment of her taste and smell in which the discantus subtly varies the pacing of the tenor. Things heat up with the arrival of spring: the pacing becomes more urgent, and the

Table 6.2. *Continental cantilenas in Q15 (stage II unless otherwise noted)*

I	224: Du Fay, Alma redemptoris I (chant in T)
I	235: Du Fay, Anima mea (chant in all voices; motet texture)
	199: Lymburgia, Regina celi (fb, chant incipit)
	183: Lymburgia, Descendi in ortum (uses chant)
	179: Reson, Salve regina (chant paraphrase, mm. 1–8)

unusual repetition of the final line "come and you will be crowned" with the rise through an octave in the tenor and a sixth in the discantus suggests that the love-making has indeed reached fruition. The basic approach of consonant homorhythmic declamation of the text in a trochaic long–short pattern has been subtly modified: Lantins alters the pace of the declamation and decreases the rhythmic synchronicity of the voices to depict the text and provide a satisfying overall shape. This is a response to the *Song of Songs*, and perhaps to *Quam pulchra*, that is just as accomplished as Dunstaple's famous cantilena.

Continental cantilenas

This subgenre consists of Marian antiphon settings that use chant. Although the subgenre is very small in Q15, it will become more important later in the century. The choice of texts and the use of chant suggest a conscious attempt to imitate English practices. Reson's *Salve regina* paraphrases chant (in an easily recognizable form) only in the first eight measures: this casual approach to chant paraphrase is found in many English cantilenas. Lymburgia's *Regina celi* begins with a chant incipit and paraphrases the chant in the discantus, as do the two English settings of this text (see Table 4.6: nos. 238 [Anon.] and 280 [Dunstaple]). Lymburgia's *Descendi*, which I have also included as a cut-circle motet, paraphrases parts of the chant in the top voice.

The two Du Fay pieces both use aspects of the cut-circle musical language, but combine it with unusual chant treatment. *Alma redemptoris I* has the standard tripartite mensural pattern, [₵]O₵, followed by a fermata section of longs and breves in typical cut-circle style. It puts the chant in the tenor in mostly equal values, perhaps in imitation of English discant; the top, meanwhile, is free and includes some florid embellishment.

In *Anima mea* Du Fay combined conventions from several different sub-genres. There is no mensuration sign, but the rhythmic language is clearly that of Ø. The Marian antiphon text and the chant paraphrase make it look like a continental cantilena; the tenor treatment is similar to that of *Alma redemptoris I*, moving primarily in equal breves with minimal ornamentation of the chant. The texture – two upper voices in the same range over a lower tenor voice – and the *Song of Songs* text ally *Anima mea* with the devotional double-discantus motets discussed below (Table 6.5), and I include it there as well. Other features are specific to this piece. The range is exceptionally low (with C3, C3, F4 clefs, rather than C1, C1, C3). All voices paraphrase the chant and carry the text; the tenor treatment is quite strict, while the other voices paraphrase the chant more freely. The voices enter one at a time after a time-interval of four longs; this quasi-canonic opening means that at any given point all the voices are singing different text. The piece is truly *sui generis*, combining the English practice of Marian antiphon settings with the cut-circle musical language, motet-style texture and a unique approach to range and the use of chant.[8]

Both of these motets are from stage I of Q15, suggesting that English models must have been available to Du Fay in the 1420s, and revealing his penchant for experimentation from the very start of his compositional career.

Unus–chorus motets

This is a small but interesting subgenre that makes use of contrasting textures and forces (see Table 6.3). Although the texts are of different genres (a troped Marian antiphon, a processional hymn, and a sequence), all of them are pre-existent and liturgically flexible. The contrasts in texture generally serve to emphasize structural features of the text: unus sections are used for the trope in Salinis's *Salve regina*, and for alternating couplets or stanzas in the others. All of the examples contrast chorus sections in a three-voice can-tilena-style texture with sections for two voices in mezzo-soprano (C2) clef and ₵ mensuration, usually marked "unus" to indicate the use of soloists for these sections.[9] *Salve regina* and *Surrexit Christus* both have an additional con-trasting texture for the full ensemble: *Salve regina* has a four-voice motet-style texture for the acclamations alternating with the tropes at the end of the piece, while *Surrexit Christus* has a monophonic alleluia refrain sung by the whole chorus.

Table 6.3. Unus–chorus motets in Q15

MS no.	Composer	Title (source)	[Chorus I] texture mens. section (cl/v)		Unus texture mens. section (cl/v)		[Chorus II] texture mens.section (cl/v)	
				Opening		Trope		Acclamations
232 (I)	Salinis	Salve Regina/Tr. Virgo (Troped Marian Antiphon)	C2/D C	1–35	C2/D1 ₵	36–53	C2/D1 ₵	54–5
			C4/Ct	(mm.)	C2/D2	56–71	C2/D2	72–3
			C4/T			78–89	C4/Ct	91–4
						(mm.)	C4/T	(mm.)
				Odd stanzas		Even stanzas		
196 (III)	Anon.	Ave Yhesu Christe (Sequence)	C2/D C	1	C2/D1 ₵	2		
			C4/Ct	3	C2/D2	4		
			C4/T	5		6		
				7		(stanzas)		
				(stanzas)				
				Opening, alt. couplets		Alt. couplets		Alleluia refrain
175 (II)	Lymburgia	Surrexit Christus hodie (Processional Hymn)	C2/D1 [O]	1–4	C2/D1 ₵	5–6	C4/tutti [O]	each 4 lines
			C2/D2	7–8	C2/D2	9–10		"chorus semper respondens"
			F3/T	11–12		(lines)		
				(lines)				

Key: cl = clef; v = voice; mens. = mensuration; alt. = alternating

Where does this subgenre come from? Numerous Mass movements composed during the first half of the fifteenth century have unus–chorus or duo–chorus markings, as do some other genres (including laude, motets and processional hymns).[10] Some English cantilenas have duet sections marked "unus": compare Q15.232, Salinis's *Salve Regina*, with Q15.240, Power's setting of the same text (Table 4.6). Both set the same trope with contrasting duet sections marked "unus."[11] The English unus texture, however, is not for two equal voices. In several of Du Fay's Mass movements we find pieces with unus or duo sections for two equal voices that contrast with a chanson/cantilena texture of a single discantus above tenor and contratenor; in these, however, the duo sections are in O rather than in C.[12] Although the unus–chorus motet is a minor subgenre, it illustrates the constant experimentation with texture and form characteristic of the early fifteenth century.

Retrospective double-discantus motets

This is a surprising group of pieces that seems to look backwards, not just to the fourteenth century, but to the thirteenth (see Table 6.4). Four of the six are from stage I of the manuscript compilation (unlike most of the other double-discantus motets). Three are by Humbertus de Salinis, whom John Nádas and Robert Nosow have identified as a Portuguese member of the chapel of the Pisan pope, Alexander V, in 1409. These three also appear together in the recently discovered Italian manuscript San Lorenzo 2211; the motets may have been written shortly after the Council of Pisa, in 1409–10.[13] The example we will focus on, Salinis's *Ihesu salvator/Quo vulneratus* (Ex. 6.2), is found in four sources, including Oxford 213, where it appears in formal black notation with a huge decorative initial.[14]

Texts

Five out of the six motets are polytextual. Polytextuality is a traditional attribute of the medieval motet, and in the fifteenth century it is usually associated with isorhythm (as in the French motet) or with some Italian motets. Two of the motets use actual thirteenth-century texts taken from the conductus and motet repertory.[15] Almost all of the texts are of a type seldom found in the fifteenth-century motet: critical of the evils of the world or the enemies of the church. This kind of text, known as *admonitio* or *cantus moralis*, was par-

Table 6.4. *Retrospective double-discantus motets in* Q15 (*stage I unless otherwise noted*)

MS no.	Composer	Title (subject, source)	v–t	final/sig.	mens.	Echo	remarks	Contratenor
171	Lymburgia (II)	Tu nephanda/Si inimicus T: Emitat celum (Jews, as enemies of Church)	4–2	G/♭	ØO/C		Conflicting mensurations almost no imitation	inessential
261	Ruttis	Prevalet simplicitas (simple life vs. duplicity)	3–1	F/♭	[C]		Cadence together, florid	—
278	Salinis (II)	Si nichil aculeris In precio precium (old conductus texts, enemies of Church)	3–2	D	[C]		Cadence together, syllabic and homorhythmic, stops a lot	—
247	Salinis	Psallat chorus in novo Eximie pater et regie rector (Old motet texts, St. Lambert)	4–2	G/♭	[C]	X	Alternates texted and untexted sections	problematic
213	Salinis	Ihesu salvator seculi Quo vulneratus scelere (Holy week)	3–2	F/♭	[C]	X	Alternates texted and untexted sections	—
260	Velut	Summe summy tu patris (D1&Ct) Summe summy tu matris (D2&T) (p–e: God and Mary)	4–2	D	[O]	X	Alternates texted and untexted sections; fermatas at end	inessential

Key: v–t = voices/texts; sig. = signature (of lower parts); mens. = mensuration; Echo = Echo imitation (discantus 1 rests while discantus 2 imitates it)

ticularly popular in the thirteenth-century conductus, but persists in the four-teenth-century French motet (especially in the *Roman de Fauvel*; see Table 4.5).[16] The text of Example 6.2 consists of a fairly standard account of how Jesus suffered for our sins; the pun on "die Veneris" and "ygnem . . . Veneris," however, emphasizes the sin of lust, and the tone of the whole motet is peni-tential.

Discantus 1

Ihesu salvator seculi	Jesus, savior of the world,
Jude traditus osculo,	betrayed by Judas with a kiss,
redemptione populi,	redemption of the people,
suspensus est patibulo.	was hanged from the gibbet.
Sanguis qui die Veneris,	Let the blood that was spilled
fusus, futuro miseris,	for future sinners on Venus's day [Friday]
ygnem extingue Veneris,	extinguish the fire of Venus,
ne crememur [in] inferis.	lest we burn in hell.

Discantus 2

Quo vulneratus scelere,	Where you were wounded by a criminal
lancea dextro latere,	by a lance in your right side,
lavasti nos a crimine,	there you have washed away our sins
manante unda sanguine.	in a pouring flood of blood.
Patri, Nato, Paraclito,	To Father, Son, and Holy Ghost,
sit honor, laus et gloria,	let honor, praise and glory be,
eiusque matri merito,	and to the worth of his mother
lux nobis pax et gracia.	our light, peace and grace.[17]

Q15.261, Ruttis's *Prevalet simplicitas*, is the only one of this group with a single text. The two upper voices cadence and declaim the text together throughout, though they do have some florid figuration. The single text and simple texture correspond to a text that praises the virtues of simplicity over duplicity and simony.

Texture and Style

Although three are found in Q15 with four voices, all of these motets proba-bly began life as three-voice pieces. All three contratenors are inessential; the contratenor for Q15.247, *Psallat chorus*, is especially problematic, and is not found in the concordant source San Lorenzo 2211, so it must have been added later.

Q15.171, Lymburgia's *Tu nephanda/Si inimicus*, uses simultaneous conflict-ing mensurations and complex overlapping phrase-structures. The rhythmic

Example 6.2 Salinis, *Ihesu salvator* (Ox 213, fol. 81)

137

complexity is another retrospective trait, reminiscent of the late fourteenth century.[18] The rest are unusual in the coincidence of phrases and cadences in all the parts and the degree of homorhythm, as can be seen in *Ihesu salvator seculi* (Ex. 6.2). While the use of echo imitation in three of the motets (see Ex. 6.2, mm. 1–5) recalls the Italian motet, the texture and style in general is simpler and more syllabic. Several of the motets alternate texted and untexted sections, recalling the textless *caudae* of thirteenth-century conductus. The sections without text use extended imitative rhythmic sequence, as can be seen in Example 6.2, mm. 11–15, where all three voices have the same four-beat rhythmic pattern, each starting at a different point in the pattern, or in mm. 23–7, where the sequence is limited to the upper voices. This kind of rhythmic episode is a fairly common way of drawing attention to talea structure in the French isorhythmic motet:[19] here, however, there is no isorhythm. Instead, the lack of text in the rhythmic episodes and their sharp separation from the texted portions of the motet result in another kind of isoperiodic formal structure. Every phrase in *Ihesu salvator* is five bars long except for the fourth (mm. 16–22), where a two-measure texted transition to the untexted section is added on. Each of the texted phrases ends with a long; the untexted phrases cadence into the beginning of the next texted phrase. The extra two measures are added to the central phrase in the motet (excluding the introitus), and thus emphasize the symmetrical structure of the piece (/=Long in all voices):

(Introitus →) Text/No text → Text/+2 → No text → Text/.[20]

In the retrospective double-discantus motet we see composers from outside Italy adapting the Italian motet style to text types and compositional techniques drawn from the early history of French polyphony: a hybrid indeed.

Devotional double-discantus motets

These motets are very different from the previous subgenre. They all have a single pre-existent text taken from the liturgy or the Bible, unlike most motet-style and cut-circle motets. Of the eight pieces six are Marian, and five of those are from the *Song of Songs*, linking them to the declamatory and the cut-circle *Song* settings. All of them would be suitable for both public and private devotions.[21] Unlike most of the other motet-style motets, all but one were copied in stage II or stage III, and they were probably composed in the late 1420s and early 1430s (see Table 6.5). I have included Du Fay's *Anima mea*

Table 6.5. *Devotional double-discantus motets in Q15 (stage II unless otherwise noted)*

MS no.	Composer	Title (source of text)	final/sig.	mens.	Echo	Øopen.	imit.	remarks	Contratenor
207	H. de Lantins	Ave gemma claritas (2 As)	F/♭	[Ø]C	X	X	X		inessential
205	Lymburgia	Puer natus in Bethleem (H)	F	[O]Ø	X		X	unus duet	inessential
193	Du Fay (III)	Gaude virgo mater (S)	G	[Ø]			X	florid; 6/8 cadence	problematic
197	Lymburgia (III)	Tota pulchra (SoS; not A)	G	[Ø]	X	(up)	X	fermatas on "Veni"; 6/8 cad.	inessential
191	Anon. (III)	Descendi in ortum (SoS: A)	F/♭	[O]			XX	fermatas on "Revertere"	problematic
202	A. de Lantins	Tota pulchra (SoS: A)	F/♭	O		X		declamation; D2 added	n/a
204	Lymburgia	Surge propera (SoS; not A)	F/♭	[Ø]		(up)		D2 added	n/a
235	Du Fay (I)	Anima mea (SoS: A)	G	[Ø]			X	chant par. in all voices	—

Key:

sig. = signature of lower parts; mens. = mensuration; Echo = Echo imitation

Øopen = begins with the opening common in cut-circle motets (see Ex. 5.2); (up) indicates that the semibreve ascends

imit. = prevalent imitation

"6/8 cadence" indicates the voice-leading for the outer voices at the final cadence (in contrast to a 10–12 "Italian" cadence)

Example 6.3 Lymburgia, cadences from *Tota pulchra* (Lewis, 14–16)

(a) mm. 34–6

(b) mm. 40–2

(c) mm. 83–8

liquefacta est (discussed above as a continental cantilena) because of its texture and use of *Song* text, though its copying date (in stage I) and its use of chant distinguish it from the others.[22]

Stylistically these pieces combine the motet-style texture of the Italian motet with the rhythmic and melodic style of cut-circle motets and chansons. Like Italian motets they use echo imitation or introitus, imitation between the discantus parts throughout, syncopated hocket-like exchanges, a variety of free rhythms in the tenor, and 10/6–12/8 ("Italian") cadences on F and G.[23] The composers – Lymburgia, Arnold and Hugh de Lantins, and Du Fay – also composed cut-circle motets, and several of these double-discantus motets use the characteristic cut-circle opening figure, while others have fermata sections or florid melismas. These motets also resemble some of Du Fay's four-voice chansons, especially *Mon cuer me fait tous dis penser*, discussed above in relation to the cut-circle motets.

Two of the pieces (Q15.202, Arnold de Lantins's *Tota pulchra es*, and Q15.204, Lymburgia's *Surge propera*) were converted from cut-circle cantilena-style motets to double-discantus motets by the addition of a second discantus part. Pieces were often arranged or adapted in the fourteenth and fifteenth centuries by the addition or substitution of voices. Such arrangements increased the possibilities for performance by making the piece suitable for different ensembles or provided a way for a performer to personalize a piece and make it his own. Popular chansons or motets (such as Lantins's *Tota pulchra*) were subject to the most arrangements, but obscure or anonymous works were sometimes arranged as well.[24] The addition of a fourth voice (whether a discantus voice or a contratenor) may also have been motivated by a desire to experiment with four-voice textures during the 1430s and in the following decades.

What is the status of the contratenor voice in these pieces? The five devotional double-discantus motets other than *Tota pulchra*, *Surge propera*, and *Anima mea* are found in Q15 with two original discantus parts, tenor, and inessential contratenor. Two of the contratenors are problematic, and were probably added later; the comparative competence of the other three, and the late copying date, suggest that they were conceived from the start as four-voice works.[25] Lymburgia's *Tota pulchra*, for example (the text of which is not the same as Lantins's *Tota pulchra*), avoids problems in many cadences by leaving the contratenor out or having it move to the third of the chord (Ex. 6.3a and 6.3b). The final cadence of the piece, however, is a 4/5 cadence (Ex. 6.3c), with a seventh between the second discantus and the contratenor. This might be considered a mistake, or a sign that the contratenor was added, except that the 4/5 cadence becomes fairly common in four-voice works in mid-century, as we shall see below.[26]

Features from a variety of traditions seem to have been assembled to form this new (and very appealing) subgenre that stands somewhere between the

141

Table 6.6. *Other double-discantus motets in Q15 (all stage II)*

275:	Brassart, Summus secretarius omnia scientis
281:	Power, Ave regina celorum (A)
173:	Du Fay, Inclita stella maris (top part in canon)

motet-style motet and the cut-circle cantilena motets. The use of liturgical and biblical texts and the more competent treatment of four-voice texture without a long-note tenor cantus firmus point toward developments in motet composition in mid-century and later.

Other double-discantus motets

Three of the double-discantus motets do not fit in well with the others, nor do they resemble each other. All have four voices and a single text in the two discantus parts. Q15.281, Power's *Ave regina caelorum*, has a liturgical text, and thus could be listed among the devotional double-discantus motets. But stylistically it is rather different, with no imitation, a problem-free contratenor, and two duet sections after the opening introitus. Q15.275, Brassart's *Summus secretarius*, has a new text. The identity of the person addressed in the text is debated: it could be a dignitary of the church (perhaps the pope), St. John the Evangelist, or the Holy Ghost.[27] The text is thus neither retrospective nor liturgical. As in Power's *Ave regina celorum* the contratenor is not problematic and the motet uses little imitation; unlike the English work, however, it avoids duets. The Brassart and Power pieces have similarities to some slightly later motets found outside Bologna Q15, to which we shall return in chapter 11.

Q15.173, Du Fay's *Inclita stella maris*, has a new Marian text and the cantus voices perform a mensuration canon. The canonic voices make cadences together, while both of the lower voices are labeled contratenor. I know of one other motet with canonic cantus voices: Carmen's *Pontifici decori speculi*, found in Oxford 213 with a new text in honor of St. Nicholas. These canonic motets may make reference to the Italian motet and its connection to the caccia.[28] But Du Fay also wrote four-voice chansons with canon (*Par droit je puis bien* and *Les douleurs*) and without (*Hé compaignons*) similar in construction to *Inclita stella maris*.[29] Once again Du Fay makes multiple references: to Italian music, to his Parisian predecessor, and to his own chansons.

Table 6.7. *Borderline motets in Q15*

2 equal voices

I	255: Ciconia, O beatum incendium
	(N: Corpus Christi; contrafactum for Aler m'en veus)
I	258: Ciconia, O Petre Christi
	(St. Peter; possibly for Petro Marcello; probably contrafactum)
I	212: Reson, Ave verum corpus natum
	(Corpus Christi)

2 equal voices plus contratenor "concordans si placet"

| II | 270: Lymburgia, Recordare virgo mater/Trope: Ab hac familia |
| | (troped offertory for the BVM) |

Others

II	210: Reson, Ave verum corpus natum
	(Corpus Christi)
III	190: Anon., Hec dies
	(Easter Gradual, with chant incipit)

Borderline motets

Six pieces in the motet section in Q15 seem to me to be problematic as motets, but interesting as case studies in the motet's fuzzy boundaries (see Table 6.7). Three are for two equal voices, and a fourth has an optional contratenor. The "two-voice motet" could perhaps be considered a minor subgenre, but there are other category problems with these pieces too.

David Fallows has identified a limited tradition of chansons for two equal voices composed between *c.* 1400 and 1425, and he discusses the two Ciconia pieces listed here as part of that tradition.[30] *O beatum incendium* began life as a chanson by Ciconia, *Aler m'en veus*, and then received a new contrafact Latin text at some point before its copying in Q15. *O Petre* is similar enough to *O beatum incendium* that it is also probably a contrafactum, but there is no earlier source to tell us for sure. We will come back to the issue of contrafacture in chapter 8; for now it is enough to say that these pieces lie on the border between the motet and the chanson, while their use of only two voices makes them atypical of both genres.[31]

Lymburgia's *Recordare* is a setting of a troped offertory text for two equal voices. It thus sits on the borderline between the motet and liturgical music, though there is no use of chant. Its optional third voice, a contratenor "concordans si placet," accompanies the upper voices in mm. 14–43, 60–70, and

82–113. Unlike the unus–chorus motets the textural contrasts fail to coincide with significant textual divisions and the unus sections do not use ₵ mensuration. A more obvious case of liturgical music is *Hec dies*, whose use of the Easter gradual text and chant incipit followed by chant paraphrase in the top voice indicates that it is a polyphonic gradual, not a motet. This piece was added to the manuscript in stage III, perhaps for want of any better place to put it.

The last two borderline pieces are settings of *Ave verum corpus* by Reson for two and three voices. The text of *Ave verum corpus* had multiple uses: as a devotional prayer, and as a prayer or chant spoken or sung during Mass at the Elevation. This kind of multi-functional text was ideal for motets, and Hugh de Lantins set the text as a florid four-voice cut-circle motet. Although neither uses chant, Reson's extremely austere settings are closer in style to the polyphonic lauda or the simplest liturgical music than to the motet.[32]

Song settings in Bologna Q15

Ten of the motets in Bologna Q15 use texts from the *Song of Songs* (see Table 6.8). Only one of them is English (Dunstaple's *Quam pulchra*); the others are by continental composers working in Italy: Du Fay, Arnold de Lantins, and Johannes de Lymburgia. These *Song* settings belong to several of the new hybrid subgenres: the cut-circle motet, the devotional double-discantus motet, and the declamation motet; most of them use elements of the cut-circle musical language. Some of the pieces (such as Ex. 6.1, Lantins's *Tota pulchra*) can be associated with more than one subgenre.

Scholars have tended to associate the origins of the tradition of polyphonic *Song* settings with England.[33] Most of the *Song* settings in the mid-century manuscripts such as the Trent Codices and Modena X.1.11 are by English composers, as we shall see below in chapter 9. We have associated the three-voice cantilena-style motet with English models, as well as the practice of setting pre-existent Marian antiphon texts to polyphony. Arnold de Lantins's *Tota pulchra* could well have been modeled on Dunstaple's *Quam pulchra*, the most widely disseminated *Song* setting of all.

Nevertheless I would like to make a case for a continental tradition of *Song* settings that is largely independent of English models. It is not clear when the English tradition of *Song* settings began, but most of the examples appear first on the Continent in the 1430s and 1440s, after these Q15 pieces.[34] The earli-

Table 6.8. Song of Songs settings in Q15 *(stage II unless otherwise noted)*

		Cut-circle	Devotional D-D	SUBGENRE Declamation	Eng. cant.	Cont. cant.
Antiphon settings						
291	Dunstaple	Quam pulchra es			X	X	X
235	Du Fay	Anima mea (I; uses chant)	X	X			
202	A. de Lantins	Tota pulchra es	X	X	X		
178	A. de Lantins	O pulcherrima mulierum					
191	Anonymous	Descendi in ortum (III)		X			
183	Lymburgia	Descendi in ortum (uses chant)	X				X?
From the Bible; nor antiphon texts						
177	Lymburgia	Pulchra es amica	X	X			
204	Lymburgia	Surge propera	X	X			
197	Lymburgia	Tota pulchra (III)		X			
279	Lymburgia/ Du Fay	Veni dilecte my		X			

est of the *Song* settings in Q15, Du Fay's *Anima mea*, was copied before *Quam pulchra*. *Anima mea* is in a motet-style texture very different from that of the English cantilena, as are several of the later continental *Song* settings. Half of the pieces are by Lymburgia, who avoids antiphon texts, preferring to take his *Song* texts directly from the Bible. The cut-circle musical language used in so many of these pieces is closer to the French chanson than it is to English style: the *Song* texts may have appealed to these continental composers because of their similarity in tone and subject matter to chanson texts. Like Du Fay's *Vergene bella*, these *Song* settings are a musical and textual hybrid of the sacred and secular.

Kinds of motet

Almost all of the Q15 motets were composed between 1410 and 1435, most probably in the 1420s, a remarkable decade of social and musical cross-fertilization. One of the most important new developments of the period was the adoption or absorption of the English cantilena and the cantilena texture into the motet on the Continent. Still, the older varieties – especially the French isorhythmic motet – continued to be highly valued as well, and cultivated in their own right. Composers and patrons thus had a strong sense of tradition and innovation, and of the status and associations of the different subgenres.

Close examination of the pieces found in the motet section of Bologna Q15 has revealed ten different kinds of motet, or subgenres, as well as some pieces that sit on the border between the motet and other genres. Some of these subgenres are large, some small; some can trace their ancestry directly back to earlier local traditions of motet composition, some have strong ties to genres outside the motet such as the chanson, liturgical music, or Mass movements, and some are of mixed parentage, deriving their features and styles from multiple genres and subgenres. These subgenres embody a flexible model of categorization in which subgenres can overlap and not every piece in a subgenre will display all the associated features.

Having established these different kinds of motet in Q15 we need now to look beyond its boundaries. The Q15 scribe was an individual collector. To what extent was his taste in motets idiosyncratic? Which of the subgenres would persist; which would die out? How did the motet continue to evolve? The best way to answer these questions is to compare the motets of Q15 with those of other manuscripts, which we will do in the next chapter.

7 The motet in the early fifteenth century: evolution and interpretation

The scribe of Bologna Q15 determined which pieces should go in the motet section. As we have seen, many different kinds of piece were considered by the scribe to be motets, and *en masse* they share few characteristics. By identifying the different subgenres, however, we have established kinds of motet that can be described and identified by means of characteristic features. Knowledge of the various subgenres thus allows us to recognize motets in other sources as well, even those without distinct motet sections. Comparison of the motets in Bologna Q15 with those found in other manuscripts of the period gives us a key to the whole motet repertory of the early fifteenth century. The comparison will also allow us to investigate the evolutionary success of the different subgenres. A subgenre (like a variety or species) can die out or it can survive and continue to evolve. Its fate is determined by the fates of the individual works that make up the subgenre: if they reproduce the subgenre will survive, if not it will die out. Reproduction, in the case of motets, takes two forms: a work can be copied in multiple manuscripts, or it can give rise to new works resembling it in various ways.

The first kind of reproduction (manuscript copies) is best observed in relation to individual works rather than subgenres. The second kind of reproduction (leading to production of new works) can be recognized by the continued presence of new examples of a subgenre in the repertory. The presence in the repertory, and presumably popularity, of a certain subgenre at any one time is determined by both kinds of reproduction combined: a subgenre with a few widely copied members may appear in every manuscript, as may a subgenre with many different members, each of which has few concordances. A subgenre that contains both widely copied pieces and many different pieces will have the greatest presence in the repertory at any one time. The size of the subgenre at any one time, however, is not a predictor of its evolutionary future. Ultimately it is the second kind of reproduction, leading to the production of new works over time, that will have the most influence on the survival of a subgenre and thus on the evolution of the genre as a whole.

Comparison with other manuscripts

I have examined the six major manuscripts containing motets from the first half of the fifteenth century (see Table 7.1): Oxford 213, Bologna 2216, Aosta, Trent 87 and 92, and Modena X.1.11. All of these manuscripts were compiled within fifteen years of the completion of Q15 and have concordances with it; they are listed in Table 7.1 in approximate chronological order.[1] In the case of the two Trent Codices I have combined the figures from Trent 87–1 and 92–2, both compiled by the same scribe at the same time, and Trent 92–1, which was bound together with Trent 92–2 early on. I call this complex of three half manuscripts "TR+."[2] For Modena X.1.11 I have listed the continental and English motet sections separately. The contents of the Trent Codices and Modena X.1.11 are discussed in detail in Part III.

In order to compile Table 7.1 I identified the motets in these manuscripts with reference to the subgenres identified in Q15 and Modena X.1.11.[3] The three generically organized manuscripts (Q15, Bologna 2216, and Modena X.1.11) all include a broad range of subgenres: motet-style motets and cantilena-style motets, English and continental motets, and pieces with *cpf* and pieces without. Individual manuscripts have their biases: Bologna 2216 leans toward cantilena-style motets, while Modena X.1.11 leans toward English music. Likewise, the kinds of pieces in the manuscripts without motet sections correspond to the subgenres found in the generically organized manuscripts. We can be confident that the pieces we have identified as motets here would also have been recognized as motets by musicians, patrons, and audiences of the period.

Careful consideration of the information in Table 7.1 is thus extremely revealing. I will point out a few of the Table's features, and then use it to answer questions about Q15 and the evolution of the motet repertory. The subgenres listed in Table 7.1 are divided into three groups: motet-style, cantilena-style, and English (both styles). This allows some particular patterns of dissemination to emerge: the Italian motets (at the top of Table 7.1) ceased

148

Table 7.1. *Representation of Q15 subgenres in other contemporary manuscripts*

	Q15	Ox 213			B2216			Aosta			TR+			Modena X.1.11 Continental			Modena X.1.11 English			Total "New"	Actual no. New motets	Q15+Actual New
		Q15	New	=	Q15	New	=	Q15	New	=	Q15	New	=	Q15	New	=	Q15	New	=			
Italian																						
no isorhythm	14	1	1	2	2	—	2	—	—	—	—	—	—	—	—	—	—	—	—	1	1	15
double-statement	6	1	2	3	—	—	—	—	—	—	—	—	—	—	—	—	—	—	—	2	2	8
Retrospective double-disc.	6	2	—	2	—	—	—	—	—	—	1	—	1	—	—	—	—	—	—	—	—	6
Devotional double-disc.	7	—	—	—	—	1	1	—	—	—	1	—	1	—	—	—	—	—	—	1	1	8
Other double-discantus	3	1	3	4	—	—	—	1	2	3	1	4	5	—	2	2	—	—	—	11	7	10
French isorhythmic	19	5	8	13	1	—	1	1	4	5	3	3	6	1	8	9	—	1	1	24	22	41
Cut-circle motet	23	6	2	8	3	1	4	—	—	—	5	3	8	2	1	3	—	—	—	7	7	30
Declamation motet	5	3	—	3	2	1	3	1	—	1	3	—	3	—	—	—	—	—	—	1	1	6
Continental cantilena	3	1	1	2	2	1	3	—	3	3	—	3	3	—	4	4	—	—	—	12	11	14
Unus–chorus motet	3	—	—	—	—	—	—	—	—	—	—	—	—	—	—	—	—	—	—	—	—	3
Borderline cases (incl. 2 vv.)	6	—	—	—	—	1	1	—	1	1	—	2	2	—	—	—	—	—	—	4	4	10
English cantilena	10	—	—	—	2	1	3	6	7	13	3	22	25	—	—	—	5	29	34	59	39	49
English isorhythmic	1	—	—	—	—	—	—	—	1	1	—	2	2	—	—	—	—	12	12	15	12	13
3-voice tenor motet	—	—	—	—	—	—	—	—	1	1	—	7	7	—	—	—	—	5	5	13	9	9
TOTALS	106	20	17	37	12	6	18	9	19	28	17	46	63	3	15	18	5	47	52	150	116	222

Key for subheadings for each manuscript: "Q15" = pieces concordant with Q15; "New" = pieces not in Q15; "=" = the total number in the MS

reproducing (in either sense) and thus died out very early, while the English repertory increased rapidly and makes up more and more of the total repertory in the later manuscripts.

For each of these five manuscripts I have listed the number of motets in each subgenre, first supplying the number of pieces also in Q15, then the number of "New" pieces, not found in Q15, and then the sum of those two figures, the total number of examples of the subgenre in the source. In the "Total 'New'" column on the right I summed up the "New" columns for each subgenre; in the "Actual no. New motets" column I eliminated the duplicate copies found in more than one source (concordances), resulting in the actual number of pieces in each subgenre not found in Q15. In the final column I summed up the number of pieces in Q15 and the number of actual new motets for each subgenre. The total at the bottom of that column (222) is the total number of different pieces in these six manuscripts (a figure that is fairly close to the total surviving motet repertory for *c*. 1410–1445).

The extent to which a subgenre is widely disseminated and copied in multiple manuscripts is shown by two sets of figures. Comparison of the figures for Q15 (in the far left column of the table) with the "Q15" column for each of the other manuscripts indicates the extent to which the Q15 pieces are concordant, and have multiple sources; the totals at the bottom indicate this for the repertory as a whole (it can be observed, for example, that the proportion of Q15 concordances diminishes as we move toward the later manuscripts). The difference between the "Total 'New'" and "Actual no. New motets" columns indicates the extent to which there is a repertory of widely disseminated pieces outside Q15. If the two numbers are the same then every piece not in Q15 is an unicum; the greater the difference between the two numbers the more concordances there are among the pieces not in Q15. For most of the subgenres the two numbers are identical or quite close: this indicates that most of the pieces outside Q15 are unica. Only in the case of the English cantilena is there a radical difference between the two columns, indicating that the English cantilenas not in Q15 tend to have multiple concordances.

The extent to which a subgenre was fruitful and gave rise to new examples is shown by the number in the "Actual no. New motets" column. If it is small (as it is for Italian motets) then the subgenre is poorly represented outside Q15; when the number is large (as it is for French isorhythmic motets or continental cantilenas) the subgenre is well represented outside Q15.

Examination of the representation of these two subgenres in the individual manuscripts indicates that new examples continue to be found in each of the successive manuscripts; thus these two subgenres continued to be productive and reproduce after the completion of Q15 in the mid-1430s.

Table 7.1 can help us answer a number of important questions. To what extent is Q15 representative? Q15 contains more motets than any other manuscript, and indeed accounts for almost half of the total repertory found in these manuscripts, with 106 motets out of a total of 222. Its repertory is also widely disseminated in the later manuscripts. Forty-four of its motets have concordances, and if we exclude the English repertory, Q15 includes most of the early fifteenth-century motets with more than three sources, while most of the pieces not found in Q15 are unica. Many of the works and subgenres in Q15, then, were successful in both kinds of reproduction: they were frequently copied, and they gave rise to new works. The repertory found in Q15 is especially close to that of the contemporary Veneto sources Oxford 213 and Bologna 2216 (look at the figures for these manuscripts at the bottom of Table 7.1, and compare "Q15" to "New"); Q15 is forward-looking, however, in its early inclusion of English music. There was no substantial tradition of motets alternative to that presented in Q15 in the Veneto, while several of the subgenres that would expand later (such as the English and continental cantilenas) are represented in embryo in Q15.

To what extent is Q15 idiosyncratic? Sixty-two motets are unique to Q15, so the manuscript contains a potentially idiosyncratic repertory larger than the motet repertories of any of the other individual manuscripts. Margaret Bent has already shown that the scribe of Q15 tended to meddle with the pieces, and he may have had individual tastes that could distort our view of the repertory as a whole. Closer consideration of the individual subgenres will allow us to answer this question.

Which of the Q15 subgenres are not included in the other manuscripts? Which are? Genres that were already old-fashioned when Q15 was compiled are poorly represented elsewhere: the Italian motets and the retrospective double-discantus motets (mostly composed in the 1410s and 1420s). Q15 thus provides us with a final glimpse of these subgenres, already on the edge of extinction. The devotional double-discantus motets are also poorly represented outside Q15, but aspects of their style may have been absorbed into the "other double-discantus" subgenre, which continued to flourish after Q15. The unus–chorus motet resulted from an experimental borrowing of a technique more common to Mass movements; since it is poorly represented outside Q15, we can conclude that the experiment failed.[4]

The subgenres that had real staying power over the period can be identified by comparison of the Q15 figures (first column) with those under "Actual no. New motets" (or by comparison of the figures in the "Actual no. New motets" column with those in the "Q15 + Actual New" column). The subgenres in which there was a substantial increase in the repertory after Q15 are the other double-discantus motets (three in Q15, seven outside), the continental cantilenas (three in Q15, eleven outside), and the English cantilenas (ten in Q15, thirty-nine outside): in all these cases the number of examples from outside Q15 far exceeds the number within it. These subgenres, then, were just beginning as Q15 was compiled, and continued to grow, develop and reproduce over the next few decades. Q15's relatively small numbers for each of these subgenres result from the fact that we are seeing the very first examples of new varieties of motet.

The number of French isorhythmic motets inside and outside Q15 is almost equal (nineteen in Q15, twenty-two outside). Here we can see healthy continuation of a substantial older repertory. It is possible that a slight decline in numbers can be observed as we move later in the century, but the picture is somewhat skewed by the emphasis in Modena X.1.11 on Du Fay's late isorhythmic motets. Ironically, the Modena motets are among the last isorhythmic motets ever composed, something that could not be predicted from these data. Only when we move one decade further (as we will in Part III) will we be able to observe the extinction of the isorhythmic motet.

The cut-circle and declamation motets, in contrast, are well represented outside Q15, but the bulk of the repertory is found in Q15. The cases are somewhat different. The declamation motets, as we have seen, are widely disseminated, but there seems to have been no substantial attempt to add to their number; five out of the total number of six are already in Q15. These pieces reproduced themselves only by being copied, not by inspiring additional examples; although they were popular and important pieces in the period, they had relatively little effect on the subsequent history of the genre.

Of the thirty cut-circle motets twenty-three are found in Q15, and most of the seven new ones were probably also written in the 1430s. This was a very productive subgenre while it survived, generating numerous new pieces but relatively few concordances. The Q15 scribe seems to have had a special fondness for the cut-circle motet, and been in a position to obtain and copy almost all of them close to the time of their creation. The period during which the manuscript was compiled seems to have coincided with the birth, flourishing, and decline of the subgenre: only one new example appears in Modena X.1.11. As mensural fashions changed (influenced in part by the increasing dominance of English music) the cut-circle motet died out.

Are there subgenres of motet not included in Q15? Two subgenres, both of them English, are not represented at all in Q15: the fifteenth-century English isorhythmic motet and the three-voice tenor motet. (The one English iso-rhythmic motet listed for Q15 in Table 7.1 is the fourteenth-century *Sub Arturo plebs*.) English isorhythmic motets are found primarily in the English motet section of Modena (with a few in Trent 92). Only one English iso-rhythmic motet, Dunstaple's *Veni sancte/Veni creator*, is widely disseminated in fifteenth-century continental sources (see the Appendix): it is found in Modena X.1.11 and in sources associated with the Council of Basel copied later than Q15. It was composed in time to be copied in Q15, but we do not know when it reached the Continent, or if it reached the Q15 scribe.[5] The three-voice tenor motet is a subgenre that combines features of the English cantilena and isorhythmic motet. I will return to this subgenre in chapter 10; like the English isorhythmic motet it seems to have arrived on the Continent too late to be copied in Q15. It is highly unlikely that lack of these two sub-genres in Q15 was the result of a bias on the part of the scribe against English music. While the absence of English music in Oxford 213 or Bologna 2216 could be explained this way, Q15 is the earliest continental source with English cantilenas, the number of which (ten) compares favorably with Aosta (thirteen), a later manuscript known for its extensive repertory of English music. It seems that the Q15 scribe copied whatever English music he could get his hands on.

English music appears much more abundantly in the later manuscripts, and in fact constitutes almost a third of the total motet repertory of the period, and close to half of the repertory of the later manuscripts Aosta, TR+, and Modena X.1.11. Individual works are also much more broadly disseminated than most continental pieces (see the Appendix). As mid-century approached, the total repertory of motets seems to have been more and more dominated by English music. Strohm's suggestion that English music first became widely available at the Council of Basel in the 1430s may thus be substantially correct, if overstated.

The rather peculiar pattern of dissemination of English music that shows up here reflects a special pattern of production, as we saw in chapter 4. The demand for English music on the Continent seems to have been high, and the supply limited, so the same pieces were copied over and over again. The real fusion of English and continental music would come in the 1440s and 1450s, and that story will be told in Part III. Still, it is apparent even in the first half of the century that the subgenres with strong English features such as the continental cantilena or the "other double-discantus" motets continue to have presence in the repertory.

The scribe of Q15 had some idiosyncratic tastes: he collected Italian motets, double-discantus motets, and cut-circle motets assiduously. In the process he preserved an older Italian repertory (the Ciconia motets) and a newer repertory composed by northerners in Italy and in many ways inspired by Italian models. Many of the cut-circle motets and the devotional double-discantus motets must have been copied very soon after composition. These repertories would be largely lost to us if Q15 had not survived. The scribe also collected examples of every other kind of motet available to him, including English music and English-influenced subgenres that would blossom over the next few decades. Study of the motets in Bologna Q15, then, has provided us with a remarkably comprehensive overview of the genre as a whole; comparison of Q15 to other manuscripts has allowed us to see where the genre was going.

Interpretation, context, and history

Each of the individual motets we have studied serves to exemplify a subgenre, and each sets its text and establishes a musical shape with the resources available within the subgenre. It is worth reviewing these pieces, however, with an eye to interpretation: how does our recognition of the intersection of text, texture, and musical style that make these pieces members of their subgenres help us to understand them? Our awareness of generic norms, of the horizon of expectation, allows us to see individual pieces more clearly. Are they conventional exemplars of a subgenre, or are they unusual? If unusual, do their peculiarities have an expressive purpose? Do they belong to more than one subgenre, or use subgeneric mixture? Let us consider our examples once more with these questions in mind.

Cristoforus de Monte: Dominicus a dono *(Ex. 4.1)*

Before Margaret Bent identified the characteristic features of the Italian motet tradition, motet-style motets without isorhythm like Cristoforus de

Monte's *Dominicus a dono* were hard to place. Now, however, we can see this as a typical Italian motet, very much part of a tradition. The motet-style texture, with its distant roots in the thirteenth century, conferred gravity on the laudatory text in praise of St. Dominic, while the playful interchange between the voices and the lively melismas in the first half recall the Italian traditions of madrigal and caccia. This is an immediately attractive example of an enjoyable subgenre. The Italian motet tradition came to an end with the generation of Italian composers after Ciconia. Many of the subgenre's most appealing features, however, would live on in the isorhythmic and double-discantus motets by northern composers working in Italy: the 10–12 Italian cadences, echo imitation and imitative exchange, and the use of textural contrasts as a way of creating large-scale form. These features provided the devotional double-discantus motets with fruitful ways of responding to their texts, and brought a new brilliance of sonority to the French isorhythmic motet.

Forest: Alma redemptoris mater *(Ex. 4.3)*

The other English cantilenas in Q15 provide us with a horizon of expectation for Forest's *Alma redemptoris*. The choice of text, the tripartite form with a central duet, and the tonal ambiguity (with F and G making competing claims for the most important pitch), are all fairly typical. Unusual for music of the Dunstaple generation are the exclusive use of duple meter (imperfect tempus) and the extreme rhythmic asymmetry. This extreme avoidance of regularity may have been Forest's way of creating innovation within tradition, by exaggerating standard style characteristics of the genre. Some of his innovations would become typical of the music of the next generation of English composers, as we shall see in chapter 9. At the same time, the asymmetry of this piece has a mysterious quality that could have struck listeners as sacred. At first this piece appears difficult, aimless, even arcane; but it grows on you. The complex rhythmic counterpoint and the search for stability separate us from our moorings, and pull us briefly into another world.

Johannes de Sarto: Ave mater, O Maria *(Ex. 5.1)*

The cut-circle motet, the largest of the new hybrid subgenres, has multiple generic affiliations. In Sarto's *Ave mater*, for example, the text is a composite of two stanzas from an Italian lauda, with the addition of a new third stanza containing a more personal plea for attention from the Virgin. This use of a lauda

155

text evokes the musical associations of the lauda as a genre – personal devotions or the communal devotions of confraternities – although the style is too ornate for amateur choral singing. One need not recognize the source of the text, however, to recognize that its style resembles that of the Italian motet, with rhyming four-line stanzas and personal reference at the end.[6] The subject of the text also recalls the English cantilena and makes the motet suitable for all kinds of Marian devotions.

The texture of the cut-circle motet resembles that of the three-voice continental Mass cycle, the chanson, and the English cantilena. Like the Mass cycles, *Ave mater* has a fermata section, and sections set off by contrasting mensuration signs. The florid melismas of *Ave mater* recall those of late fourteenth- and early fifteenth-century secular music, both Italian and French. The cut-circle rhythmic style, with its relatively long-breathed phrases and expanded metrical groupings, lends itself to great variety of rhythmic patterning. Each new phrase is characterized by emphasis on a new rhythmic device. The opening uses the standard cut-circle remote imperfection of the long; "O Maria" (mm. 3–4) has the descending suspension chain of off-beat semibreves; "Pietatis" (mm. 5–9) has constantly shifting dotted semiminim patterns; "Deploranti" (mm. 12–13) introduces chains of minims and minim triplets. Later on we have extended melismas, triplets, fermatas, hemiola block chords, imitation. Some rhythmic and melodic ideas do return, but overall there is an almost overwhelming abundance of detail and variety. We can thus see the texture and melodic style of the cut-circle motet as reaching in multiple directions – towards the solemnity of the Mass cycle, the variety and asymmetry of the English cantilena, and toward the exuberance and elaboration of high-style song.

The result of combining all these styles and generic references is a genre that is both intimate and impressive, devotional and decorative, exuberant and expressive. *Ave mater* is a votive love song to the Virgin and a passionate personal prayer; it is also a demonstration of compositional and performative virtuosity that serve to glorify both the Virgin and the patron. "Look what we can do for the glory of God" it seems to say; one cannot help but enjoy the show.

Arnold de Lantins: Tota pulchra es *(Ex. 6.1)*

In *Tota pulchra* Lantins also uses the cut-circle musical language, but rather than aiming for dazzling variety he concentrates on a single possibility within the vocabulary: the syllabic, mostly note-against-note writing with frequent repeated notes characteristic of the declamation motet. This texture (like the text of *Ave mater*) evokes the world of improvised polyphony or the polyphonic lauda, and thus endows the piece with both intimacy and a sense of community. Lantins (like Dunstaple in *Quam pulchra*) creates a fine balance in *Tota pulchra* between the warmth of communal devotions to the Virgin and the intimacy and eroticism of the love song. The text, biblical and liturgical, is appropriate to communal devotions; but on the surface it is a love lyric, and thus belongs to the world of the secular chanson. The musical style of *Tota pulchra* (unlike *Ave mater*) is simple enough that most of it could be sung by relatively unskilled singers; only the florid melismas of the opening phrase and the difficulty of the contratenor suggest that a successful performance would really demand skilled vocal soloists. Text and texture reach outside the motet in order to enrich the work's meaning by evoking the love song and shared communal devotions.

Humbertus de Salinis: Ihesu salvator seculi/Quo vulneratus scelere (Ex. 6.2)

This is one of the earliest of the new hybrid motets, stemming from the initial French/Italian cross-fertilization at the Council of Pisa. The Portuguese Salinis combines an old French type of admonitory text with an Italianate approach to motet composition using echo imitation and imitative effects, but without isorhythm. The text – unlike most fifteenth-century motet texts, but like some fourteenth-century motets, and even more like thirteenth-century motets and conductus – is a clever but gory reflection on how Christ's suffering redeems the sins of mankind. For this ancient but always appropriate subject matter Salinis chose to use motet texture, and perhaps to make musical reference to the thirteenth-century conductus with his strict separation of texted and untexted sections. But was any thirteenth-century music known at this time? Salinis's (and others') reuse of texts from these earlier genres for early fifteenth-century motets suggests that it was available in manuscript sources, even if not performed. By combining archaic techniques for an archaic subject with the textures and rhythms of the modern French and Italian motet Salinis demonstrates that old themes are still relevant. There can be little doubt that Salinis sees himself as part of a tradition of motet composition, beginning in the distant past.

<u>Supremum est mortalibus bonum</u>	Ø	The highest good for mortals is
pax, <u>optimum summi dei donum.</u>		**peace**, the best gift of God on high.

Pace vero legum prestancia	I	In **peace**time the supremacy of law
viget atque recti constantia;		has force and constancy in right;
pace dies solutus et letus,		in **peace**time the day is free and happy,	5
nocte sompnus trahitur quietus;		at night quiet sleep is prolonged;
pax docuit virginem ornare	II	**peace** taught the maiden to adorn
auro comam crinesque nodare;		her hair with gold and tie it in a knot;
<u>**pace** rivi psallentes et aves</u>		in **peace**time the streams and singing birds
patent leti collesque suaves;	III	are seen to rejoice, and the pleasant hills;	10
pace dives pervadit viator,		in **peace**time the wealthy traveller reaches his destination,
tutus arva incolit arator.		and the ploughman cultivates the fields in safety.

O sancta **pax**, diu expectata,	₵3 I	O holy **peace**, long awaited,
mortalibus tam dulcis, tam <u>grata----</u>,		so sweet and pleasing to mortals,
sis eterna, firma, sine fraude,	II	mayst thou be eternal, firm, inviolate,
fidem tecum semper esse gaude.		and ever rejoice that good faith is with thee.	15
Et qui nobis, o **pax**, te dedere	III	And may they that have given us thee, O **peace**,
possideant regnum sine fine:		possess their realms without end;

sit noster hic pontifex eternus	Ø *	Let our Eugene be our pope for ever
EUGENIUS ET REX SIGISMUNDUS.		and Sigismund our king.	20
A----men.		Amen.

Key: * Tenor for this line (mm. 101–106) is the *Magnificat* antiphon "Isti sunt due olive."

___ = fauxbourdon; CAPITALS = fermatas; Roman numerals = tenor taleae

Figure 7.1

Du Fay: Supremum est mortalibus bonum

The subgenre I have discussed least is the French isorhythmic motet. I would therefore like to end Part II with a discussion of Du Fay's *Supremum est*, the most widely disseminated isorhythmic motet of the fifteenth century (it is found in six sources). Usually classified simply as a French isorhythmic motet, this motet in fact makes multiple generic and subgeneric references.

The motet has a single text, celebrating the meeting of the Holy Roman Emperor elect, Sigismund, with Pope Eugenius IV in 1433.[7] It is essentially a hymn to peace (see Fig. 7.1, where the word "pax"/"peace" is shown in bold-face).[8] The popularity of this motet may have resulted in part from the basic message of the text, since the desire for peace is an uncontroversial good thing that is appropriate to all kinds of occasions. Only the final couplet anchors the text to any particular occasion, and the names of the two rulers would continue to be appropriate to Christians and allies or subjects of the Holy Roman Emperor as long as both pope and emperor were alive. In one manuscript the names "Eugenius et rex Sigismundus" are simply replaced with the names of the local rulers.[9]

The tenor of *Supremum est* is isorhythmic, with two colores in different mensurations, each with three taleae (marked on Figure 7.1). The motet is on a grand scale, as long as or longer than most isorhythmic motets, and its status as an occasional work is typical for the subgenre. On the other hand, almost everything else in the piece points away from the traditional isorhythmic motet. The upper voices use no isorhythm, there is only one text, the motet begins and ends with lengthy freely composed sections, and the tenor is not pre-existent (except for a brief passage during the postlude, marked on Fig. 7.1 with an asterisk). *Supremum est* is also Du Fay's first isorhythmic motet in which the two upper voices are not in the same range: here the second discantus (better called the motetus, or even contratenor) is significantly lower than the discantus (or triplum), and in the same range as the tenor. Even more unusual for an isorhythmic motet are the occasional passages of fauxbourdon (which appear while the tenor rests).

Some of the peculiarities of *Supremum est* have been explained by Willem Elders as humanist rhetorical devices.[10] Others have seen Du Fay's use of fauxbourdon as an effective way to project a text, or as an extension of "divisi" writing.[11] All of these explanations may indeed be true; but now we are in a position to see that the work's peculiarities are generic allusions that evoke meaningful associations. In fact, *Supremum est* refers to most of the subgenres of the motet in the early fifteenth century, as well as to other genres.

Let us imagine that we are highly educated listeners of the period hearing the piece for the first time. What would our reactions be as we listened to the motet?

LINES 1–2 (MM. 1–10): PRELUDE

The first thing we hear is fauxbourdon. What's going on here? Is it a hymn or a sequence? Possible – but that's not what we expected to hear in this context (presumably some sort of papal reception for Sigismund). It is very pretty, sweet and simple – reminds us of Vespers services. But what about the text? It's a single rhyming poetic text on the subject of peace. The vocabulary is grand, and tends to superlatives: "supremum," "optimum," "summi"; doesn't sound like a normal hymn text. Could it be some kind of laudatory text, as in Italian and French motet-style motets?

The mensuration is perfect tempus, which doesn't tell us much, but is typical of hymns. But wait – the piece begins with remote imperfection of a long, typical of the cut-circle mensuration. Could it be a cut-circle motet that is overdoing the parallel motion? The single top voice and the poetic text would accord with this hypothesis. Maybe the next event will give us a clue.

LINES 3–8, MM. 11–37: TALEA I AND MOST OF II

Here is a new texture, with a long-note tenor and two faster texted voices with independent rhythms and melodies. It sounds like a motet-style motet. This is more complicated and grander than the opening fauxbourdon section: the harmonic rhythm is slower, there are conflicting rhythms in the upper parts, the text is no longer sung to the same rhythm in all parts. But there are some oddities here – the faster voices are singing the same text, as in some of those old Italian motets. And the texted parts are not in the same range! The lower texted voice sometimes even crosses below the tenor. What is this? A cantilena-style or a motet-style piece? There are some English motets like this, for three and four voices, some isorhythmic, some not. They tend to be sacred works; but here the subject is law, justice, and peace.

In line 6, mm. 23–5 the tenor drops out – is this a duet in the English style? Or part of the tenor talea? The reduction in texture creates a nice effect for a reference to the "sompnus . . . quietus," "quiet sleep." Lines 7–8: this text about a maiden adorer hair certainly isn't sacred – and listen to that decorative melisma – another nice word-painting touch. The melisma and the repeated-note figure on "auro comam" (m. 33) sound like cut-circle music again, or even like some of Du Fay's songs – Du Fay is clearly evoking a sensuous secular world here.

LINE 9, MM. 38–40: END OF TALEA II

Here is a passage in fauxbourdon again – and the tenor has dropped out. Another nice word-painting effect for "rivi psallentes et aves" – psalms and antiphons are sometimes sung in fauxbourdon, so the brooks and birds are doing it too. We begin to see a pattern here – alternation of an unusual three-voice motet texture with fauxbourdon.

LINES 10–12, MM. 41–57: TALEA III, TO COLOR 2, TALEA I, FIRST NOTE

That's right, here comes the motet texture again; long note in the tenor after it has dropped out for a while; probably isorhythmic, with rests at the end of each talea. Yes – it has dropped out again (mm. 53–5) – and the upper parts have an extremely lively melisma, with conflicting rhythms – it must be build-ing up to some arrival. Yes – momentary calm (mm. 56–7) coinciding with the return of the tenor.

LINES 13–18, MM. 56–100: COLOR II, TALEAE I–III

Must be the beginning of the second color. Will there be a change in the tempo? Yes – it's a bit faster, but with the same basic mensural organization. This piece certainly acts a lot like a standard isorhythmic motet in its construction. Will there be fauxbourdon at the end of these taleae? Only one talea had it in the first half. Yes – there is fauxbourdon at the end of the first talea, a melisma on the word "grata" – pleasing sounds of fauxbourdon to represent the pleasing harmony of peace. No fauxbourdon in the other two – that's symmetrical. The end of the last talea is a duet on a melisma after the words "sine fine," "without end" – will there be another color?

LINES 19–21, MM. 101–20: POSTLUDE

The piece returns to the original tempo, but without the long-note tenor. This must be new material: it doesn't seem related to the previous isorhythm. Is the piece about to end? Very lively upper parts here – is it a drive to the cadence, or to some new event? It's a new event – a fermata section – that reminds us of cut-circle motets, or some Mass movements and chansons. The fermatas are for the names of the pope and the King of the Romans – Church and state. Perhaps this is the punchline, the key that explains the peculiarities of this piece – fauxbourdon and motet for the Church, song and motet for the state, combined here in one all embracing whole.

   Will the motet end there? Many cut-circle motets end with fermatas. No, it can't: wrong pitch. This motet is "sine fine" – this postlude seems to go on forever. The Amen begins with another passage of fauxbourdon, very remi-niscent of the very beginning of the motet in the way it rises dramatically through an octave (g down to e up to ee with cadence on ee). But here the fauxbourdon continues the phrase back down, giving way almost impercept-ibly to a final three-voice texture in which the tenor is as active as the contra-tenor. Motet texture has been abandoned completely in favor of song or cantilena-style texture. The rhythmic complexity in the top line recalls that of the duet at the end of the first color – and that of some English cantilenas and motets, with its constantly shifting groupings – and carries us, breathless, to the final cadence.

Multiple generic allusions are central to the impact and import of this work. It is a motet-style motet, part of the great French tradition, with a long-note isorhythmic tenor, two active texted voices, and a political text. It also, however, makes reference to Italian and English motet traditions. The single laudatory text recalls the political texts of the Italian tradition, while the low motetus voice and lack of isorhythm in the texted voices recall the texture of the English three-voice tenor motet. Du Fay could have known examples by this time, since they are found in Trent 92, and were probably heard at the Council of Basel.

More striking than allusions to these motet traditions are the references to the cantilena-style genres of simple liturgical music, the English cantilena, the chanson, and the cut-circle motet. The use of fauxbourdon evokes the communal devotions of the convent and the community: it is the voice of the Church, not of its soloists or leaders, but the community of souls that are its foundation. The style of the chanson and the cut-circle motet recall the world of the court (also evoked by lines 7–8, "peace taught the maiden to adorn her hair with gold and tie it in a knot"). The rhythmic writing, while closest to that of the cut-circle motet, also approaches in some passages that of the English cantilena. Both of these subgenres evoke the intimacy of private Marian devotions.

In the process of combining all these generic references Du Fay created a challenging puzzle for the audience. As hypothetical listeners we found the answer in the fermata section: just as the union of Sigismund and Eugenius, Church and state, encompasses the secular and the sacred, the temporal and the eternal, the north and the south, this motet brings together the whole world of musical possibilities: secular and sacred, poetry and politics, motet-style and cantilena-style, English, French, and Italian. More specifically it represents Eugenius and the communal voice of the Church by the use of fauxbourdon, while Sigismund and the court are represented by the use of

162

cantilena-style texture; they are brought together in the motet, a genre that has historically stood at the intersection of the sacred and the secular. And not just any kind of motet, but the great old tradition of the French isorhythmic motet, now the preferred subgenre for laudatory occasional works. Only by recognizing the wealth of Du Fay's generic references can we appreciate the breadth of his vision and achievement.

Part III

Motets in the mid-fifteenth century: the case of the Trent Codices

8 Motets in the Trent Codices: establishing the boundaries

Bologna Q15's distinct motet section allowed us to examine the repertory of motets and sort the pieces into subgenres without having to worry too much about which pieces were motets. Having established the subgenres in Q15 it was then relatively easy to identify the motets in other contemporary manuscripts. Unfortunately, there is no comparable source for the mid-fifteenth century. While the last source in Table 7.1, Modena X.1.11 (c. 1448), has a distinct motet section, its continental subsection contains only eighteen motets, and it is a little too early for the new developments of the third quarter of the century. Sources for all genres are scarce during this period, and it is particularly hard to find manuscripts containing substantial numbers of motets.[1]

The principal surviving manuscripts from mid-century for all genres are the Trent Codices, a group of seven manuscripts copied between *c.* 1430 and *c.* 1475 and now found in Trent, Italy. Fortunately, the Trent Codices contain more than 1800 compositions (counting Mass movements individually), an international repertory whose origins extend from England to Eastern Europe, from Holland to Naples, in a heterogeneous mix of genres and styles. While largely neglected for much of the twentieth century, the codices have received considerable scholarly attention in recent years. Unfortunately, while many of the other genres found in the Trent Codices – Mass Ordinary cycles, Mass Propers, hymns, *Magnificat* settings, chansons, and "cantus planus" chant settings – have received preliminary cataloging and in some cases extended study, there has been no systematic consideration of the Trent motets. The reasons are not hard to find. Establishing which of the pieces in the manuscript are motets is no easy task: there are no distinct motet sections, most of the pieces are anonymous unica, and

Table 8.1. *Dates and provenance for the Trent Codices*

MS	Main scribe	Saunders or Wright	Traditional date (*Census Catalogue*)	Probable provenance
87–2	Battre?	1434–7 (S)	*c.* 1430–40	Ciney, in Namur province
92–1	Merques?	1429–37 (S)	*c.* 1430–40	Basel/Strasbourg
87–1	Lupi	1433–45 (W)	*c.* 1430–40	Basel/Tyrol/Austria
92–2	Lupi	1439–45 (W)	*c.* 1430–40	Basel/Tyrol/Austria
93	?	1450–52/56 (S)	*c.* 1460	Trent
90	Wiser	1452–9 (S)	*c.* 1460	Trent
88	Wiser	1456–62 (S)	*c.* 1460–5	Trent
89	Wiser	1460–6 (S)	*c.* 1460–80	Trent
91	Wiser	1472–7 (W)	*c.* 1460–80	Trent

there is much contrafacture and omission of text. Nevertheless, I have established a repertory of motets in the Trent Codices. Study of this repertory (in conjunction with smaller contemporary manuscripts) illuminates the transformations in the genre that will lead ultimately to the late fifteenth-century motet of the Josquin era.

Dates and provenance

Several different sets of dates have been proposed for the Trent Codices (see Table 8.1): the traditional one, based primarily on knowledge about the repertories, is found in the *Census Catalogue*; Suparmi Elizabeth Saunders developed a new set of dates based on watermark studies; individual scholars, most recently Peter Wright, have refined and deepened her work. Saunders's dates have received cautious acceptance by the scholarly community; Wright's dating of Trent 91 (with dates for the other manuscripts to follow soon) inspires even more confidence.[2]

The exact dates for each manuscript are less important for our purposes than their order (though I will do some chronological speculation). Peter Wright has demonstrated that manuscripts 87 and 92 are in fact four different manuscripts: 87–1 and 92–2 were copied by the same scribe, Johannes Lupi, at the same time (Wright refers to them together as TR); Lupi then bound them together with two other slightly earlier manuscripts, 87–2 and 92–1, copied by unknown scribes.[3] This group of manuscripts, copied in the 1430s and early

168

1440s, includes many concordances with other early to mid-fifteenth-century manuscripts such as Bologna Q15, Modena X.1.11, and Aosta, as we saw in Table 7.1, where I referred to the contents of Tr 87–1, 92–2, and 92–1 collectively as TR+. Trent 93 and 90 are slightly later, but they still include some concordances with the earlier manuscripts (especially in the case of motets by Dunstaple and Power). Margaret Bent has shown that much of Trent 90 was largely copied from Trent 93 by the scribe Johannes Wiser, when Trent 93 was close to completion.[4] Both manuscripts, however, have sections with repertory not found in the other: it is in these sections that most of the motets appear.[5] Wiser continued collecting music well into the 1470s, doing much of the copying and supervising the compilation of manuscripts 88, 89, and 91 (see Table 8.1).[6]

Turning from dates to provenance, another question arises. Why do we find this substantial repertory in Trent? Located near the Brenner pass, Trent was a natural stopping place between Venice and Innsbruck, or between Italy and much of northern Europe. It also had political ties with the Habsburg court in Wiener Neustadt and Vienna. A great deal of music must have passed through the city. But the town itself did not apparently have the kind of substantial choir and choir school usually associated with the advanced polyphony found in the manuscripts.[7] Why then was such a huge collection of polyphonic music copied and kept in Trent? This question has not yet been fully answered, although scholars have learned a great deal about the two major scribes of the Trent Codices. This knowledge, combined with information about the possible origins of the repertory and about manuscript types, leads to some promising hypotheses.

Peter Wright has taught us a great deal about Johannes Lupi, the scribe of TR (87–1 and 92–2). A Tyrolean cleric and organist from Bolzano (north of Trent), Lupi studied at the university in Vienna beginning in 1428–9, and worked as chaplain to Duke Frederick IV (the elder) of Austria, Count of Tyrol from 1431 to 1439, and then (*c.* 1440–43) with the thirteen-year-old Sigmund, Duke of Austria, and his guardian, Frederick, Habsburg King of Germany (Holy Roman Emperor from 1452). It was during this period that he must have collected and copied the music for TR; he may also have worked as a copyist for Frederick's chapel.[8] He probably visited the Council of Basel (1431–49), where he would have obtained more music, and may have acquired 92–1 from the Basel chaplain Nicholas Merques. Battre may have brought Trent 87–2 from Namur to the court of Frederick III in 1443. Lupi became organist at the cathedral of Trent in 1446–7, bringing the manuscripts with him; he retained the position until his death in 1467.[9] Lupi was well connected and broadly traveled: he thus had the opportunity to acquire music from all over Europe. He may have collected the music for performance by a skilled musical organization, such as the Habsburg chapel, or it may have been more of a personal collection, to be performed by Lupi himself and a small circle of friends. Whatever the original intent of the manuscripts, Trent 87 and 92 became part of the Trent repertory once Lupi settled there.[10]

Johannes Wiser, the scribe in charge of the copying of the later Trent Codices (90, 88, 89, and 91), is documented in Trent beginning in 1455, though he may have arrived somewhat earlier. Johannes Lupi soon became a good friend of the young cleric, and he may have aided and advised Wiser in his collecting and copying efforts. Wiser was schoolmaster at the cathedral between 1459 and 1465, and continued his affiliation with it for the rest of his life. The manuscripts remained in the city after his death. In 1470 he became the chaplain to the prominent humanist and bibliophile Johannes Hinderbach, Provost of Trent Cathedral from 1455, and Prince-Bishop of Trent from 1465.[11]

Reinhard Strohm has suggested that Wiser's manuscripts constituted "a personal collection for his career as cantor and schoolmaster."[12] The repertory would have been sung by the boys of the choir school or *Kantorei* and additional clerics from the cathedral, and it was appropriate for all the necessary functions: endowed Masses, special devotions and processions for guild chapels, civic ceremonies and visiting dignitaries, including *"Ansingen* tours" by the choirboys and their masters. He finds much in common between the Trent Codices and later German and Central European collections such as Strahov, Speciálník, Munich 3154 (the Leopold Codex), Warsaw 2016, Berlin 40021, and Leipzig 1494 (the Apel Codex), several of which were compiled by schoolmasters like Wiser. The many scribal hands in the Trent Codices in addition to Wiser's would have included those of his students.[13] Adelyn Peck Leverett has suggested that Wiser and his circle of friends and copyists were essentially imperial appointees who formed a kind of informal chapel for Hinderbach; she thus sees the Trent repertory (especially that of the last manuscript, Trent 91) as Austrian in orientation, and closely related to that of the Imperial chapel.[14] Whatever the reasons for the origins and survival of the Trent Codices, we have reason to be thankful, for without them our knowledge of music of the mid-century would be virtually non-existent.

Establishing a repertory of motets

Deciding which pieces in the Trent Codices are motets is of course a problem of categorization. The problems are slightly different for each manuscript: each has its own repertorial emphasis, and since the motet itself was evolving during the period, recognition of motets in one source is no guarantee of familiarity with those of the next. I will begin, therefore, with a discussion of the general problems in establishing the repertory of motets.

The Trent Codices contain examples of every genre of polyphony composed in the mid-fifteenth century, and their organization is often haphazard. Sections or gatherings devoted to one genre are followed by miscellaneous assortments; multiple layers of copying (as later scribes went back and filled in the blank folios and the bottoms of pages) often obscure the organization even more. A first step in identifying the repertory of motets in the Trent Codices is to exclude from consideration those compositions that belong clearly to other genres. The only genres that are easy to distinguish from motets at first glance are *Magnificat* settings and Mass Ordinary movements and cycles (about 45 per cent of the music in the codices). Even here there can be problems of categorization, since Mass movements sometimes receive contrafact texts. The boundaries between the motet and the various genres of liturgical service music, cantio and Leise settings, contrafact secular music, and compositions without text, are fuzzy and difficult to draw clearly. The process of drawing the boundaries, however, often sheds light on the music on either side.

Liturgical service music

To a modern scholar approaching the Trent Codices the task of distinguishing motets from the genres of liturgical service music is often the most daunting, since we lack familiarity with the chant texts and melodies. To compound the problem, text alone is not sufficient to distinguish liturgical service music from motets, as we have seen in relation to Modena X.1.11. Motets often use texts derived from the liturgy (though usually from the genres with the most flexible role in the liturgy). Nevertheless, certain patterns emerge. In liturgical service music the text and music of selected chant genres are closely tied and presented as a unit in the polyphonic setting; this relationship is freer in motets, and the chant melody is treated loosely, concealed, or dispensed with altogether. In liturgical service music monophonic chant often serves to introduce the polyphony (where there is a chant incipit), or is sung in alternation with polyphony (as in hymns and sequences): while some motets use chant incipits, alternatim practice is a sure sign of liturgical function.

Each genre of service music has its own conventions of composition and manuscript presentation, and the practiced eye comes to recognize the features of each genre (such as additional stanzas of text, chant incipits, or alternatim practice) that distinguish them from motets. While individual examples of each genre of service music are found scattered through the manuscripts, many are copied in clusters, groups, or cycles (see Table 8.2); such groupings, once detected, can be very helpful in identification. The same texts are often set in more than one of the Wiser manuscripts, so one comes to recognize them.[15] I am also greatly indebted to the scholars who have provided inventories and studies of individual genres.[16]

Many different genres of service music are included in the Trent Codices; the most common are hymns and Mass Propers (especially introits; see Table 8.2). Antiphons of all kinds and sequences dedicated to the Virgin are the chant genres most likely to receive different kinds of musical settings, or to sit on the boundary between motet and liturgical service music. When it comes to deciding which settings of these texts are motets, and which are service music, it is essential to examine the style and manuscript context for the works.

The four great Marian antiphons (especially *Salve regina*) are the texts set most often as motets in the mid-fifteenth century, and the settings exhibit the whole gamut of stylistic possibilities, from large-scale multipartite four-voice tenor motets to the simplest cantus planus settings. Most of them are motets, but a few of the simplest must be considered liturgical service music. Trent 89.600, for example, is a *Salve regina* setting in alternatim style, with only the even verses in polyphony. The tenor voice carries the chant, primarily in equal semibreves.[17] This kind of setting is typical of service music, but not of the motet, so I have excluded it from consideration. In Trent 91, fascicles 8 to 18, there is a large group of three-voice pieces with very simple equal-note chant presentation that Adelyn Peck Leverett has labeled "the Passau paraphrase repertory," because they use texts and melodies found in surviving chant books of the diocese of Passau.[18] The section includes multiple settings of the great Marian antiphons *Salve regina* and *Regina celi*. It also includes set-

Table 8.2. *Liturgical genres in the Trent Codices (these are not motets)*

All the codices include Mass Ordinary movements and cycles, not listed here.
Manuscripts listed after a genre contain groups, clusters, or cycles of that genre; Roman
numerals indicate fascicles. When no manuscript is listed, individual examples are found in
more than one of the codices.

Music for Mass

Asperges and Vidi aquam settings: 93 & 90
Introits in conjunction with Mass Ordinary cycles: 92–1
Introits: 93 & 90[a]
Other individual propers (gradual, alleluia, offertory, communion)
Mass Proper cycles: 88 (many); 89 (1: BVM); 91 (1: Dedication of Church)[b]
Plenary Masses (Ordinary and Propers)[b]
   Liebert, Marian: 92–1–V–VI
   Du Fay, St. Anthony of Padua: 88 (Ordinary in 90)
   [Du Fay?], St. Anthony Abbot: 89
Sequences: 87–1–VI, 92–1 (secondary layer), 93, 91

Music for Vespers

Magnificat settings
Office hymns: 92–2, 92–1 (secondary layer), 93, 88, 89, 91[c]
Vespers antiphons: 92–1 (secondary layer), 89, 91
Psalms

Other

Processional hymns
Te deum
Benedicamus domino settings (TR)
Responsories
Gospel genealogy with responses (91)
Prosulae, tropes

Notes:
[a] See Spilsted, "Trent 93," Appendix II: "A Catalogue of Polyphonic Introits (*ca.* 1400–*ca.*
1474)," 256–85; Frohmut Dangel-Hoffmann, *Der Mehrstimmige Introitus in Quellen des 15.
Jahrhunderts*, Würzburger Musikhistorische Beiträge 3 (Tutzing: Schneider, 1975).
[b] See Gerber, "Trent 88," 143–89; Fallows, *Dufay*, 182–92, and "Dufay and the Mass Proper
Cycles of Trent 88," *I codici*, 46–59; Planchart, "Du Fay's Benefices," and "Guillaume Du Fay's
Second Style," *Music in Renaissance Cities and Courts*, 307–40.
[c] See Tom R. Ward, "The Office Hymns of the Trent Manuscripts," *I codici*, 112–29.

tings of Vespers antiphons for the Virgin often used for motet texts, such as *O florens rosa*, or the *Song of Songs* antiphons (*Ista est speciosa, Descendi in ortum meum, Anima mea liquefacta*, and *Nigra sum sed formosa*).[19] These pieces are found in a section of the manuscript clearly devoted to liturgical music, however, and the style of the chant setting is so clear and basic (with the chant in equal note values) that I have not classified them as motets. One more group of antiphon settings that I exclude because of style and manuscript presentation are those that present the cantus firmus in chant notation.[20]

Sequences are also set as liturgical service music or as motets. Liturgical settings use the chant melody and almost always alternate polyphony and monophony, so that only alternate stanzas (verse, line) are set in polyphony. The chant stanzas are usually not supplied in the Trent Codices, but liturgical sequence settings are still easy to recognize because they consist of a series of short sections separated by double bars. When set as motets, however, no alternation takes place, and often the chant melody is not used: each subsequent stanza is set to polyphony without omissions (though sometimes only the first stanzas of text are used).[21]

Each of the genres of prescribed liturgical service music deserves a separate study: knowledge of the compositional conventions of these different repertories and their development will greatly aid our understanding of music history in the fifteenth century. Inclusion of these genres under the heading "motet" in the past, however, has obscured our vision of both kinds of music. Eliminating them from the motet genre allows us to see a distinct repertory with its own characteristics and history. At the same time an understanding of the parallel developments, occasional overlaps, and historical affiliations of the motet and other genres can increase our understanding of some subgenres of the motet.

Cantiones and Leisen

Cantiones and Leisen are German devotional songs, sometimes macaronic or with German and Latin versions of their texts (thus *Christ ist erstanden* often appears as *Christus surrexit*; see Table 8.3). Like the Marian antiphons, they receive polyphonic settings in Central European sources that range from extremely simple to extremely complex; they also have a loose relationship to the liturgy. The simplest use bare-bones note-against-note polyphony, sometimes in only two voices; the most complex I know of is an eight-voice setting

Table 8.3. *Cantiones and Leisen in the Trent Codices (3 vv. unless noted; all anonymous)*

Trent no.	Text	vv.	editions; concordances; comments
88.391	Ave Jesu Christe	4	altered cantio text, but no *cpf*; contrafact?
89.667	Ave mundi spes/Gottes namen	8	DTÖ 14, EDM 80; Mu 3154; T Leise (see *REM* 532–3)
90.870	Christus surrexit		Gozzi
90.958	Christ ist erstanden/Alleluia		DTÖ 14
90.1089	Christ ist erstanden		DTÖ 14
88.392	Christus surrexit	4	
89.631	Christus surrexit	4	Text incipit only
91.1271	Christ ist erstanden		DTÖ 14
88.242	Dies est laetitiae/Der tag		DTÖ 14; cantio, *AH* 1, 42
88.388	Dies est laetitie		Gerber
93.1599	Martinus nam pusillus	2	Text also set in Strah, no. 239 (different music)
93.1848	Novus annus hodie		cantio, *AH* 20, 228 (in part)
89.595	Novus annus hodie		
89.537	Novus annus hodie	4	
93.1849	Resonet in laudibus		
88.386	Resonet in laudibus		Gerber
89.660	Resonet in laudibus	4	double discantus

of *Gottes namen fahren wir* found in Trent 89 (and in Munich 3154), in which the Leise (found in the tenor voices, and occasionally in some of the others) is combined with a Latin text, *Ave mundi spes Maria*. Clearly many of these pieces use forms and techniques derived from the motet; nevertheless, they belong to a distinct Central European tradition, and I will not discuss them further.[22]

Textless pieces and contrafacta

Text omission and contrafacture are not exclusively Central European, but they are especially typical of the region. Central Europe was the *fons et origo* of the most successful instrumentalists of the fifteenth century, and the omission of text is often a sign of instrumental performance.[23] Furthermore, the *Kantorei* or choir schools and their practice of *Ansingen* for visiting dignitaries required numerous appealing compositions suitable for schoolboys to sing, easily obtained by replacing the text of a French chanson with an appropriate Latin text.[24]

Omission of text can be complete or partial, and can occur for different reasons. Often text is omitted, but text incipits remain, helping to identify the original genre of a work. Sometimes there is no text at all, and sometimes the original text incipit is replaced by a contrafact incipit, such as a new title or catalog mark (as in many of the pieces in the Glogauer Liederbuch, in which we find series of pieces, some originally chansons, labeled only with the successive letters of the alphabet, and others with animal names).[25] The decision to omit text can be deliberate, if a piece is intended for instrumental performance (contrafact incipits often seem to be a special indicator of instrumental performance). It may be accidental: the result of a lazy or hurried scribe (or a no-show text scribe). Or the text may be omitted in anticipation of the addition of a contrafact text, to be chosen in relation to a particular occasion, and written in at that time.[26]

So what do I do with textless pieces (with and without incipits) when looking for motets? I include textless pieces that are concordant with known motets (such as the textless 93.1828, the *Alma redemptoris mater* attributed to Power and Dunstaple, and 93.1829, the *Qualis est dilectus* attributed to Forest and Plummer, which includes only the text incipit for the entrance of the tenor voice). Latin text is a preliminary generic marker for the motet, so I exclude pieces with no text at all (both those with no concordances, and those with concordances to genres other than the motet). I treat unica with Latin text incipits just as I do pieces with a complete Latin text: if a piece lacks features typical of other genres (such as liturgical service music or the Mass Ordinary), I include it provisionally as a motet.

Contrafacture also has several different forms: we find Latin contrafacta of both secular and sacred works. Contrafacta of secular works are more common, especially the replacement of the French text of a chanson with a Latin text suitable for performance by choirboys in church or school (see Table 8.4). Latin texts are also supplied for vernacular songs in other languages (especially German and Italian), and for primarily instrumental works that began life without text.[27] Many such contrafacta are thus found in

Central European schoolmasters' manuscripts such as Wiser's. Chanson contrafacta are often provided with French text incipits revealing the original genre of the work, in addition to the new Latin text. Performers would thus have the pleasure of knowing they were singing the latest love song, even if with a sacred text. Often, however, there is no such verbal clue as to the original text or genre, and we can identify the piece as a contrafact only by means of concordances. If a piece has no concordances, the form and phrase structure (and sometimes the poor fit of the Latin text) can also provide clues as to the original genre of the composition.

In some cases we really cannot tell whether a work was originally conceived as a chanson or as a cantilena-style motet. Frye's *Ave regina celorum, mater regis angelorum* (found twice in Trent 90: nos. 1013 and 1086) must be the most widely disseminated work from the mid-fifteenth century. It appears in almost twenty sources, as well as two panel paintings and a wall painting. Unlike virtually every other known motet, the piece includes internal repetition: the form is aBcB, the form of an English ballade with a "rhyming melisma" at the end of both A and B sections.[28] None of the numerous sources, however, includes even a hint of a secular text, so we are forced to believe that it was originally conceived as a motet – and in this case, "song motet" seems like the appropriate label.

In the Trent Codices there are numerous contrafacta of chansons, especially in 90 and 93 (see Table 8.4). They were identified and concordances located by David Fallows in his tremendously useful "Songs in the Trent Codices."[29] In many cases a piece's status as a contrafactum is made explicit by means of a French text incipit. Of the pieces with concordances, but without vernacular text incipits, some are well known, and might have been recognized without any such incipit (*O rosa bella*'s contrafact Latin text even begins with the same words). If we did not know of the concordances, however, there would be no way of knowing for sure that they were French chansons. So what should we do when we find short, chanson-like Latin-texted pieces for which we know no concordances? Are they motets?

My solution is to list such pieces as members of a subgenre of the motet, noting the possibility that they are contrafacta. It is important not to exclude them completely from the motet, for the presence of Latin contrafacta in the manuscripts and in the repertory may actually have sparked the composition of original "song motets" like Frye's *Ave regina*: short pieces resembling chansons in style and structure that nevertheless were composed originally to

Motets in the mid-fifteenth century

Table 8.4. *Secular contrafacta in the Trent Codices (3 vv. unless noted)*
Based on David Fallows, "Songs in the Trent Codices"

With vernacular concordances

With vernacular text incipits

93.1798	Resone unice / [Du Fay], Par le regart (R4)
90.1012	Unicus Dei / Legrant, Las je ne (R4)
88.345	Aeterne rerum conditor / [Binchois], Dueil angoisseux (Ballade, 3 or 4 vv.)
90.1022	Globus igneus / Puyllois, Quelque cose (R5)
90.1140	Beata es / Bedingham, Grant temps ay [= Myn hertis lust] (Eng. Ballade)
90.988	Nesciens mater / Parle qui parla vudra (R5?)

Without vernacular text incipits

90.1071	Virgo verbo/Sacerdos = En un gent (Ballade; 2 Latin texts underlaid)
93.1843	Qui deus natus = [Du Fay], Franc cuer gentil (R4)
90.1072	Superno nunc = [Du Fay], Le serviteur (R5)
90.990	Sancta Maria = [Bedingham/Frye], So ys emprentid (Eng. Ballade)
90.1074	O rosa bella, O tu mitis = [Bedingham/Dunstaple], O rosa bella (It. Ballata)
88.502	Gaude mater miserorum = [Busnoys], Quand ce viendra (R6)
91.1189	Gaude mater miserorum = [Busnoys], Quand ce viendra (R6; 4 vv.)
89.602	Ex ore tuo = [Cornago], Yerra con poco (Cancion)
91.1150	Da pacem domine = [Caron], Acceullie m'a la belle (R5)

Latin texts applied to textless instrumental works

89.604	O quam clara testimonia = [Barbingant], Der pfawin swancz (4 vv.; Basse danse tenor?)
89.675	Sancta genitrix = Der Fochs swantcz (instrumental reworking of rondeau, Ayme qui vouldra)

Without concordances outside the Trent Codices, but include vernacular text incipit

93.1833	Resone unice / Puyllois, Puisque fortune (R4?)
90.1009	Resone unice / Puyllois, Puisque fortune (R4?)
90.1139	Superno nunc / Bedingham, Le serviteur (not the piece attributed to Du Fay) (?)
90.1141	Imperitante Octaviano / Pour l'amour (R5) (Latin text at bottom of page)
90.1142	Virtute cuius presideat / Hellas mon cuer (Bergerette) (Latin text at bottom of page)
88.258	O edle Frucht / Martinus Abrahe (Tenorlied?)

Unica that look like chansons, but no explicit evidence: must consider motets

87.111	Protegat nos divina maiestas	?
87.141	L. de Arimino: Primi pulchri (2 vv.)	Ballade?
93.1836	Christus deus	R4?
93.1840	Virgo Maria non est tibi	Strophic?
93.1844	Bene ad te coclea	R4? (text incipit only)

Table 8.4. (*cont.*)

90.989	Altissimi Dei	R4?
90.1078	O beate Sebastiane	Eng. Ballade?
89.601	Assit herus rex (4 vv.)	Ballade?
89.603	Deus decorum inclite (4 vv.)	Ballade?
89.661	O gloriosa et laudabilis (4 vv.)	Bergerette? (not mentioned in Fallows)
Borderline cases		
92.1470	Laudo vinum datum (2 vv.)	? (Secular Latin text)
90.1082	Gayus: Dyana, lux serena	? (Text inc. only, probably not a song)

Key: / means French incipit given; = means no French incipit given; R4 is a rondeau quatrain; R5 is a rondeau cinquain. Attributions in square brackets are found in concordances; without brackets they are found in the Trent MSS.

Latin texts. The most successful of these pieces came to be widely disseminated in chansonniers as well as in manuscripts of sacred music. There was a fuzzy boundary between the short three-voice motet and the chanson in the mid-fifteenth century. (I do not list known contrafacta as motets; they are adequately represented in any case in Fallows's list.)

Contrafacture of sacred works involves replacing one Latin text with another. Three different categories emerge: the retexting of troped Kyries as motets, the retexting of sections of other Mass Ordinary movements as motets, and the retexting of motets with different texts (see Table 8.5). Each of these deserves a separate discussion.

English polyphonic Kyries (and perhaps some Central European Kyries modeled on English works) were often provided with long Latin texts (or tropes); they were comparable in length and form to Glorias and Credos, with a division into two parts being the most normal. This was very different from the rather brief tripartite Kyries composed on the Continent, and as a result, troped Kyries were often omitted or appear extensively modified in continental sources.[30] One way of using such a movement was to provide it with a new text and thus transform it into a motet. There exist several cases of Mass cycles that lack their Kyries, for which we also have surviving motets using the same tenor and often the same motto (see Table 8.5). The "Philipus" motet actually appears with three different texts: two are written under the discantus part in Trent 89, and yet another is found in Strahov (where a fifth voice is also added). This multitude of texts tends to cast doubt on the authenticity of

179

Table 8.5. *Sacred contrafacta in the Trent Codices*

(a) Probable contrafact Kyries

Composer/T	Mass	vv.	Motet	
Frye/Summe trinitati	Br 5557, G–A	3	88.240:	Salve virgo
Anon./Meditatio	Strah, G–A	4	88.416–17:	Gaude Maria
Philipus/Hilf und gib	Strah, G–A	4	89.729:	Salve regina & Gaude rosa
			Strah (5 vv.):	O gloriosa mater

(b) Motet with multiple texts associated with a Mass

Composer/T	Mass (K–A; 3 vv.)	Motet (4 vv.)	
Anon./O rosa bella I	88	Strah:	O pater eterne
		Milan 1:	O admirabile

The motet is grouped in Strah with the 4-v Missa O rosa bella III

(c) Contrafact Mass sections

Martini	Missa Coda di pavon (ModD, Milan 2, Siena)
91.1288: Flos virginum	Gloria, 1st half
91.1289: Jhesu Christe piissime, mm. 1–13	Agnus II

(d) Contrafact motets

Power	92.1456: Virgo prudentissima	Mod: Salve sancta parens (not the introit)
Du Fay	88.212: Imperatrix angelorum	Mod: Mirandas parit
Frye	90.1087: Ave regina	Sched, Strah (2x): O florens rosa
Touront	89.599: O castitatis lilium	Spec, Glog: Advocata libera
Touront	89.579: Compangant omnes	Strah, Spec: O generosa
	91.1336: No text, T & Ct. only	Bol Q16.96: O generosa (1st *pars*: O)
		Bol Q16.94: Je suis seulet (2nd *pars*: C2)

any one of them. Instability of texting is not proof that a motet originated as something else, however: another four-voice motet with two texts is closely related musically to a three-voice Mass that has its own three-voice Kyrie. For none of the proposed contrafact Kyries do we have a concordance with a Kyrie text, and only the Frye Mass and motet are definitely English; still, there is a strong case to be made that these motets began life as texted Kyries.[31]

It was not uncommon in the late fifteenth century to extract excerpts from tenor Masses for use as instrumental works or, retexted, as motets.[32] One of the earliest examples of this practice occurs in Trent 91, where two sections of Martini's *Missa Coda di pavon* appear as motets with contrafact Latin texts:

the first half of the Gloria is 91.1288, with the text *Flos virginum*, while the first thirteen bars of 91.1289, *Jhesu Christe piissime*, are equivalent to the second Agnus of the Mass.[33]

Finally, some motets have different texts in different sources. These include some of the motets associated with Masses, and a small list of other works (Table 8.5). In the case of 88.212, Du Fay's *Imperatrix/Mirandas*, the secular text in praise of the women of Florence is replaced by a sacred Marian text appropriate to many more occasions. In most other cases, however, the reasons for such retexting are obscure, since the original sacred Marian text is replaced by another such text; it is in fact difficult to determine which is the original text. The instability of texts may hint that the pieces began life as chansons: David Fallows suggests that Frye's *Ave regina/O florens rosa* is a ballade, and that Touront's *O castitatis lilium/Advocata* is a rondeau cinquain.[34] Another possibility is that the pieces were retexted to make them suitable for a devotion that required a particular text. There is no real evidence, however, to justify calling these works anything other than motets, although all are fairly brief three-voice works: they are written by composers known for their motets of this kind, and they lack the overt medial cadences or double bars that are the hallmark of the *formes fixes*.

I include all the different types of sacred contrafacture as motets, with acknowledgment of their probable origins. These works are presented in the manuscripts as motets, and may have influenced the subsequent development of the motet if they were perceived and performed as motets by other musicians.

Overview of the repertory

By eliminating the non-motets in the Trent Codices we have succeeded in establishing a repertory of motets for the manuscripts. I have sorted the motets into subgenres and prepared Table 8.6, which provides an overview of the representation of the different subgenres in the Trent Codices. (Modena X.1.11 is included to fill the chronological gap between TR+ and Trent 93.) Comparison of Table 8.6 with Table 7.1 reveals the connections and differences between the Q15 repertory and that of the Trent Codices. I have retained from Table 7.1 only the subgenres found in TR+ and Modena X.1.11, and added the new subgenres that emerge in the later manuscripts. I have also divided the English cantilenas into two groups: those of the

181

Table 8.6. *Subgenres of the motet in the Trent Codices and Modena X.1.11*

	TR+	Modena X.1.11 Cont.	/Eng.	93	90	88	89	91	total/actual no. pieces (when different from total)
French isorhythmic	6	9	1	—	—	—	1	—	17 / 15
Double-discantus	7	2	—	—	—	3	—	—	12 / 10
Cut-circle motet	8	3	—	—	—	1	—	—	12 / 11
Declamation	3	—	—	—	—	—	—	—	3
English isorhythmic	2	—	12	—	—	—	—	—	14 / 12
3-voice Tenor motet	7	—	5	—	—	1	1	1	15 / 12
English cantilena I	25	—	29	2	6	—	—	—	62 / 36
II	—	—	5	1	12	7	2	—	27 / 23
3-voice continental cantilena	3	4	—	1	—	4	1	—	13 / 11
3-voice song motet (Touront)	—	—	—	—	—	1	3	2	6 / 5
4-voice song motet	—	—	—	—	—	—	2	2	4
4- (& 5-) voice tenor motet	—	—	—	—	—	4	4	2	10
Between T & chant paraphrase	—	—	—	—	—	—	1	1	2
4-voice chant paraphrase	—	—	—	—	—	1	4	—	5
4-voice freely composed	—	—	—	—	1	1	7	1	10
Canonic	—	—	—	—	—	—	4	—	4
Probable secular contrafacta	2	—	—	3	2	—	3	—	10
Cantiones/Leisen 3 vv.	—	—	—	3	3	3	1	1	11
4+ vv.	—	—	—	—	—	2	4	—	6
Totals	63	18	52	10	24	28	38	10	243 / 200

Excluded: unidentified works without text or text incipit; known contrafacta of secular works; borderline cases.

Dunstaple/Power generation (Band I), and those of the Plummer/Frye generation (Band II) (the term "Band" comes from Curtis and Wathey's "Fifteenth-Century English Liturgical Music: A List of the Surviving Repertory"). There are some English pieces also among the four-voice pieces; these we will discuss in that context.

The earliest Trent Codices (87 and 92: TR+) have a considerable overlap with the Q15 repertory, and with the slightly later manuscript Modena X.1.11; many of the same subgenres appear in all three manuscripts. The major contrast between Q15 and these sources of the 1440s is the disappearance of the

earliest music in Q15, the expanded presence of English music, and the intro-
duction of a new English subgenre, the three-voice tenor motet. Modena
X.1.11 also introduces a few pieces by the younger "Band II" generation of
English composers represented by Plummer and Stone.

Trent 90 and 93, however, provide a definite contrast with the earlier repertories. The isorhythmic motets have disappeared, as have the cut-circle and
double-discantus motets, subgenres that may have flourished primarily in
Italy. Virtually all of the music is for three voices, but in Trent 90 there is one
four-voice motet with two *partes*. New genres include German-texted cantiones and Leisen, and short song-like pieces that may be contrafacta. English
music continues to be important, but while there are still cantilenas by
Dunstaple and Power, the new "Band II" repertory has a much larger presence, especially in Trent 90. TR+ and Modena X.1.11 have a Western
European and Italian orientation, and a slightly retrospective cast (they both
contain isorhythmic motets that were composed decades earlier). 90 and 93,
on the other hand, are the first of the Trent Codices to be copied in Trent,
and they were copied in the 1450s. They therefore contain both music from
Central European traditions (cantiones and Leisen) and a newer Western
European repertory.

The last three Trent Codices (88, 89, and 91) dispense altogether with the
English music of the Dunstaple/Power generation, and the proportion of
English music to the total repertory of motets is much smaller. The inclusion
of cantiones and Leisen and of contrafacta begun in Trent 93 continues. At
the same time, the number of four-voice pieces increases dramatically in
Trent 88 and 89 (in Trent 89, fewer than one-quarter of the motets have three
voices). While Trent 89's substantial repertory of large four-voice motets
looks ahead to Munich 3154 or even some of the collections of the 1490s
(such as CS 15 and the Gaffurius codices), Trent 91 contains primarily three-
voice music. The motets in Trent 91, however, include well-known pieces
with dedicatory texts by famous composers: Busnoys's *In hydraulis*, in praise of
Ockeghem, 1465–7; Compère's *Omnium bonorum plena*, a singer's prayer to the
Virgin that mentions Du Fay, Busnoys, Ockeghem, Tinctoris, and Josquin; and
Martini's *Perfunde celi rore*, in honor of the marriage of Duke Ercole d'Este in
1473.[35] With these three pieces we emerge from the predominantly anonymous repertory of mid-century into a more familiar world of recognizable
styles and figures. Our job in the next four chapters will be to trace the antecedents of these pieces and composers.

Several issues emerge from this overview of the motets in the Trent Codices. One is the role of English music. Its representation in the total repertory seems to reach a high point in the 1440s, only to decline gradually until it has disappeared from the repertory completely by Trent 91 (see Table 8.6). The attributions (even if only to "Anglicanus") and groupings of English works so common in the 1430s and 1440s also gradually disappear: there seems to have been less interest after 1450 in marking pieces as English, perhaps because English music no longer had such a high status. This is surely due in part to a decreasing English presence on the Continent in the 1440s and the end of the Hundred Years War in 1453, followed by a civil war in England during which English energies were no longer focused on France. It may also have to do with the increasing mastery by continental composers of aspects of English style, as we will see when examining the individual sub-genres.

Another issue is the rise of the new four-voice texture with a single dis-cantus voice and two contratenors (high and low), the texture of four-voice music of the Josquin generation. Where did this texture come from? What are its origins? How did it develop? Finally, the roots and ramifications of the new subgenres of the motet need to be investigated, with reference to earlier sub-genres and to other contemporary genres.

The Q15 repertory was characterized by incredible variety, in which the individual character of the earlier local traditions of motet composition stood out: a multicultural salad bowl or mosaic. During the 1430s, 1440s, and early 1450s some of these local traditions died out, and much more intermixing (or interbreeding) went on, as composers learned from each other and a pan-European style began to take shape. Especially striking is the extent to which continental composers began to make the genres, textures, rhythm, and melodic style of English music their own, while the idiosyncratic brilliance of Italian music seems to have disappeared. Rather than the vivid individual colors of the 1420s, a more muted palette emerged in which the various colors blended – a melting pot, not a mosaic.

9 English and continental cantilena-style motets

The number of three-voice cantilena-style motets grew extensively during the 1430s and 1440s. In the 1450s their numbers declined as the four-voice motet achieved prominence: there are only six in the last two Trent Codices. I will therefore consider all the three-voice cantilena-style motets (early and late, English and continental) in this chapter.

The English cantilena: from Dunstaple and Power to Plummer and Frye

As a glance at Table 8.6 reveals, the English cantilena is far better represented than any other subgenre of the mid-fifteenth century (and this would be true even without the English section of Modena X.1.11, since most of its English cantilenas are concordant with TR+). In their catalog of English fifteenth-century sacred music Curtis and Wathey attempted a "rough chronological grouping," with Band I including music "to the end of Dunstable's musical career," and Band II including "music of the mid century, written by a subsequent generation of composers including Frye and Plummer."[1] In the case of anonymous works they presumably used style and manuscript dating as guides. I find the division helpful and revealing (see Table 9.1).

The earlier Band I group (Table 9.1.1, including music by Dunstaple, Power, Forest, and Piamor, as well as some anonymous pieces) is larger than the later Band II group (Table 9.1.2). Not only are there more Band I pieces (thirty-six) but most are found in multiple sources. Only ten are unica, and almost half are found in three or more manuscripts.

Most of the Band I cantilenas are found in TR+; six appear only in

Modena X.1.11, and all of the Band I cantilenas in Trent 90 and 93 can also be found in earlier sources. Half (eighteen) of the Band I cantilenas are attributed to Dunstaple in at least one source (four have conflicting attributions to Power), while a surprisingly small number survives with no attribution in any source (only six pieces, two of which are identified as English). Of 167 total copies of motets (including all subgenres) in TR+, Modena X.1.11, Trent 93 and Trent 90, more than a third (sixty-two) are Band I English cantilenas (see Table 8.6). These facts suggest that most of the music of the Dunstaple generation arrived on the Continent in the 1430s and early 1440s, and quickly dominated the repertory. Six of Q15's eleven English cantilenas are still found in these later sources: in terms of style and approach to form this is the same kind of music that we saw there.

The later group of Band II English cantilenas (see Table 9.1.2) is somewhat smaller than the Band I group: there are not as many pieces (twenty-three), and most have fewer concordances (fourteen are unica). The Band II pieces are found first in Modena X.1.11 and are well represented in Trent 93 and 90, but then the numbers diminish fast, with only seven in Trent 88, two in 89, and none in 91. The Band II cantilenas must have reached the Continent primarily in the late 1440s and early 1450s. None is identified as English with a label like "De Anglia" or "Anglicanus," and only seven are attributed; of those attributions, most are found in Modena X.1.11. The music was less available, and perhaps the continental passion for English music was on the wane.

It is difficult to establish a relative chronology or stylistic development for the English cantilenas, since their first appearance in continental manuscripts may have little or nothing to do with their date of composition. Forest's *Qualis est dilectus*, for example, is found only in the later continental manuscripts (Modena X.1.11, Trent 93 and 90), so we might suspect that it is one of the later pieces of the Band I repertory (perhaps composed in the early 1440s). But it happens to survive also in the Old Hall Manuscript, and was probably copied there in the 1420s.[2] Margaret Bent did not even try to develop a chronology for Dunstaple's cantilenas in her monograph on the composer.

The works of Leonel Power, however, display a greater variety of style and approach, and Charles Hamm proposed a tentative chronology of Power's works based on a combination of stylistic evidence and manuscript dating: his first group includes the simple chant settings of Old Hall, while his last group consists of pieces in Modena X.1.11.[3] Comparing the characteristics of the Band I and II repertories confirms the findings of Hamm's chronology, as well

Table 9.1. *English cantilenas in the Trent Codices and Modena X.1.11*

Table 9.1.1. *English cantilenas, Band I*

	Mens.	Concordances; comments
Dunstaple		
Sub tuam protectionem	CO	Q15, 92.1463, Mod, Aosta, Bux (2X)
Quam pulchra es (SoS)	O¢	Q15, 92.1465, Mod, Aosta, B2216, MuEm, Pemb
Beata dei genitrix	OCO	Q15, 90.1048, Mod, Aosta, MuEm
Salve regina/Virgo tr.	OCO¢O	87.24, Mod
Beata mater	O¢O	87.131, Mod, Aosta, MuEm, Ob26, Olc89
Sancta Maria succurre	O¢	87.104, 92.1502, 90.1051, Mod, Aosta
+Ave regina celorum	OC	92.1449, Mod, F112bis; chant incipit, paraphrase
+Crux fidelis	OC	92.1504, Mod; C.f. in Ct.
O crux gloriosa	OCO	922.1523, Mod
Speciosa facta	O	922.1535, Mod
Sancta Maria non est	O	922.1542, Mod
Gaude virgo Katerina	O¢	Mod
Sancta Dei genitrix	OC2ØO	Mod
Gloria sanctorum	OCO (2)	Mod
Conflicting attributions: Dunstaple and Power		
+Alma redemptoris (A)	O¢ (2)	Q15 (@P, ~~Binchois~~), 93.1828, Mod (@D), Aosta; very free use of chant in D
+Salve regina/Virgo tr.	O¢OC¢O	922.1577 (@D), 90.1081 (@D), Mod (@P), Aosta, Columbia, Lo 5665
Alma redemptoris (B)	O¢O	922.1524 (@P), Mod (@D), Aosta (@P)
Salve mater	OC	922.1544 (@P), 922.1562, Mod (@D)
Power		
"Middle" works		
+Regina celi (C)	O¢O	92.1507, 90.1136; free use of chant
Virgo prudentissima	O	92.1456, Mod (Salve sancta)
Anima mea (A) (SoS)	O¢O	B2216 (2 vv.), Mod, F112bis, MuEm (Christus resurgens)
"Late" works		
Mater ora	O	92.1505, 922.1536, Mod
Ibo michi ad montem (SoS)	O	Mod
Anima mea (B) (SoS)	C (2)	Mod
Quam pulchraes (SoS)	O¢C (2)	Mod

Table 9.1.1. (*cont.*)

Forest

Alma redemptoris	C	Q15, 90.1052, Mod, Aosta
Ave regina celorum	O	87.102, Mod
Tota pulchra (SoS)	OCO	92.1459, Mod; some use of chant?
Qualis est (SoS)	C (2)	OH (@Forest), Mod (@Plummer), 93.1829, 90.1049

Piamor

Quam pulchra es (SoS)	C (2)	922.1526, Mod

Anonymous

+De Anglia, Benedicta es	OC	Q15, 922.1531, B2216, Olc24; chant paraphrase
Anglicanus, Regina celi	OCO (2)	922.1576
Gaude virgo	OCO	87.97 (S, text in T; copied from score?)
Sancta Maria, non est	OC	87.130, 922.1574
Salve regina/Virgo tr.	OCOCO	922.1575
O admirabile	OØO (2)	92.1492

Table 9.1.2. *English cantilenas, Band II*

Song of Songs settings

Plummer, Descendi in ortum	C (2)	Mod, 90.1030 & 995, Bux
Plummer, Tota pulchra	C (2)	Mod, 90.1050, Ob26
+Plummer, Tota pulchra	OCO (2)	Mod, Lucca, Spec.; chant in D
Stone, Tota pulchra	C (2)	Mod
+Stone, Ibo michi ad montem	C	Mod; chant in T
Anon., O pulcherrima	O (2)	93.1838, 88.239 (4 vv.), Sched (4 vv.), etc. (10 MSS)
Anon., Anima mea	CO (2)	90.1046–7, 89.640 (4 vv.), Mu 3154 (4 vv.)
(+)Anon., Ibo michi ad montem	C (2)	90.991–2; first 11 notes of chant in D
Anon., Quam pulchra es	¢O (2)	90.1053
Anon., Ego dormio	O¢	88.211; no known A with this text
Anon., Quam pulchra es	O (2)	88.444
Anon., Qualis est dilectus	C (2)	88.445
Anon., Tota pulchra	O¢O (2)	88.446–7
Anon., Tota pulchra	OCO (2)	88.448–9
Anon., Quam pulchra es	O¢	89.655

Table 9.1.2. (*cont.*)

Other Marian texts		
Frye, Ave regina coelorum mater	O	90.1086, 90.1013 (4 vv.), Sched, etc. (16 MSS)
Frye, O florens rosa	C	90.1087 (Ave regina), Sched, Strah (2X)
Anon., Salve regina/Tr. Virgo	OCO¢O(2)	90.1025–6, F112bis, Antwerp
+Anon., Salve regina	O¢3COC	90.1038, Antwerp; chant incipit, paraphrase in D
+Anon., Salve regina	O¢O	88.343; chant paraphrase in D
+Anon., Virgo mater ecclesie	O¢O	90.1061–2; trope melody in Ct.
+Anon., Sub tuum presidium	O¢	90.1135; chant in D, no duets
Anon., Nesciens mater	O¢	90.1143–4

Table 9.1.3. *Relative frequency of mensurations in Bands I and II*
For the purposes of this table I have considered C and ¢ equivalent.

	OCO	OC	O	C	SRs	CO	Ɇ	Other (OC2ØO, OØO)
Band I (36)	9	8	6	4	3	1	3	2
Band II (23)	5	4	3	7	2	2	–	–

Key: + indicates use of chant. @ = attribution to. (2) after the mensuration indicates that the piece begins with a duet. SRs = *Salve regina* settings.

as bringing to light some new directions in the English cantilena of mid-century.

Although Hamm's chronology was designed to apply specifically to Power, it can also serve as a guide to the repertory as a whole. Most of the Band I cantilenas (including Dunstaple's) conform to Hamm's description of Power's middle group: they are treble-dominated, multisectional, begin in perfect tempus, and have a fairly extensive self-contained central duet.

Hamm lists four pieces (*Mater ora filium, Ibo michi ad montem, Anima mea (B)*, and *Quam pulchra es*) as Power's late works, characterized by "equal melodic interest" for all voices, some imitation, and greater variety and sensitivity in text setting. Duets, while still common, are shorter and no longer marked off as distinct sections; they also occur between all the possible voice combinations.[4] These features of Power's late works are found in many of the Band II works as well, which confirms Hamm's hypothesis about their date. They

189

also occur in Band I works by Forest and Piamor.[5] But there is more to this story.

A new musical style for settings of the Song of Songs

When comparing Bands I and II the difference in the choice of texts is striking. Although both groups set primarily votive Marian antiphons, there is a noticeable increase in the number of texts from the *Song of Songs* in Band II: fifteen out of twenty-three, vs. eight out of thirty-six in Band I. *Song* settings appear to have become all the rage in mid-century, but there are some precedents in the Band I repertory. Of the *Song* settings in Band I, three figure among Power's four "late" works, and three are works by Forest and Piamor that resemble them. Dunstaple's *Quam pulchra* and Power's *Anima mea (A)* seem to be earlier works, lacking the "late" style characteristics. On closer examination it becomes clear that many of the *Song* settings in Bands I and II share musical features not only among themselves, but also with Power's late motets.

OPENING DUETS

Of the fifteen Band II *Song* settings, twelve begin with a duet (indicated on Table 9.1 by a "2" in parentheses following the mensuration sign). This is a strikingly high proportion, especially when it is noted that only one of the non-*Song* Band II pieces begins with a duet. Duet openings are much rarer in the Band I cantilenas – seven out of thirty-six, four of which are *Song* settings. Opening duets have many generic associations during this period: they are common in works with tenor cantus firmus such as isorhythmic motets, three-voice tenor motets, and cyclic Masses. The use of opening duets for the Band II *Song* settings may have been for the purpose of associating these cantilenas with the higher-status cantus-firmus works.

MENSURAL USAGE

While both Band I and II repertories use a range of mensural patterns, there are differences in the relative proportions of mensural usages (see Table 9.1.3), and again these seem to be associated with *Song* settings. The most striking differences between Bands I and II appear in the use of major prolation ($\mathbb{C}$) and imperfect tempus (C).

The only pieces in either Band I or II that use major prolation (℃) are three *Song* settings in Band I: Dunstaple's *Quam pulchra*, Power's *Quam pulchra*, and Forest's *Tota pulchra* (see Table 9.1.1). The uncharacteristic use of major prolation for all voices in the Forest and Power works may be a reference to Dunstaple's famous motet. Imperfect tempus (C), either as the only mensuration or as the first mensuration, is quite uncommon in the Band I works, but it accounts for about a third of the Band II cantilenas. In both Bands all but one of the works using exclusively imperfect tempus are *Song* settings.

TEXT SETTING AND TEXTURE

Other features of the *Song* settings are not apparent on Table 9.1, but accord with Hamm's description of Power's late style and with Burstyn's observations on fifteenth-century *Song* settings.[6] Most show careful attention to text setting for selected passages, including repeated notes (atypical of English style) and brief homorhythmic sections with text in all voices. Imitation is fairly common, although this varies a great deal from composer to composer (it is most extensive in the works of Plummer). It tends to be simple triadic imitation at the unison, although some duets show more extended imitation at the fifth. Duets (after the opening duet) are common between all possible pairs of voices, and they are generally fairly brief and carefully integrated into the texture. All these features (occasional full texting, homorhythm, imitation, and duets) contribute to a homogeneous texture in which all voices have a similar melodic style and rhythmic profile.

ORIGINS

Where did this *Song of Songs* style come from? If we look back at the Band I *Song* settings, it becomes clear that most of the earliest pieces (judging by manuscript dating) exhibiting features of the style are by Forest. Dunstaple's *Quam pulchra* may have been the model for homorhythmic passages, repeated notes, attention to text setting, and use of major prolation in selected works, but none of the later *Song* settings comes anywhere close to the unrelieved homorhythmic style of this most famous declamation motet. Variety of texture, in fact, became one of the hallmarks of the later *Song* settings. One of the earliest works with a single section in imperfect tempus is Forest's *Alma redemptoris mater* (Ex. 4.3), which we studied as an example of English cantilena style in Bologna Q15. Forest's *Qualis est dilectus* combines imperfect tempus with an opening duet already in Old Hall, while Piamor's *Quam pulchra* exhibits these features in Trent 92–2.[7] Power's "late" style may have been modeled on these earlier compositions. Whatever the actual chronology of composition, on the Continent the *Song* settings in the new style appeared first in the works of Piamor and Forest, and only somewhat later in the works of Power.[8] In the late 1440s and early 1450s *Song* settings in the new style came to dominate the English cantilena repertory, at least on the Continent. The success of this new sub-subgenre is shown by both kinds of reproduction. Many new pieces of the same type were composed, and one particular example – the anonymous *O pulcherrima* – became one of the most widely disseminated works of the century, appearing in ten different manuscripts (see Ex. 11.3 for the beginning of the work).[9]

Most of the later sources of *O pulcherrima* are chansonniers, making this *Song of Songs* motet one of the first of the "song motets" found at the beginning or end of many chansonniers, presumably as a kind of benediction or prayer. We saw that the continental cut-circle and double-discantus *Song of Songs* motets in Bologna Q15 often had close ties to chanson style, and there may be similar affinities here. Half of the Band II *Song* settings are in one section, with no mensuration change (six use imperfect, two perfect tempus). The use of a single mensuration is more typical of the chanson than it is of the cantilena, and imperfect tempus became more and more prevalent in the chanson at mid-century; the erotic subject matter of the texts also evokes the amorous tone of chanson verse.[10] The shorter *Song* settings (such as *O pulcherrima*) may thus have deliberately taken on some of the characteristics of the vernacular song. Nevertheless, the frequent duets (especially at the beginning) and the multiple sections of many of the pieces serve to distinguish most of these works from chanson style, and bring them closer to the large-scale works with tenor cantus firmus.

Non-Song *cantilenas in Band II*

These works can be divided into two groups: the two Frye works and the anonymous Marian antiphon settings (see Table 9.1.2). The Frye works resemble the *Song of Song* motets in their homogeneous texture, careful text setting, and occasional use of imitation. Unlike the *Song* settings both pieces have the continuous three-voice texture (with no duets) and single mensuration of the contemporary chanson. Frye's *Ave regina celorum* (as noted in chapter 8) is even in English ballade form (aBcB), although literal repetition is generally avoided in the motet. His *O florens rosa* looks less like a ballade, but the end of its third and final section also repeats material from its first. *Ave regina celorum* was the most copied piece from the mid-fifteenth century (see the Appendix), but none of the other English pieces looks much like it.[11] Frye's main imitator was the continental composer Touront, whose motets we will examine below.

Of the anonymous Marian antiphon settings in Band II three are *Salve reginas*. All the *Salve regina* settings (in Bands I and II) use variants of the same organizational plan. The main part of the *Salve regina* text (before the final acclamations) is divided into two parts in the standard OC mensuration pattern. The final acclamations ("O clemens; O pia; O dulcis Maria") become a third section. When troped this final section is often divided into three sub-sections with the mensurations OCO; the tropes are usually set as duets. The Band II settings generally incorporate additional duets into the first two sections.

Another Band II Marian cantilena is an independent setting of the three-stanza trope, *Virgo mater ecclesie* (90.1061–62), that is often inserted before each of *Salve regina*'s final acclamations.[12] The trope melody is in the contratenor (as in Dunstaple's *Crux fidelis*), and follows the traditional O¢O plan. The melody is the same for all three stanzas, but it is paraphrased differently each time. The independent trope setting might be intended for insertion into another work (perhaps a four-voice work?); it could also function as an independent votive Marian composition.

The other two Marian antiphon settings in Band II are less elaborate. *Sub tuum presidium* is fairly straightforward chant paraphrase with no duets; the main thing that distinguishes it from a piece of liturgical service music like a Vespers antiphon is its use of two different mensurations. *Nesciens mater* does not use chant, but it has the traditional self-contained central duet found in so many of the Band I cantilenas.

All these English cantilenas (Band I and Band II) share certain basic approaches to composition. They are all constructed around a primary conso-nant discantus/tenor duet to which the contratenor fits itself. All are characterized by the flexible, elusive, and elegant English approach to rhythm and melody as described above in relation to Forest's *Alma redemptoris mater* (Ex. 4.3). There are some new developments in the Band II pieces, develop-ments that may have had their roots in England as far back as the 1420s but which appear to have flourished in works found on the Continent in the late 1440s and early 1450s. Especially striking in the Band II works is the preference for *Song of Songs* texts, and the new musical developments are most clearly associated with settings of these texts, though they also influence settings of other texts. Opening duets, integrated duets for all voices throughout a work, less sectionalization (with fewer self-contained duets, and more pieces in a single mensuration), increasing interest in imperfect tempus, and occasional imitation or homorhythmic passages are some of the new developments. The movement away from a hierarchy of voice function and toward homogeneity of melodic style for all voices, plus a preference for frequent alternation between tutti and duet passages without interruption of the melodic flow, were important stylistic developments in both Mass and motet on the Continent for the next few decades.

Continental cantilena-style motets

In Bologna Q15 I divided the continental cantilena-style motets into declamation motets, cut-circle motets, and continental cantilenas. A similar classification will work for the repertory in the Trent Codices and Modena X.1.11 (see Table 9.2). Several of the continental declamation motets from Q15 appear also in the Trent Codices, but there are no new examples. The subgenre of the declamation motet died out, perhaps because of a growing preference toward mid-century for long melismatic phrases and rhythmic flexibility (a similar change is evident in the evolution of the chanson).[13] Most of the cut-circle motets originally appeared in Q15 (there are only four new ones). The continental cantilena, present only in embryo in Q15, expands, moving toward a closer and closer imitation of the English cantilena, though with certain differences in emphasis. Most of the few surviving three-voice cantilena-style pieces in the last two Trent Codices are by Johannes Touront, whose *O gloriosa regina* approaches Frye's *Ave regina celorum* in its broad dissemination. We will consider them as a separate group. Another group of three-voice cantilena motets are those that look like chanson contrafacta because of their brevity, continuous three-voice texture, and major cadences, signs, or double bars that make them resemble the *formes fixes*. A few of these works bear some resemblance to Touront's motets.

We can distinguish English and continental cantilenas from cut-circle motets on the basis of text types as well as musical style. The cut-circle motets generally use poetic texts without associated melodies, and it is rare to find more than one polyphonic setting of most of the cut-circle texts. English cantilenas, in contrast, set fairly well-known Marian texts (usually antiphons of some kind) with associated chant melodies (though they use those melodies only occasionally). Many of these Marian texts are set over and over again.

Continental cantilenas, as I define them here, are three-voice cantilena-style motets that use the texts and text types typical of the English cantilena (in contrast to the cut-circle text types). Most continental cantilenas are settings of the four great Marian antiphons, though some texts are more obscure. English composers of cantilenas usually chose to ignore the chant melody associated with the texts they set. Continental composers, in contrast, usually paraphrased the chant melody in their cantilenas, perhaps because of habits developed while composing the many new liturgical chant settings of the 1440s and 1450s.[14]

Continental cantilenas with chant

We saw the beginnings of the continental cantilena in Bologna Q15, and there are quite a few new examples in the Trent Codices and Modena X.1.11. Most of the pieces paraphrase the chant in the discantus. While the elaboration is sufficient to make the discantus resemble a freely composed melody, the tunes are so familiar that it is not difficult to detect them; two of the pieces even have chant incipits.

Of the nine pieces listed in Table 9.2, six are settings of the four great Marian antiphons (two *Salve reginas*, two *Regina celis*, an *Alma redemptoris*, and an *Ave regina celorum*). *Anima mea* is of course another Marian antiphon from the *Song of Songs*; Du Fay's setting combines multiple generic references, as we saw in chapter 6, but I have included it here because it sets a chant commonly used by English composers. Binchois's motet is a setting of the "other" *Ave regina celorum*, also a votive Marian antiphon; Binchois paraphrases the chant in the first two phrases and then drops it with a rather English casualness. *O sacrum convivium* is a *Magnificat* antiphon for Corpus Christi that was not set by English composers; its use of two contrasting mensurations, however, distinguishes it from a purely functional chant setting.

Roughly speaking, one can trace a development in these pieces from a musical style derived from that of the cut-circle motet toward a more English style. The first three continental cantilenas with chant in Table 9.2 use the

Table 9.2. *Three-voice continental cantilena-style motets in the Trent Codices and Modena X.1.11*

	Concordances; comments
Cut-circle motets	
Brassart, Te dignitas	Q15, 87.49
Brassart, O flos fragrans	Q15, 87.129, Ox 213
Sarto, O quam mirabilis	Q15, 922.1528, Ox 213
Sarto, Ave mater, O Maria	Q15, 922.1529
Lymburgia, Ave mater nostri	Q15, 922.1530
Du Fay, Flos florum	Q15, Mod, Ox 213
Du Fay, O beate Sebastiane	Q15, Mod
Du Fay, O proles/O sidus	87.88, 88.347, Mod
Du Fay, Ave virgo quae	92.1393, MuEm
L. de Arimino, Salve cara	87.144
Verben, O domina gloriosa	87.150
Declamation motets	
Grossin, Imera dat hodierno	Q15, 92.1481, B2216, Ox 213, Par 4379, MuEm
Lymburgia/Du Fay, Veni dilecte my	Q15 (@Lymburgia), 87.100 (@Du Fay), Aosta (@Du Fay)
Du Fay, Ave regina celorum (I)	Q15, 87.138, Ox 213, Par 4379, Ven

Continental cantilenas
With chant:

Brassart, Regina celi	OØ	87.158–59; chant incipit, par. in D
Du Fay, Anima mea	[Ø]	Q15, 87.142, Ox 213; chant par. in all voices
Du Fay, Alma redemptoris II	O	922.1532, Mod; chant in D, looks like cut-circle
Du Fay, Ave regina celorum II	O¢O	Mod, 88.443, MuEm; chant incipit, par. in D
Binchois, Ave regina celorum mater	O	Mod; chant in D, 1st 2 phrases
Anon., Salve regina	OC	93.1653; chant in T; A section repeats
Anon., Regina celi	¢	88.363; chant par. in D up a step; T only in Alleluias
Anon., O sacrum convivium	O¢	88.489; chant incipit, par. in D
Anon., Salve regina	O¢OØ	89.730; chant par. in D

Without chant:

Dupont, Salve mater misericordie	OCC	92.1495
Anon., Salve regina peccatorum	O	Mod; Ct. in ¢
Anon., Advenisti/Advenit	¢C¢	88.394; Motet, bishop of Trent, 2 texts

Table 9.2. (*cont.*)

		Concordances; comments
Touront song motets		
O gloriosa regina	¢	91.1298, Strah, Cas@, etc. (11 MSS)
O florens rosa	O	88.426@, Strah
Compangant omnes or O generosa	O,C2,3	89.579, 91.1336, Spec@, Strah, Bol Q16 96&94
O castitatis lilium or Advocata	O3O3O	89.599, Spec@, Glog (Advocata)
Anon., O dulcis Jhesu memoria	O3	89.777
Unica that look like 3-v. chansons, but no explicit evidence: must consider motets		
87.141	L. de Arimino: Primi pulchri (2 vv.)	Ballade?
87.111	Protegat nos divina maiestas	?
93.1836	Christus deus	R4?
93.1840	Virgo Maria non est tibi	Strophic?
93.1844	Bene ad te coclea	R4? (text incipit only)
90.989	Altissimi Dei	R4?
90.1078	O beate Sebastiane	Eng. Ballade?

cut-circle rhythmic language. Brassart's *Regina celi* uses the cut-circle mensuration sign in contrast with a section in regular perfect tempus, and Du Fay's *Anima mea*, although it has no mensuration sign, shows many of the signs associated with Ø, especially imperfect modus organization (Besseler chose to transcribe it in 6/4). Du Fay's *Alma redemptoris II* uses the regular perfect tempus sign (O), but it has all the signs of cut-circle writing, complete with the typical minim melismas and fermatas for the final phrase (Ex. 9.1).[15] There is also a central section written in black coloration, but mensurally organized in perfect tempus. Perhaps Du Fay was trying out a new way of notating the usual ØOØ form. This piece is also inventive in other ways: Du Fay took the traditional chant incipit and paraphrased it into an opening eight-measure solo for the discantus.

Du Fay's *Ave regina celorum II*, in contrast, looks very much like the Band II English cantilenas. The mensural pattern is typical for English cantilenas, and the opening and closing sections in perfect tempus have none of the cut-

Example 9.1 Du Fay, *Alma redemptoris (II)*, mm. 18–26 (DufayB, vol. V, 118)

circle mannerisms. We see here the usual English rhythmic flexibility, with constantly shifting groupings that obscure the meter, long phrases that keep you guessing about when and where they will end, and a rhythmic drive to the cadence. Band II traits include a homogeneous texture and integrated duets for all voices (Ex. 9.2). One duet even has imitation at the fifth, while none of the earlier continental cantilenas has any duet at all.[16] Du Fay's version of the English style may have a bit more sense of direction and of rhythmic vitality (note the sequence in the duet, mm. 73–7), but it is remarkable how close he gets to the "contenance angloise."

Binchois is the only continental composer with conflicting attributions to English composers, and his style is often considered English in orientation; his setting of the "other" *Ave regina celorum* is no exception, though as usual his motet is less ambitious than Du Fay's.[17] The anonymous pieces in Trent 93, 88, and 89 also adopt elements of English style, while combining them with other traditions. *O sacrum convivium* and the *Salve regina* in Trent 93 are fairly simple chant settings in the basic OC mensuration pattern with no duets. This *Salve regina* is the only one of the continental cantilenas to put the chant in the tenor: the paraphrase is not elaborate, but it is more varied than the equal-note settings we find in some of the later Trent Codices, or than the very simple cantus firmus in Du Fay's *Alma redemptoris I* (Q15.224). The *Regina celi* setting uses only one mensuration sign, a progressive ₵, but divides the piece into four sections according to the form of the text. Each section begins with a lengthy duet, because the tenor voice enters only for the last word of each section ("Alleluia"). The form of this piece thus resembles that of some three-voice tenor motets (e.g. *Ascendit Christus*) to be discussed below in chapter 10, even though here the chant is paraphrased in the top voice.

The *Salve regina* from Trent 89 has the typical English flexibility of rhythm and acceleration toward the cadence. The section in imperfect tempus

Example 9.2 Du Fay, *Ave regina celorum (II)*, mm. 62–81 (DufayB, vol. V, 122)

includes lengthy duets characterized by lots of parallel thirds and sixths and quite a lot of imitation, often (as in Du Fay's *Ave regina celorum II*) involving melodic sequence. The contratenor is usually lower than the tenor, and has an unusual amount of fourth and fifth leaps after the manner of a later bass line; this gives the piece a more "modern" sound, even though most of the major cadences still use the old leaping contratenor formula. This piece moves the English style in the direction of a more energetic, directed style characterized by rhythmic sequence.

Continental cantilenas without chant

This may not be a real category. Dupont's *Salve mater misericordie* and the anonymous *Salve regina peccatorum* are probably English. *Salve mater* is found in the middle of the twelfth fascicle of Trent 92–1, otherwise devoted to English motets, and it has the highly unusual mensural pattern of Power's *Quam pulchra*. I suspect that it is only the French sound of the composer's name that has kept this piece off the lists of English music. The anonymous *Salve regina peccatorum* was identified as English by Charles Hamm, even though it appears in the continental motet section of Modena X.1.11.[18] Neither of these texts has been identified, though both sound like glosses on *Salve regina* (rather like the text of Dunstaple's *Salve regina mater mire*, found only in Modena X.1.11).

Advenisti/Advenit, in contrast, is definitely a continental work, though possibly one with limited Central European circulation. The piece appears in

Trent 88 with two texts under the discantus part. The lower text is somewhat larger and clearer; the higher text looks as if it was squeezed in on top of the first. The original, larger text (*Advenisti*) is that of a Central European processional song known as the *canticum triumphale*, in which the Old Testament prophets greet Christ at the harrowing of hell after the Resurrection. The song was used in Easter processions and for the reception of secular rulers (including Sigismund, King of the Romans, in 1414). As here, *Advenisti* was often followed by a duple-meter trope or verse, ideal for marching, that begins *Triumphat Dei Filius*.[19] Close inspection reveals that the added text (*Advenit*) is an adaptation of the lower one designed to include local references to Trent, and probably refers to the return of Bishop Georg Hack to Trent sometime during his tenure there (1445–65).[20]

I have not been able to find the original *Advenisti* and *Triumphat* melodies, but I suspect that this piece is a setting of both the text and melody of this processional song and its trope.[21] The style throughout is extremely simple, much of it barely elaborated fauxbourdon, with a slight elaboration during the brief section in major prolation (C). The setting of the trope text at the end is even simpler, with an almost inanely repetitive melody in the top part. It lacks the contratenor, which can however be supplied by fauxbourdon. This is believable as processional polyphony to be sung by clergy of limited musical ability; while it helps to nail down Trent 88's provenance in Trent, *Advenisti* does not have much to do with the more general development of the continental cantilena.

Probable contrafacta

The three-voice Latin-texted works I have listed as probable contrafacta are short, unambitious works, most of which look at a glance like chansons, due to their use of double bars and/or prominent central cadences. I have listed them here, however, because the blurring of the generic boundaries resulting from the practice of contrafacture helped make possible mutual stylistic exchanges between the cantilena-style motet (both English and continental) and the chanson. The expansive, flexible approach to rhythm that arrived on the Continent with the English cantilenas made its way into the mid-century chansons of Du Fay, Ockeghem, and Busnoys; a more rhythmically animated continental version of that style with frequent imitation then made its way into chansons, instrumental tricinia, and the three-voice motets of Touront.[22]

It is often impossible to determine what the original form of a piece was: a prime example is Caron's *Helas que pourra devenir*, known in Glogauer as *Der seyden schwanz*, but also provided there with a Latin text, *Ave sidus clarissimum*. Frye's and Touront's motets were both profoundly informed by developments in chanson composition (just as the cut-circle motet had been) – and chanson composition was assuredly influenced in turn by the three-voice motet.

Touront's song motets

The origins and biography of Johannes Touront remain a mystery. His music appears in so many Central European sources (especially the Strahov and Speciálník codices) that most scholars assume that he worked in the region. He may be the "Johannes Tirion" named in Sarto's funeral motet for the Habsburg Albrecht II, *Romanorum rex*; this would put him in the Imperial chapel as early as 1439 (though perhaps only as a choirboy, as Strohm suggests). Trent 88 is probably the earliest source for his music, so he cannot have begun composing much before the early 1450s.[23]

Much of Touront's music, like the Central European repertory in general, is found with different texts (or no text) in different sources, so that it is often difficult to determine the original form of a composition. David Fallows has identified several new Touront concordances and contrafact texts.[24] The style of Touront's compositions often resembles that of chansons and tricinia, but no complete French text has been found for any of the compositions. Touront also wrote cantiones, similar in style to the motets, making it hard to draw clear generic distinctions. This difficulty is understandable, given that Touront's works show the influence of the chanson, the instrumental tricinium, the cantio, and of Frye's English cantilenas. I have called these Touront pieces (plus *O dulcis*) song motets because of their stylistic affinities with chansons such as Caron's. The five works listed in Table 9.2 lack the central fermatas or barlines that seem to shout out "I am a chanson in a *forme fixe*" found in so many of the attested contrafacta; I therefore believe that these Touront works started life as motets.

Like Frye, Touront uses a low contratenor, with fairly frequent "5–1" cadences, and he has very few duets, preferring a continuous three-voice texture like that of the chanson. His texts are brief votive antiphons to the Virgin, and even when there is an associated melody Touront does not use it. Touront's most famous work, *O gloriosa regina*, joined *O pulcherrima* and Frye's

Ave regina celorum as a song motet appearing in chansonniers far outside the Central European orbit (it is found in eleven manuscripts). Touront's motets are later than Frye's, and they exhibit several style features that we associate with the 1470s and the works of Busnoys, Martini, and Isaac, rather than with the earlier repertory. Especially striking in Touront's three-voice motets is the extensive use of imitation (often in all three voices), and sequential passages based on staggered rhythmic motifs.

Touront's *O florens rosa* sets a text also used by Frye, and both motets are found in the Strahov Codex as well as in the Trent Codices. Both composers use a single mensuration, and begin with a textless introduction ending with a fermata; they also use the same clefs (C2, C4, F4, with a low contratenor) and final (D).[25] It is certainly possible that Touront knew the Frye composition, and took it as a model. Nevertheless, there are also substantial differences between the works. Frye's setting is divided into three extremely melismatic sections (the work is 334 semibreves long). Touront's, in contrast, is quite concise (192 semibreves). The approach to text setting is actually closer to that of Frye's more famous *Ave regina celorum mater*. Touront takes the rhythmic flexibility typical of English music and injects it with a new vitality and dynamism, just as Du Fay did in his *Ave regina celorum II*.

One of David Fallows's additions to the Touront corpus is *O castitatis lilium* (89.599), a modest work that appears in the Glogauer Liederbuch with a different text (*Advocata*), and has an attribution to Touront in the Speciálník Codex.[26] It is in perfect tempus throughout, but includes tripla sections in which the voices bounce along in a meter equivalent to perfect tempus, major prolation. The anonymous *O dulcis Jhesu* is very much in the same style, so I have grouped it with the Touront motets, few of which are attributed in the Trent Codices.

Touront's most ambitious three-voice motet is found in Trent 89 with the text *Compangant omnes*, but in most other sources with the text *O generosa nata David* (Ex. 9.3). It is a bipartite work with the OC mensurations standard in the big four-voice motets of the 1460s, and it ends with a brief tripla section.[27] The motet begins with deliberate rhythmic ambiguity: both outer voices move in colored breves, and only the tenor hints at the actual meter. The hemiola (three against two) at the breve level gives way in m. 4 to hemiola (two against three) at the semibreve level, everyone speeds up, and they all land on a perfect breve, but without a real cadence. The piece seems to start over again in m. 11 with a metrically unambiguous subject for imitation at the

Example 9.3 Touront, *Compangant omnes* (Trent 89.579, 123'–124)

Example 9.3 (*cont.*)

fifth between tenor and discantus. The imitation continues with a dotted figure over the bar; this figure is then taken up by the discantus and transformed into a descending sequence that is four minims long and off the beat. Standard cadence formulas are avoided – instead the voices come to rest for a moment, poised before setting off on another frantic forward drive.

The end of the English cantilena

The 1430s and 1440s could be called the age of the English cantilena. Just as England dominated France during most of this period, the English cantilena assumed the dominant position in the continental motet repertory. Many of its features – the single top voice, pre-existent devotional text, and the homogeneous melodic style with integrated duets associated especially with the Band II *Song* settings – became typical of the motet as a whole over the next several decades.

Continental composers began by adopting the three-voice format and Marian subject matter of the English cantilena; only gradually did they learn to imitate the flexible, floating, almost ametrical English approach to rhythm and melody. As continental composers developed their own cantilena-style subgenres they separated out the sacred and song-like elements that are so closely entwined in the English cantilena. In the continental cantilena the sacred is emphasized by the frequent use of clear chant paraphrase. In the cut-circle motet of the 1420s and 1430s, and later in the Touront song motet of the 1460s, continental composers adopted the melodic language of secular music, choosing texts with weak or non-existent melodic associations and avoiding reference to chant melodies. Frye's exceptionally song-like English cantilenas provided a model for Touront, while Touront's more directed, energetic musical language points toward developments in the last quarter of the century.

The 1450s saw the departure of the English from the Continent, as well as the emergence of four-voice writing as the norm for sacred polyphony. Although three-voice motets continued to be composed, they were now found more often with chansons than with other motets. The age of the cantilena-style motet had come to an end, after fundamentally changing the nature of the motet on the Continent.

10 Motets with a tenor cantus firmus *c.* 1430–1450

It was relatively easy to trace the continued evolution of the three-voice cantilena-style motets in chapter 9, since their basic texture stays the same. Things are more complex when we turn to the motet-style motet and developments in four-voice writing in mid-century. The various oppositions and threads of development (English and continental, three- and four-voice, with and without cantus firmus, with and without isorhythm) become tangled. I have chosen to divide the repertory into works with tenor cantus firmus and freely composed works for more than three voices. In this chapter I focus on works of the first group, which trace the strongest line of descent from the great English and French traditions of isorhythmic motet composition. I begin with the motets closest to the Q15 repertory: the four-voice isorhythmic motets in which the top voices are in the same range (Table 10.1). I go on to consider four-voice works in which the upper voices are not in the same range: here I consider both English and continental works (Table 10.2). I turn then to a new non-isorhythmic subgenre, the three-voice tenor motet (Table 10.3). I end with the first major four-voice cantus firmus work without isorhythm, the anonymous English *Missa Caput.* Although I concentrate on works found in the earlier Trent Codices (87, 92, 93 and 90) and Modena X.1.11, I also include other contemporary pieces, in order to provide a comprehensive look at the surviving examples of these subgenres.

Table 10.1. *Four-voice isorhythmic motets in the Trent Codices and Modena X.1.11 with triplum and motetus voices in the same range*

MS	Composer	Texts	Concordances
(a) Panisorhythmic			
87.37	Du Fay	Vassilissa ergo gaude	Q15.244, Ox 213
87.143	[Du Fay?]	Elizabeth Zacharie	
Mod	Dunstaple	Gaude virgo salutata	
89.590	Anon.	O sacrum manna	
(b) Free upper voices			
87.29	Brassart	Ave Maria/O Maria	Q15.229
87.53&70	Du Fay	Ecclesie militantis (5 vv.)	
Mod	Anon.	O pia virgo Fides	

Isorhythmic motets

Four-voice isorhythmic motets with the top voices in the same range

Of all the isorhythmic motets in the Trent Codices and Modena X.1.11, the motets in this group (see Table 10.1) are the closest in style to the Q15 isorhythmic motets, and several of them are concordant with Q15. I have divided them into those that are panisorhythmic (meaning that the upper voices repeat their own rhythms when the tenor repeats its talea) and those with free rhythms in the upper voices. The two panisorhythmic motets in Trent 87 are the earliest (*Vassilissa* was composed in 1420, and *Elizabeth* resembles it closely).[1] *Gaude virgo salutata* is the only fifteenth-century English motet to use the double-discantus texture; perhaps Dunstaple was imitating continental models.[2] *O sacrum manna* combines English and continental features; probably composed in the 1430s or 1440s, it was the last isorhythmic motet to be copied in the Trent Codices, appearing in Trent 89 (1460s).[3]

The use of free upper voices in the other three motets (Table 10.1b) may be a progressive feature. Brassart's *Ave Maria* shows Italian influence, and may have been composed in the 1420s, but the others are works of the 1430s. *Ecclesie militantis* was composed *c.* 1431, and breaks new ground with its five-voice texture, since it has three lower voices (a texted contratenor and two

207

tenors); we will return to it below. The talea design of the anonymous *O pia virgo fides* shows English influence, according to Michael Allsen, suggesting a relatively late date.[4] The small number of double-discantus isorhythmic works in these sources suggests that interest in this combination of texture and form was declining in mid-century.

Four-voice isorhythmic motets with unequal triplum and motetus

While early fifteenth-century continental isorhythmic motets invariably had triplum and motetus parts in the same range, this was not the case in England, where the triplum was usually higher than the motetus. In three-voice works motetus and tenor are generally in the same range, with clefs a fifth below the triplum; in four-voice works the clef of the motetus is a third below the triplum, with various different clef combinations for the lower voices.[5] Although most of the surviving English isorhythmic motets seem to have been composed in the 1420s, they were generally not known on the Continent until the 1430s, judging by their representation in continental sources (they appear first in the Basel sources Trent 92 and Aosta). Beginning in the 1430s continental composers began to experiment with different ranges in the triplum and motetus parts, probably inspired largely by English works.[6] They also introduced range differentiation in the lower voices, as we shall see. I list here (see Table 10.2) all the surviving four-voice isorhythmic motets with triplum and motetus voices in different ranges (including one work, Sarto's *Romanorum rex*, that appears only in Aosta).

I have divided the pieces into those in which the lower voices are labeled as tenor and contratenor and those in which they are both labeled tenor. Many of these motets are occasional, and can be dated with some precision; I have listed the pieces in their probable chronological order within each group. All of these works are true four-voice works, with essential contratenors or second tenors that support fourths between the other voices.

In the three Dunstaple works the motetus voice is approximately a third lower than the triplum (with C1 and C2, or C2 and C3 clefs), which is enough to minimize crossing of the upper voices, and to allow each voice to establish a distinct range. Compare, for example, the duets opening Dunstaple's *Veni/Veni* and Du Fay's *Rite majorem* (Ex. 10.1a–b). In the Dunstaple motet the motetus generally remains below the triplum. In the Du Fay motet the upper

Table 10.2. *Four-voice isorhythmic motets with unequal triplum and motetus*

	[Tr.	Mot.]	T	Ct.
Tenor and Contratenor:				
Dunstaple, Preco/Precursor (1416) (Cant 128, 922.1538, Mod)	C1	C2	_C4_	C4 *(in-between values)
Dunstaple, Veni sancte/Veni creator (1420s) (OH, 922.1537, Ao, Mod, Mu 3224)	C1	C2	_C3_	C3
Binchois, Nove cantum (1431) (Mod, incomplete)	C2(Quad.)	C4(Tr.)	_C4_	C4 (Mot.)
Du Fay [Anon. ?], O gloriose tiro (Mod)	C1	C2	_C4_	C5
Sarto, Romanorum rex (1439) (Ao, Del Lago)	C1	C3 (Ct.1)	_C3_	C4 (Ct. 2)

		[Tr.	Mot.]	Ct.	TI	TII
Two tenors:						
Free Tr. & Mot.						
Dunstaple, Salve scema (1421?) (Mod)		C2	C3		_C4_	_F3_
Du Fay, Ecclesie militantis (1431) (87.53&70)	X	C2	C2	C4	_C4_	_C4_ (chant)
Du Fay, Nuper rosarum flores (1436) (92.1381, Mod)	X	C1	C3		_C4_	_C3_ (chant)
Du Fay, Salve flos Tuscae gentes (1436) (Mod)	X	C2	C4		_F3_	_F4_
Du Fay, Moribus et genere (1442) (Mod)		C1	C3		_C3_	_C4_
Du Fay, Fulgens iubar (1442–47) (Mod)		C1	C3		_C3_	_C4_

		[D]	Ct.	TI	TII
Anon., Missa Caput (G, C, S) (Trent 93, etc.)	X	C1	C3	_C3_	C4

Key:

__ under a clef/voice label indicates that the part uses long notes (maximas, duplex longs, longs, breves).

All dates are approximate.

Example 10.1 Contrasting introitus sections

(a) Dunstaple, *Veni/Veni*, mm. 1–12 (Dunstaple, 88)

(b) Du Fay, *Rite majorem*, mm. 1–9 (DufayB, vol. I, no. 11)

voices are in the same range and the voices cross frequently, trading off the leading role.[7]

When we turn to the ranges and rhythmic activity of the lower voices we see several different approaches even in the English works. The clefs of the tenor and contratenor voices of Dunstaple's *Preco/Precursor* and *Veni/Veni* are the same, but the contratenor spends quite a lot of time below the tenor. In *Salve scema* the second tenor is a third lower than the cantus-firmus-bearing tenor, which becomes a middle voice. The result is that each voice is in a different clef and has its own range, although the voices are close enough that a fair amount of crossing still goes on.

The degree of rhythmic activity of the contratenor/second tenor is different in each of these works. The two tenors of *Salve scema* have the same rhythmic character. In *Preco/Precursor* the rhythmic character of the contratenor is similar to that of the tenor, but it moves faster at times. In *Veni/Veni* the contratenor is much closer in character to the upper voices, and carries its own text. In some passages of this motet the range differentiation and rhythmic activity of the different voices resembles that of the later four-voice tenor motet, in that each voice has its own range and the long-note tenor functions

Example 10.2 Dunstaple, *Veni/Veni*, mm. 121–35 (Dunstaple, 91)

as a middle voice (see Ex. 10.2, especially mm. 129–34).[8] The total range (C1, C2, and C3 clefs) is very compressed, however, and the isorhythm imposes a rhythmic rigidity lacking in later freely composed four-voice motets.

These English four-voice motets thus provided examples of new approaches to motet textures for continental composers. The new elements included different ranges for the triplum and motetus voices, and the possibility of contrasting ranges and rhythmic profiles for the two lower voices. The principal composer to exploit these new approaches was Du Fay, who adopted and adapted features found in Dunstaple's works. Binchois and Sarto also produced four-voice isorhythmic works with new approaches to texture that had implications for the future of the motet.

Like Dunstaple's, the continental motets in Table 10.2 have contrasting clefs and ranges for the triplum and motetus voices. But while the clef of Dunstaple's motetus is always a third below the triplum, the clef of the continental low motetus is invariably a fifth below the triplum (as in the English three-voice isorhythmic motet). Sometimes the continental motetus voice crosses below both tenors and functions as a low contratenor. In these continental isorhythmic motets we see the motetus voice being transformed into a contratenor voice, usually a contratenor altus in the middle of the texture, but sometimes a contratenor bassus.

Most of Du Fay's late isorhythmic motets also have two voices labeled tenor rather than the usual tenor/contratenor pair. Both "tenors" move very slowly, and are governed by the same isorhythmic and mensural manipulation. This two-tenor voice-label scheme is actually used two different ways. In *Nuper rosarum* and *Ecclesie militantis* the second tenor, like the first, carries chant, and in fact lies higher in range than the first tenor.[9] In Du Fay's last three four-voice isorhythmic motets, on the other hand, the second tenor label is used for a voice with freely composed pitch materials like a normal contratenor, but with a lower range than the tenor and long note values, as in Dunstaple's *Salve scema sanctitatis.*[10] The label "tenor" had multiple meanings in the early fifteenth century: it was a voice with pre-existent material (cantus firmus), usually in long notes; it was a freely composed low voice essential to the counterpoint, as in chanson-format pieces, or three-voice motets. Both meanings are operative in the last three Du Fay motets: both tenors have long notes, both are essential to the counterpoint, so both are called tenors, even though one is pre-existent and one is newly composed.

The ranges of these low second-tenor pieces begin to approximate those of the later tenor motet: they have a single top voice, two middle voices, and a voice below the tenor. The extreme rhythmic differentiation between fast upper voices and the slow tenors, however, is very different from the more homogeneous four-voice texture found a few decades later. Furthermore, the tenors' rests often alternate in all of the two-tenor pieces, so for much of the time only one tenor is sounding. The result approaches a three-voice texture like that of Du Fay's *Magnanime gentes.*

In the three continental motets that use a contratenor rather than a second tenor, however, the contratenors have faster rhythmic values than the tenors and approach the level of rhythmic activity shown by the upper voices, as in Dunstaple's *Veni/Veni. Ecclesie militantis* can be included in this group since it has an active contratenor voice in addition to its two tenors. Each of these works labels its voices differently, and has a slightly different approach to texture. *Ecclesie militantis* and the incomplete *Nove cantum* (both of which refer to events of 1431 in their texts) use the standard combination for the early fifteenth century of two clefs a fifth apart (C2 and C4), and have three texted voices (as in *Veni/Veni*).

	Nove cantum	*Ecclesie militantis*
C2	Quadruplum	[Triplum and Motetus]
C4	Triplum & Motetus	Contratenor
	Tenor	2 Tenors

Binchois's texted voices are labeled Quadruplum, Triplum, and Motetus; Du Fay's are the unlabeled Triplum and Motetus and the contratenor. The results are very different: Du Fay uses two active voices at the top while Binchois uses two active voices at the bottom. Still, both can be seen to be experimenting within the range and clef constraints that were normal for the early fifteenth-century motet.

O gloriose tiro's clefs and ranges (C1, C2, C4, C5) are almost identical to those in Dunstaple's *Preco/Precursor*, with the exception of the contratenor, which has a lower clef than the tenor, and moves faster. Both contratenors have wide ranges, however, and spend time both above and below the tenor. *O gloriose tiro*'s mensural scheme (perfect tempus followed by imperfect: OC) is fairly uncommon in isorhythmic motets (most have more than two sections), and resembles the pattern coming into favor in mid-century. The attribution of *O gloriose tiro* to Du Fay in its one source, Modena X.1.11, is generally discounted because the work is so different from the composer's other motets, and because of occasional poor counterpoint; whatever the status of the attribution, the work's single top voice, active contratenor, expanded range (with clefs extending from C1 to C5), and mensural scheme provide important precedents for the motets of the 1450s and 1460s.[11]

Romanorum rex has the same cleffing as Du Fay's last two isorhythmic motets (C1, C3, C3, C4), but unlike those works (and like *O gloriose tiro*) it has an active contratenor part. Only the top voice is texted (though the second voice does have a fairly extended text incipit, perhaps indicating that this voice should be texted as well). The old motetus voice is now labeled first contratenor and the old contratenor is labeled second contratenor, as in the four-voice motets of the second half of the fifteenth century. Most of the tenor tacet passages are for three voices (as in *O gloriose tiro*), but there are occasional duets for the top two voices. The cleffing and texture of this work are remarkably similar to those of the early four-voice Masses and many of the four-voice motets of the 1450s and 1460s (see Ex. 10.3). The basic mensural layout is also typical of these later works, with the first half in perfect tempus, then a change to imperfect tempus, and a final return to perfect tempus for the end (OCO). Only the complex isorhythmic scheme, including isorhythmic patterning in the upper voices, marks *Romanorum rex* as a work of the 1430s.[12]

All these works are isorhythmic, but a few limit the isorhythm to the tenors. Neither *Nuper rosarum* nor *Ecclesie militantis* has isorhythmic triplum and

Example 10.3 Sarto, *Romanorum rex*, mm. 25–35 (Brassart, 44–5)

motetus voices, since their taleae are set up so that they never repeat in the same mensuration.[13] For most of *Salve flos* the upper voices are isorhythmic – except in the last section, where they break free, for a dramatic florid conclusion. In the first two works, then, Du Fay designed the structure to provide rhythmic and melodic freedom for the upper voices; in the last he made the departure from the rhythmic scheme into an exciting formal device.

The use of isorhythm in these works looks back to the venerable history of the isorhythmic motet. In their experimentation with voice function, labels, and rhythmic profiles, and their use of range differentiation, they look to the future of the four-voice motet. Many of the new features appeared first in Dunstaple's motets, but were extended and adapted in the hands of continental composers. Rob Wegman has suggested that the new four-voice texture with a low contratenor is first found in Du Fay's last isorhythmic motets, *Fulgens iubar* and *Moribus et genere*, and these works do have the high, two middle, and low voice ranges found in the *Caput* Mass.[14] But the "low contratenor" in these works – labeled as a second tenor – is so slow, and so tightly constrained by the isorhythmic structure, that it is quite different from the rhythmically active low contratenor of later four-voice works. I believe that *O gloriose tiro* and *Romanorum rex* are more convincing precedents for the new four-voice texture with low contratenor. Not only cleffing, but mensural usage, the contratenor's faster note values, and its independence from the tenor bring them very close to the later works.[15]

Inspired by English music, and especially by Dunstaple's motets, Du Fay and Sarto fundamentally altered four-voice composition in their late iso-rhythmic motets. No longer was the motet-style motet about competition and exchange between the two top voices in the same range – now the focus was on the extended melody of the single "lyric top voice," as Brothers calls it.[16] Range differentiation extended to the lower voices as well: these motets have an essential contratenor (or second tenor) lower than the tenor voice. Each of the outer voices moves in its own pitch space; although the middle voices (motetus and tenor) cross, they are differentiated by rhythmic motion.

These are still isorhythmic motets composed for state occasions, however, and their traditionally hierarchical layered character was maintained by the rhythmic contrast between the tenors and the upper voices in the two-tenor pieces, and/or by the use of panisorhythm. It is in the three-voice tenor motet, a predominantly English genre with close ties to the isorhythmic motet, that we find the first devotional non-isorhythmic motets with tenor cantus firmus.

The three-voice tenor motet

Examples of the three-voice tenor motet are found primarily in the twelfth fascicle of Trent 92–1, a collection of English motets (these are marked on Table 10.3 as being in 92–12). Some are also found in the English motet section of Modena X.1.11, with a few concordances in Trent 92–2 or Aosta (see Table 10.3).[17] Most are English, but there are some continental works, possibly written in emulation of English models. I list examples from later in the century, but I will limit the discussion to the eleven earlier works.[18] To illustrate my discussion of the subgenre I will refer to the anonymous *Regali ex progenie/ T: Sancta Maria virgo* (Trent 92–1.1494; see Ex. 10.4).

The subgenre of the three-voice tenor motet has not been previously rec-ognized, probably because of its ambiguous position between the three-voice English isorhythmic motet and the English cantilena.[19] The clef configuration of the three-voice English isorhythmic motet is identical to that of most English cantilenas (voice labels in brackets are not provided in the manu-scripts):

3-v. English isorhythmic motet			English cantilena
[Triplum]	C1	C2	[Discantus]
[Motetus]	C3 or C4		Contratenor
Tenor	C3	C4	Tenor

Table 10.3. *Three-voice tenor motets*

MSS	Composer	Texts T:	Clefs [D Ct.] T	Mens.	Comments
92–12	Anon.	Regali ex progenie (A)	C1 C3 C3	[O]	
		T: Sancta Maria virgo (A)		₵C	
92–12	Anon.	O sanctissime (R)	C2 C3–4 C4	OCO	Duet in middle
		T: O Christi (A)			section
Mod	Dunstaple	Ascendit Christus (A)	C1 C3 C3	[O]	Faster T
OH	Forest	T: Alma redemptoris (A)			

"Isorhythmic" tenors:

MSS	Composer	Texts T:	Clefs [D Ct.] T	Mens.	Comments
92–12	Anon.	Hac clara/Hac clara	G2 C2 C3	C	T 2x, 2nd dim.
		T: Nova (all one S)			
92–12	Dunstaple	Specialis virgo (A)	C1 C3 C3	Ø	*Talea* 2x +intro&coda
Mod		T: Salve parens (S)		₵	no opening duet
92–1	Dunstaple	Veni/Consolator (S)	C2 C4 C4	[O]C	T: 1–sic jacet,
Mod		T: Sancti spiritus (S)			2–inverted, 3–retro
92–1	Du Fay	Supremum est (1433)	C1 C3 C4	Ø₵3Ø	Starts w/ fauxbourdon
Q15, Mod, etc.		(*Tenor mostly free*)	(Fb "C2")		T isorhythmic
Mod	Du Fay	Magnanime/Nexus (1438)	C1 C3 C3	[O]CØ	T: 4x, 12:4:2:3
		T: Haec est vera (R)			+ intro and coda

New tenors (?)

MSS	Composer	Texts T:	Clefs [D Ct.] T	Mens.	Comments
Mod	Dunstaple	Salve regina mater mire	C2 C4 C4	[O]CO	Long duos in O sections
		T: *No incipit*; long notes			
Mod	Sandley	Virgo prefulgens	C2 C4 C4	[O]CO	
92–2	Winchois	T: *No incipit*; long notes			
92–2	Merques	Castrum/Virgo viget	C1 C3 C4	[O]	T may not be pre-existent
Ao		T: Benedicamus			

Three-voice tenor motets from later sources

MSS	Composer	Texts T:	Clefs [D] T Ct.*	Mens.	Comments
88	[Frye?]	Salve virgo mater	C1 C2 C4	[C]	K of Frye's Mass on
		T: [Summe trinitati] (R)			same T in Br 5557
89	Anon.	Ave vivens hostia	C2 C4 C5	O₵	2a *pars*, T long note
		T: *No incipit*			
91	Anon.	Alma redemptoris (A)	C2 F4 C3	₵₵	Ch. paraphrase in D
Apel		Ts: Alma end; ARC (As)			
Canti C					
Br 5557	Busnoys	Anima mea (A)	C3 F5 F5	C	T rests beginning,
CS 15		T: Stirps Jesse (R)			middle

* Note change in order of voices (as T becomes the middle voice)
Key: Mens. = mensuration. 92–12 = the twelfth fascicle of Trent 92–1.

The three-voice tenor motet uses this same clef combination (see Table 10.3 and Ex. 10.4), and combines features of both genres. Three-voice tenor motets have two texted voices like the isorhythmic motet's triplum and motetus: four have different texts, seven have the same text. Most have a foreign tenor (a pre-existent tenor based on chant with a text or text incipit different from those of the other voices). In Example 10.4, *Regali ex progenie*, the two upper voices carry the same text, a very common antiphon used for Marian feasts. The tenor carries the text and melody of a rarer antiphon used for the same feasts, *Sancta Maria virgo intercede.*[20] It is not isorhythmic, but consists primarily of a simple long-note presentation of the chant, with some livelier passages in the second half of the piece. Its values must be augmented in relation to the upper voices, which have perfect tempus throughout (making this an example of English "pseudo augmentation").

Five of the eleven motets have been considered isorhythmic motets because of their "isorhythmic" tenors, which manipulate repeated material. But these motets lack the proportional patterns typical of English isorhythm (6:4:3 or 3:2:1), and none of them exhibits the isorhythm or isoperiodic phrasing in the upper voices typical of isorhythmic motets.[21] Overstressing isorhythm has obscured the similarities among these three-voice tenor motets.

Both English isorhythmic motets and cantilenas generally include duets, during which the rhythmic profiles of the two voices are about the same: take a duet out of context and it would be difficult or impossible to identify the subgenre from which it came.[22] Three-voice tenor motets generally begin with an extended duet, with another duet after the midpoint. In this they resemble the later Band II *Song* cantilenas, and the English isorhythmic motets in which the tenor talea begins with rests. In *Regali ex progenie* the tenor is divided into two halves, of identical length: the first half in imperfect tempus, major prolation (₵, or C-dot), the second half in imperfect tempus, minor prolation (C).[23] Each half begins with an eight-measure duet for the upper voices, and then has a shorter duet later before a more protracted three-voice section (see Ex. 10.4).

The lack of isorhythm and the single lyrical upper voice of the three-voice tenor motet recall the texture of the English cantilena, especially when the tenor speeds up (as it often does, especially toward the end of a piece: see Ex. 10.4, m. 75 to the end). Without the constraints of isorhythm the motetus/contratenor voice is free to change roles and styles. *Regali ex progenie* alternates between two textures. While the tenor rests, the upper voices have lively duets in a rhythmically animated style. They share rhythmic and

217

Example 10.4 Anon., *Regali ex progenie*/ *T: Sancta Maria* (Trent 92.1494, 134′–135)

Example 10.4 (*cont.*)

melodic motifs without strict imitation. The three-voice sections, in contrast, have a treble-dominated texture in which the rhythmic style of the middle voice is closer to that of the tenor. It dips below the tenor only occasionally and is never required to harmonize fourths between discantus and tenor.[24] Texturally, then, this work looks in two directions. In the three-voice sections it resembles an English cantilena, with a single upper voice over two somewhat slower lower voices in the same range. The piece as a whole, on the other hand, resembles an English isorhythmic motet: it has two texted voices over a pre-existent tenor with a contrasting text in long note values. The middle voice plays two roles: it is an inessential contratenor in the three-voice sections, and an essential motetus in the duets.[25]

This double role of the middle voice is reflected in the voice labels in continental manuscripts. Text-bearing voices (triplum and motetus in the isorhythmic motet, discantus in the cantilena) are generally not labeled, and the disposition of the voices on the page is different in English and continental manuscripts. This sometimes led to confusion on the part of continental scribes, who also expected the motetus voice of a motet-style motet to be in the same range as the triplum.[26] In the three English pieces on the list with the best claim to be considered isorhythmic motets (*Hac clara die* and Dunstaple's *Specialis virgo* and *Veni/Consolator*), the scribe of Trent 92 added the label "Contratenor" to the motetus voice.[27] These labels seem to have been an afterthought, because they are not written under the music, but added in the margin or above the staff. The motetus voice thus begins to be perceived as a contratenor, at least by continental scribes (and possibly by continental composers as well).

Three-voice tenor motets must be distinguished, however, from chant settings (English and continental) in which the chant is in the tenor voice. These include Dunstaple's *Crux fidelis* (in which the chant is actually in the contratenor), Du Fay's *Alma redemptoris* I and *Anima mea liquefacta est* (in which the chant is paraphrased in all voices), and an anonymous *Salve regina* (Trent 93.1653). These works lack the duets and bipartite structure of the three-voice tenor motets, and the text of the tenor cantus firmus can easily be sung by all three voices; I include them with the cantilena-style motets discussed in chapter 9 (see Tables 9.1 and 9.2).

Contrasting approaches to the subgenre

The three-voice tenor motets, although they share a basic approach to texture and construction, also display a wide variety of approaches. Almost every work finds a different balance between cantilena and isorhythmic motet. Most of the completely non-isorhythmic pieces on the list have been considered English cantilenas in spite of peculiarities of texting and texture. Cantus firmi have not been identified in Dunstaple's *Salve regina mater mire* and Sandley's *Virgo prefulgens*, and the voices do not appear to resemble chant melodies. Both, however, have long-note tenors and lengthy duets at the beginning and in the middle; both also have otherwise unknown poetic motet-like texts to the Virgin underlaid in the discantus and contratenor parts. Even if these works do not have pre-existent tenors, texturally and formally they count as three-voice tenor motets.

Ascendit Christus/T: Alma has a pre-existent tenor, but presents it in short note values like those of the other voices. The paraphrase technique in the tenor voice resembles that usually used for the upper voices of chant-bearing cantilenas, and the character of the tenor voice is not that of a cantus firmus. Although the piece remains throughout in perfect tempus, it divides into two halves, each of which begins with a lengthy duet almost the same length as the three-voice section that follows: 2vv. (30 mm.); 3vv. (26 mm.); 2vv. (24 mm.); 3vv. (28 mm. + L). This kind of structure, in which the tenor rests for half of the piece (54 mm. out of a total of 108), resembles that of some English isorhythmic motets, in which the tenor talea begins with rests for a substantial portion of its total length (a "talea introduction").[28] The homogeneous texture of this piece, in which all voices use similar kinds of rhythmic and melodic motion, is closer to the cantilena than to the isorhythmic motet; the structure and form, with a foreign tenor and extensive duets beginning each half, are closer to the isorhythmic motet.

Although most of the three-voice tenor motets appear to be English, there are also examples by the continental composers Merques and Du Fay, both of whom were at the Council of Basel;[29] the three-voice tenor motet may have first appeared on the Continent there. The texts of the upper voices of Merques's *Castrum/Virgo/T: Benedicamus* are those of a thirteenth-century motet based on the "Flos filius" tenor; the tenor may be freely composed.[30] Like most of the other three-voice tenor motets it divides into two halves, each of which begins with an extended duet; the two texts of the discantus and contratenor (or triplum and motetus) make it look even more like an isorhythmic motet. The tenor starts with long values and speeds up toward the end, as in *Regali ex progenie*. By borrowing old motet texts Merques evokes the new subgenre's connection with the past.

Du Fay's *Magnanime/Nexus* and *Supremum est* are usually considered isorhythmic, though they lack isorhythm in the upper voices. We have already discussed the multiple generic referents of *Supremum est*; suffice it to say here that its texture and form also resemble those of several of the other three-voice tenor motets. Although the tenor of *Magnanime/Nexus* undergoes a fairly complex scheme of mensural reinterpretation, it is designed in such a way that isorhythm in the upper voices is impossible, since there is no repetition of the tenor talea within any one mensuration.[31] The overall effect is of a tripartite three-voice tenor motet, with a form similar to that of *Salve regina mater mire* and *Virgo perfulgens*.

The three-voice tenor motet and the English tenor Mass

The three-voice tenor motet, while combining features of the English cantilena and the isorhythmic motet, is perhaps closest in style and construction
to the English three-voice cantus firmus Mass. Both use a foreign cantus firmus
and lack isorhythmic organization in the upper voices. Both use a variety of
approaches to tenor construction (including some tenors that may not be pre-
existent).[32] And both have the same texture, with two texted voices about a fifth
apart and a long-note tenor in the same range as the lower texted voice.[33]

The tenor treatment in *Regali ex progenie*, for example, is very similar to that
of Power's *Missa Alma redemptoris mater*: both use "pseudo augmentation," and
in both the tenor is divided into two equal sections in ₵ followed by C. In
most of Power's Mass the upper voices change to duple mensuration to
accord with the tenor for the second half, but in much of the Sanctus and all
of the Agnus the discantus voice remains in O, and for part of the Agnus both
upper voices have O against the tenor's C, as in the motet (see Ex. 10.4).[34] Both
works are also characterized by rhythmic conflict or tension between the
tenor and the other voices. Although theoretically the mensurations in the
first half coincide, the presence of colored notes in the tenor voice means that
the beginnings of tenor notes frequently fail to coincide with the perfections
(or barlines) in the upper voices (see Ex. 10.4, mm. 12, 14, 25–6, 30, 32).
During the second half the tenor is working in multiples of two against the
triple meter of the upper voices. The upper voices of both works also exhibit
constant displacement of rhythmic figures and rhythmic flexibility. The result
is a suspension of audible metrical organization, resolved at the moments of
stasis at the beginnings and ends of the three-part sections. This almost ametrical style is typically English, as we have seen in Forest's *Alma redemptoris
mater* (Ex. 4.3). In Power's Mass and in *Regali ex progenie*, however, the seeming
irrationality is encompassed by overall symmetry, since the tenors both divide
into two halves of equal length.[35]

Another similarity between the three-voice tenor motet and the three-
voice cantus firmus Mass is the approach to form. Most movements from the
early cantus firmus Masses use the mensuration patterns OC or OCO (or O₵,
O₵O); if OCO, the final return to perfect tempus is significantly shorter than
the opening section.[36] These are favorite patterns for the English cantilena
too, but they become almost mandatory for fifteenth-century Mass move-

ments. The same can be said of the three-voice tenor motets. Five of the eleven early pieces use some version of the OCO mensuration pattern (sometimes with diminution). *Regali ex progenie,* as we have seen, is essentially in OC, given the tenor augmentation, as are *Crux fidelis* and *Veni/Consolator.* The four pieces with no change of mensuration are still bipartite, with a major cadence near the midpoint and followed by a duet to begin the second section, or a bipartite isorhythmic structure.

The relationship between Mass and motet is further demonstrated by one of the later three-voice tenor motets, *Salve virgo mater,* found in Trent 88 (mentioned in chapter 8 as a sacred contrafactum). It shares its tenor with Walter Frye's Mass cycle *Summe trinitati,* and is probably a contrafact of the Mass's original troped Kyrie. On the Continent, however, it was copied as a motet independent from the Mass, and became a potential model for other motets. Although the tenor of this motet carries the text of the other parts in the manuscript and does not use long notes (making it resemble the tenor of *Ascendit/T: Alma*), it is still a foreign tenor. It has now moved into the middle range (note the clefs in Table 10.3), and there are occasional fourths between it and the discantus, as it moves to the fifth degree in cadences.[37]

In the three-voice tenor motet, as in the early English cyclic Masses, we see many of the features of the later four-voice tenor motet: pre-existent cantus firmus with optional rhythmic organization, a single discantus voice distinct in range from the lower voices, and a tenor that occasionally lies in the middle of the texture. The old motetus voice of the isorhythmic motet has become a contratenor: contratenor altus, as in *Regali ex progenie,* or even contratenor bassus, as in Frye's *Salve virgo.* Developments in the English Mass and the motet were interdependent: on the one hand, the independent motet *Regali ex progenie* shares approaches to style and structure with Power's *Missa Alma redemptoris*; on the other hand, Frye's Kyrie is transformed into a motet in continental sources.

The *Caput* Mass and the *Caput* texture

No four-voice non-isorhythmic motet with a single discantus voice and a tenor cantus firmus appears in the earlier Trent Codices (87, 92, 93, and 90) or in Modena X.1.11, although there are several in Trent 88. Some of the four-voice isorhythmic motets provided promising precedents to the four-voice tenor motet – but they were all isorhythmic. The three-voice tenor motet had all the required ingredients except for the fourth voice. Are there any examples of the new non-isorhythmic four-voice texture with a tenor cantus firmus before the motets in Trent 88? The connections between the three-voice tenor motet and the three-voice cyclic Mass point toward the four-voice cyclic Mass as a possible source of this new texture. Rob Wegman and Reinhard Strohm have recently stressed the importance of the widely disseminated anonymous English *Missa Caput* as the first four-voice cyclic Mass with a low contratenor. They suggest that it may have arrived on the Continent first in the southern Netherlands, perhaps Antwerp, in the late 1440s.[38] The Mass's earliest surviving source is Trent 93, copied *c.* 1451–5, where three of its movements are found in a group of six Masses copied at the beginning of the Mass Ordinary section of Trent 93 (see the bottom of Table 10.2). Strohm has suggested that these were the six Masses sold to the singer Jean Philibert in Ferrara in 1447, and that they were subsequently brought to Trent in the early 1450s; Wegman, on the other hand, proposes that the Mass was copied in Cambrai in 1448, and then moved on to Trent.[39] Whatever the status of these speculations, there is little doubt that *Caput* is the first non-isorhythmic work with the high/two middle/one low scoring (C1, C3, C3, C4) copied on the Continent. Other Masses and motets using this scoring first appear in Trent 88, copied in the late 1450s and early 1460s.[40]

The texture, structure, and style of the *Caput* Mass can be seen as a mixture of elements derived from the three-voice tenor motet, the three-voice tenor Mass, and the four-voice isorhythmic motet with a single discantus.[41] It is often said that the cyclic Mass took over the techniques developed for the iso-rhythmic motet; this may be true in part, but it is not the whole truth, as we shall see.[42]

The form of each movement of the *Caput* Mass is the common bipartite structure, moving from perfect to imperfect tempus (OC) (as in most of the earlier three-voice English cyclic Masses and many of the tenor motets there is no final return to perfect tempus). The tenor melody, derived from chant, is heard twice in each movement (this is known as double cursus), but there is no proportional or mensural transformation: the tenor pitches are provided with completely new rhythms for the second half. Rests, cadences, and choice of long versus short notes differ in the two halves.[43] While repetition of the tenor pitch material or color is reminiscent of isorhythm, the deliberate differences between the two rhythmicizations marks the *Caput* technique as

fundamentally different from isorhythm's proportional or mensural transformation.[44]

Each half of each movement of *Missa Caput* begins with a fairly lengthy
rhythmically animated duet for the top two voices. This recalls the introitus
and "talea introduction" of isorhythmic motets, many of which begin with
extended duets for the triplum and motetus; it also recalls the duets that open
each half of most three-voice tenor motets. Unlike English isorhythmic "talea
introductions," however, the lengths of the duets in *Missa Caput* vary in
unpredictable ways from section to section and movement to movement.[45]
After the opening duet there is alternation between tutti sections and duets in
which all the voices, including the tenor, are involved. No longer are the roles
and functions of each voice type sharply differentiated: all the duets are of a
similar character. This is a major step toward the homogeneous texture of the
High Renaissance.

During the tutti sections the texture changes to a treble-dominated texture
of a faster top voice over three slower supporting voices.[46] The tenor has more
longs than the other voices, and virtually no minims (there is one minim close
to the end of the section in perfect tempus), but the contrast in rhythmic
values between the tenor and the upper voices is not immediately obvious, as
it is in the opening sections of isorhythmic motets. The moderate pace of the
tenor (not extremely slow) contributes to the sense of a homogeneous style,
and makes possible the duets involving the tenor. The rhythmic style of the
second tenor (or low contratenor) is closer to that of the high contratenor
than it is to the tenor (as in *O gloriose tiro* and *Romanorum rex*). The rhythmically flexible "melodic garlands" (as Bukofzer calls them) of the discantus float
freely and almost unpredictably in the English cantilena style, very different
from the stiffer, more regimented upper voices of pan-isorhythmic motets.
The treble-dominated texture is much closer to that of the tutti sections in
Regali ex progenie – i.e., like that of the English cantilena – than it is to the stratified two fast/two slow voices of most four-voice isorhythmic motets.

The main thing that *Missa Caput* has in common with the four-voice isorhythmic motets, in fact, is the four-voice texture (see Table 10.2). As in the
isorhythmic motets the second tenor/low contratenor is essential, and there
are numerous fourths between the tenor and both upper voices (including the
initial tenor entrance in the Kyrie on b-natural).[47] Like *Caput* in its earliest
source, many of the motets in Table 10.2 use a two-tenor designation; many
have a high/two middle/low texture; and three use the identical cleffing (C1,

C3, C3, C4). The second tenor is a low contratenor, and rarely crosses above the tenor, even at the final cadences to each section, most of which have "5–1" motion in the contratenor (this contrasts with the isorhythmic motets, where 5–1 cadences are quite rare).[48] This "modern" 5–1 cadence is often combined, however, with 4–5 motion in the first contratenor, resulting in a dissonant 4/5 cadence like that in Lymburgia's *Tota pulchra* (Ex. 6.3c); evidently some aspects of four-voice writing had not been completely worked out.[49] Still, the *Caput* texture (as Strohm calls it) looks to the future in important ways.

It is hard to know whether the anonymous composer of *Missa Caput* could have known the continental isorhythmic motets of the 1430s and early 1440s, since as far as we know music traveled from England to the Continent and not vice versa. Perhaps the *Caput* composer independently came to a solution similar to that of Du Fay and Sarto, by adding the low second tenor of Dunstaple's *Salve scema* to the C1, C3, C3 texture of the three-voice tenor Mass and motet. Or perhaps he acquired some of the continental pieces from English friends who had been on the Continent, or even attended the Council of Basel. Although *Missa Caput* is the first non-isorhythmic four-voice piece with a single discantus, a low contratenor, and a tenor cantus firmus, there are precedents for almost every individual aspect of its style and texture. As we will see, the *Caput* Mass would go on to be an important formal and textural model for the Mass and the motet for the next three decades.

This chapter has described how three different kinds of English music influenced the development of the motet on the Continent. Their novelty, the timing of their arrival, and the importance of England in European power politics of the period all contributed to their impact on continental composers. A large amount of English music reached the Continent for the first time in the early 1430s at the Council of Basel. Among this music may have been Dunstaple's isorhythmic motets and the English three-voice tenor motets. Du Fay was at Basel, and Sarto may have been; their experimentation in the 1430s with the texture of four-voice isorhythmic motet appears to have been inspired by the motets of Dunstaple. The English three-voice tenor motet, found first in the Basel manuscript Trent 92, is the first devotional non-isorhythmic motet with tenor cantus firmus. The continental examples of this subgenre are by Du Fay once again and by Merques, another composer known to have been at Basel. The *Caput* Mass arrived in Antwerp more than a decade later and was quickly disseminated and imitated. Its bipartite structure and high/two-middle/low scoring became standard for later Masses and motets. All three of these English genres – isorhythmic motet, three-voice tenor motet, and cyclic Mass – would go on to contribute essential features of structure, form, and style to the four-voice tenor motet of the second half of the fifteenth century.

II Freely-composed four-voice writing in transition

In this chapter we will examine the four-voice motets without cantus firmus found in the earlier Trent Codices (TR+, 93, and 90), in Modena X.1.11, and in a few fragmentary sources. Most of these works are representatives of sub-genres we have already examined (double-discantus motets, cut-circle motets, or English cantilenas); several are three-voice works to which a fourth voice was added later. The diverse approaches to four-voice texture found in these works are suggestive of a period of experimentation, and point to some of the ways in which the new four-voice textures of the second half of the century were created.

The end of the double-discantus texture

Two upper voices in the same range were standard for four-voice pieces on the Continent from *c.* 1415 to *c.* 1430; tenor and contratenor were also in the same range (with clefs a fifth lower than the upper parts). Virtually all of the four-voice motets in Q15, Du Fay's earlier isorhythmic motets, Brassart's four-voice motets, and many others use this double-discantus texture, which was a defining feature for continental motet-style compositions for three and four voices, both isorhythmic and free. Although it became less and less popular during the 1430s and 1440s, and essentially died out in the 1450s, the double-discantus subgenre continued to evolve during the period (see Table 11.1). I have included in this Table a few additional pieces found in later manuscripts (Trent 88 and the Ferrara fragment), since they seem to be the last representatives of this subgenre and are best discussed here.[1]

The double-discantus pieces can be divided into several different types,

Table 11.1. *Double-discantus motets copied in mid-century*

MS	Composer	Texts	Concordances; comments. mensurations
Q15, 87	Du Fay	Anima mea	Ox 213
Q15, 87	Velut	Summe/Summi	Retrospective double-discantus
92–2	Anon.	Gaude Dei genitrix	Ox 213; resembles Summus Secretarius, Q15.275
87	Brassart	Fortis cum quaevis	Ox 213. [Ø]
87	[Brassart?]	Lamberte vir inclite	Aosta. [Ø]OØ
87	[Brassart]	Christi nutu sublimato	Aosta2x, MuEm. O
88	[Quadris]	Gaudeat ecclesia	ØO₵O
92–1&2	[Power]	Ave regina celorum	Q15, Ao, Ob26
Mod	Power	Gloriose virginis	F112bis
	Anon.	Ibo michi ad montem	MuEm, Ithaca
88, Mod	Du Fay	Mirandas parit	88: Imperatrix angelorum. [Ø]₵. Imitation. 3vv.
88	Anon.	O sidus Hispanie	5 vv. O₵

according to style and probable origin. The first two are found also in Bologna Q15, and were discussed in chapter 6. The anonymous *Gaude Dei genitrix* is very close in style to one of the other double-discantus motets in Q15, Brassart's *Summus secretarius*: they begin almost identically and use similar harmonic and melodic language throughout. These two resemble the devotional double-discantus motets, in that they use the [Ø] mensuration and features of the cut-circle musical language, especially the minim melismas (here passed back and forth between the upper voices), and they lack extended duet sections (unlike Brassart's other motets). Yet *Gaude Dei genitrix* and *Summus secretarius* are also substantially different from the devotional double-discantus motets in other ways. They have longer notes in the lower voices, less suited to carrying text; they have D finals, resulting in a more sober tone; they lack Italianate echo imitation; and they have new texts.

Brassart's other three double-discantus motets form the next group, along with *Gaudeat ecclesia*, a motet attributed to Johannes de Quadris in Gaffurius.[2] These works, while they also use the cut-circle musical language, have extended duet sections for the discantus voices at the beginning and once or twice in the body of the work. They also use minim declamation, often on repeated notes, in rhythmic unison or in alternation between the discantus voices.[3]

Extended duet sections for the discantus voices are not found in the Q15

Italian and devotional double-discantus subgenres, though they are common at the opening of isorhythmic motets. They are also found in English double-discantus motets, only three of which survive: Power's widely disseminated *Ave regina celorum* (it survives in four sources) and his *Gloriose virginis*, plus an anonymous *Song* setting in MuEm, *Ibo michi ad montem* (see Table 11.1).[4] *Ave regina celorum* begins both sections with duets for the discantus voices and includes one internal duet in the first section; *Gloriose virginis* lacks the opening duet, but includes a central duet for the two discantus parts (in addition to duets for first discantus and tenor, and second discantus and contratenor). The use of duets is characteristic of English music in all genres, and Brassart may well have been inspired by these examples.

In Brassart's double-discantus motets in the Trent Codices, then, we can see a further evolution of the devotional double-discantus motet, away from the Italianate *Song* settings of Q15 and toward the larger scale and variety of texture found in the isorhythmic motet or the English double-discantus motet. This subgenre, then, continued to evolve after Q15, but by the mid-1440s it faced the same extinction as the isorhythmic motet.

The last two double-discantus motets in Table 11.1, and probably the last to be composed, are Du Fay's three-voice *Mirandas parit* and the anonymous five-voice *O sidus Hispanie*. Both use the mensuration plan that became standard in mid-century, perfect followed by imperfect tempus (OC), although the perfect tempus in *Mirandas parit* still retains traces of cut-circle writing. *Mirandas parit* is characterized by extensive imitation in three voices. Like so many of Du Fay's works in this period it is a hybrid, combining the imitative Italianate cut-circle language of the Q15 devotional double-discantus motets (and the three-voice texture that was probably the original form of most of those pieces) with an occasional text in classical hexameters and a forward-looking approach to form and to integration of all three voices in the texture.[5] *O sidus Hispanie* is a five-voice work, with two discantus parts over three lower voices; we will return to it below.

Fewer and fewer works with two upper voices in the same range were composed around mid-century; four-voice works from the second half of the century almost always have a single discantus over three lower voices. Double-discantus texture thus looks to the past; it is to the four-voice motets with a single discantus that we must look for the origins of the new motet style of the second half of the century.

Transitional freely composed motets with a single discantus

Four-voice non-isorhythmic motets with a single discantus are surprisingly rare in the first half of the century (see Table 11.2). In addition to the relevant works from the manuscripts TR+, 93, 90, and Modena X.1.11, I have included in Table 11.2 the single example from Bologna Q15 (Hugh de Lantins's *Ave verum corpus*), a five-voice double-discantus work from Trent 88 (*O sidus Hispanie*), and three pieces found only in contemporary English sources. I have also included works that appear in some sources with only three voices. The resulting list includes only ten motets, three of which were definitely written originally for three voices, and three more may have been (their fourth voices look like later additions, and are marked with an asterisk in square brackets in Table 11.2). As isorhythm and the double-discantus texture died out *c.* 1450, four-voice motet composition almost ceased: there is only one motet composed originally for four voices in the mid-century manuscripts Trent 93 and 90 (Johannes Puyllois's *Flos de spina*, to which we will return).

Most of the ten motets listed in Table 11.2 come out of the English cantilena tradition (of the anonymous works, only *O sidus Hispanie* is believed to be continental). They have relatively short sacred texts, most of which are Marian, some of them antiphons, but virtually all of them lack pre-existent musical material. Three consist of a single section in one mensuration (O: perfect tempus); most have two or three sections in contrasting mensurations, after the manner of most English cantilenas. Of these, four have perfect tempus followed by imperfect (OC or OCO), the preferred mensural sequence in mid-century. They all lack isorhythm or other large-scale rhythmic organization. The texture of these works is quite homogeneous: all the voices have the same basic rhythmic and melodic style. The top voice may be somewhat more active than the others, and duets also tend to use smaller note values, but there is none of the hierarchic distinction between lines that we find in isorhythmic motets or even in three-voice tenor motets. This is a different musical world from that of the large-scale isorhythmic motet, with its polytextuality and multiple sections governed by strict proportional relationships. How does this cantilena tradition contribute to the development of the four-voice motet in mid-century?

At first glance Table 11.2 seems to show a bewildering variety of cleffing patterns, and there can be little doubt that here, as in the late isorhythmic

Table 11.2. *Transitional four-voice non-isorhythmic motets with a single discantus*

	[D]	T	Ct(1)	Ct2	Final	Mensurations
(a) Two clefs, two ranges						
H. de Lantins, Ave verum corpus (Q15)	C1	C4	C4	C4	F	[Ø]
(b) Tenor in the middle						
Du Fay, O proles/O sidus (87, 88, Mod)	C1	C3	C4	C4[*]	G	ØOØ
Frye, Ave regina, (90.1086, etc.)	C1	C3	C4		F	O
Added voice: 90.1013	(c-dd)	(E-f)	(C-d)	C1* (b-dd)		
Added voice: Verona 757				C3* (G-bb-flat)		
Added voice: Spec				C3* (F-f)		
(c) Tenor on the bottom	[Tr.	Med.	Ct.	T]		
Dunstaple, Descendi (2 Eng. Frags.)	G2	C2	C4	C5	C	[O]
Anon., Cantemus Domino/T: Gaudent (Eg)	G2, C1	C2	C4	C5 (chant)	F	[OC]
(d) Tenor on the bottom, 3 vv.	[D]	Ct(1)	T	Ct2		
Anon., O sidus Hispanie (88; 5 vv.)	C1,C1	C4	C4	C3[*?]	F	OȻ
Plummer, Anna mater (Oc87)	C1*	C3	C4	C4	F	OCO
Anon., O pulcherrima (93, etc.)	C2	C3–4	C5		D	O
Added voice: 88, Sched (mm. 1–24)	(G-aa)	(C-f)	(A-a)	C4–5* (A-e)		
Anon., Anima mea (90)	C2	C4	F3		D	CO
	(a-aa)	(C-e)	(A-b)			
4th up, rewritten: 89, Mu 3154	C1	C2	C4	F4*	G	CC(2v)Ø
	(d-dd)	(G-a)	(D-e)	(F-b-flat)		
Puyllois, Flos de spina (90)	C2	C4	F3	F3	D	OȻ
(Strah, CS 15, Milan 1)	(a-cc)	(C-f)	(A-c)	(A-d)		

Key: * = added or optional voice; Tr. = Triplex; Med. = Medius (English voice labels).

motets, there was a great deal of textural experimentation. On closer scrutiny, however, certain patterns appear. I have divided the motets into four groups, based primarily on cleffing patterns.

Two clefs, two ranges

In the first group, consisting only of the early *Ave verum corpus*, a single discantus voice is accompanied by a tenor about an octave below and two contratenor voices in the same range as the tenor. This is a cut-circle motet that uses
the usual discantus/tenor contrapuntal framework; the first contratenor per-

forms the usual tasks of connecting sections, adding rhythmic momentum, and supplying fifths at cadences. The piece works well without the second contratenor, but the voice has none of the contrapuntal problems that usually mar later additions. Here we have a composer experimenting with four-voice textures within the range and clef constraints of a normal three-voice cut-circle motet.

Most of the Q15 repertory uses only two clefs, usually a fifth apart (C1 and C3), sometimes a seventh, as in *Ave verum corpus*. When a voice was added (to a two- or three-voice original) it was usually in the same range and clef as one or more of the original voices: a new contratenor in the same range as the tenor, a second discantus in the same range as the first. In the first third of the fifteenth century voice-crossing was the norm. While voice-crossing continued to be practiced throughout the fifteenth century, voice ranges gradually became more differentiated over the course of the century as the total range of compositions expanded.

Tenor in the middle

The second group in Table 11.2 consists of two three-voice works to which a fourth voice (or voices) has been added. In the case of Frye's *Ave regina celorum* three different fourth voices are found in three different sources; in the case of the Du Fay motet, the same fourth voice is found in all sources, but it shows signs of being a later addition or perhaps an experimental afterthought on the part of the composer. In both pieces the original three-voice texture already demonstrates range differentiation, with the tenor voice in the middle and a low contratenor.

Once again Du Fay seems to have been in the forefront of experimentation on the Continent. His *O proles/O sidus*, a setting of two antiphons in honor of St. Anthony of Padua, is essentially a cut-circle motet with the common ∅O∅ mensuration plan and a fermata section. It is probably the earliest piece in Table 11.2 after *Ave verum corpus*.[6] The work is unusual in that it has not one but *two* low contratenor voices.[7]

Examination of the second contratenor reveals that it is cleverly integrated into the texture: it fills in the middle voice in some double leading-tone cadences, and participates in one set of imitative entries (Ex. 11.1: mm. 79–82). Nevertheless, it is completely inessential, both contrapuntally and texturally. When both discantus and tenor are sounding, they form a self-contained duo,

Example 11.1 Du Fay, *O proles/O sidus*, mm. 79–83 (DufayB, vol. I, 18)

and make cadences together in the usual manner (by moving in contrary motion to the octave). Both discantus and tenor rest occasionally in this piece (though never at the same time): when one rests, the first contratenor makes cadences with the remaining voice. Although the second contratenor causes no problems, it also plays no structural role: it never moves sixth to octave in cadences with discantus or tenor, nor does it harmonize fourths above the tenor.[8] Furthermore, the second contratenor is always present when discantus or tenor rests, thus turning all the duets into trios (Ex. 11.2: mm. 16–26). It was presumably easier to add the contratenor to sections with two voices than to those with three, but the lack of duets is atypical for the period; I find that the piece works better with only three voices.[9]

The distribution of texts in *O proles/O sidus* is also odd: discantus and tenor have one text, the two contratenors have the other.[10]

[D]: O proles   Ct. 1 O sidus
T: O proles   Ct. 2 O sidus

This texting looks more normal if we eliminate the second contratenor and consider the discantus and first contratenor as triplum and low motetus, after the manner of the three-voice tenor motet.

[Tr.]: O proles   [Mot.]:   O sidus
T: O proles   [Ct. 2 ---- O sidus]

The result is two different texts for triplum and motetus, while the tenor, which is not pre-existent, carries the triplum text by default. The manuscript layout accords with this proposal, in that discantus and first contratenor are in the positions usually held by triplum and motetus.

Like so many of Du Fay's motets, *O proles/O sidus* combines features of many different subgenres of the motet. The form (ØOØ) and the rhythmic and melodic language are closest to the cantilena-style cut-circle motet. The

Example 11.2 Du Fay, *O proles/O sidus*, mm. 14–26 (DufayB, vol. I, 15–16).

use of polytextuality recalls the motet-style motet and the three-voice tenor motet. The antiphon texts and duet (or trio) sections recall features of English music. But the free four-voice texture is something new, a first attempt at a four-voice texture with a single discantus voice. The experiment does not seem to have been a success from an evolutionary point of view (I know of no other work with exactly this texture), but the isolation of an upper voice over three lower voices and the use of the low contratenor do point toward later developments.

Frye's *Ave regina caelorum* has three different added voices. In one of the earliest sources for the piece, Trent 90, the work appears twice: once for three voices (90.1086), and once for four (90.1013). Two of the later sources (Verona 757 and Speciálník) also include a fourth voice. The addition of a fourth voice to a three-voice composition both provided a way of experimenting with different textures, and exemplifies one possible method for original composition in four voices.

The added voice in Trent 90 is probably a later addition to the manuscript (perhaps added in order to differentiate this copy of the piece from the other one in the manuscript). Although it is a second discantus part, in the same clef as the discantus, it is copied on the bottom-right side of the opening in a different hand.[11] The resulting four-voice texture is that of the old-fashioned double-discantus motet; the technique is the same as in the four-voice version of Lantins's *Tota pulchra*. Whoever added the voice looked to the past for textural models rather than experimenting with lower contratenor parts.

235

The two later fourth voices are both in the same clef as the tenor voice. This results in a texture with single high and low voices and two middle voices, one of which is the tenor (essentially the *Caput* texture). The added voices behave quite differently, though. The Verona voice spends much of its time near the top of its range, and occasionally crosses with the top voice (it often has the same pitches as the added voice in Trent 90). The Speciálník voice spends more time at the bottom of the range, and crosses with the contratenor. Both of these voices are fairly awkward, obvious fillers, with many ungainly leaps and no clear sense of direction.

The first half of the Speciálník version ends with the 4/5 cadence that we saw at the end of Lymburgia's four-voice *Tota pulchra* (Ex. 6.3) and in the *Caput* Mass, resulting in a seventh just before the resolution. The transitional dissonant cadence form was thus no longer deemed appropriate for the *end* of a piece by the time the Speciálník voice was composed (perhaps in the 1480s?), though it was still possible for an internal cadence.

Ave regina celorum is a typical song-format composition, with a contrapuntally complete discantus–tenor duet. Its original contratenor was presumably added after the two-voice framework; others then added new fourth voices. There are no duets or contrasts in texture: all voices sing throughout. The results are sometimes clumsy or busy, but they demonstrate the changing preferences in four-voice textures: from a saturated upper register with two discantus parts toward more saturated middle and lower registers.

More than three voices with the tenor on the bottom

In the third group, consisting of two motets found only in English sources, the tenor is the lowest voice, the contratenor slightly higher. The triplex voice of *Cantemus Domino* splits into two for the duets that open each section; once the other voices enter there is only one triplex voice, in the G2 clef. *Cantemus Domino* is also the only piece in this group to have a tenor cantus firmus; I have included it here as another example of the English approach to four-voice writing.[12] Both *Descendi* and *Cantemus Domino* include lengthy duets, but while *Cantemus* duets are restricted to the upper voices, in *Descendi* every voice participates in a duet at some point during the piece. *Descendi* also paraphrases the chant antiphon from which it takes its texts during the first several bars, after which it is freely composed. Several features in these two works appear progressive: they seem to have been conceived from the start for four voices; each voice has its own clef, resulting in relatively little voice-crossing; and the overall range (from G2 to C5 clefs) is quite broad. Nevertheless, this particular approach to four-voice texture, with the tenor alone at the bottom of the texture, does not seem to have been used on the Continent.[13]

Tenor on the bottom, three voices

In this final group of pieces the tenor is on the bottom of the original three-voice texture. The basic cleffing pattern for discantus, contratenor, and tenor is C1, C3, C4 for F-final pieces, C2, C4, C5(=F3) for D-final pieces. The position of the fourth voice varies.

Anna mater matris Christi has a comment in its one source, an English fragment, to the effect that the top voice ("triplex") is optional.[14] The piece is set up so that the two voices that approach the octave in the few four-voice cadences are the tenor and the second voice down; it is also true that the top voice does not participate in imitation as much as the three lower voices. The three-voice version would thus consist of three low voices, with the tenor and one contratenor in the same range. On the other hand, the top voice is integrated into the texture, involved in duets with the other voices, and often in imitation, so the piece would feel rather thin without it. I think the motet was probably conceived in four voices, but composed so that it would still be performable if the choirboys were absent. It spends long sections over F pedals, to lovely effect. This is one of the first pieces with the high/middle/two low, four-voice texture.

O sidus Hispanie is the five-voice double-discantus work that we mentioned above. The second contratenor, copied last on the page, is higher than the tenor and first contratenor, which may be because the voice was added later. If we reverse the order of the two contratenors, however, the cleffing of the motet is the same as that of *Anna mater*. The basic texture of this work looks back to the Italian or double-discantus motet, with two imitative active voices on top, while tenor and first contratenor have long notes and cross frequently. The second contratenor (like the contratenor in *Ecclesie militantis*, Du Fay's five-voice isorhythmic motet) has a rhythmic profile like that of the upper voices, though it does not join their imitative exchange. The broader total range, the use of three distinct ranges, with two voices at the bottom of the texture, and the bipartite O¢ mensural pattern – all of these features look to the future.

The two anonymous English settings of *Song of Songs* antiphons, *O pulcher-rima* and *Anima mea*, were originally for three voices but are also found in four-

Example 11.3 Anon., *O pulcherrima*, mm. 1–24, three- and four-voice versions (3 vv.: Trent 93.1838, 368′–369; 4 vv.: Trent 88.239, 69′–70, Sched 39′–40)

voice versions.[15] The motets are rather similar: both have D finals, both begin with fairly extended duets for the discantus and contratenor (as do so many of the English Band II *Song* settings of the Plummer generation) and the flexible asymmetrical rhythms are typically English. The total range of the first contratenors are just about the same (*O pulcherrima*'s is C–f, while *Anima mea*'s, C–e: see Table 11.2d). But *O pulcherrima*'s contratenor spends more time at the top of the range, returning to the f repeatedly, resulting in a slightly more plangent tone (see Exx. 11.3 and 11.4); it also uses more imitation, almost completely absent from *Anima mea*. *O pulcherrima* is a modest composition, in only one section (like Frye's *Ave regina*), and its status as a "song motet" is attested by its appearance in numerous chansonniers later in the century. *Anima mea* is a more ambitious piece, with a much longer opening duet and two sections in different mensurations.

In *O pulcherrima* the second contratenor is a rather clumsy addition, with a

238

very broad range (A–e), equal to that of the tenor and the first contratenor. The added voice careens from the top to the bottom of its range, fits in wherever it can find a place, and turns all the duets into trios (see Ex. 11.3).

The transformation of *Anima mea* for four voices was much more extensive (see Ex. 11.4). The discantus–tenor duet is contrapuntally complete in both versions, and the contratenor is not essential in the three-voice version. In the four-voice version the discantus and tenor are transposed up a fourth, and the contratenor is rewritten to fit with an added low contratenor (and partially rewritten even in the opening duet: see Ex. 11.4, mm. 7 and 12). The rewritten high contratenor has numerous fourths above the tenor, making the low contratenor essential (Ex. 11.4, mm. 19–21, marked with an asterisk). A new duet was added in the middle (using a repeated phrase of text), increasing the size of the work temporally as well as sonorously. It is thus possible to build a motet with an essential low contratenor around the discantus–tenor duet of the three-voice cantilena motet, although it involves adapting the original contratenor as well as adding a new voice.

The result is, as far as I know, the earliest surviving example of a motet with ranges corresponding to soprano, alto, tenor, and bass clefs (SATB, C1, C3, C4, F4), the standard clef-combination for four-voice music in the sixteenth century, and on up to Bach.[16] This four-voice version of *Anima mea* is at least a decade later than any of the other motets we have looked at so far, seeing as it is found in Trent 89 and Munich 3154 (it was probably composed in the early 1460s). The author of the adaptation was a skilled composer, and there is no way of knowing whether he was English or continental. This example is a vivid illustration of how a large-scale multipartite four-voice motet typical of the 1460s or 1470s could develop out of an English cantilena.

Flos de spina

The last motet in Table 11.2, Puyllois's *Flos de spina*, appears to be the earliest surviving non-isorhythmic continental motet with a single discantus voice originally conceived in four voices. With the exception of the four-voice arrangement of Frye's *Ave regina celorum* this is the only four-voice motet in Trent 90, the first of the Wiser manuscripts. The next, Trent 88, contains half-a-dozen four-voice motets in a similar style, and there are almost twenty in Trent 89. Since this then appears to be one of the very first examples of this new kind of motet, it is worth considering its composer, style and its precedents at some length (see Ex. 11.5).[17]

Example 11.4 Anon., *Anima mea*, mm. 7–21, three- and four-voice versions (3 vv.:
Trent 90.1046–1047, 334′–335′; 4 vv.: Trent 89.640, 195′–197)

Example 11.5 Puyllois, *Flos de spina* (Trent 90.1122, 434′–436)

Example 11.5 (*cont.*)

Example 11.5 (*cont.*)

Johannes Puyllois

Who was Johannes Puyllois, and when might he have written this motet? Recent research by Pamela Starr has provided us with a rich portrait of the composer, while Gerald Montagna has emphasized his importance for the development of the chanson.[18] Puyllois was born in Brabant, and worked as a choral vicar, and probably the choir master, at the collegiate church of Notre Dame in Antwerp from 1443 to 1447. There he began his life-long association with Ockeghem (who worked there in 1443–4).[19] After failing an audition for admittance to the Burgundian chapel, Puyllois set out for the papal chapel in Rome in 1447, where he remained from December 1447 to August 1468. He returned to Antwerp and spent ten years as a residential canon there until his death in August 1478. During his years in Rome Puyllois became a master of the benefice system, serving as a procurator for Ockeghem, among others, and becoming a rich man himself.

In Antwerp Puyllois was in a good position to acquire and perform English music; Wegman suggests that the *Caput* Mass arrived in Antwerp with a lot of other English music before 1448.[20] Strohm suggests that Puyllois was one of the "two Frenchmen" who sold six Masses to a singer in Ferrara in the spring of 1447, *en route* from Antwerp to Rome. Furthermore, he suggests that the Masses in question are the six Masses (mostly English, including *Caput* and Puyllois's three-voice Mass) copied together in Trent 93.[21] Both Puyllois's Mass and this motet may have been composed in conscious imitation of English music.

Puyllois composed *Flos de spina* in time for it to be included in Trent 90. Saunders dates the fascicle of Trent 90 in which *Flos de spina* is copied to 1456; the next source for the motet is SP B80, in the layer deriving from copies of 1458–63.[22] But it might have been composed somewhat earlier: a date of composition in the very early 1450s is entirely plausible.

Melodic style

The overall style of this work is closest to that of the English cantilena, especially Band II *Song* settings such as *Anima mea* or *O pulcherrima*. The melodic style includes triadic figures, frequent irregular groupings and rhythmic displacement, especially toward the end of a phrase, creating the familiar floating ametrical sensation so familiar from English music. The tutti passages generally begin with long note values (we saw this also in *Regali ex progenie*), and then accelerate, resulting in a definite drive to the cadence, as in much late Du Fay or Ockeghem.

Although Puyllois seems to have had an almost uncanny ability to imitate English style, he also exhibits some individual features of his own. He was particularly fond of dotted-minim/semiminim figures (transcribed as dotted-quarter/eighth), often off the beat. There are also more long note values (breves and longs, transcribed as whole notes and double whole notes) in *Flos de spina* than in the three-voice cantilenas, but this is appropriate for a longer piece, in which the phrases have more time to breathe; they may signal generic references to subgenres using tenor cantus firmus, such as the three-voice tenor motets or the *Caput* Mass.

The alternation of tutti passages with duets (and one brief trio, mm. 33–4) also recalls English music. By far the longest duet is the one that begins the second half. It is the only duet to involve the discantus voice, and it is also self-contained, ending with a fermata before the entrance of the other voices. As such it recalls the central duets in most Band I English cantilenas, although

244

its position at the beginning of a section also recalls the triplum/motetus duets during tenor rests in isorhythmic motets (and three-voice tenor motets), and the duets beginning most sections of mid-century tenor Masses. *Flos de spina* also features integrated duets involving all voice combinations like those in the *Song* settings of the Plummer generation and in Dunstaple's late four-voice *Descendi*. As in these English works the duet passages are lively and feature flexible rhythmic displacement of groups of two and three minims or semibreves.

Imitation

Flos de spina uses two different kinds of imitation. The first kind occurs over sustained notes in the tenor during the tutti sections that begin and end the piece: unison imitation between the contratenors (and sometimes the discantus as well) on triadic figures or 5–6–5 embellishes the cadential arrivals. At the opening of the first half the tenor comes to rest on long notes every five or six measures, for an almost periodic effect: on F (mm. 6–7), D (mm. 12–13) and again D (mm. 18–19). (The discantus sometimes sustains a note, sometimes moves in free counterpoint.) The two imitative passages over tenor Ds (mm. 12–13 and 18–19) are almost identical, and the last one leads into the first duet in the work (mm. 18–22). In the final section held notes in the tenor on D and C prompt imitation of a descending triad figure in three voices, from bottom to top (mm. 100–102, and 105–9). This kind of imitation over a pedal point is a common feature of English music.[23] Plummer's *Anna mater* exhibits it to an unprecedented extent, and there is a certain amount in *O pulcherrima* as well (Ex. 11.3, mm. 18–21). Here the pedal-point imitation seems to serve the formal functions of highlighting periodic structures and emphasizing cadential arrivals, while providing a transition to the next phrase. The use of this kind of imitation near the beginning and end of the piece also results in a rounding effect for the motet as a whole.

The second kind of imitation takes place in almost all the duets. Unlike imitation in the High Renaissance the imitative passage often does not start at the beginning of the phrase (Ex. 11.5, mm. 34–40), or is not exact in terms of rhythmic values (mm. 18–22). The intervals used are the unison, octave, and fifth; in imitation at the fifth, thirds and seconds are sometimes interchanged (mm. 73–4). The second voice often follows at the shortest possible time interval (the minim). This kind of concealed, rhythmically intricate imitation

Example 11.6 Du Fay, *Ave regina celorum (III)*, mm. 138–49 (DufayB, vol. V)

is found in the duet sections of some English music, such as the Band II English cantilenas and the *Missa Caput*. It is also found in English-influenced continental music, such as the duets in Du Fay's *Nuper rosarum* or *Missa Se la face*, or in his continental cantilena, *Ave regina celorum II* (Ex. 9.2). It became even more common in another decade: it is found in some of Regis's motets, and it is greatly extended in the climactic trio near the end of Du Fay's *Ave regina celorum III* (Ex. 11.6, mm. 138–49).[24]

Texture

The discantus voice is clearly distinguished in range from the other voices (the clef is C2), while the three lower voices are similar in range (C4, F3, F3). Although the clefs (and ranges) of the tenor and the second contratenor are the same, the second contratenor spends much of its time below the tenor part.[25] Major cadences use the 6/3–8/5 or leaping-contratenor cadence formulas, in which both contratenors arrive on the fifth above the tenor, but there are quite a few "5–1" cadences along the way (Ex. 11.5: mm. 10, 11, 27, 44, 49).[26] The first contratenor also occasionally crosses below the tenor voice and enters into imitation at the unison with the second contratenor. The texture is rich, complex, and fairly homogeneous, like that of the Band II English cantilenas, with all voices exhibiting the same kind of rhythmic motion.

The clef configuration, with a single high and middle and two low voices, resembles almost all of the four-voice versions of the pieces in Table 11.2d,

Table 11.3. *Constructing a four-voice texture*

	Anima mea	O pulcherrima	Flos de spina	Puyllois Mass
D	C2	C2	C2	C2
Ct. (1)	C4	C3–4	C4	
T	F3	C5	F3	F3
Ct. (2)	F3	C4–5*	F3	F3

but it is closest to those of *O pulcherrima* (compare the voice ranges shown in Table 11.2d). Like the added voice in *O pulcherrima*, Puyllois's second contra-tenor leaps about and covers a broad range. Puyllois's second contratenor is better integrated in the texture as a whole, however, since *Flos de spina* was conceived from the start as a four-voice piece. As in virtually all cantilena-style motets the discantus and tenor work as a contrapuntally complete duet throughout (without dissonant fourths). Unlike three-voice cantilenas there are numerous fourths between the tenor and the first contratenor (Ex. 11.5: mm. 5, 15, 25, 26, 42, 45, 46, 84, etc.) which make the second contratenor essential (as in the four-voice version of *Anima mea*). Unlike *Anima mea*, however, every voice is involved in at least one duet,[27] and both contratenors move to the octave in cadences, not only during duets, but also in tutti sec-tions (Ex. 11.5: Ct. 1: mm. 11, 29; Ct. 2: m. 8; both, mm. 42, 51, 86). For the first time in the freely composed four-voice motet the discantus/tenor cadence functions are available to all voices in the texture; all voices are integrated into the piece and essential to it.

The four-voice versions of *Anima mea* and *O pulcherrima* suggest one way in which Puyllois might have composed the piece: he could have begun with the discantus/tenor duet, leaving the appropriate gaps for duets in which they were not involved. He would then have added the higher contratenor, allow-ing himself fourths above the tenor, since he knew that he could remedy them with the lower contratenor (see Table 11.3, left-hand side). He would end by filling in and completing the duet sections, then adding the lowest voice to the tutti sections.

On the other hand, Puyllois's decision to put the second contratenor in the same range as the tenor may derive from the long tradition of doing just that in three-voice music. All of Puyllois's other surviving music uses only two clefs, with the two lowest voices in the same clef, sometimes a fifth below the clef of the discantus, but often a seventh. If he began with this kind of three-voice texture (as in his *Missa sine nomine*) then he would have added the first contratenor last (see Table 11.3, right-hand side).[28] The most likely method of composition probably involved adding the two contratenors phrase by phrase, beginning with whichever one came most easily.

In any case, the resultant texture was an effective and flexible solution to the problems of writing in four voices. As we shall see, it became one of the principal four-voice textures in the 1450s and 1460s, especially for freely composed works. From now on I will call the texture with high, middle, and two low voices and a consonant discantus/tenor framework the "*Flos de spina* texture."[29]

Form and Structure

Although several scholars have assumed that there is a tenor cantus firmus in *Flos de spina*, no pre-existent material has been identified.[30] Strohm has pointed out that the tenor of *Flos de spina* resembles that of Puyllois's widely disseminated three-voice *Missa sine nomine*, including the "motto-like beginning in the tenor in long notes," and suggests that together they may constitute a freely composed Mass-motet cycle.[31] This is a stimulating idea that reinforces our growing sense of connections between developments in the motet and the cyclic Mass, though it is hard to say whether the similarities between the works extend beyond the common language to be expected in two sacred works with the same final by the same composer. Puyllois's Mass belongs to the tradition of English three-voice "sine nomine" Masses (including works by Benet/Dunstaple/Power, Bedingham, and Plummer) in which the tenor is not pre-existent but "plays with modal cliches in the tenor," and all voices share a common mensural layout.[32] Gareth Curtis believes that the Benet and Puyllois Masses, at least, have pre-existent cantus firmi that are very freely paraphrased, but Strohm finds his examples unconvincing, as do I.[33]

Christopher Reynolds has recently pointed out that the Puyllois Mass draws extensively on musical material from *Puisque je suis infortunée*, a chanson by Horlay (whose chansons are copied with Puyllois's in the chansonnier Escorial IV.a.24).[34] While such quotations are not necessarily inconsistent with the use of a pre-existent tenor (Reynolds notes many other chanson borrowings or allusions in Masses with attested tenor cantus firmi), they do suggest a basis for musical unification distinct from the tenor. None of the passages from the chanson that Reynolds cites is found in the motet; this circumstance weakens claims about musical connections between the Mass and the motet.

In any case, the tenor of *Flos de spina* does not behave like those of the genuine tenor motets in Trent 88 and 89, almost all of which exhibit double cursus (i.e. the pitches of the tenor are repeated for the second section of the motet). Nor does the shape of the tenor resemble that of a pre-existent chant or chanson – it moves through its whole range too rapidly, and has too many leaps (see, for example, Ex. 11.5, mm. 51–8, the end of the first *pars*). Unlike *Flos de spina*, virtually all of the attested tenor motets also begin with duets for the upper voices. I believe that both motet and Mass are freely composed, and that the motet derives its texture and style largely from the freely composed English cantilena tradition. The resemblance between the Mass and the motet, however, confirm our sense that Puyllois was a master of the English style. Curtis finds the Mass to be almost indistinguishable from English music, and suggests that either Puyllois is a much more important figure than we realized, or the attribution is incorrect and the Mass is in fact English (though few scholars accept this last hypothesis).[35] It is worth noting in any case that Puyllois, as Rob Wegman put it, "either wrote, or was widely held capable of writing, a cycle in the English style."[36]

Puyllois may have composed *Flos de spina* to accompany his Mass, but I think it is very likely that he had another Mass cycle in mind as well. Wegman and Strohm have suggested that some of the earliest continental four-voice Mass cycles, copied in Trent 88, were modeled on the *Missa Caput*: Petrus de Domarto's *Spiritus almus*, Ockeghem's *Caput*, Simon de Insula's *O admirabile commercium*, and Du Fay's *Se la face*.[37] There are some striking similarities between *Missa Caput* and *Flos de spina*: I would like to suggest that Puyllois's four-voice motet *Flos de spina* was another, more modest, response to *Missa Caput*.

Flos de spina is a larger work than the English cantilenas (such as *O pulcherrima*) to which it has its closest stylistic ties. As Puyllois looked for a piece on which to model his new, large-scale, four-voice motet, he may have turned to the newest four-voice composition to arrive from England. There can be little doubt that Puyllois knew the work, and he may have been one of its first performers on the Continent when it arrived in Antwerp.

Both the motet and individual movements of the Mass are divided into two

Example 11.7 Anon., *Missa Caput*, Kyrie, mm. 117–33 (Planchart, 8)

large *partes* of similar length, the first in perfect, the second in imperfect tempus, with no return to triple meter at the end.[38] Puyllois' Mass, in contrast, returns to perfect tempus at the end of most movements.[39] Both mensural schemes, as we have seen, were common around mid-century in all genres, though OCO may have been slightly more popular.[40] After *Caput* and *Flos de spina*, however, almost all of the four-voice motets in Trent 88, 89, and 91, use the pattern OC (or O₵).

Both *Caput* and *Flos de spina* have a single discantus voice and use frequent integrated duets involving all voices. The second section of *Flos de spina* begins with a protracted duet in the upper voices, like those beginning every section in *Caput*. Example 11.7 shows the end of the duet that opens the duple meter section of the *Caput* Kyrie, and the entrance of the lower voices; compare it to Example 11.5, *Flos de spina*, mm. 73–80. Both duets feature imitation at the fifth, then move into free counterpoint as they approach the cadence. Both pieces make use of flexible rhythmic displacement of groups of two or three minims (*Flos de spina*, mm. 73–5 in both voices and mm. 77–8 in the discantus; *Missa Caput*, mm. 123–4 in the contratenor and m. 128 in the discantus). When the lower voices enter there is a moment of harmonic and rhythmic stasis before the parts continue in a somewhat more sedate style. The rhythmic motion and melodic style of the voices in the tutti sections are also similar – both have slightly longer note values in the bottom voice, phrases beginning with quarter-note (semibreve) pickups, somewhat aimless melodic motion, and a seamless texture. Lively duets with flexible rhythms,

250

general pauses at the beginning of tutti sections, and the overall melodic language are of course common to much English music, or music influenced by the English style; we saw them also in *Regali ex progenie*. Still, we can see Puyllois emulating the English style here, and perhaps more specifically the style of *Missa Caput*.

There are also, of course, many differences in style between *Flos de spina* and the *Caput* Mass. *Caput* has a cantus firmus, and a more stratified treble-dominated texture. It also has fourths between discantus and tenor, and two voices (tenor and high contratenor) in the middle range, with a single low contratenor in the low range. These differences may seem to call into question my proposal of a relationship between *Caput* and *Flos de spina*. But as both Wegman and Strohm point out, each of the early Masses modeled on *Caput* is also very different from the English Mass. "Each of them adds something new: Du Fay the secular tenor, Domarto the rhythmic transformations, Ockeghem the unprecedented harmonies. These new traits are, at the same time, the most important ones of each work."[41] We can see *Flos de spina*'s lack of tenor cantus firmus and low tenor voice as elements in another such individualized response. In particular, we can see Puyllois combining features of *Missa Caput* – use of four voices, contrasting duets, bipartite structure – with those of the Band II English cantilenas.

Text and text setting

The text of *Flos de spina* is a five-stanza cantio for Christmas in honor of the Virgin and of Jesus.[42]

Flos de spina procreatur	A flower is born of a thorn
et flos florum fecundatur	and the flower of flowers is made fertile
misso rore celitus.	by dew sent from heaven.
Rorant celi, nubes pluunt	The heavens bedew, clouds rain,
stillant montes, colles fluunt,	mountains distill, hills flow,
unda patet veritas.	like a wave is truth revealed.
Quod celerat umbra legis	What the shadow of the law concealed
in natali summi regis	at the birth of the highest king
totum patet homini.	is all revealed to man.
Elyseus incurvatur,	Elisha bows down,
verbum patris incarnatur	the Father's word is made flesh,
verbum per quod filia	the word by which the daughter
Babilonis visitatur	of Babylon is visited,
per quod salus predicatur	by which salvation is preached
illis de Samaria.	to them of Samaria.

The first stanza refers to the miracle of the Incarnation: as the dew coming down from heaven waters the plants and makes them fertile, so the Holy Spirit came down from heaven and made Mary fertile. The first two lines resonate with passages from the *Song of Songs* understood to refer to the Virgin: "Flos de spina" (Jesus from Mary) recalls 2.2, "sicut lilium inter spinas" ("like a lily among the thorns"), while "Flos florum" (the Virgin) recalls the previous line, 2.1: "ego flos campi, et lilium convallium" ("I am a flower of the field, and the lily of the valley"). In the second stanza the dew imagery is expanded: the Holy Spirit that came from heaven as dew is now the flowing water of truth.

The third stanza is transitional: it explains that the birth of Jesus revealed the truth that had been hidden by the shadow of the old law, the law of the Old Testament. This allows the last two stanzas to discuss Elisha, or Eliseus, a miracle-working prophet in the Old Testament understood to be a prefiguration of Christ, and referred to by Jesus: Elisha, who himself preached the word of God in Samaria, bows down to the highest king, overjoyed to see his message finally come true.[43] Within this brief text, then, we have traveled from the sensual imagery of the Virgin, the *Song*, and flowing waters, to sterner images of the prophet preaching to the wicked.

The overall musical structure of the motet responds extremely well to the structure of the text. The first two stanzas correspond to the first section in perfect tempus. The contrast in tone introduced in the third stanza, with its harsh evocation of the "shadow of the law" is complemented by the change to imperfect tempus; the transitional status of the stanza is reflected in the fact that it is set as a lengthy central duet. All voices come in again for the last two stanzas.

The text setting of the motet is quite melismatic, and the underlay varies considerably in the different sources. In the earliest source, Trent 90 (the basis for the edition in Ex. 11.5), each line of text receives a phrase of music. The end of the first stanza is set off by a four-measure duet, while the grammatical elision between the last two stanzas is cleverly managed by means of a brief duet that both finishes the text from the fourth stanza and leads into the fifth. The sudden entrance of B-flat for the word "Babilonis" provides some harmonic color, perhaps to illustrate the exotic wickedness of Babylon.

While *Flos de spina* is a pre-existent text, it is not a common one, and this is the only polyphonic setting of it that I know. The verse form and subject matter of this text, with its arcane imagery and typological references, are similar to the new texts of the medieval motet and some of the early fifteenth-century motet-style motets.[44] By choosing a pre-existent text for the Virgin with textual echoes of the *Song*, Puyllois was referring to the text types of the English cantilena, especially the many *Song* settings of the English Band II repertory. In choosing a rare, abstruse, poetic text Puyllois may have been deliberately referring to the text types and generic associations of the medieval motet. The text of *Flos de spina*, like its music, has multiple generic referents.

Puyllois, like Du Fay, was a northerner who worked in Italy. During his early years in the Netherlands he was exposed to the newest in English music. He may have been an important disseminator of English music when he traveled from Antwerp to Rome in the late 1440s. A key participant in a pan-European musical culture, Puyllois kept his connections to France and the Netherlands while working in Rome, the center of Italian musical life. In *Flos de spina* he successfully combined a rich and allusive continental text with aspects of English style and structure derived from the cantilena and the cyclic Mass. His use of imitation derives partly from English models, but it also points toward the styles of late Du Fay and Regis.

Puyllois thus succeeded in naturalizing English style on the Continent. He drew on contemporary experiments in four-voice writing, both English and continental, to devise a successful four-voice texture that was used for the next several decades. The homogeneous texture with a single discantus voice, bipartite structure, and carefully placed use of duets and imitation make *Flos de spina* the first surviving example of the new four-voice motet, and it was successful enough to be copied up to the end of the fifteenth century. The *Flos de spina* and *Caput* textures proved to be effective solutions to the problems of four-voice writing with a single discantus; the exploitation of these textures in the service of the various subgenres of four-voice motet will be the subject of the last chapter.

12   The four-voice motet *c.* 1450–1475

We will conclude our study of the motet in the fifteenth century with the different subgenres of four-voice motet copied between *c.* 1455 and 1475, concentrating on the motets in Trent 88, 89, and 91, but including also a few other motets from sources copied during the same period (see Tables 12.1–5). The later Trent Codices contain significant numbers of four-voice motets. Some are lingering remnants of earlier traditions: 89.590, *O sacrum manna*, is a double-discantus isorhythmic motet (see Table 10.1), while 88.347, Du Fay's *O proles/O sidus*, is a four-voice cut-circle motet also found in Trent 87 (see Table 11.2). Most, however, resemble the four-voice motets found in late fifteenth-century sources such as the Gaffurius codices or CS 15: they use the new *Flos de spina* and *Caput* textures, with a single discantus part and homogeneity of melodic style. We have traced some of the precedents for these new kinds of motet in chapters 10 and 11: it is in the later Trent Codices that substantial numbers first make their appearance. I will begin with a small group of four-voice song motets with a single section, and then go on to the large-scale multipartite motets that make up the bulk of the repertory.

Four-voice song motets

In Trent 89 and 91 there are a few four-voice pieces with a single section that resemble the three-voice Touront song motets and the contemporary repertory of four-voice chansons and instrumental works (see Table 12.1). Among them I have included one known contrafact chanson – Busnoys's *Quand ce viendra* (91.1189), supplied with an additional fourth voice – and three other probable contrafacta that sit on the borderline between motet and chanson.

254

Table 12.1. *Four-voice song motets*

Chanson contrafacta		
91.1189	Gaude mater miserorum	= Busnoys, Quand ce viendra
89.601	Assit herus rex	Ballade?
89.603	Deus decorum	Ballade?
89.661	O gloriosa	Bergerette?
The *Peacock's tail* complex		
89.604	O quam clara	= Barbingant, Der pfawin swancz
91.1288	Flos virginum	= Martini, M. Coda di pavon, Gloria, 1st half
91.1289	Jhesu Christe	mm. 1–13 = Martini, M. Coda di pavon, Agnus II
No known model or source		
89.654	O florens rosa	Text = Frye and Touront 3-v. motets
89.616	Tu ne quesieris	Setting of Horace *Odes* I,11

Another group of four-voice song motets is related to the four-voice text-less instrumental piece known as the *Peacock's tail* (*Der pfawin swancz, Der Pfobenschwanz,* or *Coda di pavon*). This piece is believed to be a polyphonic setting of a *basse danse* tenor, and is now usually attributed to Barbingant. *O quam clara* is a simple contrafactum of the instrumental work. The other two share most of their material with sections of Martini's *Missa Coda di pavon*: *Flos virginum* is equivalent to the first half of the Gloria, while the first thirteen measures of *Jhesu Christe* are equivalent to the second Agnus (the rest seems to be freely composed). In the Gloria (and in *Flos virginum*) the musical material is very close to that of the model: both discantus and tenor of the model are quoted almost exactly (with some rhythmic alterations), while the two contratenors are paraphrased.[1] The use of the model in the Agnus (and in *Jhesu Christe*) is much freer. It is entirely possible that the two motets in Trent 91 were written before the Mass: the long notes in *Flos virginum* are not divided into shorter values to accommodate the long Gloria text as they are in the Mass, and the second half of *Jhesu Christe* is not used in the Mass at all. All three members of the *Peacock's tail* complex, then, can be seen as motets derived from an instrumental work. The first simply adds a Latin text; the second slightly recomposes the *basse danse* setting, and adds another Latin text; and the third is a free fantasy on the material, set to yet a third text.

There are two single-section four-voice pieces in Trent 89 with no known source or model: *Tu ne quesieris* (89.616), a setting of a Horace ode (I, 11), and *O florens rosa* (89.654), a setting of a Marian text also used by Frye and Touront. Both can be seen as stemming from the continental song motet tradition. The Horace text is more secular than sacred,[2] while *O florens rosa* is very much in the Touront style: like Touront's *O castitatis lilium* it begins with a lengthy melisma during which the tenor rests, and has a brief tripla section in the middle. All of the four-voice pieces listed in Table 12.1 belong to the Central European repertory that could move across generic boundaries, from instrumental work and chanson to motet and even Mass.

Large four-voice motets with two or more sections

In contrast, the rest of the four-voice motets in the later Trent Codices (see Tables 12.2–5) have ties to large-scale Mass movements and liturgical music. All share basic approaches to form and construction. They are big pieces (usually taking up two openings) with two (and sometimes more) *partes* or sections, very much after the *Flos de spina* plan. The sections are distinguished from each other by double bars and change of mensuration, almost always from perfect tempus to imperfect tempus (O to C or ₵). The *Missa Caput* may have been responsible for the widespread adoption of this mensural pattern in the motet.

Texture in these works is fairly homogeneous: all the voices (with the exception of some tenor cantus firmi) have a similar range of rhythmic motion. This homogeneity of texture distinguishes these pieces sharply from most of the late four-voice isorhythmic motets, where the tenor and contratenor move much more slowly than the other voices. Most of the motets in Tables 12.2–5 use either the *Caput* texture (high/two middle/low) or the *Flos de spina* texture (high/middle/two low). I have marked these textures in Tables 12.2–5 with M for two middle voices, and L for two low voices. The tenor is always one of the pair of voices in the same range. The pieces with soprano, alto, tenor, and bass clefs, the texture that became the norm in the sixteenth century, are marked with an S, for SATB texture; the few five-voice pieces are marked "5." There is one double-discantus work, marked "H" (for two high voices).

Evidence of the novelty of these homogeneous four-voice textures comes from the use of the dissonant 4/5 cadence type found in many of the pieces (marked with an asterisk in Tables 12.2–5), a cadence that we saw in

Lymburgia's *Tota pulchra es* (Ex. 6.3), in the *Missa Caput*, and in Frye's *Ave regina celorum* in the Speciálník version. Here the low contratenor often goes 5–1 or includes both the root and fifth in the final chord, combining "5–1" and leaping contratenor formulas. It occurs most often in the cadence ending the *prima pars* (just as in Frye's *Ave regina celorum*), and it may have been considered an effective way to end the first half, but too strident for the end of a piece. The 4/5 cadence gradually died out in favor of the standard four-voice 5–1 cadence, where the high contratenor sustains the fifth degree: it no longer appears in the Trent 91 motets. In one case (89.729, the *Salve regina/ T: Hilf und gib rat* by Philipus) the 4/5 cadence was rewritten in the later source (the Strahov Codex) in order to eliminate the dissonance.[3]

Although they share size, mensural practice, and approaches to texture, these four-voice motets demonstrate several contrasted approaches to construction. I have divided them into three main subgenres: the tenor motet (derived from the isorhythmic motet and the cyclic Mass), the chant-para-phrase motet (derived from the continental cantilenas with chant and from utilitarian liturgical chant settings), and the freely composed motet (derived from *Flos de spina* and its predominantly three-voice English antecedents).

Tenor motets

I include in Table 12.2 all the works from the last three Trent Codices with tenors that either are labeled in the source or have been identified by modern scholars. They can be further divided into three different types: occasional motets, motets associated with cyclic Masses, and other tenor motets. In spite of their differences, all three categories of tenor motet have features in common: foreign tenor, double cursus, and opening duets.[4] I will discuss first their common features, and then examine the three different categories of tenor motet individually.

Pre-existent foreign tenor

In all but two of the motets in Table 12.2 the tenor is identified in the manu-script with a text incipit different from that of the other voices (tenor identifications not shown in the manuscript are in square brackets in Table 12.2). The use of a foreign cantus firmus follows from the basic conception of both the occasional motet and the cyclic Mass. In the case of motets in which

257

Table 12.2. *Tenor motets*

(a) Occasional or dedicatory motets with new texts and foreign Tenors

88.452	Advenisti: Venisti nostras	S	For Bishop of Trent, 1446–65, Georgius II
	T: Advenisti/Lauda Sion		(Georg Hack). Text inaugural (1446?).
			Begins with 4-v acclamation, then trio
			before each T entrance; triple cursus.
89.585	Adoretur beata trinitas/	5	On reconquest of Bordeaux, 1451. 5 vv.
	In ultimo lucente Junii/		T is phrase from Alleluia Virga Jesse.
	Dies datur/Lilia nunc		
	T: Pacem deus reddidit		
MC, F2794	Du Fay, O tres piteulx	M	Mentioned by Dufay in letter of 1455.
	T: Omnes amici		Lament on the fall of Constantinople.
91.1162	Busnoys, In hydraulis	M	In praise of Ockeghem, 1465–7.
Mu3154	T: Constructed, ratios		Fourfold cursus.
91.1161	Compère, Omnium bonorum	M	Musicians' motet, before 1474 (1470–3).
SP B80	T: De tous biens pleine		T is a rondeau by Hayne van Ghizeghem.

(b) Motets associated with Mass cycles

(1) Mass-motet cycles: four-voice motets for three-voice masses

Strah	O pater eterne	L	Mass in Tr 88, K-A, 3 vv.
Milan 1	=O admirabile (Mil)		O, 1 *pars*, T single cursus.
	T: O rosa bella		T by Dunstaple or Bedingham.
88.204	Le Rouge, Stella celi	M	Mass in Tr 90, SP B80, K-A, 3 vv.
	[T: So ys emprentid]		OO; no duet 2da *pars*; 1 1/2 cursus.
			T by Frye.
88.496	Gaude Maria	L	Mass in Tr 88, K-A, 3 vv.
	T: Esclave puist		T by Binchois.

(2) Contrafact Kyries (?)

[88.240	[Frye], Salve virgo	3 vv.	Mass in Br 5557, G-A. C, 1 pars.
	[T: Summe trinitati]		T Responsory, single cursus.
88.416–17	Gaude Maria (E)	M	Mass in Strah, G-A.
	T: Meditatio cordis		T Introit.
89.729	Philipus, Salve regina (E?)	L*	Mass in Strah, G-A.
Strah	=Gaude rosa		OC2. Strah w/ extra Ct.,
	=O gloriosa mater (Strah)		"concordans cum omnibus."
	T: Hilf und gib Rat		T is found in a quodlibet in Glog.

Table 12.2. (*cont.*)

(c) Independent devotional tenor motets			
89.615	Perpulchra Sion filia	M*	CO; opening trio, no duets; triple cursus.
89.638	Salve regina	S	Does not go with the Le serviteur Masses.
	T: Le serviteur (up a step)		T by Du Fay? 2nd cursus incomplete.

Key:

* = 4/5 cadence, combining 5–1 motion in one contratenor with 4–5 motion in another

@ = attribution in that source

M = two voices in the same, middle range ("*Caput* texture")

L = two voices in the same, lowest range ("*Flos de spina* texture")

S = all voices in different ranges (SATB texture)

5 = 5-voice motet

E = may be English, according to Curtis and Wathey, "List"

the primary text is written for a specific occasion, or to honor a contemporary person, it is impossible for a pre-existent cantus firmus to have the same text as the other parts. In the cyclic Mass the original text of the cantus firmus is necessarily different from the text of the five movements of the Mass Ordinary; motets associated with cyclic Masses work on the same principle. As in the Mass, cantus firmi for motets can be chant or secular songs.[5]

Motets with foreign cantus firmus raise some interesting questions of presentation and performance: what text did the tenor sing? Most motets in the Trent Codices are only texted in the top voice: the other voices generally have text incipits for the text of the top voice, or, if the voices enter later, the text sung by the top voice at their entrance. In tenor motets the tenor text incipit at the beginning of the work is that of the cantus firmus, but at the *secunda pars* it will have a text incipit derived from the text of the top voice when the tenor enters. The first incipit served to identify the cantus firmus, while the second could have served as a rehearsal letter ("let's start at 'O pulcherrima'"). Did the tenor sing the text of the cantus firmus, the text of the other voices, or no text at all? I would suggest that all three were (and are) possible options. Some of the time the tenor must have sung the same text as the other parts (occasionally we have bits of upper-voice text inserted in the middle of the tenor, perhaps as a guide to text placement). Alejandro Planchart and Gareth Curtis have shown that in some fifteenth-century Masses the tenor cantus firmus was sung to its original text;[6] the same must apply to motets. Sometimes the lower voices must also have vocalized without text when it was too difficult to reconstruct any suitable text for the part.

The two four-voice pieces in which the tenor cantus firmus is not identified are both exceptional cases. The tenor of Le Rouge's *Stella celi* is clearly based on Frye's *So ys emprentid*, but it also resembles a tune associated with the *Stella celi* text (both begin with two upward leaps D–a–c). The "Stella celi" text incipit in the tenor voice may have been designed to bring out that similarity.[7] *Perpulchra Sion filia* is fully texted in all voices, unlike most other pieces in the Trent Codices. It may be that the desire to supply the full text (which is long and fairly complex) overrode the usual practice of labeling the tenor.

Double cursus

Almost all the tenor motets are characterized by double cursus, in which the tenor is repeated in the second section.[8] Strict tenor repetition with mensural transformation was of course characteristic of isorhythmic motets; here, in contrast, the tenor returns in the second section in a freely varied form. This approach to tenor repetition was another English invention, best known in *Missa Caput.*[9] In later fifteenth-century cyclic Masses double cursus was rather rare, perhaps because the tenor is repeated at least five times over the course of the cycle in any case, but it remained the norm for the tenor motet.[10]

Opening duets

Both *partes* of tenor motets usually begin with fairly extensive duets for the upper voices, the discantus and the first (high) contratenor, while the tenor and second (low) contratenor rest.[11] The opening duet had associations with exalted positions in the genre hierarchy: with the duets beginning many four-teenth- and early fifteenth-century motets, and with contemporary cyclic Mass movements.

Foreign tenor, double cursus, and opening duets are common to almost all tenor motets. They can be further subdivided, however, into three sub-sub-genres with individual characteristics.

Occasional or dedicatory motets

These motets (see Table 12.2a) have new texts that refer to specific occasions or people. They thus participate in the early fifteenth-century tradition of occasional motets, most of which were isorhythmic. In these works (as in the older isorhythmic motet) the tenor cantus firmus often has a symbolic as well as a musical function.

The text of *Advenisti: Venisti* (88.542) refers to a certain "Georgi," "princeps," presumably the Georg Hack who was Prince-bishop of Trent from 1446 to 1455.[12] The nobles and people ("proceres" and "turba") rejoice at his long-awaited arrival, greet him, and wish him long life. The text has an inaugural sound to it, but it could refer to the bishop's return to the city after a long absence (1446 seems too early for the work, in terms of style). The motet begins with sustained homophonic chords for all voices, set to the word "Advenisti" ("you have arrived"). The tenor cantus firmus is marked with the text "Advenisti desiderabilis," the first words of the *canticum triumphale* also set as a continental cantilena (88.394: see Table 9.2). The melodies for the tenor of the four-voice motet's opening invocation and the beginning of its cantus firmus are the same; they are also essentially the same as the opening of the discantus in the cantilena-style setting. There can be little doubt that this is the melody of the *canticum triumphale*, a superbly appropriate cantus firmus for the occasion. The tenor cantus firmus is also labeled "Lauda Sion," but there is no melodic resemblance to the famous Corpus Christi sequence. The text of this sequence's first stanza, however, is ideally suited to the occasion: "Lauda Sion Salvatorem, Lauda ducem et pastorem, In hymnis et canticis" ("Praise the Saviour, Zion, praise the leader and shepherd, in hymns and songs"), and it was probably added as another symbolic reference.

Adoretur beata trinitas is a five-voice polytextual motet with texts that refer to the reconquest of Bordeaux by the French (from the English) in 1451.[13] The tenor text ("Pacem Deus reddidit," "God restores peace") is appropriate to the occasion. Of all the tenor motets listed here, this one looks most like the late isorhythmic motets, with its multiple texts in the upper voices, active upper parts, and slow-moving tenor and "contra primus" in the same range. Nevertheless, the work is not isorhythmic, and its fluidity of texture, with integrated duets and trios between various different voice combinations, is reminiscent of English music.

I have included Du Fay's *O tres piteulx* among the tenor motets in spite of its French text, because of its tenor cantus firmus, bipartite structure, and occasional text. In F2794 it is entitled *Lamentio Sancte Matris Ecclesie Constantinopolitane* (*Lament of the Holy Mother of the Church of Constantinople*) and

261

the French text presents the Virgin/Mother of the Church complaining to God the Father about a "forfait . . . gref tourment, et douloureulx oultrage" ("crime, grievous torment, and tragic outrage") that has been perpetrated against her son: the reference must be to the Fall of Constantinople in 1453.[14] The tenor of this work paraphrases a lesson tone and spends most of its time on a single pitch. The text of the tenor, from the Lamentations of Jeremiah 1.2, refers to the destruction of Jerusalem: "All her friends have despised her; there is none to comfort her among all them that were dear to her." Here Du Fay once again mixes genres for expressive purposes: the French text of the upper voices belongs to the genre of the secular lament, while the form and cantus firmus treatment belong to the motet. Just as Jeremiah spoke about Jerusalem as if the city were a beloved woman friend, Du Fay laments the fall of Constantinople in the language of courtly love.[15]

The text of *In hydraulis* praises Ockeghem as a new Pythagoras, and Busnoys constructed his tenor according to Pythagorean ratios.[16] This is, as far as I know, the first motet with a constructed tenor, and it would beget distinguished progeny.[17] *In hydraulis* is a "singer's motet" about a single musician. Compère's *Omnium bonorum plena* is a prayer to the Virgin on behalf of a whole group of musicians, many connected to Cambrai Cathedral: among them are Du Fay ("the light of all music and the light of singers"), Busnoys, Caron, Tinctoris, Ockeghem, Faugues, Regis and the young Desprez, as well as Compère himself.[18] Not named is the composer of the tenor cantus firmus, Hayne van Ghizeghem. The cantus firmus is the tenor of his most famous chanson, *De tous biens pleine est ma maitresse*, the first words of which are cleverly translated into Latin and applied to the Virgin in the main text of the motet ("Omnium bonorum plena, Virgo parensque serena"). Here a secular chanson is treated as a straightforward allegorical reference to the Virgin. This work is complementary to *O tres piteulx*, in which a sacred tenor enriches the meaning of a French text; in *Omnium bonorum* a chanson tenor is used for a Latin-texted work.

The foreign cantus firmus serves to enrich and amplify the meaning of these occasional and dedicatory works, just as in older isorhythmic motets. Many of these works are also compositional *tours de force*: their composers were deliberately showing off new techniques within a subgenre with ancient roots. *Advenisti* is for five voices; *O tres piteulx* combines sacred and secular in a new way; *In hydraulis* and *Omnium bonorum* are huge works requiring virtuoso singers.

Motets associated with Mass cycles

The Mass-motet cycle, in which the same tenor is found in a cyclic Mass and in a motet, was identified by Robert Snow (see Table 12.2b).[19] Like the tenors of occasional tenor motets, the cantus firmi of Mass cycles can also have symbolic significance: they can make the text of the Ordinary "proper" to particular feasts, occasions, or institutions.[20] Many Mass tenors are chansons, probably intended for Marian feasts, or important occasions in Marian churches and cathedrals. The associated Marian motets could have been used at these Marian Masses, or for other Marian devotions.

Strohm and others have recently suggested that in fact some of the motets identified by Snow as part of Mass-motet cycles are really contrafact Kyries (discussed in chapter 8: see Table 8.5). I have therefore divided Snow's six Mass-motet cycles into two groups: true Mass-motet cycles, and Masses with contrafact Kyries.[21]

MASS-MOTET CYCLES (TABLE 12.2B.1)

In this group four-voice motets share their tenors with three-voice Masses for which all five movements survive. All three cycles belong to a group of early Masses based on chanson tenors, in which the rhythms but not the pitches of the chanson melodies are varied freely and differently in every movement (this is known as "isomelic" treatment).[22] *Esclave puist* and *So ys emprentid* (to a lesser extent) occasionally quote the chanson's top line as well, making them early examples of "imitation" or "parody" technique, while *O rosa bella* uses the opening of the discantus voice as a motto for all movements before the entrance of the tenor.[23] The motets were probably performed along with the Mass cycles when first composed, but some at least then went on to circulate individually as independent motets.[24]

Christopher Reynolds has tentatively identified Le Rouge with a certain Rubino who came to St. Peter's in Rome in 1447 (the same year as Puyllois), and then moved on to work in the chapel of Charles of Orléans from 1451 to 1465.[25] Reynolds identified multiple musical references between Le Rouge's *So ys emprentid* cycle and three other Mass cycles, one of them being the Puyllois three-voice Mass.[26] He also suggests that Compère worked at St. Peter's in 1465–6. This would make Rome a center for the development of the new style of four-voice motet in the 1450s and 1460s.[27]

CONTRAFACT KYRIES (TABLE 12.2B.2)

This group is made up of three four-voice Masses for which no Kyrie survives. It makes sense, therefore, to assume that the four-voice motets with the same tenors are contrafact versions of the missing movements. I have included Frye's three-voice *Summe trinitati* in order to present all the contrafact cases together. We can be fairly confident that the original Kyrie of Frye's Mass was troped; this is why it was supplied with a new text on the Continent. Are the other two also English Masses that began life with troped Kyries? *Meditatio cordis* looks extremely English, *Hilf und gib Rat* by the unknown "Philipus" less so – and it is hard to imagine an English composer writing a Mass on a German song. The Philipus motet is actually found with three different texts, at least two of which must be contrafacta (two are found, one on top of the other, in Trent 89, the third in the Strahov Codex). Perhaps *Hilf und gib Rat* is not the original text of the tenor; or perhaps this is a rare example of a Central European Mass with a troped Kyrie.[28]

There is a considerable variety in the tenor treatment of these three Masses. *Summe trinitati* uses strict (or "isorhythmic") cantus firmus treatment (like the *Caput* Mass), in which the rhythmicization of the chant tenor is the same in every movement. *Meditatio cordis* has a chant tenor that is given only slightly different rhythms in each movement (the rhythms are more different in the motet). *Hilf und gib Rat* varies the rhythms freely in the different movements (as in the "isomelic" tenors of the chanson Mass-motet cycles). It also has a recurring motto opening.

None of the six motets associated with Mass cycles follows exactly the form and structure of the *Caput* Mass (OC, double cursus, strict cantus firmus treatment). All are essentially bipartite, however, even those in a single mensuration (*O rosa bella*, *Esclave puist*, and *Summe trinitati*): they come to a major cadence near the middle of the work and begin the second half with a fairly lengthy duet. Four out of the six use double cursus (though the second cursus of *So ys emprentid* is abbreviated). Unlike *Caput*, all the four-voice Masses use some kind of free cantus firmus treatment (though *Meditatio cordis* is much less free than the others), and only two use the *Caput* texture, with two voices in the middle range. Ironically, the motets associated with Mass cycles are less like the *Caput* Mass than the occasional tenor motets, most of which use the *Caput* texture, and none of which uses a single cursus. The tenor Mass had been around long enough by the 1450s that the problem was to differentiate new cycles from their predecessors, so composers kept trying new approaches to tenor structure and form; the motets associated with those Masses were, by definition, also subject to such experimentation. The big four-voice motet was brand new, however, so that composers of independent motets may have felt safer conforming to generic norms, some of which were borrowed from the *Caput* Mass.

The existence of these "Mass motets" confirms our sense of the mutual influence of the big motets and the cyclic Mass during this period. Both the contrafact motets and the four-voice motets for three-voice Masses circulated independently of their Masses quite early: only two are found in the same manuscripts with their Masses, and texting was unstable for motets in both groups (both *O pater eterne* and the Philipus *Salve regina* have multiple texts, and a motet from each group uses the text *Gaude Maria*, perhaps a favorite of the Trent 88 scribe). All of these motets must have become models for other independent motets, just as contrafact chansons or instrumental tricinia served as models for song motets like those of Frye and Touront.

Independent devotional tenor motets

There is a small number of Marian tenor motets that do not fit into the other two categories (Table 12.2c). The *Salve regina* with the tenor *Le serviteur* may be part of a Mass-motet cycle, but if so the Mass is lost.[29] The combination of the Marian antiphon *Salve regina* with the chanson tenor confirms the Marian symbolism of chansons. I have not identified either the text or the tenor of *Perpulchra Sion filia*. It has a tuneful long-note tenor melody that is repeated twice in a freely varied fashion (Ex. 12.1: triple cursus, with a brief free insertion for the end of a duet). I strongly suspect that this melody is pre-existent, and therefore class this work with the tenor motets.

The existence of these two devotional tenor motets demonstrates that the tenor motet was becoming a truly independent genre: no longer necessarily associated with the Mass, with devotional rather than occasional texts, these works could take their place with the other devotional motets for use as an embellishment for Vespers, Mass, Salve services, or private devotions. Membership in this group grew by leaps and bounds: most of the tenor motets composed in the last quarter of the fifteenth century were just such independent devotional works.

The four-voice tenor motets, then, can be seen as a cross between the late

Example 12.1 Anon., *Perpulchra Sion filia*, tenor (Trent 89.615, 166'–168)

isorhythmic motets and the tenor Mass. The occasional motets have the new occasional texts and symbolic cantus firmi of the isorhythmic motets, with the four-voice texture and double cursus of the *Caput* Mass. The tenor continued to have a symbolic function in the context of the Mass cycle, but more and more the symbolism was Marian. The use of chanson tenors in the early Mass-motet cycles may have inspired the slightly later dedicatory musicians' motet *Omnium bonorum plena*. The motets associated with Masses that circulated as independent motets also served as models for a growing group of independent devotional tenor motets.

Chant-paraphrase motets

While tenor motets tend to use chant fragments or chansons as cantus firmi, and place them in the tenor, chant-paraphrase motets paraphrase a complete chant in the discantus voice (see Table 12.3).[30] The paraphrase can be quite ornate, but the melodies (most of which are well known – only *O beata infantia* is at all obscure) are fairly easy to trace throughout the piece. Another way in which these motets differ from the tenor motets is their lack of opening duets – they maintain their four-voice texture throughout most of the composition, with few rests in any part longer than two or three breves. All voices also have the same text incipits and presumably sing the same text:

Table 12.3. *Chant-paraphrase motets*

88.235	Salve regina (E)	L	OȻOȻO (some internal duets). Very free chant treatment.
89.727 @Mu 3154, Milan 1	Du Fay?, Salve regina	M	OȻOȻ. Chant incipit.
89.639 Mu 3154, SPB80, CS15	O beata infantia	M	Antiphon, Xmas season.
89.591–92 Glog, Spec, @Strah	Touront, Recordare virgo	M	Offertory; troped.
89.637	Regina celi	L	Marian antiphon; troped.

Key:
@ = attribution in that source
E = may be English, according to Curtis and Wathey, "List".

there is no foreign cantus firmus. Chant-paraphrase motets thus resemble their humbler relations, the smaller-scale liturgical chant paraphrases, such as hymns and Mass Propers. But unlike utilitarian service music these are long pieces, with the bipartite structure now mandatory for the motet (*Salve regina* settings tend to have more *partes*). The four continental works are closer in style and scale to the three-voice "continental cantilenas with chant" (see Table 9.2), most of which are multipartite and paraphrase Marian antiphons in the top voice. These motets, then, are essentially four-voice cantilenas that use chant. With the addition of a voice, however, composers seem to have felt required to lengthen the compositions: the four-voice chant-paraphrase motets are comparable in length to tenor motets.

Within these basic parameters there is a range of styles. Variables include the ornateness of the chant paraphrase, the extent to which the chant is quoted in the other voices, and the extent to which the four-voice texture is relieved by occasional duets and trios.

The *Salve regina* attributed to Du Fay in Munich 3154 is the most straightforward.[31] It makes its ties to humbler genres clear through the use of a chant incipit, fairly transparent paraphrase with clear cadences in all voices at the end of each chant phrase, and lack of duets and trios.[32] It is built around a consonant discantus–tenor duet without fourths; the chant migrates to other voices for the final acclamations. The motet's length (it takes up three openings in the manuscript) and multi-partite form serve to distinguish it from

Example 12.2 Touront, *Recordare*, mm. 1–14 (Trent 89.591–92, 137′–139)

utilitarian service music. The anonymous *O beata infantia* is similar, but has more textural variety, with several trios and one duet. *O beata infantia* was widely disseminated, perhaps because of its appropriateness for the celebratory Christmas season.[33]

Touront's *Recordare* (a setting of an offertory text) and the anonymous *Regina celi* take this basic approach to chant paraphrase and enrich it by means of imitation between the discantus and tenor, resulting in chant quotation in more than one voice. Both use the trope text for the *secunda pars*, and can be distinguished from utilitarian service music by their bipartite form and overall length. In Touront's *Recordare* there is a great deal of imitation between the tenor and the discantus voices. The tenor sometimes anticipates the entry of the discantus, and when the beginning of the next phrase is triadic and thus easy to present in imitation over a sustained note (as it often is in this chant), the other voices participate as well: this is *vorimitation* in embryo (see Ex. 12.2, mm. 1–14). During the *secunda pars* the imitation between discantus and tenor becomes so pervasive that free material in the tenor voice almost disappears: the work is like a free canon, in which the time interval is always shifting and the *dux* and *comes* can change places at will (Ex. 12.3, mm. 39–53). Touront also incorporates into this motet techniques derived from his freely composed three-voice motets. The rhythms of the opening, carefully calculated to obscure the meter, are almost identical to those at the beginning of *Compangant omnes* (Ex. 9.3). The one duet in the work comes right at the end of

Example 12.3 Touront, *Recordare*, mm. 30–53

the *prima pars*, with a jaunty tripla section in almost canonic imitation between the discantus and tenor (perhaps as a foreshadowing of the extensive imitation to come in the *secunda pars*; see Ex. 12.3, mm. 31–8).[34]

Regina celi has no duets, but several integrated trios, including a lengthy one that begins the *secunda pars*. The imitation between discantus and tenor is less extensive than in *Recordare*, but some of the imitative passages are combined with faster note values and rhythmic sequence for exciting drives to the cadence. One such passage, during a trio leading up to an important cadence, resembles some of Puyllois's imitative duets (the imitation starts in the middle of the phrase, the time interval is one minim, and the pitch interval is a fifth). It ends with a zippy sequential pattern using parallel tenths between

269

Example 12.4 Anon., *Regina celi*, mm. 44–50 (Trent 89.637, 189a'–191)

the outer voices (Ex. 12.4, mm. 44–50). Another canonic passage for discantus and tenor, this time at the octave in a four-voice context, brings the *prima pars* to an exciting close. The imitative and sequential writing are reminiscent of the Touront song motets and tricinia extending beyond the end of the century.

The Trent 88 *Salve regina* uses the freest approach to chant paraphrase: the chant melody comes in and out of focus, and occasionally recedes from view completely, returning for the last "O dulcis" in grand long-note presentation. This approach to chant paraphrase is typical of English music, and this motet is in fact listed as an English work by Curtis and Wathey.[35] Another English feature is the presence of a lengthy self-contained duo at the beginning of the *secunda pars*, as well as several integrated trios. The texture is close to that of *Flos de spina*, with almost identical ranges and the same clefs and final. What we have here is an English cantilena expanded in both directions (number of voices and length).

The four-voice chant-paraphrase motets, then, combine elements from the liturgical chant setting, the cantilena (English and continental), and the *Caput* Mass (bipartite form and texture, in most cases). The result is an elevation of the chant paraphrase in the genre hierarchy: rather than an intimate cantilena or a utilitarian chant setting, these four-voice chant-paraphrase motets approach the status of tenor motets or Mass movements.

Between tenor and chant-paraphrase motet

Having established generic norms for the tenor motet and chant-paraphrase motet, we can detect the existence of a small hybrid group (see Table 12.4). Like the chant-paraphrase motets, these hybrids paraphrase a complete chant in a single voice once through and have the same text in all voices. They thus

Table 12.4. *Hybrids of the tenor and chant-paraphrase motets*

89.728	Ave beatissima civitas	L*	Chant in D & T.
Lucca CS 15	Vidi speciosam	M	Opening trio; Duet 2a *pars.* Chant mostly in T.
91.1318	Ave Maria T: Ave Maria, A	M	Both halves begin with duets. Chant in T, 1a *pars*; free 2a *pars*.
SP B80	Du Fay, Ave regina celorum T: ARC (whole chant)	M	Copied in Cambrai, 1464 (no. III, troped). Chant in T, single cursus. Short duet in ₵.

Key:
* = 4/5 cadence, combining 5–1 motion in one contratenor with 4–5 in another

lack the tenor motet's double cursus and the foreign tenor. As in the tenor motet the cantus firmus is in the tenor voice, and there are more duets and trios. In some cases the chant material is also treated imitatively in the contratenor voices. We can see this hybrid subgenre as growing out of the imitative chant treatment characteristic of the second half of Touront's *Recordare*, but with more influence from the tenor motet. Each of these hybrid motets exhibits a slightly different mixture of characteristics.

Ave beatissima is closest to the chant-paraphrase motet (see Ex. 12.5, mm. 55–end).[36] It lacks the extended duet sections of the tenor motet, and passages in reduced texture are extremely short. At the beginning of the piece only the discantus has the chant, which moves primarily in colored breves, as in the opening of Touront's *Compangant* and *Recordare* (Exx. 9.3 and 12.2), but here extending for the whole first phrase. From m. 15 on, however, the discantus and tenor paraphrase the chant so completely and closely that for most of the piece the two voices are in a kind of loose canon, with the lead passing back and forth between the voices. During the *prima pars* the imitation is limited to discantus and tenor, except for one phrase near the end where the low contratenor joins in with a neighbor-note motif around E (Ex. 12.5, mm. 55–65). During the *secunda pars* many of the phrases begin with imitation in three parts (these could be called proto-points of imitation), and there is even one passage where all voices participate in two successive points of imitation, the first including a modified entrance at the fifth as well as the unison and octave (Ex. 12.5, mm. 84–96). Toward the end of the *secunda pars* the neighbor-note motif heard in three voices at the end of the *prima pars* (Ex. 12.5, m. 55) occurs

Example 12.5 Anon., *Ave beatissima*, mm. 55–152 (Trent 89.728, 352′–354)

Example 12.5 (*cont.*)

again for tenor and discantus, in two forms: first an augmented version (Ex. 12.5, m. 104 ff.), and then the original dotted version, now superimposed on the duple meter (m. 116 ff.). After a sequential passage in which tenor and discantus exchange one-measure phrases (m. 129 ff.) the discantus returns to long-note chant presentation while the tenor and high contratenor engage in an imitative tripla section for a climactic conclusion (m. 142–End). Here we find Touront's imitation for two voices expanded to include the whole texture.

Texture, rhythm, and imitation in *Ave beatissima* are handled with great skill – which makes its numerous problematic cadences all the more surprising. *Ave beatissima* paraphrases a fourth-mode chant and thus features numerous cadences on E. E cadences are phrygian, with a half-step down in the tenor voice (F–E): this works fine for two voices, or for three when the middle voice goes from A to B (e.g. m. 89). But leaping contratenor or "5–1" cadences do not work, because of the conflict between the fifth degree (B) and the lowered second (F). Solutions to this problem include doubling the A in both contra-tenors, then moving in contrary motion to B and G (see mm. 114 and 125); or a "plagal" harmonization, in which the lowest voice moves from D to A, so that E becomes the fifth rather than the root of the sonority (mm. 81, 105). But many of the cadences on E are treated as if they were normal cadences with a whole-step descent in the tenor, resulting in prominent Bs in the contra-tenor against the tenor's Fs (see m. 103).[37] The problems are especially acute in the final cadence. Here there is a fermata over the B–F sonority, after which natural signs have been added to the final Bs in the contratenor voices.[38] Should we flat the Bs under the fermata, leading to a leap of an augmented octave in the low contratenor? Should we raise the F to F-sharp (and the d to d-sharp) to produce a normal cadential progression that eliminates the phry-gian quality at the end of a phrygian piece? Or should we accept the tritones, even dwell on them during the fermata? I don't know the answer. The use of an E final for polyphony was new in the 1460s, and it remained very uncom-mon: this composer was obviously still working out the problems.[39]

Vidi speciosam, like *Ave beatissima*, is a setting of chant with an E final (third mode in this case), and the chant appears in both discantus and tenor. Unlike *Ave beatissima*, however, *Vidi speciosam* carries the chant primarily in the tenor voice: it appears in the discantus at the beginning of each *pars* and in a few other spots, but almost never in the other voices.[40] A striking feature of this motet is the predominance of trios and duets: tutti sections make up only thirty of the sixty-seven breves in the *prima pars*, and thirteen of the thirty-eight longs in the *secunda pars*. The motet begins with two trios: the first lacks the discantus, and paraphrases the chant in the tenor, while the second lacks the tenor and paraphrases the chant in essentially the same way in the dis-cantus. After a brief tutti section there are two more brief trios, then two duets, and the section ends with another short tutti section. The *secunda pars* (Ex. 12.6) begins with duets for high and low voices, the second of which basi-cally repeats the first down an octave (allowing for repetition of the chant paraphrase as in the opening trios) (Ex. 12.6, mm. 68–83). We then hear two brief trios, and end the motet with a thirteen-measure tutti section. The transparency of texture and alternating duets and trios recall Josquin's *Ave*

Example 12.6 Anon., *Vidi speciosam, secunda pars* (CS 15, 199′–201)

Maria, although the use of imitation is rudimentary in comparison with *Ave beatissima.*

Unlike *Ave beatissima* there are relatively few E cadences in *Vidi speciosam*, and none of them is problematic. This motet is first found in the Lucca Codex, copied c. 1467–72, so it may be a bit later than the motets in Trent 89, by which time the difficulties of E-final pieces had been worked out. Both *Ave beatissima* and *Vidi speciosam* point toward the imitative motet of the Josquin era. These works highlight imitation by placing it at the beginning of a phrase, associating it with a new line of text, and separating entries by two or more beats, an approach to imitation very different from Puyllois's in *Flos de spina*. *Ave beatissima* succeeds in presenting material in all voices, while *Vidi speciosam* introduces the transparent texture that makes Josquin's imitation so easy to hear. The use of structural imitation may have originated in the chant-para-phrase motet, and especially in these hybrids of the tenor motet and the chant-paraphrase motet.[41]

The *Ave Maria* in Trent 91 looks at first like a tenor motet because of its opening duets, tenor cantus firmus in the *prima pars*, and identical opening of the tenor in both *partes*. Other features make it look like a chant-paraphrase motet. The cantus firmus is not foreign, since it has the same text as the other voices (although not the complete text of the motet), and it is paraphrased in both the discantus and the tenor voices. Finally, the *secunda pars* appears to lack pre-existent material, making it at least partially a freely composed motet.[42]

The text of the *prima pars* of *Ave Maria* consists of the standard text of the angelic salutation (or "Hail Mary"):

> Ave Maria, gratia plena, dominus tecum,
> Benedicta tu in mulieribus,
> et benedictus fructus ventris tui.

As Daniel Freeman has shown, this text was set repeatedly in the Renaissance, often with additional text at the end.[43] The text of the *secunda pars* is an additional text known in no other *Ave Maria* setting: it goes on to praise Mary's mother ("Et benedicta sit mater tua sancta Anna") to whom Mary owes her immaculate conception ("sine peccato originali es concepta, O Maria"). Only discantus and tenor are texted in the *prima pars*. The text of the *secunda pars* would have been unfamiliar to the singers, so all voices are texted there (the first contratenor's text disappears after "Anna").

The chant on which the motet is based is an Annunciation antiphon, which sets only the first two lines of the motet text ("Ave Maria . . . mulieribus"). The chant is paraphrased in the discantus for the opening duet, which sets the first line of text ("Ave Maria . . . tecum"); the discantus repeats the first line of text to free material once the tenor voice enters with its own chant paraphrase. The tenor then continues with its paraphrase until the end of the chant (which comes before the end of the *prima pars*). In the *secunda pars* the tenor paraphrases the *Ave Maria* chant once again at its first entrance, and then continues with free material.

The combination of chant paraphrase in more than one voice (resulting in imitation, even if at a long time-interval), and the mixture of pre-existent and free material in both text and music points to the motets of the Josquin era, and in fact Josquin set the first phrase of the same antiphon in his so-called "little" *Ave Maria*.[44] As here, Josquin's motet begins with chant paraphrase for the opening of the angelic salutation, then goes on to new text set to freely composed music. Both motets have a triple-meter section near the end: Josquin's is just before the final phrase, while the Trent 91 motet puts it at the very end, for the final acclamation ("O Maria"). Although Josquin's motet is formally and musically very different – it is quite syllabic, uses pervasive imitation with alternating pairs of voices, has only one *pars*, and is in $\math0{C}$ throughout – many of the musical and textual techniques can be seen in embryo in the Trent 91 motet. But I do not want to suggest that the Trent *Ave Maria* is a beginner's attempt at the Josquin style: in its own way it is just as impressive, with its lively rhythms, continuous counterpoint, and grandeur of scale. The composer of the Trent *Ave Maria* demonstrated a lively and inventive ability to combine features and techniques from all the different subgenres of the large four-voice motet to create a new hybrid that would be very fruitful in the decades to come.

Du Fay's *Ave regina celorum III*, perhaps the best-known composition considered in this book, was copied in Cambrai in 1464.[45] The only surviving copy is in San Pietro B80, where it is found just before *Omnium bonorum plena*. Among the chant-paraphrase/tenor motet hybrids it is the closest to being a tenor motet. The chant is paraphrased in the tenor voice throughout and only makes occasional appearances in the other voices. The work begins with extended duets that Alejandro Planchart has recently compared to the opening of the *Caput* Mass.[46] The personal trope in the outer voices mentioning Du Fay by name recalls the new texts of the occasional or dedicatory motets. The delayed entrance of the tenor results in simultaneous presentation of two different texts (chant and trope), as in the motet with a foreign tenor.[47] The sacred Marian text and the existence of the related cyclic Mass recall the Mass-motet cycles.[48]

Like the chant-paraphrase motet, however, *Ave regina celorum* paraphrases a complete Marian antiphon in a single voice once through; for much of the motet all voices sing the same text. The opening duets paraphrase the tenor's chant melody in anticipation of the tenor, as in the second half of *Vidi speciosam* or the beginning of *Ave Maria*.[49] The duet beginning the second half is much shorter than those of most tenor motets (only two measures). This work, usually considered a fairly typical tenor motet, is another unique Du Fay creation. By combining the grandeur of the occasional motet and the cyclic Mass with the sacred liturgical associations of the chant paraphrase, Du Fay created a motet with encyclopedic references to the subgenres of the large-scale motet of the time.

Freely composed motets

The last group of pieces consists of those in which no one has yet identified any pre-existent material (see Table 12.5). The existence of a freely composed subgenre of the four-voice motet during this period has gone largely unrecognized until now. The pieces among this group that have been considered at any length have been assumed by some to be tenor motets, and the tendency is to generalize this assumption, essentially ignoring the possibility that they could be freely composed.[50] Almost all of them begin at least one section with a fairly extensive duet, and in many cases the tenor voices of these pieces begin with large note values, in the style of a long-note cantus firmus, so they do resemble tenor motets to some extent.

Still, there are reasons for suspecting that they are not tenor motets: (1) the tenor voice is not identified by a contrasting text incipit; (2) it does not exhibit double cursus, which is to say, that the tenor in the *secunda pars* is significantly different from the *prima pars*; and (3) the style of the tenor voice differs from the style of both chant and chanson tenors.

(1) Lack of identifying label. If the tenor is pre-existent there are two possibilities: either it is based on a chant with the same text as the other voices (as in the hybrid tenor/chant-paraphrase motets) or it is foreign (as in the tenor motets). Use of a chant with the same text is unusual, but it is relatively easy to track down, because all you have to do is find the melody associated

Table 12.5. *Freely composed motets*

89.640 Mu 3154, Tr 90 a3	Anima mea liquefacta est (**E**)	S*	CO or CØ (!); 3 & 4 vv.; duet 1a *pars*. 4-v version rewritten, up a fourth.
89.583–4	Regina celi (JC: **E**?)	S	OCO; T lowest part.
89.617–18	Gaude flore virginali (**E**)	L*	[O]CO; 3 *partes*; duets 1a and 3a *partes*.
89.567 Lausanne	Ave regina celorum (**E**)	5	Duet 1a *pars* only.
90.1122 @Strah, CS 15 SP B80, Milan 1	Puyllois, Flos de spina	L	Cantio BVM, Christmas. Duet 2a *pars* only.
88.238	O quam luce glorifica	L	R, Assumption BVM; pseudo-double cursus. Duet 1a *pars* only.
89.580–1	Gregatim grex audet	L	Sts. Gregory and Nicholas. Trio 2a *pars*.
89.582	Gaude regina	L*	No duets.
89.656	Levavi oculos	L*	Ps. 121; pseudo-double cursus.
89.577–8	Odas clangat (D1 & 2) Yesse produxit (T & Ct.)	H	OCC̸Ø; text incipits only; very imitative. Pseudo-double cursus; double-discantus.
91.1169–70	Martini?, Perfunde celi	M	Marriage of Duke of Ferrara, 1473. Pseudo-double cursus; trio 2a *pars*.

Key:
* = 4/5 cadence, combining 5–1 motion in one contratenor with 4–5 motion in another
@ = attribution in that source
M = two voices in the same, middle range ("*Caput* texture")
L = two voices in the same, lowest range ("*Flos de spina* texture")
S = all voices in different ranges (SATB texture)
H = two high voices in the same range (double-discantus texture)
5 = 5-voice motet
E = may be English, according to Curtis and Wathey, "List"

with the text of the upper voices and see if it is used. In the case of the foreign tenor it is much more difficult to determine whether the voice is pre-existent, since it could come from virtually anywhere. Nevertheless, such foreign tenors are usually labeled, because the emblematic function is lost if the tenor is not identified.[51] Lack of such an identifying label, then, is in itself grounds for suspicion of free composition, especially when combined with the other features discussed below.

(2) Lack of double cursus. Almost all the tenor motets listed here exhibit double cursus, while none of the freely composed motets does. There can be little doubt that double cursus is a strong indicator of a pre-existent tenor, since varied manipulations are usually carried out on a pre-existent melody. While the converse – lack of double cursus indicates a freely composed tenor – does not carry strict logical force, the motets assembled here do seem to bear it out.[52] Some of these motets begin the two *partes* with the same pitches, but then proceed very differently. This "pseudo-double cursus" may indeed be a reference to the tenor motet.[53]

(3) Melodic style of the tenor part. Pre-existent tenors are usually recognizable as such. A chant tenor is either stated almost exactly in long note values, and thus is recognizable as a cantus firmus (as in the contrafact Kyrie *Gaude Maria / T: Meditatio cordis*), or rhythmicized in such a way as to make the line resemble the other voices of the motet. In this second case (of which the only good example here is the three-voice *Salve virgo / T: Summe trinitati*) the contour of the melody and its phrasing remain very close to the chant, making it easy to identify.[54] In the case of chanson tenors many quote the original rhythms and pitches exactly (at least in the section of the motet that occurs in the same mensuration as the chanson). Others show free treatment of the original rhythms, but they tend to stick close to the original pitches. Chanson tenors also have phrases of more or less equal length, ending with recognizable cadences. The tenor of *Stella celi*, for example, treats the rhythms of the tenor of Frye's chanson, *So ys emprentid*, very freely, but quotes the pitches quite literally; the phrase structure of the original is still detectable.[55] Chant and chanson tenors both have a tendency to leap up, hover a bit, and then fall fairly gradually.

When we examine the tenors of the "freely composed" motets such as *Flos de spina*, they look rather different, especially in melodic contours and range of rhythmic motion. Freely composed tenors move around abruptly through a large range, occasionally careening from the top to the bottom; they lack the tuneful quality and the carefully modulated melodic arches of the pre-existent melodies. While chanson tenors often have a fairly restricted range of note values, freely composed tenors begin phrases with longs and breves, very quickly speeding up to the level of minims and semiminims, as in *Flos de spina* (Ex. 11.5). Most of the freely composed pieces also have the "*Flos de spina*" texture, with two low voices, both of which move rapidly through their range. These tenor lines lack the melodic decorum that we associate with chant and with chanson tenors; I am confident that these works are freely composed.

The earliest of the motets listed here (at least judging by copying dates) is *Flos de spina*, which, as we have already seen, derives from the English cantilena tradition, while incorporating features from the *Caput* Mass and, perhaps, the largely English tradition of freely composed three-voice "Sine nomine Masses." It may well have provided a model for many of the later works. There is also evidence of more direct contact with English music of the period. *Anima mea liquefacta est*, as we have seen, is actually a reworking for four voices of a three-voice English cantilena. *Regina celi* may be an English work, though no one has suggested it previously: its unusual texture, with differentiated ranges and the tenor on the bottom, resembles that of Dunstaple's *Descendi* and the anonymous *Cantemus domino* discussed in chapter 11.[56]

Two other works in Table 12.5 are English as well. The five-voice *Ave regina celorum* (89.567) is found in an English fragment now housed in Lausanne; it has an unusual texture, with two high voices, a tenor in the middle, and two low voices.[57] This work may represent a proto Eton Choirbook style, as Strohm suggested. As soon as four-voice writing became the norm, composers began experimenting with five-voice textures for special effects.

Gaude flore virginali sets an English text believed to have been written by St. Thomas Becket. As he was meditating on the poem *Gaude virgo mater Christi* about the five Joys of the Virgin in this life, the Virgin appeared to him and suggested that he consider the seven joys she experiences in paradise, upon which he wrote the poem *Gaude flore virginali*.[58] Eleven settings are found in the index to the Eton Choirbook, while there are no firmly attested continental settings. This is one of the few four-voice motets of this period with more than two *partes*, and it is fully texted in Trent 89. Much of the piece is given over to duets that alternate between imitative writing and chains of parallel thirds and sixths; one duet often gives way to another pair of voices before return of the full texture. There is homorhythmic declamation on "A Jesu dulcissimo," and brief melodies in triplets. The constant changes of texture keep the lengthy work interesting. The F final, triadic melodies and parallel thirds give this motet a bright major-mode sound, quite different from the denser and more somber sonorities of *Flos de spina* (even though it uses the same basic texture, with two low voices). These two motets illustrate the best in the freely composed four-voice motet of the 1450s.

The freely composed motet, then, owes a great deal to English music, and

English examples of the subgenre continued to be found on the Continent well into the 1460s. The English pieces tended to set texts with associated melodies (such as Marian antiphons), and then ignore those melodies, while the continental composers chose texts without such strong musical associations (such as the psalm motet, *Levavi oculos*, whose text could be sung to any psalm tone but was associated with no real melody). The English works were also more likely to have more than two *partes*: the association of this form with the motet had not become fixed in England.

Most of the continental freely composed motets resemble *Flos de spina* in terms of voice ranges and texture. They retain the predominantly consonant discantus–tenor framework, now with the occasional fourth slipped in on the sly in expectation of the other voices still to be composed.

O quam luce and *Levavi oculos* come closest to *Flos de spina*. Both use the *Flos de spina* texture (*Levavi* in the high-clef version C1, C3, C4, C4, because of its higher final, G). *O quam luce* begins with a lengthy duet (twenty breves), and there is another in the middle of the *secunda pars*. Otherwise duets and trios are few and limited to two or three breves. The work as a whole has very little imitation, with the exception of a few triadic exchanges, or brief imitative exchanges between the contratenors over sustained notes in the tenor.[59] *Levavi oculos*, a setting of Psalm 121, may be the first surviving psalm motet. In addition to the opening duets for the upper voices, each *pars* has a central duet; each duet uses a different voice combination. There is little imitation, but cadences are formed between any two voices, even in the tutti sections, leading to a highly integrated texture.

Gregatim grex and *Gaude regina* both use a variant of the *Flos de spina* texture in which the two contratenors are in the same range: they have the same lowest note as the tenor, but also rise high above it, for a total range of an octave and a sixth. This texture resembles that of Du Fay's *O proles/O sidus*, with one high part and three low ones, and all three voices move rapidly up and down through their total range, resulting in constant voice-crossing. The second contratenor's behavior is especially surprising, participating at one moment in imitation at the unison with the discantus (and even crossing above it), the next moment dropping down for the typical low-contratenor cadential harmonization (see Ex. 12.7, *Gaude regina*, mm. 50–4).[60] *Gaude regina* has no duets and only one brief trio. It is a shorter piece than the others (only one opening) and its pleasing melodies, frequent parallel thirds and fifths, and passing of motifs from voice to voice are very appealing. *Gregatim grex* fea-

Example 12.7 Anon., *Gaude regina*, mm. 50–4 (Trent 89.582, 126′–127)

tures lengthy, often imitative duets and trios with lots of minims and semi-minims.

Odas clangat is in some ways a throwback to the 1420s and 1430s. It uses the old-fashioned double-discantus texture (C1, C1, C4, C4) and its opening duets recall the imitative introitus sections of Italian motets of Du Fay's *Vassilissa* or *Ecclesie militantis*. Nevertheless the sequence of mensurations and the general melodic and harmonic language are closer to those of the 1440s and 1450s. The music of the final Ø section looks exactly like that of the opening O section, and bears no resemblance to the old cut-circle style. This piece is an extremely attractive mix of old and new.[61]

Our last motet, *Perfunde celi rore*, is also among the latest of the motets in the Trent Codices. The text reveals that the motet was composed for the wedding of Duke Ercole I d'Este and Eleanor of Aragon in Ferrara in 1473.[62] We would expect such a grand occasional work to be a tenor motet, and it has many of the tenor motet's trappings: reduced scoring and then long notes in the tenor at the beginning of both *partes*, *Caput* texture, and occasional text. The scribe included the complete text in all the voices, so he would probably have included a tenor label if one had been present in his exemplar. But there is no such label, and the tenor voice moves at the same rate as the other voices (after the long-note openings); it also uses pseudo-double cursus. I believe that *Perfunde celi rore* is freely composed.

The work as a whole is rhythmically animated, with strings of minims, dotted rhythms, and even the occasional fusae. One striking rhythmic figure involves the alternation of minims and semiminims (a kind of six-eight pattern in transcription) that can start on any beat. This figure occurs every few measures and serves to shake things up rhythmically.[63] Martini is also fond of the dotted figures so common in Puyllois's *Flos de spina*. While there is relatively little strict imitation, Martini is constantly passing around small rhythmic figures and scale fragments, or doubling them momentarily in thirds or sixths, so that the texture as a whole is integrated rhythmically and melodically.[64] The few real imitative passages are highlighted by abrupt reduction in texture, as at the word "Hercules" (Duke Ercole), for first contratenor and tenor, with related figures in the other voices immediately before and after,[65] or at the opening of the *secunda pars*, where there is a three-voice point of imitation. In *Perfunde celi rore* Martini combined the trappings of the tenor motet with the freedom of the freely composed motet. He then added the rhythmically animated motivic style that we saw in Touront's song motets: the result is an exciting, almost frenetic, grandeur.

Conclusion

Part III, like Part II, concludes with a review of some of the individual pieces with an eye to interpretation. (I do not discuss the four-voice tenor motets here, since most are discussed elsewhere.) Knowledge of the origins and associations of the subgenres to which these pieces belong allows us to determine the motets' fields of reference, to recognize what is new and important about them, and to position them in the genre hierarchy. With this knowledge we can begin to enjoy what is special about these motets and recognize some of what their composers were trying to do.

Touront: Compangant omnes *(Ex. 9.3)*

Compangant omnes looks back to the English cantilena's three-voice cantilena-texture and flexible rhythms. It is especially close to Frye's cantilenas. Its bipartite, triple-to-duple form is unusual for a song motet; it should perhaps be seen as a three-voice analog of the four-voice freely composed motet. It looks over at the chanson (its two sections are found separately in a chansonnier, Bologna Q16, with French text incipits) recalling the formal eroticism of courtly love. *Compangant omnes* also belongs to the world and the repertory of the professional instrumentalists: the town trumpeters and dance bands that played so many functions in daily life in the courts and towns, especially in Central Europe and the Netherlands. It belongs to the repertory of three-voice, rhythmically animated, often imitative works that move easily across generic boundaries and contribute to the cross-fertilization of genres in the second half of the fifteenth century.

Regali ex progenie/T: Sancta Maria *(Ex. 10.4)*

This three-voice tenor motet also makes multiple generic references: to the cantilena, the isorhythmic motet, and the tenor Mass. The careful division of the tenor cantus firmus into two parts of equal length recalls the precise proportional relationships of isorhythm, while the flexible rhythmic style of the top part and its mensural conflicts with the tenor suggest the fluid, ametrical rhythms of the Band II cantilenas, as does the use of a single top voice carrying a pre-existent text. The dual role of the motetus/contratenor underscores the generic ambiguity of the whole subgenre. Is this an intimate Marian cantilena, or a severe, hieratic isorhythmic motet? It is both and neither: the informal intimacy of the cantilena is given new dignity, while the rigid motet is given a more human voice. Just as the motet lies in the middle of the genre hierarchy, *Regali ex progenie* lies in the middle of the subgenre hierarchy.

Puyllois: Flos de spina *(Ex. 11.5)*

This is the first surviving four-voice freely composed motet. Both its text and music make multiple generic references that point toward the origins of the subgenre. The use of a pre-existent Marian text with language that recalls the *Song of Songs* seems at first to belong to the English cantilena tradition. But the poetic form and the more abstruse typological second half are more reminiscent of isorhythmic motet texts. Likewise, the lack of pre-existent material, the flexible approach to rhythm, the imitation over sustained tenor notes, and the integrated duets recall the English Band II *Song* cantilenas. But the long notes in the tenor at the beginnings of sections, the lengthy duet in the second half, and the length of the piece recall the tenor motet or the English Mass movement, specifically *Caput*. English musical innovations are integrated into continental compositional styles and genres in *Flos de spina*. The intimate cantilena has given birth to a new four-voice subgenre that aspires to the status of the tenor motet.

Touront: Recordare virgo *(Exx. 12.2 and 12.3)*

This four-voice chant-paraphrase motet makes several explicit references to liturgical chant settings. The chant paraphrased is an offertory, one of the Mass Propers often set to polyphony as part of a complete set of Propers; the piece also begins with a chant incipit. Nevertheless, *Recordare* is not part of a set of Mass Propers, and its number of voices, bipartite structure, and overall length move it up the genre hierarchy toward the Mass Ordinary movement and the tenor motet. Touront's use of imitation and rhythmic sequence were apparent in his freely composed song motets: here they are used in conjunction with the text and melody of a chant, resulting in text-based mostly syllabic imitation between discantus and tenor. The inserted tripla section at the end of the *prima pars* may point toward the tripla sections so common in the motets of the Josquin generation. Humble service music is here raised to the status of the motet by musical means.

Ave beatissima *(Ex. 12.5) and* Vidi speciosam *(Ex. 12.6)*

These two pieces both paraphrase E-final chants. The use of an E final for polyphony was almost unheard of before *c.* 1450; these motets are thus part of a new mid-century development that included the E-final chansons of Ockeghem and Du Fay, and Ockeghem's *Missa Mi-mi*. Our knowledge of the different subgenres of the four-voice motet makes it possible to recognize these pieces as hybrids of the chant-paraphrase and tenor motets. As such, they combine the piety of chant settings with the musical ambitions of tenor motet. The chant paraphrase in these works is combined with imitation, resulting in a texture that points toward the late fifteenth-century imitative motet.

Du Fay: Ave regina celorum III

In Du Fay's last motet our master of generic mixture once again makes multiple references to other genres, to the subgenres of the motet, and to the genre's history. *Ave regina celorum III* is a chant-paraphrase motet that makes reference to simpler chant settings and continental cantilenas. It is a tenor motet that recalls the isorhythmic motet tradition: it has a long-note cantus firmus in the tenor, lengthy opening duets, and new text in the upper voices (interpolated into the Marian antiphon text). It recalls the four-voice freely composed motet and the English cantilena, with its Marian text and flexible homogeneous texture; freely composed sections of the motet use the closely spaced imitation at the minim (Ex. 11.7), derived from English music, that we saw in *Flos de spina* (Ex. 11.5). It has the bipartite form and four-voice texture of the *Caput* Mass. It uses the same tenor, and served as the model for Du Fay's last cyclic Mass, making it part of a Mass-motet cycle. Thomas Brothers sees in the motet's "Terzfreiheit" a reference to the high-style chanson.[66] Du Fay's lifetime of experimentation with all kinds of music came to fruition in his motet *Ave regina celorum III*. It is no wonder that he asked that it be sung at his death bed.

Conclusion

In the preceding pages I have mapped out the radical transformation of the motet over the course of Du Fay's lifetime. This map looks something like Darwin's great evolutionary tree: some subgenres die, while others branch off from old ones. The motet's evolutionary tree, however, has even more interconnections and intertwinings than Darwin's, since many of the subgenres have multiple antecedents. I have summarized my findings in Tables C.1–3 (pp. 298–303). The different subgenres, their antecedents and descendants, are listed in Table C.1; other genres that influenced the motet are listed in Table C.2; and a diagram of the subgenres and their interconnections is given in Table C.3. We are now in a position to look back and narrate the history of the motet during the first three-quarters of the fifteenth century, and to bring into relief the "selection pressures" – features of the political, social, cultural and musical environment – that help explain why the motet evolved the way it did.

Subgenres in Bologna Q15

The Council of Constance (1414–18) and the French victory over the English at Agincourt (1415) meant that musicians and composers from many different regions were exposed to each other and to each other's music. During and after these events composers began to travel as never before: English musicians came to the Continent, while composers and singers trained in the North increasingly traveled south to Italy in search of more rewarding employment. Bologna Q15 can be seen as a testament to and an artefact of that confluence and mobility. It contains continuations of fourteenth-century local traditions of composition from France and the Low Countries, England, and Italy; it also contains new hybrid subgenres that combine elements from these different

288

local traditions and from genres outside the motet. The Italian motet and the French isorhythmic motet are straightforward continuations of continental traditions of motet composition. New and ultimately very significant to the history of the motet on the Continent is the inclusion of the English cantilena in the motet section of Bologna Q15. I have suggested that the absorption of the English cantilena into the motet on the Continent resulted in part from the lack of any better generic category on the Continent for the cantilena and in part from the similarly indeterminate liturgical function of both the cantilena and the motet. New devotional practices on the Continent, including more Marian services and the specification of polyphony for obits, memorials, and endowments, made the predominantly Marian imports very welcome: they also created a market for continental music composed along similar lines.

The texture of the English cantilena (a single texted top voice over two lower accompanying voices) was not new on the Continent: it was well known from the chanson, the lauda and the Mass. What was new was the use of this texture in subgenres of the motet. The cantilena texture opened up the motet to new kinds of generic references and new kinds of register and tone: the sense of community associated with the lauda and improvised polyphony, and the intimacy of the chanson. These could be combined with the more traditional text types and subjects of the motet, resulting in an astonishingly rich expressive range for the genre as a whole.

New hybrid subgenres found in Q15 and in other contemporary manuscripts (especially the Italian Oxford 213 and Bologna 2216) include both motet-style and cantilena-style textures. The retrospective double-discantus motet looked back to the early history of the motet and conductus in France for its text types, while drawing heavily on the Italian motet for its basic texture and style. The devotional double-discantus motet also resembles the Italian motet, but its subject matter – the Virgin Mary – is that of the English cantilena. The other double-discantus motets, which continue into the 1440s, use devotional texts, but the style is closer to that of the few surviving English double-discantus motets.

The most important of the new cantilena-style hybrids, judging simply by numbers, was the cut-circle motet: it combined the texture of the English cantilena with continental melodic and rhythmic styles developed in the Mass and especially the chanson. As in the English cantilena, the texts of the cut-circle motet are primarily devoted to the Virgin, but they tend to use the rhyming stanzaic poetic forms of the continental motet-style motets rather than prose antiphon texts. The range of subject matter is also broader, extending to saints, doges, and important churchmen of the time. The declamation motets, while extremely popular in the 1430s, sparked few imitations and had no direct descendants. More important evolutionarily, because longer-lived, was the continental cantilena, a response to the English cantilena that used the votive antiphon texts favored by the English in conjunction with their associated melodies.

Subgenres in the Trent Codices and Modena X.1.11

The musical developments in the decades around mid-century are hard to associate with any one locale. One important location was the choir schools in the collegiate churches and cathedrals of the Netherlands. These schools, the training ground for most of the composers of the Renaissance, also benefited from their strategic location across the channel from England. Du Fay in Cambrai and Puyllois in Antwerp are witness to the importance of this area. Another musical center was Rome, the administrative center of the world for a beneficed musician. Once again we find Du Fay and Puyllois as well as Le Rouge (composer of a Mass-motet cycle) and possibly Compère. Yet another center may have been the Habsburg court, with which we can associate Brassart, Sarto, and probably Touront. These centers, and many others, were tied together by the flow of musicians up and down and across Europe.[1] Du Fay and Puylloys are just two of the many musicians who traveled back and forth between north and south, and who retained contact with distant colleagues. The sources we have examined are testimony to this musical mobility. Ferrara and Trent are both located along north–south routes. The Ferrarese Modena X.1.11 contains a substantial collection of English music as well as almost all of Du Fay's late motets, while the Trent Codices contain music from all over Europe. The musical developments on the Continent in the decades around 1450 belong to no one locale: they are the product of a pan-European musical culture in which English and local elements are blended into something new.

The "contenance angloise"

The earlier Trent Codices (87, 92, 93 and 90) and Modena X.1.11 were copied during and shortly after the Council of Basel (1431–49). It was during the early 1430s, perhaps at Basel, that English music in really large quantities first reached the Continent. From 1430 to 1450 English music dominated the motet repertory, both in terms of sheer quantity of music copied and in terms of influence on continental genres. Features that in Q15 were found only in the English cantilena – the single discantus voice combined with a pre-existent votive or devotional text – became defining features of virtually the whole motet repertory for the rest of its history. The English approach to melody and rhythm – a floating, long-breathed melody that avoided clear presentation of meter – became standard for composers in every genre in mid-century.

The "contenance angloise" has become a commonplace of music history thanks to Martin le Franc and Tinctoris, but there has been little agreement about what exactly it was. The usual features proposed are increased use of imperfect consonances and greater control of dissonance. It is also generally admitted that the cyclic cantus firmus Mass was an English invention. David Fallows has recently suggested that we avoid associating the "contenance angloise" with specific traits or specific moments of transformation.[2] When we look at the motet in the 1430s and 1440s, however, there is no escaping the overwhelming impact of English music: composers such as Puyllois and Du Fay did indeed take up the styles, textures, and subgenres of English music. A look at the English subgenres of the motet and at the other English genres that influenced the motet makes this abundantly clear.

ENGLISH CANTILENAS

The most numerous and important of the imported English genres was the English cantilena, which dominated the repertory in terms of numbers of pieces and especially numbers of copies. The English cantilena was also evolving, however, and the music of the generation of Power and Dunstaple (Band I) gradually gave way in the 1440s to a new generation of composers including Plummer and Frye (Band II). A substantial portion of the Band II cantilenas featured motets with texts from the *Song of Songs* and a new approach to composition: integrated duets for all pairs of voices (including opening duets for discantus and contratenor), a similar rhythmic and melodic style in all voices, and more extensive use of imperfect tempus. All these features would become important for later continental music. Frye's Band II cantilenas, in contrast, were closer to the chanson, with continuous three-voice texture and even repetition of musical material.

These two approaches to the English cantilena led to two different continental cantilena-style subgenres: the continental cantilena, and the three-voice song motet. Although new three-voice English cantilenas stop appearing in the sources after about 1460, two live on in the chansonniers of the last quarter of the century, along with Touront's *O gloriosa regina*: Frye's *Ave regina celorum* and the anonymous *Song of Songs* setting, *O pulcherrima*. The presence of these pieces in the chansonniers may point to English influence on the French chanson. *Anima mea*, another Band II *Song of Songs* motet, was converted into a four-voice freely composed motet, and *Flos de spina* recalls many aspects of the English *Song* settings. The English cantilena's reach was long.

ENGLISH ISORHYTHMIC MOTETS FOR THREE AND FOUR VOICES

English isorhythmic motets, unlike most continental ones in the first third of the fifteenth century, generally had differentiated ranges for the triplum and motetus voices. The resultant texture, as Thomas Brothers has suggested, had a single lyrical top voice that resembled the discantus of the cantilena or even the chanson.[3] In the three-voice motets the clef of the motetus was a fifth below that of the triplum/discantus, in the same range as the tenor, and could thus function as a low contratenor. The four-voice motets also often featured differentiated ranges and/or rhythmic motion between the tenor and contratenor parts. This kind of range differentiation, with a single top voice and sometimes a low contratenor, may have paved the way in England for the development of the *Caput* texture. The introduction of these motets on the Continent in the 1430s, probably at Basel, seems to have inspired textural experiments in the continental isorhythmic motets of the 1430s and 1440s that point toward the new four-voice textures of the second half of the century.

THE THREE-VOICE TENOR MOTET

This English subgenre combines features of the cantilena and three-voice isorhythmic motet; it is also close in style to the English three-voice tenor Mass. It seems to have arrived on the Continent in the early 1430s, inspired imitations by continental composers who attended the Council of Basel (Merques and Du Fay) quite early on, and then survived in a modest way until late in the century. This is the first motet subgenre in which we find a tenor cantus firmus but no use of isorhythm, and it provides an important precedent for the later four-voice tenor motet.

THE ENGLISH CYCLIC MASS

English Masses and the continental cycles inspired by them were essential textural and stylistic models for motets. The three-voice tenor motet evolved along with the three-voice Mass. Contrafact Kyries for three and four voices circulated as motets. Four-voice motets were composed to go with three-voice chanson Masses. The anonymous English *Caput* Mass, a model for four-voice writing in all genres, was particularly important for the treatment of form and cantus firmus (OC, double cursus) in the four-voice tenor motet. The English "sine nomine" Mass provided a model for the composition of *Flos de spina* and the development of the freely composed motet.

WHY?

How can we explain the attraction and influence of English music during the second quarter of the fifteenth century? England's control of much of France and its alliance with Burgundy and the Burgundian Netherlands made it a major power in Europe, both politically and economically. The expanding market for polyphony in churches and courts meant that there was constant demand for new music. English Masses, motets and cantilenas, often composed decades earlier, fit the bill.

Generic change in any medium at any period is largely a function of the competing claims of tradition and novelty. English music was a source of novelty, of new ways of composing for continental musicians – but there was enough familiar English music around that it also acquired the comfort of the traditional. The gradual disappearance of English music from the Continent after the early 1450s was to a large extent a result of political events (the defeat of the English in France and political turmoil in England). But it is also possible that English music became less attractive as its novelty wore off. Having mastered the English subgenres and taken over their texts and text-types, continental composers began to move in new directions: toward a more rhythmically animated style with a greater use of sequence and toward the use of structural imitation in four voices.

Continental subgenres

Most of the really distinctive new hybrid subgenres found in Q15 died out around 1440. As English subgenres and style became more popular and the approach to rhythm changed, the brilliant and extroverted melodic language of the chanson-influenced cut-circle motets and the Italian-influenced devotional double-discantus motets went out of favor. Likewise the declamation motet failed to survive, perhaps because its extreme homorhythm was considered too much of a special effect.

The continental cantilena lived on, however, into the 1460s. It moved away gradually from the cut-circle rhythmic language and simple declamatory style of the Q15 repertory, towards a more fluid, flexible approach, often with integrated duets in the English manner. Composers of continental cantilenas are more likely than the English to limit themselves to the four great Marian antiphons, and to use the associated chant melodies, perhaps because of habits developed while composing the increasing numbers of liturgical chant settings in the 1440s (such as Du Fay's hymn cycle or the Mass Proper cycles in Trent 88).

Gradually, a more energetic continental rhythmic style marked by sequence developed, perhaps influenced by developments in the chanson. We can see this in some of the late continental cantilenas such as Du Fay's *Ave regina celorum II*, but it is even more common in Touront's freely composed song motets of the 1450s and 1460s. The continued interchange between cantilena-style genres and the chanson was encouraged by the practice of contrafacture in Central Europe and by the inclusion of three-voice motets in chansonniers. In Touront's song motets the text types and forms resemble those of Frye's cantilenas, while the approach to rhythm, imitation and melody is closer to that of continental chansons and tricinia of the period. As four-voice writing became more common, freely composed four-voice motets with a single section began to emerge very much after the Touront model.

The French isorhythmic motet lived on as well, but only through the mid-1440s. During its last decade it underwent important textural modifications as it abandoned the double-discantus texture for a new texture with a single top voice and a voice below the tenor. Why did the isorhythmic motet die out? As the oldest of the subgenres, with its beginnings in the early fourteenth century or even in the thirteenth, it may just have become too rigid and old-fashioned at a time when the dominant musical aesthetic moved toward an unpredictable flexibility of melody and rhythm. Many of the most important functions and features of the isorhythmic motet were taken over by its descendants, the tenor Mass and tenor motet, which sometimes used tenor repetition or rhythmic and mensural manipulation reminiscent of older isorhythm.[4] The use of occasional or dedicatory texts, associated in the early fifteenth century primarily with isorhythm and with motet-style subgenres like the Italian motet, continued in the tenor motet (and occasionally in other subgenres of the motet as well).[5]

TEXTURAL EXPERIMENTATION

While the last examples of the isorhythmic motet were experimenting with various approaches to texture, there was also considerable experimentation with four-voice textures in the non-isorhythmic subgenres, away from the older double-discantus textures toward textures with a single top voice, like those of most of the English imports. Judging by the numerous different four-voice textures, and the numbers of pieces with added voices, there was a continuing search for satisfactory four-voice textures both in England and on the Continent. In pieces with cantus firmus this involved experimentation with the relative ranges and degree of rhythmic motion of almost all the voices; in freely composed works much of the experimentation involved adding a fourth voice to three-voice pieces. The two successful textures that emerged are the high/two-middle/low *Caput* texture, associated especially with cantus firmus works, and the high/middle/two-low *Flos de spina* texture, associated especially with freely composed works.

NEW FOUR-VOICE SUBGENRES

In the last three Trent Codices (especially Trent 88 and 89) and in some of the smaller contemporary manuscripts, we can identify four fully developed subgenres of the four-voice motet with a single discantus voice, and one hybrid. With the exception of the four-voice song motet with a single section, they almost all use the mensural pattern OC or O¢, sometimes returning to triple meter at the end, and either the *Caput* or the *Flos de spina* texture. Each of the different subgenres of four-voice motet can trace its roots back to different antecedents; all continue into the sixteenth century.

The four-voice tenor motet descends from the late continental four-voice isorhythmic motet and the four-voice tenor Mass, especially *Caput*. Some have occasional or dedicatory texts, as in the fifteenth-century continental isorhythmic motet, and some are linked by tenor and/or contrafacture to contemporary tenor Masses, both English and continental; others are independent motets with pre-existent devotional texts. The tenor motet continued to flourish through the Josquin era; as four-voice writing became more and more commonplace, tenor motets, always the grandest of the sub-

295

genres, were composed more often for five voices so that they would remain at the top of the genre hierarchy.

The chant-paraphrase motet descends from the three-voice continental cantilena with chant, the English cantilenas with chant, and the numerous liturgical chant settings composed in the 1440s. Lacking the contrasts in texture typical of the tenor motet, it does sometimes feature imitation or *Vorimitation* of the chant material, usually in the tenor part. Because the imitation is based on the chant material, it is text-linked and often syllabic. This is very different from the kinds of imitation found in English motets or in *Flos de spina*, and points toward the structural imitation of the Josquin era.

In the hybrid chant-paraphrase/tenor motet, the tenor motet's textural variety is combined with the chant-paraphrase motet's paraphrase of a single chant in a single voice. These pieces are often characterized by extensive imitation between the two possible chant-bearing lines (discantus and tenor). This free use of chant and extensive use of imitation signaled by the use of the same segment of text and a substantial time-interval of imitation will become standard features of the motet for the rest of the Renaissance.

The freely composed motet derives primarily from the Band II English cantilenas, while its form and scale resemble that of the English Mass movement, either the *Caput* Mass or the three-voice "sine nomine" Masses. Free composition is generally associated with secular genres such as the chanson, and does not usually come to mind when we think of the continental motet of the late Middle Ages and early Renaissance. This is an inappropriate stereotype, even in the fourteenth century: many Italian and English motets had no cantus firmus, while in the Q15 repertory most of the cantilena-style subgenres and the double-discantus motets lack pre-existent material. With Puyllois's *Flos de spina* we see a new subgenre of freely composed motet comparable in size to the four-voice tenor motet. It could even take on the tenor motet's ceremonial role, as in *Perfunde celi rore*. Free composition with similar rhythmic and melodic motion in all voices would become the rule rather than the exception in the motet.

One of the most important developments in fifteenth-century music was the establishment of a homogeneous four-voice texture with a single top voice as the norm for sacred vocal polyphony.[6] One subplot of this story of the motet has been concerned with that development. The texture subplot is far from over in the 1470s: throughout the next several decades the *Flos de spina* texture would die out, a single low contratenor "bassus" would become the norm, and the two middle parts would gradually move apart, resulting in the SATB cleffing and texture that would be standard for several centuries. Some of the first examples of that texture appear among our Trent motets, but it is not yet the norm.

The motet style or subgenre sometimes known as the "Milan motet" is not yet found in the Trent Codices.[7] Characterized by a four-voice texture with many duets, syllabic text setting, text-based "syntactic" imitation, occasional homorhythmic passages, and duple meter with occasional tripla insertions, the style of the "Milan motet" is best known in Josquin's famous *Ave Maria...virgo serena*; it is first found in the *motetti missales* cycles composed by Compère and Weerbecke. The dates for the creation of this new kind of motet (1470s or 1480s?) and Josquin's role in its creation are hotly debated topics.[8] In any case little is known about its stylistic origins: the "Milan motet," like Athena, appears to have leaped forth fully formed from the minds of its creators.

Knowledge of the four-voice motets of the later Trent Codices, however, provides a context for this development: virtually all the ingredients are there, ready to be combined. Free composition is found in the freely composed motets and the song motets. Use of exclusively duple meter is on the rise in the Band II English cantilenas, and is fairly common in both Frye's and Touront's song motets. "Syntactic" imitation, often text-linked, and occasional tripla passages, especially at the ends of sections, are found in the chant-paraphrase and hybrid chant-paraphrase/tenor motets such as *Ave beatissima* and Touront's *Recordare*, and in the three- and four-voice imitative song motets. Homophony is a rare commodity in mid-century, but the four-voice song motet *Tu ne quesieris* is predominantly homorhythmic, and homophonic passages are found in some of the freely composed motets (*Gaude flore* and *Gregatim grex*).[9] The development and eventual triumph of imitative polyphony belongs to the period after the death of Du Fay. The essential background for that story, however, is found earlier, in the motets of the later Trent Codices.

A central task of this book has been to establish how the motet evolved during Du Fay's lifetime. Study of the origins, growth, decay, and transformation of the branches of the motet's evolutionary tree has provided a new, clearer view of music history in the fifteenth century. The repertories and subgenres described here provide essential background to the later developments of the Josquin era. They also provide an interpretive framework and a historical context for a great deal of anonymous music and for the achievements of composers like Monte, Forest, Sarto, Salinis, Arnold de Lantins, Puyllois, Touront, and above all Du Fay.

Table C.1. *Subgenres, with their antecedents and descendants*

Ch[a]	Subgenre,[b] dates, description	Antecedents	Descendants
4	French isorhythmic motet with 2 Ds 1400–1430s Motet-style, 3 and 4 vv. cantus firmus	14th-c. French isorhythmic motet	Isorhythmic w/ 1 D; ultimately 4-v tenor motet
4	Italian motet 1400–1420s Motet-style	14th-c. Italian motet caccia	Devotional D-D; Other D-D; French isorhythmic
9	English cantilena (Band I) comes to Continent 1420s–1440s Cantilena-style, 3 vv. occasional chant paraphrase	14th-c. English cantilena and polyphonic votive antiphon	Cut-circle Continental cantilena 3-v tenor Band II Eng. cantilena 4-v freely composed
6	Retrospective double-discantus motet 1405–1420s Motet-style	13th-c. French conductus and motet 14th-c. Italian motet	None
6	Devotional double-discantus motet	Italian motet cut-circle motet	Other double-discantus
11	Other double-discantus motets 1420s–c. 1440 Motet-style	Italian motet, English double-discantus, devotional double-discantus	None (possibly a few big 4- and 5-v motets)

5	Cut-circle motet 1420s–1430s Cantilena-style	English cantilena French chanson	Some continental cantilenas, devotional double-discantus motets
6 9	Declamation motet 1420s–1430s Cantilena-style	English cantilena (esp. *Quam pulchra*), lauda, cut-circle, improvised polyphony	None
6	Continental cantilena 1420s–1450s Cantilena-style, usually uses chant	English cantilena	4-v chant paraphrase Touront song motet 4-v song motet
6	Unus–chorus motet 1420s–1430s Cantilena- and motet-style	Mass movements	None
10	English isorhythmic motet, 3vv. comes to Continent 1430s–1440s T cantus firmus, 1 D above lower motetus/contratenor	14th-c. English motet, possibly French isorhythmic motet	3-v tenor motet, tenor Mass cycle
10	English isorhythmic motet, 4 vv. comes to Continent 1430s–1440s T cantus firmus, 1 D (triplum) above lower motetus	14th-c. English motet, possibly French isorhythmic motet	Later continental isorhythmic motets with 1 D, tenor Mass(?), 4-v tenor motet
10	3-v tenor motet (mostly English) comes to Continent 1430s; some later continental exx. to 1470s (?) Foreign T cantus firmus, 1 D above lower motetus/contratenor	3-v English isorhythmic motet, English cantilena, 3-v tenor Mass	3-v tenor Mass, later continental isorhythmic motets, 4-v tenor motet

Table C.1. (*cont.*)

Ch[a]	Subgenre,[b] dates, description	Antecedents	Descendants
10	Continental isorhythmic motet with 1 D 1430s–1440s lower motetus	French isorhythmic motet 3- and 4-*v* English isorhythmic motet	4-*v* tenor motet, continental tenor Mass
9	English cantilena (Band II) 1440s–1450s *Song* texts common, opening duets, integrated texture, use of imperfect tempus; also Frye song motets	Band I cantilenas Chanson?	Later continental cantilenas 4-*v* freely composed 4-*v* chant paraphrase Touront song motet
9	Touront song motet (3 *vv.*) 1460s–1490s, possibly beyond freely composed, imitative, animated off-beat rhythmic figures in sequence	Band II cantilenas continental cantilena (w/o chant) chanson and tricinium	More 3-*v* song motets tricinia, chansons; possibly motet-chansons; 4-*v* song motet
12	4-*v* song motet 1460s– freely composed, one section	Touront "song motet" transitional 4-*v* motets chanson and instrumental works	"Milan" motet, motets with structural imitation, freely composed motets with devotional texts
12	4-*v* tenor motet 1450s–1500 (and beyond) Foreign T w/ double cursus single discantus, *Caput* texture OC mensurations/form	3-*v* tenor motet 4-*v* isorhythmic motet (Eng. and continental) *Caput* Mass other cyclic Masses	5-*v* tenor motet of Regis through Mouton (at least)

12	4-v chant-paraphrase motet 1450s–1500 (and beyond) single discantus, few duets OC mensurations/form	English and continental cantilenas liturgical chant settings	"Paraphrase" motet, motets with structural imitation, "Milan" motet
12	4-v hybrid tenor/chant-paraphrase motet 1450s–1500 (and beyond) single discantus, cpf in D & T OC mensurations/form	4-v tenor motet 4-v chant-paraphrase motet and their antecedents	"Paraphrase" motet, motets with structural imitation, "Milan" motet, motets with free use of chant
12	4-v freely composed motet 1450s–1500 single discantus, opening duets OC mensurations/form Flos de spina texture	English and continental cantilenas Caput Mass Transitional 4-v motets 3-v sine nomine Mass Touront song motet	Freely composed motets with devotional texts for the rest of the Renaissance

Notes:

[a] Ch = Chapter(s) in which these subgenres are discussed.

[b] See Tables 7.1 and 8.6 for numbers of motets in each subgenre.

Table C.2. *Genres outside the motet that influenced the motet*

Genre	The subgenres it influenced
English cantilena	See Table C.1: Band I English cantilena Band II English cantilena
French chanson and instrumental tricinium	All the cantilena-style genres, especially the cut-circle motet Touront song motet 4-v song motet but also including the English cantilena continental cantilena declamation motet
Subgenres of the Mass and Mass cycle	
Early continental unus–chorus movements	unus–chorus motet
Early continental cycles (w/o cantus firmus)	cut-circle motet
3-v English tenor Mass	3-v tenor motet, 4-v tenor motet
Caput Mass	All the 4-v subgenres from *c.* 1450 on
Troped Kyries of 4-v cycles	4-v tenor motet (contrafact Kyries)
Mass-motet cycles for 3 and 4 vv.	4-v tenor motet (companion motets w/same tenor) and *possibly:* 4-v freely composed motet (Puyllois Mass and *Flos de Spina*) 4-v hybrid of the tenor and chant-paraphrase motet (Du Fay *Ave regina celorum III*, motet and Mass)
Sine nomine Masses	4-v freely composed motet

Table C.3. *Map of motet subgenres and related genres over time, showing their interrelationships*

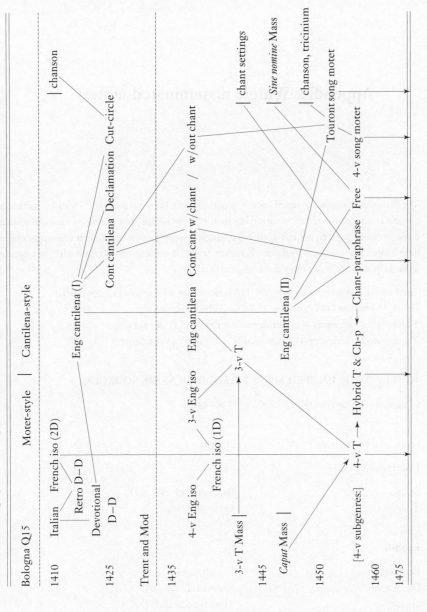

Appendix: Widely disseminated motets

The following figures are based on the repertory of motets listed in the Index of works (q.v.), not the complete repertory of surviving motets. This means that the figures for the motets in three or fewer sources are not accurate (though the proportion of English to continental may have some validity). I am confident, however, that I have identified all the widely disseminated motets (those with more than three sources).

Total no. of motets considered: 279 (186 continental, 93 English [33 per cent])
Unica: 163 motets (117 continental, 46 English [28 per cent])
Two sources: 61 motets (42 continental, 19 English [31 per cent])
Three sources: 28 motets (17 continental, 11 English [39 per cent])

WIDELY DISSEMINATED MOTETS (FOUR OR MORE SOURCES)

27 motets (10 Continental, 17 English [63 per cent])

FOUR SOURCES: 7 MOTETS (2 CONTINENTAL, 5 ENGLISH [71 PER CENT])

Continental

Salinis	Ihesu salvator (Ex. 6.2)
Touront	Recordare virgo

English

De Anglia	Benedicta es
Dunstaple	Regina celi
Forest	Alma redemptoris (Ex. 4.3)
Forest/Plummer	Qualis est dilectus
Power	Anima mea (A)

FIVE SOURCES: 11 MOTETS (4 CONTINENTAL, 7 ENGLISH [64 PER CENT])

Continental

Du Fay	Ave regina celorum (I)
Puyllois	Flos de spina (Ex. 11.5)
Touront	Compangant or O generosa (Ex. 9.3)
Anon.	O beata infantia

English

Dunstaple	Veni sancte/Veni creator
Dunstaple	Sancta Maria succurre
Dunstaple	Sub tuam protectionem
Dunstaple/Power/Binchois	Alma redemptoris
Dunstaple/Binchois	Beata dei genitrix
Power	Ave regina celorum
Plummer	Descendi in ortum

SIX SOURCES: 5 MOTETS (3 CONTINENTAL, 2 ENGLISH [40 PER CENT])

Continental

Lantins, A. de	Tota pulchra (Ex. 6.1)
Grossin	Imera dat hodierno
Du Fay	Supremum est

English

Dunstaple/Binchois	Beata mater
Power/Dunstable	Salve regina

SEVEN OR MORE SOURCES: 4 MOTETS (1 CONTINENTAL, 3 ENGLISH [75 PER CENT])

Continental

11	Touront	O gloriosa regina

English

7	Dunstaple	Quam pulchra es
10	Anon.	O pulcherrima
16	Frye	Ave regina celorum mater

Total MS copies of motets: 526 (16 are in English MSS)
Total MS copies of English motets: 217 (41 per cent of total MSS copies)
   Subtracting the 16 copies of pieces in English MSS, English motets make up 39.4 per cent of the pieces in continental MSS considered here

Notes

INTRODUCTION

1 In a music dictionary article on "genre" Carl Dahlhaus comments that:

> The historical transformations that musical genres undergo reach so deeply into their substance, that one wonders whether we are dealing with the same genre at all at the end of its development. The motets of the 13th and 17th centuries have no single feature in common: not only social function and text type, but also texture and performance practice are fundamentally distinct.

"Gattung," *Brockhaus-Riemann Musiklexikon*, ed. Carl Dahlhaus and Hans Heinrich Eggebrecht (Wiesbaden: Brockhaus; Mainz: Schott, 1978–9), vol. I, 452 (my translation). The implication is that the motet changed gradually over the course of four centuries. In fact the major transformation of the motet took place during the fifteenth century.

2 Two scholars have looked into the history of the motet in the mid-fifteenth century: Edgar H. Sparks, *Cantus Firmus in Mass and Motet, 1420–1520* (Berkeley and Los Angeles: University of California Press, 1963); and Wolfgang Stephan, *Die Burgundisch-Niederländische Motette zur Zeit Ockeghems* (Kassel: Bärenreiter, 1937; repr. 1973). Sparks was concerned with one subset of the motet (the works with cantus firmus), while Stephan was concerned primarily with the second half of the century.

3 After discussing and rejecting various possible ways of defining the motet (by text type, function, or compositional technique) Ludwig Finscher comments that "a history of the motet as a system of genres and generic evolution is therefore scarcely possible." Finscher and Annegrit Laubenthal, "'Cantiones quae vulgo motectae vocantur': Arten der Motette im 15. und 16. Jahrhundert," in *Die Musik des 15. und 16. Jahrhunderts*, ed. Ludwig Finscher, *Neues Handbuch der Musikwissenschaft* (Laaber: Laaber-Verlag, 1990), vol. III, Teil 2, ch. 4, 280–2.

4 Sparks, for example, includes "liturgical items such as antiphons, hymns, and sequences" among the motets for the purposes of his study (*Cantus Firmus*, 3). Editions of composer's works, on the other hand, often make strict distinctions between motet and liturgical music on the basis of text alone, disregarding musical style. Thus Besseler includes Du Fay's Marian antiphon settings and his four-voice through-composed setting of a sequence text,

Gaude virgo, with the much more modest Vespers antiphons and alternatim sequences in the volume of minor liturgical works (V), rather than with the motets (I); see Heinrich Besseler, ed., *Guillaume Dufay, Opera Omnia*, Corpus Mensurabilis Musicae 1 (Rome: American Institute of Musicology, 1951–66); henceforth DufayB. Modern manuscript inventories generally equate "genre" with "genre of text" and use motet as the fall-back term for pieces where they cannot determine the text genre: see, for example, Charles Hamm and Ann Besser Scott, "A Study and Inventory of the Manuscript Modena, Biblioteca Estense, α.X.1.11 (ModB)," *Musica Disciplina* 26 (1972): 117: "Classification: Where possible, the Inventory supplies the liturgical classification of the text, even for those works described in the Index as *motteti* (*Flos florum*, 56'-57, and following). Works with non-liturgical texts are classified according to musical genre: isorhythmic motet or, simply, motet." For a general discussion of the term motet see Rolf Dammann, "Geschichte der Begriffsbestimmung Motette," *Archiv für Musikwissenschaft* 16 (1959): 337–77. He has little to say, unfortunately, about the fifteenth century (pp. 354–5).

5 For studies of the motet that include references to function, see Ludwig Finscher, "Motette, II, Von Dufay bis Lasso," *MGG*, vol. IX, cols. 646–56; Ernest Sanders, "Motet: I: Medieval," *NG*, vol. XII, 617–28, esp. 626; Leeman Perkins, "Motet, II, Renaissance" *NG*, vol. XII, 628–37, esp. 628; Jacquelyn A. Mattfeld, "Some Relationships between Texts and Cantus Firmi in the Liturgical Motets of Josquin de Prez," *Journal of the American Musicological Society* 14 (1961): 159–83; Anthony M. Cummings, "Toward an Interpretation of the Sixteenth-Century Motet," *Journal of the American Musicological Society* 34 (1981): 43–59 (see especially his footnotes 1 and 2, which include references to many works relevant to the fifteenth century); Jeremy Noble, "The Function of Josquin's Motets," *Tijdschrift van de Vereniging voor Nederlandse Muziekgeschiedenis* 35 (1985): 9–31; Christopher A. Reynolds, "Sacred Polyphony," in *Performance Practice: Music before 1600*, ed. Howard Mayer Brown and Stanley Sadie (New York: Norton, 1989), 185–200, esp. 185–6.

6 See Cummings, "Toward an Interpretation," 45–6.

7 I have limited my study to works found in sources copied before 1475; as a result, I do not discuss the motets of Regis, Ockeghem, or Busnoys (with the exception of *In hydraulis*) because their motets appear in later sources. For similar reasons I do not discuss the "Milan motet," the new syllabic imitative motet type that may have emerged in the early 1470s.

1 APPROACHES AND ANALOGIES

1 Alastair Fowler, *Kinds of Literature: An Introduction to the Theory of Genres and Modes* (Cambridge, Mass.: Harvard University Press, 1982), 118.

2 *Ibid.*

3 *Ibid.*, 120.

4 Fowler wishes to retain the novel as a genre, "even if one badly in need of subdivision" (*ibid.*, 120). See p. 123 on subgenres that act like kinds, or genres, and pp. 60–1, 72, and 112–13.

5 On the role of generic mixture in generic change see Fowler, *Kinds of Literature*, 171–2 and 179–88. See also Heather Dubrow, *Genre* (London: Methuen, 1982), esp. 28–9.

6 See David Fishelov, *Metaphors of Genre: The Role of Analogies in Genre Theory* (University Park, Penn.: The Pennsylvania State University Press, 1993), 19–35. For a critique see René Wellek, "The Concept of Evolution in Literary History," in his *Concepts of Criticism* (New Haven: Yale University Press, 1973), pp. 37–53.

7 See Fishelov, *Metaphors*, 3–7; he goes on to discuss Kuhn and Boyd on metaphors in science. See also M. H. Abrams, *The Mirror and the Lamp: Romantic Theory and the Critical Tradition* (New York and London: Oxford University Press, 1953), 31: "Metaphor, however, whether alive or moribund, is an inseparable element of all discourse, including discourse whose purpose is neither persuasive nor aesthetic, but descriptive or informative." On the essential role of metaphor in human language and cognition, see also George Lakoff and Mark Johnson, *Metaphors We Live By* (Chicago: University of Chicago Press, 1980).

8 Fishelov, *Metaphors*, 2–3.

9 *Ibid.*, 68. Fishelov, like Fowler, recognizes the "elusiveness" of the novel, and judges it especially suitable for family resemblance analogies (p. 58).

10 *Ibid.*, 19.

11 See George Lakoff, *Women, Fire, and Dangerous Things: What Categories Reveal about the Mind* (Chicago: University of Chicago Press, 1987), 6–11 (on classical or Aristotelian categories), and 118–25 (on folk models of categorization); and John R. Taylor, *Linguistic Categorization: Prototypes in Linguistic Theory* (Oxford: Clarendon Press, 1989), 21–37, 72–4, 75 (on folk models).

12 For an intriguing discussion of the shifting borderline between boots and shoes, see Willet Kempton, *The Folk Classification of Ceramics: A Study of Cognitive Prototypes* (New York: Academic Press, 1981), 27 ff.

13 Ludwig Wittgenstein, *Philosophical Investigations*, trans. G. E. M. Anscombe (Oxford: Blackwell, 1953), 31–2.

14 For discussions of Wittgenstein's family resemblance theory (often including qualifications or quarrels) see Fowler, *Kinds of Literature*, 41–2; Lakoff, *Women, Fire, and Dangerous Things*, 16–18; Taylor, *Linguistic Categorization*, 38–40, Fishelov, *Metaphors*, 53–62, and John M. Swales, *Genre Analysis: English in Academic and Research Settings* (Cambridge: Cambridge University Press, 1990), 49–51.

15 Maurice Mandelbaum has suggested this as a necessary addition to Wittgenstein's proposal: see "Family Resemblances and Generalizations Concerning the Arts," *American Philosophical Quarterly* 2 (1965): 219–28.

16 See Fishelov, *Metaphors*, 65–72.

17 See Taylor, *Linguistic Categorization*, 44, and Eleanor Rosch, "Cognitive Representations of Semantic Categories," *Journal of Experimental Psychology: General* 104 (1975): 192–233, esp. 229.

18 See Taylor, *Linguistic Categorization*, 68; Sharon Lee Armstrong, Lila Gleitman, and Henry Gleitman, "What Some Concepts Might Not Be," *Cognition* 13 (1983): 263–308.

19 Eleanor Rosch and Carolyn Mervis, "Family Resemblances: Studies in the Internal Structure of Categories," *Cognitive Psychology* 7 (1975): 575.

20 See Fishelov, *Metaphors*, 62–3; Taylor, *Linguistic Categorization*, 38–58; Swales, *Genre Analysis*, 51–2.

21 Fishelov, *Metaphors*, 63.

22 Marie Laure Ryan, "Introduction: On the Why, What, and How of Generic Taxonomy," *Poetics* 10 (1981): 118.

23 See Fishelov, *Metaphors*, 66; Fowler, *Kinds of Literature*, 160–4 on "Primary, Secondary, and Tertiary Stages" in the history of genre; and Gary Saul Morson, *The Boundaries of Genre: Dostoevsky's 'Diary of a Writer' and the Traditions of Literary Utopia* (Austin: University of Texas Press, 1981), 74–5, on the status of the exemplar in the formation of genres.

24 This is the fundamental point of Lakoff, in *Women, Fire, and Dangerous Things*; see chapter 21, "Overview," where he comments that human imaginative processes enable people to "extend categories from central to non-central members using imaginative capacities such as metaphor, metonymy, mythological associations, and image relationships" (p. 371). See also Taylor, *Linguistic Categorization*, for many different kinds of categories and methods of category extension.

25 Morson comments that "genre does not belong to texts alone, but to the interaction between texts and classifier" (*Boundaries of Genre*, viii). He emphasizes, however, the crucial role of the "purposes of classifiers" in his definition. Dubrow comments that genre is like a code of social behavior or a contract between writer and reader (*Genre*, 2–3, 31–6).

26 For stimulating hypotheses about the mental mechanics that permit humans to recognize and classify things see Paul M. Churchland, *The Engine of Reason, the Seat of the Soul: A Philosophical Journey into the Brain* (Cambridge, Mass.: MIT Press, 1995), esp. 49–54, and Steven Pinker, *How the Mind Works* (New York: Norton, 1997).

27 In *Engine of Reason*, Churchland explains how a computer network was taught to recognize faces. First the network learned about faces from being shown many different faces. It gradually learned to distinguish faces from non-faces, and male faces from female faces. "These *categories*, for there is nothing else to call them – slowly emerged and stabilized during the course of the network's training. . . . What the network has developed during training is a family of rudimentary *concepts*" (pp. 49–50). This research suggests how one might build up an abstract representation from many different concrete examples. See also p. 51 (on fuzzy boundaries that represent "maximally *ambiguous* input images") and pp. 54, 289–90 (on prototypes).

28 Hedges can also provide evidence as to how a category is structured. See George Lakoff, "Hedges: A Study in Meaning Criteria and the Logic of Fuzzy Concepts," *Proceedings of the Chicago Linguistics Society* 8 (1972): 183–228; Lakoff, *Women, Fire, and Dangerous Things*, 122–4, 138–9; and Taylor, *Linguistic Categorization*, 75–80: "Hedges require us to distinguish between central and peripheral members of a category (*par excellence, strictly speaking*), as well as between different degrees of non-membership in a category (*strictly speaking*). They show that category boundaries are flexible (*loosely speaking*) and that categories can be redefined by an *ad hoc* selection and re-weighting of attributes (*in that*)" (p. 80).

29 For a stimulating discussion of a piece with characteristics of more than one genre, see Laurence Dreyfus, *Bach and the Patterns of Invention* (Cambridge, Mass.: Harvard University Press, 1996), 103–33, on the G-minor gamba sonata.

30 If she waited for the radio announcer she would be deferring to an "expert category" (see Taylor, *Linguistic Categorization*, 68–75, "Folk categories and expert categories") or deferring

to the steward of the club for a decision on category membership (to extend Ryan's metaphor from "Why, What, and How").

31 For a thorough discussion of this work, see Julie E. Cumming, "Concord out of Discord: Occasional Motets of the Early Quattrocento" (Ph.D. dissertation, University of California, Berkeley, 1987), 337–64.

32 In "Why, What, and How," Marie-Laure Ryan comments that "the 'communicative competence' of the members of a culture includes a generic component . . . and the purpose of genre theory is to lay out the implicit knowledge of the users of genres" (p. 112).

Thus John Swales, a linguist who teaches academic writing to inexperienced graduate students (often non-native speakers of English), developed a list of features for a typical introduction to a research paper, one of which is a "centrality claim" (*Genre Analysis*, 137–66, esp. 140–2). Before reading this I had never consciously thought about making "centrality claims," although I am an experienced academic writer: they are of course present in most academic articles, including the introduction to this book.

33 Fishelov, *Metaphors*, 22–5.

34 For a masterful account of modern evolutionary theory see Richard Dawkins, *The Blind Watchmaker* (New York: Norton, 1987).

35 I have chosen to refer to the first edition of *The Origin of Species*, often said to be the most eloquent and effective. References are to the reprint with introduction for Penguin by J. W. Burrow: Charles Darwin, *The Origin of Species by Means of Natural Selection, or the Preservation of Favoured Races in the Struggle for Life* (London: John Murray, 1859; London: Penguin, 1968).

36 See Lakoff, *Women, Fire, and Dangerous Things*, 187–95; Ernst Mayr, *Animal Species and Evolution* (Cambridge, Mass.: Belknap Press, 1963); and articles by Mayr, Hull, and Sokal and Crevello in Elliott Sober, ed., *Conceptual Issues in Evolutionary Biology* (Cambridge, Mass.: MIT Press, 1984).

37 *Origin*, 108.

38 *Origin*, 397; also 113. Darwin spends most of chapter 2, "Variation under Nature" (pp. 101–13), discussing the fluid boundaries between species, variety, and individual difference; see also chapter 13 on classification (pp. 397–434, esp. 402–13).

39 *Ibid.*, 53, 66.

40 *Ibid.*, 67, 66.

41 *Ibid.*, 68.

42 *Ibid.*, 130–1.

43 "A species may under new conditions of life change its habits, or have diversified habits, with some habits very unlike those of its nearest congeners. Hence we can understand . . . how it has arisen that there are upland geese with webbed feet, ground woodpeckers, diving thrushes, and petrels with the habits of auks" (p. 231; see also pp. 211–17). In this example, the habits have changed, and features evolved to suit one locale have persisted in another. See also the comments in chapter 2, pp. 101–13, "Variation under nature," in which the distinction between species and variety is discussed.

44 *Ibid.*, 170.

45 *Ibid.*

46 *Ibid.*, 171–2.

47 See Fishelov, *Metaphors*, 35–6.

48 In "The History of Remembered Innovation: Tradition and its Role in the Relationship between Musical Works and their Performances," *Journal of Musicology* 11 (1993): 164–6, José A. Bowen uses the evolutionary analogy to explain change in performing traditions:

> "The evolutionary model also works on a principle of variation and response. . . . The biological metaphor provides insight because it is the environment/audience and not the organism which determines which varieties will reproduce. . . All music is re-creation, and music that is not so reproduced (performed) dies. The life of a musical work is like the life of a species that changes and reproduces in response to its environment."

49 *Origin*, 90.

50 *Ibid.*, 89.

51 See Fishelov, *Metaphors*, 38, on the possibility that a "genre, unproductive in one literary period, will become productive in the next."

52 See Jonathan Weiner, *The Beak of the Finch: A Story of Evolution in our Time* (New York: Alfred A. Knopf, Inc., 1994).

53 See Darwin, *Origin*, 83–4.

54 For more detailed treatments of the motet in the thirteenth century, see the following: Richard L. Crocker, "French Polyphony of the Thirteenth Century" and "Polyphony in England in the Thirteenth Century," *New Oxford History of Music* II: *The Early Middle Ages to 1300*, 2nd ed. (Oxford: Oxford University Press, 1990), 636–720; and Ernest H. Sanders, "The Medieval Motet," in *Gattungen der Musik in Einzeldarstellung: Gedenkschrift Leo Schrade*, ed. Wulf Arlt and Ernst Lichtenhahn (Bern: Francke Verlag, 1973), 497–573.

55 Gilbert Reaney suggests that the motet was paraliturgical, in "The Isorhythmic Motet and its Social Background," in *Bericht über den internationalen musikwissenschaftlichen Kongress Kassel, 1962*, Gesellschaft für Musikforschung (Kassel: Bärenreiter, 1963), 25–7. Most scholars support the idea of the isorhythmic motet as "a sort of aristocratic chamber music for an educated elite," as Peter Lefferts puts it in *The Motet in England in the Fourteenth Century* (Ann Arbor: UMI Research Press, 1986), 9. For text types of the French fourteenth-century motet, see Cumming, "Concord," Table II, 124–6, and discussion on pp. 101–5.

56 See Crocker, "Polyphony in England," 681–3 and 703–11, and Lefferts, *The Motet in England*. There is some debate about the centers for polyphonic production: see Roger Bowers, "Choral Institutions Within the English Church: Their Constitution and Development, 1340–1500" (Ph.D. dissertation, University of East Anglia, 1975); and William J. Summers, "The Effect of Monasticism on Fourteenth-Century English Music," in *Actes du XIIIe Congrès de la Société Internationale de Musicologie: La Musique et le rite Sacré et Profane*, ed. Marc Honneger and Paul Prevost (Strasbourg, 1986), vol. II, 104–42.

57 Lefferts, *The Motet in England*, 86–7, 92, 182–4. See also Margaret Bent and David Howlett, "*Subtiliter alternare*: The Yoxford motet *O amicus/Precursoris*," *Current Musicology* 45–7 (1990): 60–5, and Andrew Wathey, "The Peace of 1360–1369 and Anglo-French Musical Relations," *Early Music History* 9 (1990): 129–74.

58 See Margaret Bent, "The Fourteenth-Century Italian Motet," in *L'Ars nova italiana del trecento* vol. VI, Atti del Congresso internazionale "L'Europa e la musica del trecento,"

Certaldo 1984, ed. Giulio Cattin and Patrizia Dalla Vecchia (Certaldo: Edizioni Polis, 1992), 85–125.

59 On English–French musical relations, see Roger Bowers, "Some Observations on the Life and Career of Lionel Power," *Proceedings of the Royal Musical Association* 102 (1975–6): 103–27; Andrew Wathey, "Dunstable in France," *Music and Letters* 67 (1986): 1–36; and David Fallows, "The Contenance Angloise: English Influence on Continental Composers of the Fifteenth Century," *Renaissance Studies* 1 (1987): 189–208.

60 See Manfred Schuler, "Die Musik in Konstanz während des Konzils 1414–1418," *Acta Musicologica* 38 (1966): 150–68, and David Fallows, *Dufay* (London: Dent, 1982; rev. ed., 1987), 18–20.

2 SUBGENRE, INTERPRETATION, AND THE GENERIC REPERTORY

1 See, for example, Jeffrey Kallberg, "The Rhetoric of Genre: Chopin's Nocturne in G Minor," *Nineteenth-Century Music* 11 (1988): 238–61; Laurence Dreyfus, *Bach and the Patterns of Invention* (Cambridge, Mass.: Harvard University Press, 1996), 105–6, 138–9, 141; Fowler, *Kinds of Literature*, 20–4; Marie-Laure Ryan, "Why, What, and How," 111; Swales, *Genre Analysis*, 44–58; and Gary M. Olson, Robert L. Mack, and Susan A. Duffy, "Cognitive Aspects of Genre," *Poetics* 10 (1981): 283–315.

2 Dubrow, *Genre*, 1–3.

3 Hans Robert Jauss, "Literary History as a Challenge to Literary Theory," in *Toward an Aesthetic of Reception* (Minneapolis: University of Minnesota Press, 1982), 28, Thesis 4.

4 *Ibid.*, 28.

5 See also Fowler, *Kinds of Literature*, 256–76, especially the section on the "construction of the original work" (pp. 256–63), where he invokes a "generic horizon" essential to criticism (p. 259).

6 Peter J. Rabinowitz, *Before Reading: Narrative Conventions and the Politics of Interpretation* (Ithaca: Cornell University Press, 1987), 20–42. The text, according to Rabinowitz, is like an "unassembled swing set": in order to put it together you must have equipment, skills, and knowledge (p. 38). Both Jauss ("Literary History," 22) and Rabinowitz see the concept of the authorial audience as a way of getting away from the problems of authorial intention; we attempt to join "a particular social/interpretive community," rather than searching for "the author's private psyche" (*Before Reading*, 20).

7 On the status of the "authorial reading" vs. other readings, see Rabinowitz, *Before Reading*, 29–32, and the works mentioned in his notes; on its impossibility, see pp. 32–6. The problem of the composer's hearing is especially vivid in the case of music, since it is virtually impossible to forget the sounds, harmonies, and repertories we are most familiar with. Rabinowitz himself calls it the "authentic-performance paradox"; see also his article "Circumstantial Evidence: Music Analysis and Theories of Reading," *Mosaic* 18 (1985): 159–73, and more generally, Peter Kivy, *Authenticities: Philosophical Reflections on Musical Performance* (Ithaca: Cornell University Press, 1995). Fowler distinguishes between the "then-meaning" and the "now-meaning" of a work; both are essential, but "competent readers take the work's original meaning as an especially relevant piece of knowledge" (*Kinds of Literature*, 269).

8 See Thomas Brothers, "Vestiges of the Isorhythmic Tradition in Mass and Motet, ca. 1450–1475," *Journal of the American Musicological Society* 45 (1991): 1–56.

9 See Cumming, "Concord," *passim*, but esp. 148, 171–6, 377–81.

10 Fowler, *Kinds of Literature*, 55.

11 *Ibid.*, 55: "distinguishing features, it is worth noting, may be either formal or substantive. . . . The best of the older theorists, in fact, always kept external and internal forms together in discussing the historical kinds."

12 *Ibid.*, 60–72.

13 *Ibid.*, 58.

14 *Ibid.*, 73.

15 *Ibid.*, 59–60.

16 There is of course the standard contrast between homophonic main theme and contrapuntal development in the Classical sonata form, and the reintegration of contrapuntal writing into the high Classical style. But discussion has not moved much beyond this: see Janet Levy, "Texture as a Sign in Classic and Early Romantic Music," *Journal of the American Musicological Society* 35 (1982): 482–531, where she comments that texture's "role in the delineation of structure and process in Classic and early Romantic music has gone relatively unexplored" (p. 482). Levy's own article is one of the welcome exceptions to her statement, as are some other works listed in her note 2.

17 See Frank A. D'Accone, "The Performance of Sacred Music in Italy During Josquin's Time, c. 1474–1525," in *Josquin des Prez: Proceedings of the International Josquin Festival-Conference, New York, 1971*, ed. Edward E. Lowinsky with Bonnie J. Blackburn (New York: Oxford University Press, 1976), 601–18; David Fallows, "Specific Information on the Ensembles for Composed Polyphony, 1400–1474," in *Studies in the Performance of Late Medieval Music*, ed. Stanley Boorman (Cambridge: Cambridge University Press, 1983), 109–59; and Reynolds, "Sacred Polyphony."

18 In "Vestiges" Thomas Brothers warns against making genre classifications purely on the basis of number of voices (p. 33, n. 53).

19 For a fascinating and thorough study of changing relative voice ranges for the three-voice Mass repertory, see Andrew Kirkman, *The Three-Voice Mass in the Later Fifteenth and Early Sixteenth Centuries: Style, Distribution, and Case Studies* (New York: Garland, 1995), esp. chs. 1 and 2 ("Towards a Typology of the Three-Voice Mass" and "Paradigms and Patterns").

20 See David Fallows, "Specific Information," 116–17.

21 *The Rise of European Music, 1380–1500* (Cambridge: Cambridge University Press, 1993), 161. (This book will henceforth be referred to as *REM.*) See also Margaret Bent, "Some Factors in the Control of Consonance and Sonority: Successive Composition and the Solus Tenor," in *Report of the Twelfth Congress, Berkeley 1977*, ed. Daniel Heartz and Bonnie Wade (Kassel: Bärenreiter, 1981), 625–34; Andrew Hughes, "Some Notes on the Early Fifteenth-Century Contratenor," *Music and Letters* 50 (1969): 376–87; and Kevin Moll, ed. and trans., *Counterpoint and Compositional Process in the Time of Dufay: Perspectives from German Musicology* (New York: Garland, 1997). This is a collection of articles by Besseler, Ficker, and others on the subject of how fifteenth-century music is constructed; Moll's introduction is especially useful.

22 See Bent, "Some Factors": these pieces belong to her situation "(2) where there is no self contained discant–tenor duet" (p. 626). Among the kinds of pieces she mentions are a two-part canon with a free accompanying voice, in which there are fourths between the canonic voices; isorhythmic motets for three and four voices, in which there are fourths between the two upper voices, that require the tenor voice below; and motets in four voices in which both tenor and contratenor are essential (pp. 628–30).

23 This voice is sometimes seen as a primitive version of the "functional bass line" of common practice harmony: see especially Heinrich Besseler, *Bourdon und Fauxbourdon: Studien zum Ursprung der Niederländischen Musik* (Leipzig: Breitkopf und Härtel, 1950), ch. 3, "Der Bourdon-Kontratenor," 44–67. We, however, will be more concerned with the voice as one possible contrapuntal solution to four-voice writing.

24 Margaret Bent has recently objected to the use of the term isorhythm, arguing that it "anachronistically and artificially isolates certain forms of tenor repetition"; see Bent, "The Yoxford Credo," in *Essays in Musicology: A Tribute to Alvin Johnson,* ed. Lewis Lockwood and Edward Roesner (N.p.: American Musicological Society, 1990), 39. Nevertheless, isorhythm is a useful well-understood term in musicology that can encompass many different kinds of rhythmic organization, and I will continue to use it in this inclusive way, as does Jon Michael Allsen, in "Style and Intertextuality in the Isorhythmic Motet 1400–1440" (Ph.D. dissertation, University of Wisconsin, Madison, 1992); see his discussion of the term, pp. 1–2, 6–7. For related kinds of rhythmic construction in later music, see Brothers, "Vestiges."

25 Sparks, *Cantus Firmus*; Stephan, *Burgundisch-Niederländische Motette.*

26 See Fowler, *Kinds of Literature:* "every characteristic feature, as a means of communication, must be recognizable" (p. 73).

27 Andrew Wathey, for example, has discovered that the texts of Philippe de Vitry's motets circulated without their music within a Petrarchan humanistic literary tradition, especially among fifteenth-century German humanists. See "The Motets of Philippe de Vitry and the Fourteenth-Century Renaissance," *Early Music History* 12 (1993): 119–50. Several early fifteenth-century motets use thirteenth-century motet texts: these include three motets from Bologna Q15 (Johannes de Lymburgia's *O Maria maris stella,* and the anonymous *O Maria virgo davitica/O Maria maris stella;* Humbertus de Salinis's *Psallat chorus/Eximie pater*) and one motet found in Aosta and Trent 92–2 (Merques's *Castrum pudicie/Virgo viget*).

28 For a discussion of text types in the fourteenth century and early fifteenth century, see Cumming, "Concord," 102–5, 107, 108–10, 124–9, 137–42, 156–62.

29 These composite texts fall largely outside the chronological scope of this study; see Perkins, "Motet," 631.

30 Fifteenth-century tenor Masses may also have been performed with a different text for the tenor part: see Alejandro Enrique Planchart, "Parts with Words and without Words: The Evidence for Multiple Texts in Fifteenth-Century Masses," in *Studies in the Performance of Late Medieval Music,* ed. Stanley Boorman (Cambridge: Cambridge University Press, 1983), 227–51.

31 On this subject see Frank Ll. Harrison, "Tradition and Innovation in Instrumental Usage 1100–1450," in *Aspects of Medieval and Renaissance Music: A Birthday Offering to Gustave Reese,* ed. Jan LaRue (New York: Norton, 1966), 319–35; Gilbert Reaney, "Text Underlay in Early

Fifteenth-Century Music Manuscripts," in *Essays in Musicology in Honor of Dragan Plamenac on his 70th Birthday*, ed. Gustave Reese and Robert J. Snow (Pittsburgh: University of Pittsburgh Press, 1969), 245–51; and Margaret Bent, "Text Setting in Sacred Music of the Early 15th Century: Evidence and Implications," in *Musik und Text in der Mehrstimmigkeit des 14. und 15. Jahrhunderts*, ed. Ursula Günther and Ludwig Finscher (Kassel: Bärenreiter, 1984), 291–326, esp. 303–5. See also the articles on performance practice listed in note 17, above.

3 FIFTEENTH-CENTURY USES OF THE TERM "MOTET"

1 Linguists and ethnographers have long considered the role of "elicited metalanguage": "The elicitation of labels for categories of talk is clearly not adequate to assure a full inventory and must be supplemented by other discovery procedures, but it is basic to ethnography that the units used for segmenting, ordering, and describing data should be those of the group." Muriel Saville-Troike, *The Ethnography of Communication* (Oxford: Blackwell, 1982), 34; see also Swales, *Genre Analysis*, 38–40, 54–8.

2 See Daniel Leech-Wilkinson, *Compositional Techniques in the Four-Part Isorhythmic Motets of Philippe de Vitry and his Contemporaries* (New York: Garland, 1989), vol. I, 15–24.

3 For a discussion of the term as used by these theorists, see Robert Nosow, "The Florid and Equal-Discantus Motet Styles of Fifteenth-Century Italy" (Ph.D. dissertation, University of North Carolina, Chapel Hill, 1992), 21–3. For Prosdocimus see *Expositiones tractatus pratice cantus mensurabilis magistri Johannis de Muris*, ed. F. Alberto Gallo, *Antiquae musicae italicae scriptores* vol. III, pt. 1 (Bologna: Istituto di Studi Musicali e Teatrali, 1966), 206 ff. For Ugolino see *Declaratio musicae disciplinae*, ed. Albert Seay, 3 vols. (Rome: American Institute of Musicology, 1959–62), vol. II, 258–66.

4 See Santorre Debenedetti, "Un trattatello del secolo XIV sopra la poesia musicale," *Studi medievali* 2 (1906–7): 79–80. The treatise of 1332, *Summa artis rithimici vulgaris dictaminis*, is quoted, translated and discussed in Margaret Bent, "Italian Motet," 105–6.

5 Johannes Tinctoris, *Terminorum Musicae Diffinitorium* (*Dictionary of Musical Terms*), Latin and English edition, translated and annotated by Carl Parrish (London: Collier-Macmillan, 1963), 12–13, 42–3, 40–1.

> Cantilena est cantus parvus, cui verba cuiuslibet materiae sed frequentius amatoriae supponuntur.
>
> Motetum est cantus mediocris, cui verba cuiusvis materiae sed frequentius divinae supponuntur.
>
> Missa est cantus magnus cui verba Kyrie, Et in terra, Patrem, Sanctus, et Agnus, et interdum caeterae partes a pluribus canendae supponuntur, quae ab aliis officium dicitur.

6 nec tot nec tales varietates uni cantilenae congruunt quot et quales uni moteti, nec tot et tales uni moteti quot et quales uni missae. Omnis itaque resfacta pro qualitate et quantitate ejus diversificanda est.

Johannes Tinctoris: Theoretical Works, II, ed. Albert Seay (N.p.: American Institute of Musicology, 1975), 155. For Albert Seay's more literal translation see Johannes Tinctoris,

Liber de arte contrapuncti (N.p.: American Institute of Musicology, 1961), 139, from "Chapter VIII: Concerning the eighth and last general rule, which teaches that variety must be most accurately sought for in all counterpoint."

7 See Traugott Lawler, ed. and trans., *The Parisiana Poetria of John of Garland* (New Haven: Yale University Press, 1974), 40–1 (Fig. 3), 86–9, and Lawler's commentary, 230–1. See also Fowler, *Kinds of Literature*, 240–1, and Ernst Robert Curtius, *European Literature and the Latin Middle Ages* (Princeton: Princeton University Press, 1953), 231–2.

8 This section of Cortese's treatise is reproduced in facsimile, translated, and discussed in Nino Pirrotta, "Music and Cultural Tendencies in Fifteenth-Century Italy," *Journal of the American Musicological Society* 19 (1966): 127–61, esp. 142–3, 150–1, 154–5.

9 *Ibid.*, 144 and 146; Pirrotta's translation of "De vitandis passionibus deque musica adhibenda post epulas."

10 The Latin for these and the following quotes is in *ibid.*, 150–1; Pirrotta's translation, 154–5.

11 "nemine*m* in praestantiu*m* musicoru*m* numeraru*m* referendu*m* esse censet qui minus gnarus litatorii modi faciendi sit." Expanded abbreviations are in italics.

12 "Praecentoria autem ea dicuntur quae q*uamquam* sint litatorio permixta cantu ascriptitia tamen et insititia videri possunt cum in his libera sit commutandi optio idq*ue* ob eam casam factum esse volunt ne uniusmodi servarentur in canendo modi quibus litatoria continuata cadunt."

13 "omnes tamen sunt scienter: in hoc praecentorio genere versati ex quibus multa ad senatorium usum transferri possint."

14 Reinhard Strohm, *Music in Late Medieval Bruges* (Oxford: Clarendon Press, 1985; rev. ed., 1990). Library catalogs and inventories also sometimes make reference to lost motet manuscripts. See Martin Staehelin, "Mehrstimmige Repertoires im 14. und 15. Jahrhundert: Das Problem der verlorenen Quellen," in *Trasmissione e recezione delle forme di cultura musicale. Atti del XIV Congresso della Società Internazionale di Musicologia*, ed. Angelo Pompilio *et al.* (Turin: EDT, 1990), vol. I, 153–9, and the discussion on pp. 162–7. (These congress proceedings will henceforth be known as Pompilio, IMS.)

15 Maria Carmen Gómez Muntané, *La música en la Casa Real Catalano-Aragonesa durante los años 1336–1437*, 2 vols. (Barcelona: Bosch, 1979) doc. 223; see corrections in Giampaolo Mele, "Una precisazione su un documento di Giovanni Duca di Gerona e promogenito d'Aragona, riguardante la sua cappella musicale," *Anuario Musical* 38 (1983): 255–60. Ten years later the duke requested a book "where there are notated between fifteen and twenty motets, . . . and where there are ballades, rondeaux and virelais of prime quality" (doc. 243).

16 For this manuscript type see the discussion in Reinhard Strohm, chair, Round Table "Costituzione e conservazione dei repertorii polifonici nei secoli XIV e XV," in Pompilio, IMS, vol. I, 163–4.

17 Strohm, *Bruges*, 21.

18 Peter Wathey, "Dunstable," 12. "En la maniere de France" may suggest that the motets were by an Englishman in the French style (French motets would have been "motetz français") – perhaps English isorhythmic motets like those of Dunstaple.

19 Strohm, *Bruges*, 29.

20 Paula Higgins, "Music and Musicians at the Sainte-Chapelle of the Bourges Palace, 1415–1515," in Pompilio, IMS, vol. III, 691.

21 Strohm, *Bruges*, 21 and 28.

22 *Ibid.*, 29–31.

23 Barbara Haagh, "Crispijne and Abertijne: Two Tenors at the Church of St Niklaas, Brussels," *Music and Letters* 76 (1995): 336–7.

24 See Barbara Haagh, "The Meeting of Sacred Ritual and Secular Piety: Endowments for Music," in *Companion to Medieval and Renaissance Music*, ed. Tess Knighton and David Fallows (London: Dent, 1992), 60–8; see also Strohm, *REM*, 284–7.

25 Strohm, *Bruges*, 14–15.

26 *Ibid.*, 57.

27 *Ibid.*, 53.

28 Douglas Salokar, "*Ad augmentationem divini cultus*: Pious Foundations and Vespers Motets in the Church of Our Lady in Bruges," in *Musicology and Archival Research*, ed. Barbara Haagh, Frank Daelemans, and André Vanrie (Brussels: Algemeen Rijksarchief, 1994), 306–25.

29 Strohm, *Bruges*, 46; *REM*, 429.

30 Craig Wright, "Dufay at Cambrai: Discoveries and Revisions," *Journal of the American Musicological Society* 28 (1975): 209.

31 Strohm, *Bruges*, 23, 29 and 87.

32 Strohm, *REM*, 438.

33 For example, an entry for the feast of St. Catherine of Siena reads as follows (Salokar, "Pious Foundations," 313):

> Ad primas vesperis . . . ad processiones in capella sancte crucis exeundo cum Responsorio Regnum mundi et redeundo cum antiphona Regina celi in qua processione succentor cantabit cum pueris suis unam motetum.
> At first Vespers, at the procession to the chapel of the holy cross, leaving with the responsory *Regnum mundi* and returning with the antiphon *Regina celi*, in which procession the succentor will sing one motet with his boys. [My translation.]

34 See Frank Ll. Harrison, *Music in Medieval Britain* (New York: Praeger, 1958), 81–97, 156–94, 295–329, 337–8.

35 Morson, *Boundaries of Genre*, vii–viii.

36 See Masakata Kanazawa, "Polyphonic Music for Vespers during the Fifteenth Century" (Ph.D. dissertation, Harvard University, Cambridge, Mass., 1966), 159–78, 384–93; Hamm and Scott, "Inventory," 102; and Lewis Lockwood, *Music in Renaissance Ferrara, 1400–1505* (Cambridge, Mass.: Harvard University Press, 1984), 51–63.

37 Tom R. Ward, *The Polyphonic Office Hymn 1400–1520: A Descriptive Catalogue*, Renaissance Manuscript Studies 3 (Neuhausen-Stuttgart: American Institute of Musicology, Hänssler-Verlag, 1980), 9. The "Du Fay" hymn cycle found in Modena X.1.11 occurs also in the manuscripts Bologna Q15, Trent 92, SP B80, and CS 15; individual hymns also appear in many other manuscripts, including MuEm, MC, and F112bis. See Ward, *Office Hymn*, 12–13 (and *passim*); Kanazawa, "Vespers," 42–3; and Fallows, *Dufay*, 135–46, esp. 144–5.

38 See Lockwood, *Ferrara*, 54–5, 57, and Kanazawa, "Vespers," 170–1, 384–93.

39 On the varieties of antiphon see Huglo, "Antiphon," *NG*, vol. 1, 476–80, and David Hiley, *Western Plainchant: A Handbook* (Oxford: Clarendon Press, 1993), 88–108. For a look at the shifting functions of Marian antiphons see Ruth Steiner, "Marian Antiphons at Cluny and

Lewes," in *Music in the Medieval English Liturgy*, ed. Susan Rankin and David Hiley (Oxford: Clarendon Press, 1993), 175–204.

40 My classification follows Kanazawa, "Vespers," 386–8. I include the six antiphons added on blank pages at the end of the previous fascicle by a new scribe (see Lockwood, *Ferrara*, 55). The texts for three of the pieces in the section have not been identified (shown as "?" in Table 3.1), but the chant intonations and the nature of their texts makes their identification as antiphons certain. The antiphon to the Virgin is Benoit's *Virgo Maria non est tibi similis*, fol. 51.

　The section also includes two settings of the text *Felix namque*, usually classified as offertories for the BVM. The text is also used as a Vespers antiphon (see Steiner, "Marian Antiphons," 194 and 203) and neither setting uses the offertory chant. It would make more sense for these pieces to be antiphons, given the organization of Modena X.1.11, but I omit them from Table 3.1 because of their uncertain status.

41 See Ernest Trumble, *Fauxbourdon: An Historical Survey*, Musicological Studies 3 (Brooklyn: Institute of Medieval Music, 1959), 68–80.

42 Unlike the hymns, the antiphons are not in calendar order, nor are they all identical in function (although this is hard to know with any certainty). The antiphon section does however resemble the later Vespers antiphon cycle found in Trent 89 and SP B80, including settings of three of the same texts. See Christopher Reynolds, *Papal Patronage and the Music of St. Peter's 1380–1513* (Berkeley: University of California Press, 1995), 82–3 and 345–6.

43 The division is not watertight: there is a four-voice antiphon setting by the English composer Leonel Power in the continental section, and an isorhythmic motet by Du Fay in the English section.

44 Almost any piece of chant with a Marian text could be used as a votive antiphon: Harrison mentions psalm antiphons, processional antiphons, devotional poems, and a sequence (*Medieval Britain*, 81–8).

45 In England directions concerning the performance of votive antiphons were contained in special statutes or chapter acts, reflecting the flexible or paraliturgical nature of the observances (Harrison, *Medieval Britain*, 81–8). Craig Wright describes a similar situation in Paris, where Marian antiphons after Compline were "viewed as an extraliturgical devotion, one which need not be added to the choir books and processioners of the church of Paris." *Music and Ceremony at Notre Dame of Paris, 500–1550* (Cambridge: Cambridge University Press), 108.

46 See Lockwood, *Ferrara*, 53, and Kanazawa, "Vespers," 384–5.

47 See Martin Just, *Der Mensuralkodex Mus. ms. 40021 der Staatsbibliothek Preussischer Kulturbesitz Berlin: Untersuchungen zum Repertoire einer deutschen Quelle des 15. Jahrhunderts* (Tutzing: Hans Schneider, 1975), vol. I. 56–63; for a photograph of the table of contents see vol. II, 8–9. Martin Just edits the whole manuscript in EDM 76–8 (Kassel: Bärenreiter, 1981).

48 Chansonniers are too numerous to list. Manuscripts limited to Masses include Vatican City, Biblioteca Apostolica Vaticana, Archivio della Cappella Sistina MSS 14, 41, 49 and 51; Verona, Biblioteca Capitolare, MS DCCLVI; and ModD. Manuscripts of liturgical service music for Vespers include Verona, Biblioteca Capitolare, MS DCCLIX and Modena, Biblioteca Estense, MS α. M.1.11–12.

49 For a discussion of the relationship between manuscripts and repertories, see Strohm, "Introduction" to the Round Table "Costituzione," 93–6, and the contribution by Margaret Bent, "Manuscripts as Répertoires, Scribal Performance and the Performing Scribe," 138–52.

50 See Charles Hamm, Jerry Call, and Herbert Kellman, "Sources, MS, IX: Renaissance Polyphony," *NG,* vol. XVII, 674–701; Charles Hamm and Herbert Kellman, eds. *Census-Catalogue of Manuscript Sources of Polyphonic Music, 1400–1550* (Neuhausen-Stuttgart: American Institute of Musicology, 1979–1988); and Strohm, *REM.* I omit small and fragmentary sources; additions to my list of sources are unlikely to alter my general findings.

51 I have omitted sacred songs in the vernacular, such as Italian laude and German "Leisen," and their Latin-texted relations, Latin laude and *cantiones.* These genres turn up in the all-purpose collections, and thus make no difference in terms of the categorization of manuscript types.

52 For a discussion of this manuscript type see the discussion for Strohm, chair, Round table "Costituzione," 163–4.

53 See Margaret Bent, "A Contemporary Perception of Early Fifteenth-Century Style; Bologna Q15 as a Document of Scribal Editorial Initiative," *Musica Disciplina* 41 (1987): 183–201; and *eadem,* "Manuscripts as Répertoires."

54 Strohm, *REM,* 253–4.

55 Strohm, *REM,* 291; see also 137–8 and 250–63 on the Basel manuscripts; 287–96 on the *Kantorei* and the universities, 507–18 on the Trent Codices and the later German and Central European sources.

56 The exceptions to this pattern include mostly manuscripts with small numbers of motets, often added to the manuscript as an afterthought: Brussels 5557, CS 35, and Milan 2. Milan 4 also has no clear motet section, but most of the manuscript is devoted to the groups or cycles of motets that substitute for Mass movements, so the distinction between motets and Masses is obscured.

57 See Kanazawa, "Vespers," chapters 4 and 8.

58 Only Verona 758 begins with motets, then goes on to hymns and *Magnificat* settings.

59 Where only Vespers manuscripts survive (Modena X.1.11, from Ferrara, or the Genoese F112bis) we may have lost the complementary Mass manuscripts.

60 Italian chansonniers often include some motets. Many have corrupt, incomplete, or missing texts, and they may have been used for instrumental performance: without text motets and chansons are equally satisfactory as instrumental works. One such manuscript is the instrumental collection Bologna Q18, which contains about twenty motets out of ninety-three total pieces in the manuscript; see Susan Forscher Weiss, "Bologna Q18: Some Reflections on Content and Context," *Journal of the American Musicological Society* 41 (1988): 63–101.

61 See Strohm, *REM,* 293–4 and 495–503. Glogauer is edited in EDM 4, 8, 85 and 86; for a facsimile see Jessie Ann Owens, ed., *Kraków, Biblioteka Jagiellońska, Glogauer Liederbuch* (3 partbooks) Renaissance Music in Facsimile 6 (New York: Garland, 1986). A facsimile of the Schedel Liederbuch is found in EDM 84: Bettina Wackernagel, ed., *Das Liederbuch des Dr. Hartmann Schedel* (Kassel: Bärenreiter, 1978).

62 See Adelyn Peck Leverett, "A Paleographical and Repertorial Study of the Manuscript

Trento, Castello del Buonconsiglio, 91 (1378)," 2 vols. (Ph.D. dissertation, Princeton University, 1990), vol. I, 73–96, and vol. II, 29–58, for a discussion of what she calls the "Passau paraphrase repertory." (This study will henceforth be referred to as Leverett, "Trent 91.")

4 THE MOTET SECTION OF BOLOGNA Q15 AND ITS RAMIFYING ROOTS

1 See Charles Hamm, "Manuscript Structure in the Dufay Era," *Acta Musicologica* 34 (1962): 166–84, esp. 175. Many contemporary manuscripts are not organized generically; others (such as Aosta) lack a distinct motet section.

2 See Guillaume de Van, "Inventory of Manuscript Bologna Liceo Musicale, Q15 (olim 37)," *Musica Disciplina* 2 (1948): 231–57. For discussion and transcription of most of the motets in the manuscript, see Bobby Wayne Cox, "The Motets of MS Bologna, Civico Museo Bibliografico Musicale, Q15" (Ph.D. dissertation, North Texas State University, 1977) (henceforth "Q15"). Margaret Bent is working on a study of the manuscript; see "A Contemporary Perception." See also Allsen, "Style," 9, and Cumming, "Concord," 130–70.

3 Two subgenres are not found in Q15: the fifteenth-century English isorhythmic motet, and what I call the "three-voice tenor motet," also largely an English subgenre.

4 "A Contemporary Perception"; "Contexts for the Repertory Formation of Bologna Q15," unpublished paper presented at the American Musicological Society Meeting at Austin, Texas, in 1989; and "Pietro Emiliani's Chaplain Bartolomeo Rossi da Capri and the Lamentations of Johannes de Quadris in Vicenza," *Il Saggiatore Musicale* 2 (1995): 5–16.

5 Northern Italian manuscripts include the Paduan fragments (including Pad B and Pad D), Chantilly, Oxford 213, Bologna 2216, and Modena, Biblioteca Estense, MS α.M.5.24. Florentine manuscripts include the Squarcialupi Codex and F2211.

6 See Reinhard Strohm, "European Politics and the Distribution of Music in the Early Fifteenth Century," *Early Music History* 1 (1981): 305–23; and *REM, passim.* See also Andrew Wathey, "Dunstable," and Manfred Schuler, "Die Musik in Konstanz."

7 Bent, "A Contemporary Perception," 185.

8 For the structure of the manuscript see Van, "Inventory," 246–54, and Besseler, *Bourdon,* 11–12. At the beginning of fascicle 18 (stage II), before the beginning of the motet section, there is a miscellaneous section including music of almost every kind – two *Magnificat* settings, a Mass movement, a lauda, and two motets, in no particular order. I have decided to include the two motets (164: *Alma redemptoris,* attributed to Forest in Modena X.1.11; and 167: Lymburgia's *Ostendit mihi angelus*) because they clearly belong to subgenres found in the motet section.

9 These figures are based on the rough table found in Bent's "Contemporary Perception," 198, and the discussion on pp. 185–9, but that table does not account for the details: there was a certain amount of recopying and insertion, and some of the pieces found in stage I were completed in stage II, while others from stage I were recopied in stage II. The figures will thus have to be modified once Bent has published her findings in more detail.

10 Two motets (262: Rubeus's *Caro mea vere est cibus;* and 279: Lymburgia's *Veni dilecte my*) were used as page fillers. They were clearly added with the generic constraints of the section in

mind, and will be included in the discussion. For a list of the pieces excluded from my discussion, see Cumming, "Concord," 169.

11 The hymn, Q15.282, Lymburgia's *Magne dies leticie*, is listed in Ward, *Office Hymn*, 193, and transcribed in Kanazawa, "Vespers," vol. II, 25. It is near the beginning of the following hymn section, and stylistically identical to the pieces in that section, so I have not included it.

12 Two laude (198: Lymburgia's *Imnizabo regi meo*; and 268: Brassart's *Gratulemur christicole*) appear at the tops of pages (though *Imnizabo* appears on a blank page between fascicles, so it was probably a page filler as well). Robert Nosow chooses to classify the three settings of the text "Ave verum corpus" as "liturgical works or polyphonic *laude*," and thus excludes them from the motet section of Bologna Q15 ("Florid," 6, note 10, and 207–15); I have chosen to include them as borderline cases, since they lack strophic texts. For a detailed study of the lauda during this period see Elisabeth Diederichs, *Die Anfänge der mehrstimmigen Lauda vom Ende des 14. bis zur Mitte des 15. Jahrhunderts* (Tutzing: Schneider, 1986); see also Sylvia Kenney, "In Praise of the Lauda," in *Aspects of Medieval and Renaissance Music: A Birthday Offering to Gustave Reese*, ed. Jan LaRue (New York: Norton, 1966), 489–99.

13 "A Contemporary Perception," 185, 189.

14 Robert Nosow, for example, puts three of my subgenres together into his "Equal-discantus motets" – my Italian motets, and the three kinds of double-discantus motets (retrospective, devotional, and other); see "Florid," 38–151, and "The Equal-Discantus Motet Style After Ciconia," *Musica Disciplina* 45 (1991): 221–75. Michael Allsen divides up the isorhythmic motets into national groups, primarily in terms of where they were composed (England, France, Italy); see "Style," *passim*. Neither of these classifications contradicts mine: they just draw the boundary lines at different levels.

15 The same piece is often texted differently in different sources: a piece can have all voices texted in one manuscript, cantus and tenor texted in another, or just the cantus texted in the third. The texting may also change during the course of a piece (see Reaney, "Text Underlay"). For that reason I do not consider texting of cantilena-style motets significant for subgenre.

16 *Bourdon*, 29, 135–6; *Guillaume Dufay, Opera Omnia* (Rome: American Institute of Musicology, 1951–66), vol. I, 1 (henceforth DufayB).

17 "What's in a Name? Reflections on Some Works of Guillaume Du Fay," *Early Music* 16 (1988): 165–75.

18 "Johannes Brassart and Johannes de Sarto," *Plainsong and Medieval Music* 1 (1992), 47.

19 Hannah Stäblein-Harder divides fourteenth-century Mass music into "motet style," "discant style" and "simultaneous style"; see *Fourteenth-Century Mass Music in France* (N.p.: American Institute of Musicology, 1962), 15–19 and 83–5. Her "motet style," like mine, is primarily determined by a pair of upper texted voices, and includes works with and without isorhythm. Her "discant" and "simultaneous style" would both fit into my "cantilena-style": both have a single upper voice over supporting tenor and contratenor, but in the "simultaneous style" all voices are texted and declaim the text together, as in my "declamation motets."

20 See Cumming, "Concord," 156, Table V.A.

21 The earliest motets, of course, were created by the application of texts to pre-existent discant clausulae. For discussion of the compositional order of music and text in later repertories, see Bent, "Text Setting"; Bent and Howlett, "Yoxford Motet."

22 Italy as a unified entity did not exist in the fifteenth century. As Robert Nosow notes, however, the concept of "Italia" is alluded to in several motets of the early fifteenth century, in spite of continuing rivalry among warring city states ("Equal-discantus," 223, n. 10).

23 Although Ciconia was not born in Italy his motets are thoroughly Italian in style; see Bent "Italian Motet," 111, where she comments that "there is nothing French about Ciconia's motets"; see also Bent's and Anne Hallmark's introduction to *The Works of Johannes Ciconia* (Monaco: L'Oiseau-Lyre, 1985) (henceforth *Ciconia*).

   The birthplace and nationality of the composer identified in Q15 as "P. Rubeus" remain obscure, but the style of his motets makes it very likely that he was Italian too. Gilbert Reaney and Giulio Cattin identify him with the composer of two Italian songs in Oxford 213, Pietro Rosso or Rossi, who was either from Parma (1374–1438; Reaney), or from Treviso (1418–48; Cattin). See Reaney, *Early Fifteenth-Century Music* (N.p.: American Institute of Musicology, 1955–83) vol. V, XI (henceforth Reaney), and Cattin, "Formazione e attività delle cappelle polifoniche nelle cattedrali. La Musica nelle città," in *Storia della cultura veneta III: Dal Primo Quattrocento al Concilio di Trento*, pt. 3 (Vicenza, 1981), 283, n. 97. On the Treviso Rosso see also Robert Nosow, "Du Fay and the Cultures of Renaissance Florence," in *Hearing the Motet: Essays on the Motet of the Middle Ages and Renaissance*, ed. Dolores Pesce (Oxford: Oxford University Press, 1997), 116 and 121, n. 38.

24 Bent sees the motets of Ciconia's followers as continuing the fourteenth-century tradition: "the list however could be extended to over forty pieces belonging to a coherent and continuing tradition of north Italian motet composition, were we to add about twenty motets by Ciconia's followers, notably Antonius de Cividale, Antonius Romanus and Christoforus de Monte" ("Italian Motet," 94). The eight Ciconia motets and Q15.227: *O Maria virgo davitica/O Maria maris stella* in Table 4.2, are also discussed by Bent. See also Nosow, "Equal-discantus" and "Florid," and Cumming, "Music for the Doge in Early Renaissance Venice," *Speculum* 67 (1992): 324–64.

25 See discussion by Cox, "Q15," vol. II, 290–9.

26 Suzanne Clercx, *Johannes Ciconia: un musicien liégeois et son temps (vers 1335–1411)* (Brussels: Palais des Académies, 1960), vol. I, 69; Nosow, "Florid," 61. See also Anne Hallmark, "Gratiosus, Ciconia, and Other Musicians at Padua Cathedral: Some Footnotes to Present Knowledge," in *L'Ars nova italiana del trecento* VI, ed. Giulio Cattin and Patrizia Dalla Vecchia (Certaldo: Edizioni Polis, 1992), 69–84, and Cattin, "Formazione," 291; neither one mentions Cristoforus de Monte in connection with Padua.

27 "Italian motet": on tenors see pp. 99–100, on the caccia see pp. 104–6.

28 Occasionally this interval succession is inverted, resulting in motion from the third to the unison. And very occasionally the tenor descent by step is replaced by a descent of a fifth: see *Dominicus*, mm. 17–18.

29 Most current thinking assumes that performers added accidentals at cadences as needed to bring the penultimate imperfect interval (third or sixth) as close as possible to the succeeding perfect interval. Thomas Brothers, however, has recently argued against the wholesale

addition of unnotated accidentals: see *Chromatic Beauty in the Late Medieval Chanson: An Interpretation of Manuscript Accidentals* (Cambridge: Cambridge University Press, 1997), esp. 21–44. For now I am concerned primarily with interval size (thirds and fourths), not interval quality (major, minor, perfect).

30 See Bent, "Italian Motet," 103–4.

31 See Bent, "A Contemporary Perception," 193–5; "Italian Motet," 100–3; *Ciconia*, 205–8; see also Nosow, "Florid," 42–3 and 49–50.

32 Bent remarks about Dunstaple's works that "archaic cadence forms are most commonly found in four-part cadences, where the superimposition of barely-compatible formulae and the presence of prominent consecutive fifths or octaves provide the most audible reasons for Dunstaple's preference for three-part textures." See *Dunstaple* (London: Oxford University Press, 1981), 29.

33 See Nosow, "Florid," 50.

34 This kind of form does not require the kind of pre-compositional planning typical of French isorhythm, and Bent prefers not to call it isorhythm; see "Italian Motet," 97–8, 103. Michael Allsen, however, sees links with the single-color two- and three-talea structures found in quite a few French motets, especially the Cypriot works found in the Turin manuscript; see "Style," 112.

35 See Cumming, "Concord," 213–50 on *Doctorum principem*; see also Allsen, "Style," 96–111, for discussion of isorhythm in the Italian motet.

36 The term "introitus" is found in Q15 in connection with the two-voice introductions to the isorhythmic motets *Ave virgo* by Johannes Franchois and *Apostolo glorioso* by Du Fay (Nosow, "Florid," 44–5).

Not all Italian motets are imitative: Antonius Romanus seems to have deliberately eschewed imitation in his polytextual motets, perhaps to further emphasize the autonomy of the two texts and two discantus parts. See Cumming, "Music for the Doge," 343.

37 On echo imitation, see Cox, "Q15," vol. I, 87, Nosow, "Florid," 44, and Allsen, "Style," 91, n. 9. In echo imitation at the beginning of a piece the discantus parts are usually accompanied by the tenor; the result is still reduced texture at the beginning of the piece. Openings using echo imitation range dramatically in length, from 2+2 breves to 18+18. None of the double-statement motets have imitative openings, and only Ciconia's *Albane misse celitus* has reduced texture at the opening; this introduction is part of the "double-statement" rhythmic structure, and recurs in the second half.

38 There are two other motets in praise of Dominican saints and ecclesiastics by the Florentine Dominican friar Antonius de Civitato, *Pie pater Dominice* and *O felix flos Dominici*. On this composer and his motets see Nosow, "Florid," 69–71, 77–82.

39 On *Principum nobilissime* see Cumming, "Concord," 260–2, and Plamenac, "Another Paduan Fragment of Trecento Music," *Journal of the American Musicological Society* 8 (1955): 181. Other Italian motets in which the composer's name is mentioned in the text include Antonius de Civitato's *O felix flos Florentia*, and Ciconia's *O felix templum jubila*, *O Padua sidus preclarum*, *Venecie mundi splendor*, *Albane misse celitus*, and *Petrum Marcello venetum*. See Anne Hallmark, "*Protector, imo verus pater*: Francesco Zabarella's Patronage of Johannes Ciconia," in *Music in Renaissance Cities and Courts: Studies in Honor of Lewis Lockwood*, ed. Jessie

Ann Owens and Anthony M. Cummings (Warren, Mich.: Harmonie Park Press, 1997), 153–68.

40 Three of the Italian motets listed here have pre-existent texts from the liturgy. Matheus de Brixia's *Jhesus postquam* is listed as a hymn "De Transfiguratione" in *AH*, vol. XI, 18, but it is not found in Ward, *Office Hymn*, so it should probably be considered a devotional poetic text (see Nosow, "Equal Discantus," 248–50). The texts of the two Rubeus pieces derive from the Gospels: *Caro mea* quotes John 6.56–7, but the excerpt is also the verse of an alleluia for Corpus Christi. *Missus est Gabriel* paraphrases Luke 1.26–32, but is based on four antiphons for Annunciation. The anonymous *O Maria virgo Davitica/O Maria maris stella* uses thirteenth-century motet texts (see Bent, "Italian Motet," 101, and "A Contemporary Perception," 195–6).

41 See Bent, "Italian Motet," 102. For the possibility that form of text may have had a major influence on the form of the work, at least in Ciconia's motets, see Allsen, "Style," 107–8.

42 Monte's *Plaude decus mundi* and Romanus's *Carminibus festos* (Cumming, "Music for the Doge"). Dates proposed for Q15.219, Antonius Romanus's *Aurea flamigeri,* include 1414, 1420, and 1432; the last certainly seems too late. See Cox, "Q15," vol. I, 139–40; Nosow, "Florid," 53–4; and F. Alberto Gallo, ed., *Antonii Romani Opera* (Bologna: Università degli studi di Bologna, 1965).

43 Michael Allsen's dissertation, "Style," is the most recent and most thorough discussion of isorhythm in the fifteenth century. See also Fallows, *Dufay*, 103–23; Bent, *Dunstaple*, and "The Late-Medieval Motet," in *Companion to Medieval and Renaissance Music*, ed. Tess Knighton and David Fallows (London: Dent, 1992), 114–19; Charles Turner, "Proportion and Form in the Continental Isorhythmic Motet c. 1385–1450," *Music Analysis* 10 (1991): 89–124; Samuel Emmons Brown, "The Motets of Ciconia, Dunstable, and Dufay" (Ph.D. dissertation, Indiana University, 1962); and Erna Dannemann, *Die Spätgotische Musiktradition in Frankreich und Burgund vor dem Auftreten Guillaume Dufays* (Strasbourg: Heitz & Co., 1936), 56–78.

44 Important studies include Ursula Günther, "The Fourteenth-Century Motet and its Development," *Musica Disciplina* 12 (1958): 27–59; Sanders, "The Medieval Motet," 497–573; Leech-Wilkinson, *Compositional Techniques*; Sarah Fuller, "Modal Tenors and Tonal Orientation in Motets of Guillaume de Machaut," *Current Musicology* 45–7 (1990): 199–245, and "On Sonority in Fourteenth-Century Polyphony: Some Preliminary Reflections," *Journal of Music Theory* 30 (1986): 35–70.

45 Allsen, "Style," 5, n. 12.

46 Detailed notes on the texts and music of each of the isorhythmic motets listed here, plus many others of the period, can be found in Allsen, "Style."

47 Bent, "The Yoxford Credo," 39; see also chapter 2, note 24, above (p. 314). Sanders uses the term "mensuration motet," in reference to early motets in which the color is coextensive with the talea, and the talea is repeated in different mensurations ("Motet" I, *NG*, vol. XII, 626–8). Robert Nosow adopts the term "proportional motet" ("Florid," 1, n. 1).

48 *Cuius fructus* is anonymous, but found in the only surviving French source of the period. Benenoit, the composer of Q15.195, *Gaude tu baptista Christi*, is generally believed to be the Benoit whose works are also found in Modena X.1.11; on his nationality see Pamela F.

Starr, "The 'Ferrara Connection': A Case Study of Musical Recruitment in the Renaissance," *Studi Musicali* 18 (1989): 8–12. She establishes his origins in Sens, in Haute Bourgogne; he worked in Florence, Ferrara, and Rome. See also Allsen, "Style," 339–40 and 420–1 respectively.

49 See Bent and Howlett, "The Yoxford Motet," 60–4; Bowers, "Fixed Points"; Lefferts, *The Motet in England*, 183. In "Style" (131–5, 174, 539) Allsen argues that this work may have been a model for many of the developments in the fifteenth-century English isorhythmic motet.

50 According to Allsen ("Style," 354–7 and 456–7), the only other work with a similar texture is a brief anonymous *Regina seculi* found in Oxford 213.

51 See Fallows, *Dufay*, 104–8; Nosow, "Florid," 103–7; and Allsen, "Style," 113–15 and 479–80.

52 The two other English pieces are the fourteenth-century *Sub Arturo*, and Power's *Ave regina caelorum*, a double-discantus motet.

53 On the term "cantilena," in general, see Ernest H. Sanders, "Cantilena and Discant in 14th-Century England," *Musica Disciplina* 19 (1965): 24–53; *idem*, "Cantilena (i)," *NG*, vol. III, 729–31; and Hans H. Eggebrecht, *Studien zur musikalischen Terminologie* (Mainz: Akademie der Wissenschaften und der Literatur, 1955), 843–4 (27–8). The mid-fifteenth-century Polish music theorist Paulus Paulirinus de Praga uses the term in the most general sense: "Cantilena is generally every piece of figured music. . . . Therefore, all the varieties of mensural song are called by this one word, cantilena." Cited and translated in Charles Brewer, "The Introduction of the Ars nova into East-Central Europe: A Study of the Late Medieval Polish Sources" (Ph.D. diss., City University of New York, 1984), 437; for the word in the texts of some Polish compositions see pp. 341–2.

54 Ernest Sanders, "Cantilena and Discant"; William Summers, "Fourteenth-Century English Music: A Review of Three Recent Publications," *Journal of Musicology* 8 (1990): 130–3, and "The Effect of Monasticism," 113–14.

55 The precise nature of the technique of English discant is much debated by modern scholars. In "Discant, II: English," *NG*, vol. V, 493–5, Sanders shows that discant, as described by the theorists, generally refers to two-voice polyphony. The term is widely used, however, to refer to three-voice compositions: see Andrew Hughes, "The Old Hall Manuscript: A Re-Appraisal," *Musica Disciplina* 21 (1967): 97–129, esp. 99–100. Margaret Bent describes "English descant" in the Old Hall manuscript as follows: "there is usually a plainsong cantus firmus in the middle part, while the two outer parts move simultaneously with it in sonorous chords, featuring full triads and contrary motion. The effect is one of steadily-moving, non-metrical steps in which the words are very clearly projected" (*Dunstaple*, 10).

56 Summers, "Review," 131–2.

57 See Summers, "The Effect of Monasticism," 113–14.

58 For a list of the eighty-seven whole and fragmentary surviving fourteenth-century cantilenas, see Peter M. Lefferts, "Cantilena and Antiphon: Music for Marian Services in Late Medieval England," *Current Musicology* 45–7 (1990): 270–2. This is an excellent article which has greatly influenced my thinking on the subject of the English cantilena.

59 Lefferts, *The Motet in England*, 166.

60 Sanders, "Cantilena and Discant," 14, n. 33.

61 As Lefferts points out ("Cantilena and Antiphon," 267), settings of this type of text never disappear: consider *Benedicta es celorum regina* or *Inviolata, integra et casta* set by Josquin *c.* 1500.

62 Margaret Bent remarks on this point, in connection with Dunstaple's cantilenas: "To divide settings which present the plainsong melody complete from those which allude to it, treat it freely or make no use of it, may be invidious and misleading. Such a division also obscures the fact that the two categories artificially divide pieces of similar liturgical status. Most are antiphons, and many are prescribed for more than one situation" (*Dunstaple*, 39).

63 For the earlier "layered" style of score-format antiphon and cantilena settings with *cpf* see Charles Hamm: "The Motets of Lionel Power," in *Studies in Music History: Essays for Oliver Strunk*, ed. Harold Powers (Princeton: Princeton University Press, 1968): "Each is written for three voices clearly differentiated in range." Andrew Hughes comments that "almost the whole story of English fifteenth-century music is concerned with the clash and partial blending of these two contrasting styles: the chordal texture of descant with the contra-puntal texture of chanson"; see "The Old Hall Manuscript: A Re-Appraisal," 100–2.

64 It could be said that the cantilenas, originally composed for Mass, were assimilated into the genre of polyphonic votive antiphon settings. See Harrison, *Medieval Britain*, 295–329, for the history of the polyphonic votive antiphon from its beginning through the repertory of the Eton Choirbook.

65 Sometimes cantilenas use votive texts in honor of Jesus or the Cross, as in Dunstaple's *O crux gloriosa*.

66 Lefferts comments that "counting pieces up to but not including the Eton Choirbook, this is a repertory of approximately 150 works setting over fifty different Marian texts; approx-imately 20 percent of these texts are rhymed, strophic, accentual Latin poetry" ("Cantilena and Antiphon," 264, n. 49). Lefferts's lists of texts and settings from the fourteenth and early fifteenth centuries are on pp. 270–3 and 277–82.

67 While the cantilena and the isorhythmic motet existed side-by-side in England until about 1440, ultimately the isorhythmic motet was supplanted by settings of the texts and melodies associated with the cantilena. Although such pieces were known as motets on the Continent, in England they were known as antiphons. "Antiphons" became "anthems" after the Reformation.

68 An anonymous setting of a Sarum antiphon, *Sancta Maria virgo*, is the only example I know of an English cantilena found in score format in an English source (Ob26, fol. 3') and in choirbook format in a continental source (Aosta, fol. 158'), but there must have been many more. The piece is transcribed by Andrew Hughes in *Fifteenth-Century Liturgical Music I: Antiphons and Music for Holy Week and Easter*, Early English Church Music 8 (London: Stainer and Bell, 1964), 3–4; commentary 169–70; *cpf* 180 (henceforth EECM 8).

69 In *Changes in the Land: Indians, Colonists, and the Ecology of New England* (New York: Hill and Wang, 1983), 8–9, William Cronon describes "the natural tendency for colonists to apply European names to American species which only superficially resembled their counterparts across the ocean."

70 The two anonymous motets, *Regina celi* and *Spes nostra*, are listed as English in Charles Hamm, "A Catalogue of Anonymous English Music in Fifteenth-Century Continental Manuscripts," *Musica Disciplina* 22 (1968): 75 and 76, and in Gareth Curtis and Andrew

Wathey, "Fifteenth-Century English Liturgical Music: A List of the Surviving Repertory," *RMA Research Chronicle* 27 (1994): 27 (henceforth "List").

71 See Bent, *Dunstaple*, and "Power, Leonel," *NG*, vol. XV, 174–9; Charles Hamm, "A Catalogue," esp. 56–60, and "A Group of Anonymous English Pieces in Trent 87," *Music and Letters* 41 (1960): 211–15; Strohm, *REM*, 211–22.

72 As Bent says, "the general features of 'Englishness' can be safely described and distinguished from foreign work" (*Dunstaple*, 9); see also Fallows, "Contenance Angloise," 193–4. A few English pieces (including Q15.192, *Alma redemptoris mater*) are attributed to Binchois; they all have conflicting attributions to Englishmen, however, and there is general scholarly agreement on their Englishness (see Strohm, *REM*, 190–6 and 244–8).

73 Lefferts, "Cantilena and Antiphon," 264–9, 273; Harrison, *Medieval Britain*, 81–8, and Hamm, "Catalogue," 47–76.

74 Shai Burstyn claims that Q15.164, Forest's *Alma redemptoris mater*, paraphrases the chant melody very freely in the tenor voice, omitting the first phrase ("Fifteenth-Century Polyphonic Settings of Verses from the Song of Songs," Ph.D. diss. Columbia University, 1972, 180–2). I am not convinced.

75 For a detailed discussion of this work, see Cumming, "The Aesthetics of the Medieval Motet and Cantilena," *Historical Performance* 7 (1994): 71–83.

76 Compare Bent (*Dunstaple*, 45): "The normal pattern is a triple-time opening with a change to duple time around the midpoint, followed by a shorter concluding section in triple time."

77 Bent, *Dunstaple*, 20 and 36; "Power, Leonel," 177.

78 Bent, "Forest," *NG*, vol. VI, 705; Planchart, "The Early Career of Guillaume Du Fay," *Journal of the American Musicological Society* 46 (1993): 354.

79 The cantilena is found in Q15, Trent 90, Aosta, and Modena X.1.11. The attribution is found only in Modena X.1.11, and there also the contratenor has its own text, the antiphon *Anima mea liquefacta est*. Burstyn ("Song of Songs," 178–82), thinks this text is meant to be sung with the *Alma redemptoris* text as a polytextual motet, while Bent thinks it is supplied as an alternative text ("Forest," 705). In Trent 90 the clefs are positioned incorrectly on the staff (C2, C4, C4), so that the piece begins on A and ends on E, and the occasional B-flats in the discantus become G-flats (!). The correct clefs (C1, C3, C3) are found in the other sources. Trent 90 provides two endings for the contratenor voice. I have transcribed the piece from Trent 90, correcting the clefs, adding signature flats to the tenor and contratenor from Modena, and using the second, more complex, ending for the contratenor.

80 See Bent, "Forest," 75; Curtis and Wathey list only four settings of *Alma*, including this one ("List," 53).

81 See Bent, *Dunstaple*, 51: "The final cadence of a piece cannot be predicted from the opening tonality."

82 Compare Bent, *Dunstaple*, 24–5, 31–2, on the melodic style.

83 The phrases are Bent's, in "Power, Leonel," 177. She comments also that "Forest's style has much in common with that of the 'later' Power, including an instability of meter"; see "Forest," 705.

84 See, especially, Brian Trowell, who finds proportional symmetries in virtually all the works of Dunstaple: "Proportion in the Music of Dunstable," *Proceedings of the Royal Musical*

Association 105 (1978–9): 100–41. Bent, however, comments that "exact symmetries outside the isorhythmic motets and proportioned Masses are rare" (*Dunstaple*, 41, n. 1), though she admits that Trowell's findings "have important implications."

85 Thus "(4)" means the work is found in four sources, one of which is Q15. "(4/1E)" means that one of the four sources is English. "(5/4+2Bux)" for Q15.190, Dunstaple's *Sub tuam protectionem*, indicates that the piece is found in five manuscripts, one of which is the Buxheim Organ Book, which contains two different intabulations.

86 *REM*, 138, 238–66. Bent, on the other hand, comments (*Dunstaple*, 6): "it seems, in addition, that the remarkable flow of English music to the Continent during Dunstaple's presumed period of activity started before he himself was established: the demand for English music by continental musicians extends to pieces from as early as *c.* 1410 which do not yet bear the fully-developed hallmarks of the style we associate with Dunstaple." See also Fallows, "Contenance Angloise," 193–4.

87 Bologna 2216 (a "non-Basel" manuscript of the late 1430s) also includes four English compositions, as Strohm points out (*REM*, 137). Oxford 213 lacks English music; but it is generally more orientated toward songs, in any case.

88 *REM*, 115–18.

89 Wathey, "Dunstable"; Strohm, *REM*, 43.

5 A NEW HYBRID SUBGENRE: THE CUT-CIRCLE MOTET

1 Thomas Brothers sees the continental "cantilena motet" as the result, at least in part, of English influence. See "*Contenance angloise* and Accidentals in Some Motets by Du Fay," *Plainsong and Medieval Music* 6 (1997): 29.

2 There have been several previous suggestions of a subgenre like this, but no one has recognized how extensive it is. See Fallows, *Dufay*, 124–8; Besseler, *Bourdon*, 136, 131; and Wright, "Johannes Brassart," *passim*; Nosow "Florid," chs. 5 and 6.

3 *Bourdon*, 121–38.

4 Robert D. Reynolds, Jr., "Evolution of Notational Practices in Manuscripts between 1400 and 1450" (Ph.D. dissertation, Ohio State University, 1974), ch. 6, esp. 354–7.

5 See "Q15," vol. I, 187–91, and Cox's article "'Pseudo-Augmentation' in the Manuscript Bologna, Civico Museo Bibliografico Musicale, Q 15 (BL)," *Journal of Musicology* 1 (1982): 422, 436.

6 According to Michael Collins "tempus perfectum diminutum" is not a fifteenth-century term; see Cox, "'Pseudo-Augmentation'" 421, n. 14a. For a survey of theorists who discuss Ø see Anna Maria Busse Berger, *Mensuration and Proportion Signs: Origins and Evolution* (Oxford: Clarendon Press, 1993), 126–7; only two theorists mention it before Tinctoris, and they are both after 1450.

7 Charles Hamm, *A Chronology of the Works of Guillaume Dufay, Based on a Study of Mensural Practice* (Princeton: Princeton University Press, 1964), 43; Cox, "'Pseudo-Augmentation',," *passim.* See also Bent, *Fifteenth-Century Liturgical Music II: Four Anonymous Masses*, Early English Church Music 22 (London: Stainer & Bell, 1979), 170 (henceforth EECM 22), and Anna Maria Busse Berger, *Mensuration and Proportion Signs*, 99.

8 See Anna Maria Busse Berger, "The Myth of *diminutio per tertiam partem*," *Journal of*

Musicology 8 (1990): 398–426; *eadem, Mensuration and Proportion Signs*, 120–48; *eadem*, "Cut Signs in Fifteenth-Century Musical Practice," in *Music in Renaissance Cities and Courts: Studies in Honor of Lewis Lockwood*, ed. Jessie Ann Owens and Anthony M. Cummings (Warren, Mich.: Harmonie Park Press, 1997), 101–12. See also Eunice Schroeder, "The Stroke Comes Full Circle: Ø and ₵ in Writings on Music, ca. 1450–1540," *Musica Disciplina* 36 (1982): 119–66; and Rob Wegman, "What is 'acceleratio mensurae'?" *Music and Letters* 73 (1992), 515–24. They all argue for a strict 2:1 proportion. Alejandro Enrique Planchart argues for diminution by a third: see "Tempo and Proportions," in *Performance Practice: Music Before 1600*, ed. Howard M. Brown and Stanley Sadie (New York: Norton, 1990), 135, 137, 142–3; *idem*, "What's in a Name," 169; and "The Relative Speed of *Tempora* in the Dufay Period," *RMA Research Chronicle* 17 (1981): 33–51. Robert Nosow supports this interpretation, but arrives at it by a different route: see "Equal-Discantus," 255–7.

9 "The Early Use of the Sign Ø," *Early Music* 24 (1996): 219, where she comments that in *Vergene bella* "[nothing] / O / Ø may simply mark three successive sections, two *piede* and a *sirma*, in perfect time in the same tempo."

10 *Ibid.*, 219: She goes on to say that "within a few decades the primary meaning of Ø indeed came to be some kind of acceleration, precise or imprecise, and that must derive from the indisputable proportional meaning."

11 Cox, "'Pseudo-Augmentation'," 439–40. French to Italian: Kurt von Fischer, "Zur Entwicklung der italienischen Trecento-Notation," *Archiv für Musikwissenschaft* 16 (1959): 87–99; Eugene Fellin, "The Notation Types of Trecento Music," *L'Ars nova Italiana del Trecento* IV (Certaldo: Comune di Certaldo, 1978), 213–20. Italian to French: Bent and Hallmark, *Ciconia*, XIII and 198–226. English to French: Hamm, *Chronology*, 53–5, 94–5; and Bent, EECM 22, x.

12 On *Ducalis/Stirps* see Cox, "Q15," vol. I, 187–91, and "'Pseudo-Augmentation'," 432–4. On *O lux et decus* see J. Michael Allsen, "Intertextuality and Compositional Process in Two Cantilena Motets by Hugo de Lantins," *Journal of Musicology* 11 (1993): 174–202.

A renotated chanson is discussed in Reynolds, "Notational Practices," 236–7 (Binchois's *Jamais tant*). Ursula Günther found an earlier example (Borlet's *He, tres doulz roussignol*); see "Die Anwendung der Diminution in der Handschrift Chantilly," *Archiv für Musikwissenschaft* 17 (1960): 1–21, and "Der Gebrauch des *tempus perfectum diminutum* in der Handschrift Chantilly," *Archiv für Musikwissenschaft* 17 (1960): 277–97.

13 For lists of pieces using pseudo-augmentation, see Hamm, *Chronology*, 43–5, 56 and 74. There do not seem to be any continental examples of pseudo-augmentation in which the mensuration sign O is used explicitly against ₵; either no mensuration sign is given, or Ø, or O2. In English sources, however, this is fairly common (Hamm found seven in Old Hall; see *Chronology*, 47). Berger claims to find plenty of examples of ₵ combined with O, but all the examples she cites are English (*Mensuration and Proportion Signs*, 98).

14 These advantages were first mentioned by Besseler, *Bourdon*, 123–35; see Reynolds, "Notational Practices," 357–64.

15 Nosow, "Equal-Discantus," 241, n. 30.

16 Nosow discusses Ø characteristics in "Equal-Discantus," 241, n. 30, 252, n. 45, and 255–60; Reynolds discusses them in "Notational Practices," 350–7.

17 Nosow says that "composers write semiminims in ₵, but tend to write nothing smaller than

minim triplets, notated in 3 or in coloration, in both C and O" ("Equal-Discantus," 259). See also Graeme Boone, "Dufay's Early Chansons: Chronology and Style in the Manuscript Oxford, Bodleian Library, Canonici misc. 213" (Ph.D. dissertation, Harvard University, 1987), 164. Reynolds says that semiminims and minim triplets are found in both O and Ø ("Notational Practices," 353), but his data suggest a somewhat greater use of semiminims in Ø (see pp. 283 and 352).

18 Reynolds finds two pieces in Oxford 213 that seem to mix the mensurations ("Notational Practices," 356, 244–6, 157–8). Q15.282, Sarto's *Ave mater* (Ex. 5.1), also exhibits a mixture of traits.

19 On this piece see Wright, "Johannes Brassart," 46–51.

20 I omit Grossin from this discussion; he is a French composer from the diocese of Sens who worked as a clerk of Matins at Notre Dame de Paris in 1421. See Craig Wright, *Notre Dame*, 301–2.

21 On Du Fay and the Lantins at the Malatestas, see Alejandro Enrique Planchart, "Guillaume Du Fay's Benefices and his Relationship to the Court of Burgundy," *Early Music History* 8 (1988): 124, and "The Early Career," 361–2. For Vicenza, see F. Alberto Gallo and Giovanni Mantese, *Richerche sulle origini della cappella musicale del duomo di Vicenza* (Venice: Istituto per la collaborazione culturale Venezia–Roma, 1964). For the Papal chapel, see Manfred Schuler, "Zur Geschichte der Kapelle Papst Martins V," *Archiv für Musikwissenschaft* 25 (1968): 30–45, and "Zur Geschichte der Kapelle Papst Eugens IV," *Acta musicologica* 60 (1968): 220–7; and Franz X. Haberl, "Die römische 'schola cantorum' und die päpstlichen Kapellsänger bis zur Mitte des 16. Jahrhunderts," *Bausteine für Musikgeschichte* III (Leipzig: Breitkopf und Härtel, 1888). For other biographies see Keith Mixter, "Brassart, Johannes" (*NG*, vol. III, 208–9); "Feragut, Beltrame" (*NG*, vol. VI, 468); "Johannes de Lymburgia" (*NG*, vol. IX, 666–7); "Johannes de Sarto" (*NG*, vol. IX, 668); and Hans Schoop, "Lantins, de (4) Arnold; (5) Hugo" (*NG*, vol. X, 457–8). For Brassart and Sarto, see Wright, "Johannes Brassart," 41–3; for more on the connections among these composers, see Nosow, "Florid," 236–41.

22 See Etheridge, "The Works of Johannes Lymburgia" (Ph.D. dissertation, Indiana University, 1972), 9–11.

23 For the resemblances among the openings of six of these works, see Nosow, "Florid," 217–22. Q15.222, Hugh de Lantins's *Ave verum corpus*, begins with the characteristic rhythm but starts on the wrong note (f) and goes up.

24 There exist a few Ø motets with an F final that do not use this opening in other manuscripts; see, for example, Du Fay's *Ave virgo quae de celis*. An F-final piece with two flats in the bottom voices does not use the standard opening: Q15.189, Lymburgia, *In hac die celebri*. One of the illegible pieces in Q15 also has an F final, but I cannot tell if it has the characteristic opening.

25 Robert Nosow considers these florid pieces a separate subgenre, the "florid motet style," in which the discantus voice is predominant, and contrasts it with what he calls the "discantus–tenor" or "song" motet, where discantus and tenor have a more equal role ("Florid," 152–279). I find that the florid pieces are one end of a continuum of rhythmic activity, and that the fundamental approach to composition is broadly similar in all my cut-circle motets.

26 See Wright, "Johannes Brassart," 46–9.

27 *Ibid.*, 48, for more occurrences of "melisma x" in *Flos florum* and *O flos fragrans*.

28 See, for example, *I occhi d'una ançoleta* by Prepositus Brixiensis, Reaney, vol. V, 89–90. Brothers ("*Contenance angloise*," 29, n. 22) finds French precedents in chansons by Velut, Grenon, and Haucourt. Nosow ("Florid," 195–215) sees the origins of the "florid motet style" in the Mass.

29 On the centrality of *Flos florum* see Nosow, "Florid," 216–58. Wright suggests that influence traveled from Du Fay, to Brassart, to Sarto ("Johannes Brassart," 48 and 59).

30 For speculation on what the fermatas could mean, see Charles W. Warren, "Punctus Organi and Cantus Coronatus in the Music of Dufay," in *Papers read at the Dufay Quincentenary Conference*, ed. Allan W. Atlas (Brooklyn: Brooklyn College, 1976), 128–43.

31 See Cox, "Q15," vol. I, 65, 68–70, 75–8; Etheridge, "Lymburgia," 166; Wright, "Johannes Brassart," 50 and 53.

32 Alejandro Planchart discusses devotional poetic texts in "What's in a Name," 171–3. He comments that they are frequently found in non-musical sources such as orationals and books of hours.

33 On the lauda text see Lorenz Welker, "New Light on Oswald von Wolkenstein: Central European traditions and Burgundian Polyphony," *Early Music History* 7 (1987): 207–10; Kurt von Fischer, "Die Lauda 'Ave Mater' und ihre verschiedenen Fassungen," *Colloquium Amicorum: Joseph Schmidt-Görg zum 70. Geburtstag*, ed. Siegfried Kross and Hans Schmidt (Bonn: Beethovenhaus, 1967), 93–9; and F. Alberto Gallo, ed., *Il codice musicale 2216 della Biblioteca Universitaria di Bologna* (Bologna: Forni Editore, 1966–71), vol. II, 48–9. Welker and von Fischer show that the widely disseminated lauda *Ave mater* is found in one of the Wolkenstein manuscripts ("WoB") where it has seventeen stanzas. The stanzas' first words yield the angelic salutation ("Ave / [O] Maria / gratia / plena / Dominus / tecum / bene- dicta / tu / in / mulieribus . . . ."). See Hans Ganser and Rainer Herpichböhm, eds., *Oswald von Wolkenstein-Liederbuch: Eine Auswahl von Melodien* (Göppingen: Kümmerle Verlag, 1978). Welker points out that Sarto's *Ave mater* does not use the lauda melody, but it does use two stanzas of the lauda text (the first and eighth, which Welker calls the seventh): "*Ave* mater, O Maria" . . . "*Tu* in valle delictorum." Sarto's third stanza ("Salve virgo mater Dei") is not found in WoB nor does it fit in the angelic salutation, so it was presumably written for the motet.

34 See Ann Lewis, ed., *Johannes de Lymburgia: Four Motets: The Song of Songs* (Newton Abbot: Antico, 1985): "Lymburgia seems to have derived his texts directly from the Vulgate rather than from liturgical antiphons." She finds that *Descendi in ortum*, in contrast, refers to the antiphon melody in the discantus at the beginning of each of the two verses.

35 See Allsen, "Compositional Process," for a discussion of the text and music of Q15.181, *O lux et decus Hispanie*. English composers occasionally wrote cantilenas in honor of saints, but the practice seems to have been more widespread on the Continent.

36 For a discussion of the possible origin and function of the laudatory cantilena-style motet (including those not in Q15), see Cumming, "Music for the Doge," 346–53.

37 See Nosow, "Florid," 207–15; he stresses its similarities to Du Fay's *Flos florum*. See also below, Table 11.2.

38 The four-voice version is edited in Charles van den Borren, *Polyphonia Sacra* (London: The Plainsong and Mediaeval Music Society, 1932), 262–6, with commentary on xlviii–l (henceforth *PS*). The three-voice version is found in Bologna 2216 and Oxford 213; the four-voice version in Q15 and MuEm.

39 Nosow ("Florid," 131–42) also points this out.

40 In sources other than Bologna 2216; see the critical commentary in *PS*, xlviii.

41 The Mass is edited in Etheridge, "Lymburgia," 100–13. The notational issues are discussed in Cox, "'Pseudo-Augmentation'," 427; the unity of the cycle is discussed by Philip Gosset in "Techniques of Unification in Early Cyclic Masses and Mass Pairs," *Journal of the American Musicological Society* 19 (1966): 215–18, and the incipits (with all voices, original mensurations shown) in ex. 2, pp. 216–17. The Sanctus and Agnus have four voices in motet-style texture, with two discantus parts.

42 Strohm, *REM*, 176–7. He also discusses it in "Einheit und Function früher Messzyklen," in *Festschrift Rudolf Bockholdt zum 60. Geburtstag,* ed. N. Dubowy and S. Meyer-Eller (Pfaffenhofen: Ludwig, 1990), 141–60. The Mass and motet are edited in *PS*, nos. 1–5 and 43. Arnold de Lantins's Mass music is also edited and discussed in Jean Widaman, "The Mass Ordinary Settings of Arnold de Lantins: A Case Study in the Transmission of Early Fifteenth-Century Music," 2 vols. (Ph.D. dissertation, Brandeis University, 1987); see esp. vol. I, 30, 177–8. See also Nosow, "Florid," 229–30. I find Strohm's connections to the motet a bit unconvincing, since so many of them fall into the basic stylistic framework of cut-circle-style music. But for just that reason the evidence from the Mass is still applicable to the larger consideration of the Ø signature and its origins.

43 The Sanctus and Agnus have a few semiminims in Ø which would not be possible in ₵. Without them, however, the Sanctus and Agnus could have been written just as well in ₵. The Sanctus also has one florid minim melisma very much in the standard cut-circle mold, though in the middle O section (see *PS*, 33, m. 90).

44 *Dufay*, 22 and 30. Allan Atlas agrees: see "Dufay's *Mon chier amy*: Another Piece for the Malatesta," in *Music in Renaissance Cities and Courts: Studies in Honor of Lewis Lockwood*, ed. Jessie Ann Owens and Anthony M. Cummings (Warren, Mich.: Harmonie Park Press, 1997), 3–20.

45 Bent suggests that it was copied in stage I before being recopied in stage II, in a personal communication to Robert Nosow, 29 January 1992 (cited in "Florid," 215). Nosow ("Florid," 259) also suggests that *Vergene bella* was written during Du Fay's Malatesta years, 1420–4.

46 See Planchart, "What's in a Name," 166–8, and Nosow, "Florid," 31, 259–74, and 214–15.

47 Besseler, DufayB, vol. VI, no. 16. Both 1433 and 1437 have been proposed; Fallows (*Dufay*, 40–1, 48) leans toward 1433, as do I.

48 Thomas Brothers refers to this practice as "pre-cadential lowered thirds," and finds them in chansons by Du Fay and his predecessors, and in some of his motets. See "*Contenance angloise*," 19, and n. 40, where he lists another use of A-flat in this context; and *Chromatic Beauty*, 195–202.

49 Like Arnold de Lantins's motet *O pulcherrima*, *Resvellies vous* shares musical material with a Mass by the same composer: Fallows suggests that Du Fay's *Missa sine nomine* be called *Missa Resvellies vous* (*Dufay*, 165–8).

50 See Reynolds, "Notational Practices," 360–4, for discussion of Besseler's categories.

51 Pseudo-augmentation is common in English music, but the Ø sign is never used in English sources; it must have been supplied by the Q15 scribe. *Salve regina* paraphrases the chant *Alma redemptoris mater.* Another English cantilena found in Q15 with a section in Ø is the anonymous *Regina celi,* attributed by Hamm to Power. In this piece all voices are in Ø, but the style is still different from that of the cut-circle motets.

52 See Fallows on the "careful exploitation of rhythms" in Du Fay's cut-circle motets. On *Ave virgo* (not in Q15) he comments: "not until bar 25 is the rhythm of one bar repeated in another bar . . . a fascinating and continuous unravelling of musical ideas" (*Dufay,* 126). Compare Bent, *Dunstaple,* 36: "each successive bar in a phrase . . . normally has a different rhythm."

53 Q15.185, De Anglia's *Benedicta es* has fermatas on "Ave," and Q15.291, Dunstaple's *Quam pulchra,* has fermatas on "Veni."

6 OTHER NEW HYBRID SUBGENRES

1 Nosow ("Equal-Discantus," and "Florid," 38–151) includes the Italian motets in the category, and fails to distinguish between text types as I do. My term is inspired by his, and by Wolfgang Stephan's "imitierende Doppeldiskantmotette": see *Burgundisch-Niederländische Motette,* 63–5, 104.

2 In "John Dunstable: A Quincentenary Report," *Musical Quarterly* 40 (1954): 47–8, Bukofzer says that "*Quam pulchra es* prompted a vogue of declamation motets, especially among English composers, that lasted well beyond the middle of the century." He cites Forest's *Tota pulchra es* as a later example modeled on Dunstable's *Quam pulchra,* and suggests that the style derives from the English "conductus-like" cantilenas written in score. See also *idem,* "John Dunstable and the Music of his Time," *Proceedings of the Royal Musical Association* 65 (1938–9): 26–7, and Burstyn, "Polyphonic Settings," 158–61.

3 Robert Nosow's definition of the "discantus-tenor" or "song" motet shares some features with this subgenre ("Florid," 161–94), but it is a much broader category, including most of my non-florid cut-circle motets.

4 Nosow considers *In Pharaonis* a lauda ("Florid," 6). *Ave regina celorum* is found in the later lauda manuscript, Ven 145, though its text is more typical of the English cantilena.

5 See Strohm, *REM,* 327–39: "the English cantilena and carol, the Italian *lauda,* and the Central European cantio . . . are just the best-known results of what may have been a widespread tendency of creating religious lyrics which were less venerable, but more accessible to congregations, than liturgical chant" (p. 327).

6 In Q15 and MuEm only the two discantus voices are fully texted; in Oxford 213 only the discantus is texted; Paris 4379 is an untexted tenor part, and Str is lost.

7 Text from the *Song of Songs,* 4: 7, 4: 11, 4: 10, 2: 11, 2: 12–13, 2: 10, 4: 8; translation from *The Holy Bible: Douay Rheims Version* (Baltimore: John Murphy Company, 1899; reprinted Tan Books and Publishers, 1971), 692–3. Burstyn lists the appearance of the antiphon in early antiphonaries ("Polyphonic settings," 68; see also 414–15).

8 See Fallows, *Dufay,* 127–8.

9 I have not included motets with single brief duet sections marked "unus," but only those in which contrasts in texture are a major structural feature.

10 See Manfred Bukofzer's "The Beginnings of Choral Polyphony," in *Studies in Medieval and Renaissance Music* (New York: Norton, 1950), 176–89. See also Etheridge, "Lymburgia," 167–72.

11 On this trope (*Virgo mater*) and its polyphonic settings, see Giulio Cattin, "Virgo Mater Ecclesiae: Un tropo alla Salve regina nelle fonti monodiche e polifoniche dei sec. XIV–XV," in *L'ars nova italiana del trecento* IV (Certaldo: Comune di Certaldo, 1978), 149–76. The Power and Salinis settings use different versions of the trope.

12 Fallows, *Dufay*, 168–72 and 179–81; *idem*, "Specific Information," 122–30; Planchart, "Parts with Words," 237–42.

13 On Salinis see Nosow, "Equal-Discantus," 221–2, and "Florid," 87–98.

14 It is the first piece in fascicle 5, the first fascicle to be copied, containing mostly music composed before 1415. See Boone, "Dufay's Early Chansons," 21–34, and David Fallows's facsimile edition of the manuscript, *Oxford, Bodleian Library, MS Canonici Misc. 213* (Chicago: University of Chicago Press, 1995), 45 and fol. 81; I have transcribed the piece from this facsimile.

15 Q15.247, Salinis's *Psallat chorus/Eximie pater*, uses texts from a motet found in the Montpellier and Bamberg Codices with the tenor *Aptatur*. There the texts are in honor of St. Nicholas; here they are adapted to St. Lambert. The texts of Q15.278, Salinis's *Si nichil/In precio*, are the two strophes of the text of a three-part conductus found in the sixth fascicle of the Florence MS, fols. 227r–227v (also found in the Fauvel manuscript with one voice and one strophe). Discantus 1 has the second strophe and discantus 2 has the first. See Reaney, vol. VII, XVIII.

16 On the conductus tradition of *admonitio* or *cantus moralis*, see Leo Schrade, "Political Compositions in French Music of the Twelfth and Thirteenth Centuries: The Coronation of French Kings," in Leo Schrade, *De Scientia Musicae Studia atque Orationes*, ed. Ernst Lichtenhahn (Bern and Stuttgart, 1967), 153, and Ruth Steiner, "Some Monophonic Latin Songs composed around 1200," *Musical Quarterly* 52 (1966): 56–70.

The texts of Q15.260, Velut's *Summe summy*, are found in *AH*, vol. XXVIII, 253; see Giulio Cattin, "Testi tropati nei Codici Trentini," in *I Codici Musicali Trentini a cento anni dalla loro riscoperta: Atti del Convegno Laurence Feininger, la musicologia come missione*, ed. Nino Pirrotta and Danilo Curti (Trent: Provincia Autonoma di Trento, 1986), 136. (This collection will be known as *I Codici* henceforth.)

17 Discantus 1, line 6, emended from "fusas" to "fusus."

18 See Ann Lewis, "Anti-Semitism in an Early Fifteenth-Century Motet: *Tu, nephanda*," *Plainsong and Medieval Music* 3 (1994): 45–55. She suggests that the motet be dated *c.* 1434–5.

19 For a discussion of this kind of rhythmic episode in the delineation of talea structure in isorhythmic motets, see Allsen, "Style," 47–54 and 82–6.

20 The extension of the central phrase also serves to help fit texts that divide naturally into two four-line stanzas into the three sections required for this piece: Introitus (line 1); Text 1 (lines 2–3); Text 2 (lines 4–5); extra two mm. (line 6); Text 3 (lines 7–8).

21 *Ave gemma* combines the texts of two antiphons in honor of St. Catherine; for a discussion

334

and transcription see Nosow, "Equal-Discantus," 251–4. *Puer natus* uses the text of a processional hymn for the Christmas season (not one of the normal Vespers hymns). For a discussion of *Gaude virgo mater Christi* that links it to the world of religious confraternities, see Nosow, "Renaissance Florence," 112–17.

22 Hamm ("A Catalogue," 74) and Curtis and Wathey ("List," 27 and 57) list Q15.191, the anonymous *Descendi in ortum meum*, as English presumably because of its text and manuscript position (next to another English work); its style, however, is emphatically not English. Robert Nosow agrees ("Equal-Discantus," 234–5, n. 21) and proposes that the piece is by Cristoforus de Monte ("Florid," 64–6). I find its use of a *Song* text and its relatively late copying date (stage III) ally it more with the devotional double-discantus motets by northerners.

23 In "Italian Motet," 103, Margaret Bent comments that Italian motets generally end on F, G, or D.

24 Several of Du Fay's chansons have additional or optional voices: *Donnés l'assault* is found in three- and four-voice versions; *Pour l'amour*'s second discantus (or triplum) can substitute for the contratenor; *Par droit je puis bien* and probably *Hé compaignons* can be sung with three or four voices; and *Invidia nimica*'s fourth voice may have been added by Du Fay (Hamm, *Chronology*, 8). See the works list in Fallows, *Dufay*, 238–41. Chanson arrangements were even more common in the second half of the century, with some songs receiving as many as thirty arrangements; for a recent study, see Honey Meconi, "Art-Song Reworkings: An Overview," *Journal of the Royal Musicological Society* 119 (1994): 1–42. We will be examining several other arrangements of motets in Part III, chapter 11.

25 On some of the problematic contratenors see Nosow, "Florid," 124, and "Equal-Discantus," 234, n. 25, and 251–4.

26 The same cadence is found at the end of Du Fay's *Par droit je puis bien*, DufayB, vol. VI, no. 43.

27 See Cox, "Q15," vol. I, 277–8, and Nosow, "Florid," 114–21.

28 Ursula Günther suggests that *Pontifici* is a "mixed form oriented toward the caccia" in Round Table, "Critical Years in European Musical History 1400–1430," *International Musicological Society, Report of the Tenth Congress, Ljubljana 1967* (Kassel: Bärenreiter, 1970), 48.

29 See Besseler, *Bourdon*, 84, for a list of "Dufays vierstimmige Sätze ohne 'Tenor'." In addition to the works listed here he adds the Gloria "ad modum tubae" and *Ma belle dame souveraine*. To this list could be added Lymburgia's *Recordare*; see below, under "Borderline cases." See also Fallows, *Dufay*, 131–3, on the canonic works, and 101–2 on *Hé compaignons* and *Gaude virgo*; as he says (p. 133): "there is a certain community of expressive and technical means that unites the Latin cantilena with the secular song."

30 "Two Equal Voices: A French Song Repertory with Music for Two More Works of Oswald von Wolkenstein," *Early Music History* 7 (1987): 227–41. For the Ciconia examples see pp. 239–40.

31 See Bent and Hallmark, *Ciconia*, XIII and 209 on *O Petre*. In "Italian Motet," Bent comments that "Ciconia's two equal-voiced pieces in Q15, not counted here as motets, are madrigal-motet hybrids, or, perhaps, tenorless motets" (p. 112, n. 57).

32 Nosow comments that "Ave verum corpus" settings should be considered "either liturgical

works or polyphonic *laude*" ("Florid," 6, n. 10, and 207–10 for the history of the text). See also Charles Hamm, "The Reson Mass," *Journal of the American Musicological Society* 18 (1965): 15–20.

33 See Burstyn, "Polyphonic Settings," 105–36, and Strohm, *REM*, 221.

34 Aside from *Quam pulchra*, the only English *Song* setting I know of from before *c.* 1430 is Forest's *Qualis est* in Old Hall. The piece is also found in the mid-century continental collections, Modena X.1.11, Trent 93 and 90. Another early candidate discussed by Burstyn and others is a *Quam pulchra* by Piamor, who probably died *c.* 1431 (see "Polyphonic Settings," 137–42); its earliest source is Trent 92.

7 THE MOTET IN THE EARLY FIFTEENTH CENTURY: EVOLUTION AND INTERPRETATION

1 The only substantial manuscript I omitted was MuEm; it has few motets that are not concordant with these five, and should not change the picture presented here. For approximate copying dates, see Table 1.2; the contents of the Trent Codices and Modena X.1.11 will be studied at more length in Part III.

2 "TR" is the label given to the combination of 87–1 and 92–2 by Peter Wright; see "The Compilation of Trent 87–I and 92–II," *Early Music History* 2 (1982): 237–71; "On the Origins of Trent 87–I and 92–II," *Early Music History* 6 (1986): 245–70; and *The Related Parts of Trent, Museo Provinciale d'Arte, MSS 87 (1374) and 92 (1379): A Paleographical and Text-Critical Study* (New York and London: Garland, 1989). On Trent 92–1 see Tom Ward, "The Structure of the Manuscript Trent 92–I," *Musica Disciplina* 29 (1975): 127–47. I have not considered the pieces in Trent 87–2, since it seems to be an idiosyncratic repertory with few concordances: Hans Tischler comments that 87–2 "is generally known as the Battre – or better Batty – fascicle" in "A Three-Part Rondellus in Trent MS 87," *Journal of the American Musicological Society* 24 (1971): 449. See Richard James White, "The Battre Section of Trent Codex 87," 2 vols. (Ph.D. dissertation, Indiana University, 1975).

3 This involved a certain amount of oversimplification, since each piece could be counted in only one subgenre in order to make the numbers add up. For the Q15 motets that belong in more than one subgenre I made the following decisions for the sake of tabulation. Du Fay, *Anima mea*: devotional double-discantus, not continental cantilena. Dunstaple, *Quam pulchra*: English cantilena, not declamation. Grossin, *Imera dat hodierno*: declamation, not cut-circle. A. de Lantins, *Tota pulchra*: declamation, not cut-circle or devotional double-discantus. Lymburgia, *Surge propera*: devotional double-discantus, not cut-circle. Lymburgia, *Descendi*: cut-circle, not continental cantilena. For other manuscripts I assigned each piece to one subgenre.

4 The category "borderline case" is not truly comparable, since problematic cases were not included in the counts for other manuscripts.

5 For a thorough discussion of the English isorhythmic motet, see Allsen, "Style," 129–86. *Veni sancte/Veni creator* appears as an addition to Old Hall, and thus was probably copied sometime after 1421; it may have been composed, however, as early as 1416. See Allsen, "Style," 179, 502–4; Bent, *Dunstaple*, 7–8; and on the additions to Old Hall after 1421, see

Roger Bowers, "Some Observations on the Life and Career of Lionel Power," *Proceedings of the Royal Musical Association* 102 (1975–6): 106–10, and Bent, "The Progeny of Old Hall: More Leaves from a Royal English Choirbook," in *Gordon Athol Anderson (1929–1981): In Memoriam* (Henryville: Institute of Medieval Music, 1984), 25–32.

6 The text is especially close in form to that of *Venecie/Michael:* see Bent and Hallmark, *Ciconia*, 221, for discussion of the text by Michael Connolly; and Allsen, "Style and Intertextuality," 107–8.

7 See Fallows, *Dufay*, 34–5, 115–17; Cox, "Q15," vol. 1, 34–9; Finscher and Laubenthal, "Cantiones," 301–2; Allsen, "Style," 198–9, 212–17, 477–8.

8 Edition and translation of text from Leofranc Holford-Strevens, "Du Fay the Poet? Problems in the Texts of his Motets," *Early Music History* 16 (1997): 140–1.

9 Sigismund died only four years later, in 1437; Eugenius lived until 1447. In MuEm the words "rex Sigismundus" are replaced by references to local aristocrats, "dux beatus" and "ducissa beatrix," probably Duchess Beatrix of Munich and her husband Pfalzgraf Johann of Neuburg; see Ian Rumbold, "The Compilation and Ownership of the 'St Emmeram' Codex (Munich, Bayerische Staatsbibliothek, Clm 14274)," *Early Music History* 2 (1982): 166.

10 Willem Elders, "Humanism and Early Renaissance Music: A Study of the Ceremonial Motets by Ciconia and Dufay," *Tijdschrift van de Vereniging voor Nederlandse Muziekgeschiedenis* 27 (1977): 65–101; "Humanism and Music in the Early Renaissance," in *International Musicological Society, Report of the Twelfth Congress, Berkeley, 1977*, ed. Daniel Heartz and Bonnie Wade (Kassel: Bärenreiter, 1981), 883–7, with responses on pp. 888–93; "Guillaume Dufay as Musical Orator," *Tijdschrift van de Vereniging voor Nederlandse Muziekgeschiedenis* 31 (1981): 9–14; and "Guillaume Dufay's Concept of *Faux-bourdon*," *Revue Belge de Musicologie* 13 (1989): 173–95.

11 For text projection see Bonnie J. Blackburn, "On Compositional Process in the Fifteenth Century," *Journal of the American Musicological Society* 40 (1987): 228, n. 29; for divisi, see Allsen, "Style," 215–16.

8 MOTETS IN THE TRENT CODICES: ESTABLISHING THE BOUNDARIES

1 See Gerald Montagna, "Johannes Pullois in the Context of his Era," *Revue Belge de Musique* 42 (1988): 83; and Fallows, "Songs in the Trent Codices: An Optimistic Handlist," in *I codici*, 170–9, for the chanson. See also Brothers, "Vestiges," 35: "the sad fact is that there are not many sources for motets from the period 1460 to about 1495."

2 Suparmi Elizabeth Saunders, *The Dating of the Trent Codices from Their Watermarks, With a Study of the Local Liturgy of Trent in the Fifteenth Century* (New York: Garland, 1989). Wright: see *Related Parts* and "Paper Evidence and the Dating of Trent 91," *Music and Letters* 76. (1995): 487–508. See also Strohm, *REM*, 252–6, 291, 507–11, 520, 524.

3 See Tom Ward, "Trent 92–I"; for TR (Trent 87–1 and 92–2), see Wright, *Related Parts*, "The Compilation" and "On the Origins"; for Trent 87–2, see White, "The Battre Section."

4 See Bent, EECM 22, x–xi, and *eadem*, "Trent 93 and Trent 90: Johannes Wiser at Work," *I codici*, 84–111. See also Saunders, "The Dating of Trent 93 and Trent 90," *I codici*, 60–82;

Wright, *Related Parts*, 302–11; Gary Spilsted, "The Paleography and Musical Repertory of Codex Tridentinus 93" (Ph.D. dissertation, Harvard University, 1982); and Marco Gozzi, *Il manoscritto Trento Museo Provinciale d'Arte, cod. 1377 (Tr 90) con un'analisi del repertorio non derivato da Tr 93*, 2 vols. (Cremona: Centro di Musicologia "Walter Stauffer," 1992).

5 The sections containing motets are Trent 93–2, gatherings 31–3, fols. 356–382, 93.1821–64; and Trent 90–2, gatherings 24–39, fols. 282–465, 90.988–1143. Two motets are found in 93–1: the cantio *Martinus nam pusillus* (93.1599) and the continental cantilena *Salve regina* (93.1653). They are not copied into Trent 90, and were probably added later, perhaps at the same time that 93–2 was being copied; see Peter Wright, *Related Parts*, 306.

6 On 88 see Rebecca Lynn Gerber, "The Manuscript Trent, Castello del Buonconsiglio, 88: A Study of Fifteenth-Century Manuscript Transmission and Repertory" (Ph.D. dissertation, University of California, Santa Barbara, 1985), henceforth "Trent 88"; she is preparing a complete edition of the manuscript. On 89 see Louis Gottlieb, "The Cyclic Masses of Trent Codex 89" (Ph.D. dissertation, University of California, Berkeley, 1958). On Trent 91 see Peter Wright, "Paper Evidence," and Leverett, "Trent 91." On Trent 89 and 91, see Robert Mitchell, "The Paleography and Repertory of Trent Codices 89 and 91, together with Analyses and Editions of Six Mass Cycles by Franco-Flemish Composers from Trent Codex 89," 2 vols. (Ph.D. dissertation, University of Exeter, 1989).

7 Leverett compares Trent to Brixen, a nearby city further north on the Brenner Pass with abundant documentation of a choir school and the performance of polyphony ("Trent 91," vol. I, 16–17 and n. 28).

8 See Wright, "On the Origins," 260; *Related parts*, 107–8; and "The Aosta–Trent Relationship Reconsidered," in *I codici*, 138–57. See also Leverett, "Trent 91," vol. I, 46.

9 On Lupi, see Wright, *The Related Parts*, 101–9, "On the Origins," 255–61, and Strohm, *REM*, 252–6, 507.

10 A late addition to Trent 87 is in the same hand as pieces found in two of the Wiser manuscripts 88 and 89, suggesting that Lupi's manuscripts became part of Wiser's, or the cathedral's, library (Wright, "On the Origins," 262, n. 45).

11 Leverett, "Trent 91," vol. I, 30, n. 53, and Table 1.1 (vol. II, 16–17), which lists documents that name Wiser at the cathedral from 1465 to 1480. Strohm points out that Wiser became a "non-resident court chaplain" for Duke Sigismund in 1471 (*REM*, 520).

12 Strohm, *REM*, 510.

13 *Ibid.*, *REM*, 503–21, esp. 509–16.

14 Leverett, "Trent 91," vol. I, 27–31 and 110–11.

15 This is particularly true of sequences, such as *Grates nunc omnes*, some of the more obscure prosulae (such as *Alle dei filio*), and cantiones (such as *Novus annus hodie*; for settings of this text see Table 8.3).

16 For studies of individual codices, see notes 3, 4, and 6 above. On individual genres, see the articles listed in the notes to Table 8.2. For Vespers music, see also Kanazawa, "Vespers." Studies of polyphonic sequences and Vespers antiphons of the period are badly needed. For a useful list of the most common monophonic sequences, see Nancy van Deusen, "Sequence Repertories: A Reappraisal," *Musica Disciplina* 48 (1994): 107–11.

17 Fols. 146'-148; ed. *DTÖ* 53, 50–5. This volume of *DTÖ* contains a large selection of

Salve regina settings and provides a good sample of the various different styles of composition.

18 The Passau rite was also used at the Imperial court. See Leverett, "Trent 91," vol. I, 73–111. Many of these pieces are also found in the Glogauer Liederbuch: see her Table 2.1, vol. II, 31–40.

19 See 91.1201–1214, fols. 84–95′. Leverett's findings show that the four great Marian antiphons are often used as simple *Magnificat* or *Benedictus* antiphons in the Passau paraphrase repertory (see "Trent 91," Table 2.6, vol. II, 49–51). Multiple settings of *Salve regina* and *Regina celi* using primarily equal-note cantus firmus technique are also found in Berlin 40021, listed among the "cantica. hymni. sequentiae" section of the index, rather than the "muteti et alia" section.

20 On equal-note cantus firmus treatment and the use of chant notation in Central Europe see Strohm, *REM*, 525–8; Just, *Mensuralkodex*, vol. I, 137–96; and Leverett, "Trent 91," vol. I, 76–7.

21 This contrast can be observed easily in Besseler, DufayB, vol. V, where Q15.193, *Gaude virgo mater Christi*, a four-voice double-discantus motet setting of a sequence text, is followed by simple three-voice alternatim sequences that clearly belong to the class of liturgical service music. Categorization by text alone kept this piece out of the motet volume where it belongs.

22 See Strohm, *REM*, 327–33 and 343 on cantio and Leise; 532–3 for *Ave mundi/Gottes nahmen*.

23 See Keith Polk, "Innovation in Instrumental Music 1450–1510: The Role of German Performers within European Culture," in *Music in the German Renaissance: Sources, Styles, and Contexts*, ed. John Kmetz (Cambridge: Cambridge University Press, 1994), 202–14; and Polk, *German Instrumental Music of the Late Middle Ages* (Cambridge: Cambridge University Press, 1992). See also Louise Litterick, "Performing Franco-Netherlandish Secular Music of the Late Fifteenth Century: Texted and Untexted Parts in the Sources," *Early Music* 8 (1980): 474–85; and Strohm, *REM*, 357–74, 489–503, 557–70.

24 See Strohm, *REM*, 290–6, 495, n. 355, and 510–14.

25 See Heribert Ringmann and Joseph Klapper, EDM 4 & 8, and Christian Väterlein, EDM 85–6. For a brief introduction to the manuscript in English, see Owens, ed., *Glogauer Liederbuch*, v–xi. Many of the pieces with animal names turn out to be French chansons with their texts omitted. See Howard Mayer Brown, ed., *A Florentine Chansonnier from the Time of Lorenzo the Magnificent: Florence, Biblioteca Nazionale Centrale, MS Banco Rari 229* (Chicago: University of Chicago Press, 1983), Text volume, 127.

26 Strohm calls these textless pieces a "reservoir for contrafactum texts fitting various occasions" (*REM*, 514–15).

27 For 89.604, *O quam clara/Der pfawin swancz*, see Strohm, *REM*, 362–4. For 89.675, *Sancta genitrix/Der Fochs swantcz* (= Glog no. 122), see Brown, *Florentine Chansonnier*, Text Volume, 128, 287; and Strohm, *REM*, 362 and 367.

28 The only motets I know of with internal repetition are Grossin's *Imera dat hodierno* (Q15.203) and Touront's *O gloriosa regina*, which may have been modeled in part on the Frye work. On *Ave regina celorum* see Sylvia Kenney, *Walter Frye and the Contenance Angloise* (New Haven: Yale University Press, 1964), ch. 7, and "Contrafacta in the Works of Walter Frye,"

Journal of the American Musicological Society 8 (1955): 181–202; Strohm, *REM*, 394–8; and Paolo Emilio Carapezza, "Regina angelorum in musica picta: Walter Frye e il 'Maître au feuillage brodé'," *Rivista italiana di musicologia* 10 (1975): 134–54. The term "rhyming melisma" was coined by John Stevens, in *Music and Poetry in the Early Tudor Court* (London: Methuen, 1961), and adopted by David Fallows in "English Song Repertories of the Mid-Fifteenth Century," *Proceedings of the Royal Musical Association* 103 (1976–7): 66–9.

29 See also Gozzi, *Trent 90*, 153–7.

30 On the usual forms of English and continental Kyries see Gareth Curtis, "Musical Design and the Rise of the Cyclic Mass," in *Companion to Medieval and Renaissance Music*, ed. Tess Knighton and David Fallows (London: Dent, 1992), 154–9. See also Andrew Kirkman, "The Transmission of English Mass Cycles in the Mid to Late Fifteenth Century: A Case Study in Context," *Music and Letters* 75 (1994): 192–6.

31 The proposal that the Frye motet began life as the Kyrie of the Mass was first published by Brian Trowell ("Frye, Walter," *NG*, vol. VI, 877). See also Kirkman, "The Transmission of English Mass Cycles." On "Mass-motet cycles" see Robert J. Snow, "The Mass-Motet Cycle: A Mid-Fifteenth-Century Experiment," in *Essays in Musicology*, ed. Gustave Reese and Robert Snow (Pittsburgh: University of Pittsburgh Press, 1969), 301–20; Strohm, "Messzyklen über deutsche Lieder in den Trienter Codices," in *Liedstudien: Festschrift für Wolfgang Osthoff zum 60. Geburtstag*, ed. Martin Just and Reinhard Wiesend (Tutzing: Schneider, 1989), 77–106; and *REM*, 426–9. On the issue of which *O rosa bella* Mass *O pater eterne/O admirabile* goes with, see Wegman, "An Anonymous Twin of Johannes Ockegem's Missa Quinti Toni in San Pietro B 80," *Tijdschrift van de Vereniging voor Nederlandse Muziekgeschiedenis* 37 (1987): 36. We will return to Mass-motet cycles in chapter 12.

32 See Brown, *Florentine Chansonnier*, Text Volume, 135, 139.

33 Fallows made these identifications in "Songs in the Trent Codices," 179. On the Mass's relationship to its model, see J. Peter Burkholder, "Johannes Martini and the Imitation Mass of the Late Fifteenth Century," *Journal of the American Musicological Society* 38 (1985): 486–9 (the first half of the model and the beginning of the Gloria are given on 488–9).

34 "Songs in the Trent Codices," 178–9. The French text incipit in Q16 for the *secunda pars* of Touront's *Compangant/O generosa* might suggest origin as a chanson, but the motet's length and classic bipartite form argue against it; here the contrafacture seems to have gone from Latin to French. See Leverett, "Trent 91," vol. I, 243, n. 47, and vol. II, 144.

35 For the date of *In hydraulis*, see Paula Higgins, "*In Hydraulis* Revisited: New Light on the Career of Antoine Busnoys," *Journal of the American Musicological Society* 39 (1986): 69–76: it was probably composed between 13 April 1465 and 15 June 1467. Leverett believes that both sources for *In hydraulis* (Trent 91 and Munich 3154) were copied from the same exemplar ("Trent 91," vol. I, 118–19, 124–8).

   Omnium bonorum plena is believed to have been copied before the death of Du Fay in 1474; see Ludwig Finscher, *Loyset Compère* (N.p. American Institute of Musicology, 1964), 14–15, 131–9; Fallows, *Dufay*, 78; Strohm, *REM*, 479; and Gerald Montagna, "Caron, Hayne, Compère: A Transmission Reassessment," *Early Music History* 7 (1987): 110–15.

   Perfunde celi rore has no attribution, but Martini was the court composer in Ferrara at the time of the wedding and is the most likely composer. The attribution was first made by

Stephan, *Burgundisch-Niederländische Motette*, 65, n. 28; see also Lockwood, *Ferrara*, 258, and Leverett, "Trent 91," vol. I, 150.

9 ENGLISH AND CONTINENTAL CANTILENA-STYLE MOTETS

1 Curtis and Wathey, "List," 1.

2 See Bent, "Forest," *NG*. On the dating of later additions to Old Hall in the 1420s, see Bent, "Progeny of Old Hall," 26–32.

3 Charles Hamm, ed., *Leonel Power: Complete Works*, I, *The Motets* (Rome: American Institute of Musicology, 1969), XIV–XIX (henceforth Hamm, *Power*). The chronology sketched here is only slightly different from that presented in Hamm's earlier article, "The Motets of Leonel Power," 127–36. In "Power, Leonel," 175, Bent endorses Hamm's chronology.

4 Hamm, *Power*, XVII ff. See also Bent, "Power, Leonel," 176: "the last four motets of Hamm's edition . . . clearly anticipate the smooth discant writing of Frye's generation, with their well-integrated duets and increasing participation of the lower parts in the evolution of a more homogeneous texture."

5 Bent comments that "Forest's style has much in common with that of the 'later' motets of Power" ("Forest," 705).

6 Burstyn, "Polyphonic Settings," 134–6, and *passim*.

7 Piamor apparently died in 1431; see Harrison, *Medieval Britain*, 462.

8 Dunstaple does not seem to have written any three-voice compositions in the new *Song* style. His four-voice *Descendi*, however, exhibits features of the style; it will be discussed below in chapter 11.

9 Reinhard Strohm attributes *O pulcherrima* to Plummer in *Bruges*, 133; Fallows doubts this attribution in his review, *Early Music History* 6 (1986): 289. Bukofzer attributes it to Frye in his *MGG* article on the composer ("Frye," *MGG*, vol. IV, col. 1070) because he claims (inaccurately) that it often appears with other works by Frye, and Burstyn follows ("Polyphonic Settings," 208). The piece will be discussed more in chapter 11.

10 On the increasing use of imperfect tempus in the chanson, see Miriam Tees, "Chronology and Style in the Laborde Chansonnier" (M.A. thesis, McGill University, 1995), 47.

11 For a transcription and detailed discussion of the work see Strohm, *REM*, 394–8; he comments there that Tinctoris believed that Frye's works were composed in the 1460s. See also Trowell, "Frye, Walter," 877–8.

12 For more on this trope, which is typically English, see Giulio Cattin, "Virgo Mater Ecclesie," and "Testi Tropati."

13 For a useful discussion of developments in chanson composition see Fallows, *Dufay*, 161–4. On *Par le regard* he comments: "the discantus line seems at first to have no clear shape or parallelisms: each line begins with a different rhythmic figure, each has a different melodic direction" (p. 162), comments that could apply to most English cantilenas.

14 See Alejandro Planchart, "Guillaume Du Fay's Second Style," in *Music in Renaissance Cities and Courts*, ed. Jessie Ann Owens and Anthony M. Cummings (Warren, Mich.: Harmonie Park Press, 1997), 308–40.

15 Fallows comments (*Dufay*, 128): "its discantus figuration is similar [to *Flos florum*, etc.] and it

too must have Ø mensuration, even though one of its sources states otherwise." Hamm places it in his group 2b, *c.* 1423–33 (*Chronology*, 35).

16 Fallows comments that "the voices are more equal in importance than in most of the pieces mentioned so far. The free way in which the rhythmic shapes cross the barlines makes them a classic case of the . . . new style of flowing rhythm. . . . It would be difficult to date this setting before 1440" (*Dufay*, 134). Hamm puts it in his group 8, c. 1435–60 (*Chronology*, 138).

17 On Binchois and English music, see Strohm, *REM*, 244–8, and Fallows, "Binchois, Gilles de Bins dit," *NG*, vol. II, 712.

18 Hamm, "A Catalogue," 75; it is also included in Curtis and Wathey, "List."

19 On the original *Advenisti* text and melody see Strohm, *REM*, 305 and 332, and Gerhard Pietzsch, *Zur Pflege der Musik an den deutschen Universitäten bis zur Mitte des 16. Jahrhunderts* (repr. Hildesheim and New York: Olms, 1971), 97. On the Trent 88 setting see Gerber, "Trent 88," 4, 10, n. 12 and 13, and 244–5. See also the discussion in Adler and Koller, *DTÖ* 14 (Vienna: Artaria, 1900), XVII: they suggest that the Tridentine adaptation of the text was added by Johannes Wiser.

20 For a transcription of the two texts side by side see *DTÖ* 14, XVII and 88; for a translation of the Tridentine text see Gary Spilsted, "Toward the Genesis of the Trent Codices: New Directions and New Findings," *Studies in Music from the University of Western Ontario* 1 (1976): 65.

21 Part of the same melody is used as the cantus firmus in a four-voice tenor motet discussed in chapter 12: *Advenisti: Venisti* (88.542).

22 See Stephan, *Burgundisch-Niederländische Motette*, ch. 2: "Die Liedmotette (Ausbildung der Duettform – Übergang ins Tricinium)," 51–9.

23 On Touront see Tom R. Ward, "Touront [Tauranth], Johannes," *NG*, vol. XIX, 99; Strohm, *REM*, 439, 505, and 511–13; and Leverett, "Trent 91," vol. I, 99–100, 242–9, 254–5, vol. II, 144 (Table 5.5) and 153–4 (Table 5.10).

24 "Songs in the Trent Codices," 178–9.

25 Frye's *O florens* is found in Trent 90 with the text *Ave regina celorum, ave domina* (the famous *Ave regina* text), but in the Schedel Liederbuch and both times in Strahov it uses the *O florens* text, presumably the original one. The contratenor in Touront's *O florens* begins with an F3 clef, but changes to F4 half way through the piece.

26 *Castitatis lilium/Advocata* is not listed on either of the most recent works lists for Touront: Ward, "Touront [Tauranth], Johannes," or Leverett, "Trent 91," Table 5.10 (vol. II, 153–4).

27 Touront uses C2 instead of the more normal ₵ for the second section; perhaps he felt that C2 had a more precise proportional meaning. The text of *Compangant* is extremely difficult to read in Trent 89 and 91, so I have omitted it from my edition in Ex. 9.3.

10 MOTETS WITH A TENOR CANTUS FIRMUS *C.* 1430–1450

1 In "Style," Allsen classes these works as "Franco-Italian," and (following Hamm, *Chronology*, 70–3) finds that *Elizabeth* is so similar to *Vasilissa* that he attributes it to Du Fay (pp. 113–16, 282–6, 357–9, 479–80); see also "Two New Motets by Dufay?" unpublished paper presented at the American Musicological Society Conference, New York, November 1995.

2 See Allsen, "Style," 161–3, 181, 490–2.

3 D2 is labeled Ct. 1, in the manner of the other four-voice motets in Trent 89, but it is in the same range and clef as D1. Although the work has three sections in successively smaller proportions, the overall effect is that of a bipartite motet. See Allsen, "Style," 194–6, 221–4, 352–4.

4 On Brassart's *Ave Maria/O Maria* see Allsen, "Style," 121–3, 428–9; he sees it as "the most direct imitation of native Italian motet style in an isorhythmic motet by a northern composer" (p. 121); on *O pia virgo* see pp. 192–3, 350–1.

5 For an excellent discussion of English isorhythmic motets, see Allsen, "Style," 129–86 (list on pp. 183–6); see also Bent, *Dunstaple,* 52–71.

6 See Fallows, *Dufay,* 115–21, and Allsen, "Style," 190–1. Allsen calls the non-English works in this group "Cosmopolitan," and sees in them evidence of various kinds of English influence. In "*Contenance angloise,*" 24–5, 30–1, 48–51, Brothers sees the adoption of the "lyric top voice" and a new kind of melodic style in the isorhythmic motet around 1435 as a sign of exposure to English music.

7 Many of Du Fay's motets begin with imitation at the unison, leading to immediate voice crossing; I chose *Rite majorem* because it does not begin with imitation, and the incorporation of the opening duet into the tenor talea resembles the English procedure (see Allsen, "Style," 151–9, on what he calls the "talea introduction").

8 See also mm. 19–21, 37–42, and 103–4.

9 In *Nuper rosarum* both tenors have the same chant; the "primus tenor" presents it a fifth down, while the "secundus tenor" presents it at the original pitch. In *Ecclesie* the two tenor parts use different chants; both are called tenor (with no first and second).

10 On this point see also Allsen, "Style," 191, and Brothers, "*Contenance angloise,*" 30, n. 25.

11 On the authorship of *O gloriose tiro,* see Besseler, DufayB, vol, I, 25; Fallows, *Dufay,* 291, n. 3; Allsen, "Style," 480–2; and *idem,* "Two New Motets by Dufay?"

12 The tenor voice of *Romanorum rex* is attributed to Johannes de Sarto in a letter written by Del Lago in 1533; see Bonnie Blackburn, Edward Lowinsky, and Clement Miller, eds., *A Correspondence of Renaissance Musicians* (Oxford: Oxford University Press, 1991), 387, 397–8, 658–9, 662–4, 693–4, 704–5. See also Allsen, "Style," 221, 519–21, and his references to earlier literature. Little is known of Sarto's life; he is closely associated with Brassart, who was at Basel, and his status as a member of the chapel of the Habsburg Albrecht II is attested by his authorship of the motet and the inclusion of his name among the list of singers in the text. See Wright, "Johannes Brassart," 42–3, and Pamela F. Starr, "Letter to the Editors," *Plainsong and Medieval Music* 1 (1992): 215–16.

13 See Allsen, "Style," 233, for a list of isorhythmic motets indicating which have single-talea tenors and free upper voices.

14 "Petrus de Domarto's *Missa Spiritus almus* and the Early History of the Four-Voice Mass in the Fifteenth Century," *Early Music History* 10 (1991): 296. Brothers makes the same point in "*Contenance angloise,*" 34–5, n. 34.

15 There is a passage in the second tenor of *Moribus et genere* (units 13 and 14 of the talea) where it speeds up while the first tenor is resting; this passage resembles the tenor tacet trios in *O gloriose tiro* and *Romanorum rex.*

16 *"Contenance angloise,"* 24–5.

17 The texts of *O sanctissime/ T: O Christi* derive from the liturgy of St. Donatian in Bruges, and Strohm believes that the motet was composed for the church, but possibly by an English composer (*Bruges*, 118–20; *REM*, 241).

   The presence of three-voice tenor motets in both parts of 92 but not in 87 suggests that Wright's claim that 87–1 and 92–2 are two parts of one manuscript (in *Related Parts*, and related articles) may be overstated. Tom Ward has also shown that the nature and place-ment of the hymn repertory is fundamentally different in 87–1 and 92–2 ("The Office Hymns of the Trent Manuscripts").

18 For Busnoys's *Anima mea* see Sparks, *Cantus firmus*, 222–3; Wegman, "Petrus de Domarto," 241–4; Richard Taruskin, *Antoine Busnoys: Collected Works*, Part 3: *The Latin Texted Works*, Commentary (New York: The Broude Trust, 1990), 62–4; and Paula Higgins, "Love and Death in the Fifteenth-Century Motet: A Reading of Busnoys's *Anima mea liquefacta est/ Stirps Jesse*," in *Hearing the Motet: Essays on the Motet of the Middle Ages and Renaissance*, ed. Dolores Pesce (Oxford: Oxford University Press, 1997), 142–68. For *Alma redemptoris* see Sparks, *Cantus firmus*, 209–12.

19 Bukofzer came close to describing this subgenre: "compositions with double structure: these depend, as the name implies, on two factors – a borrowed or freely composed tenor which serves merely as a scaffold for the entire movement, and a treble as the predominant voice," "English Church Music of the Fifteenth Century," in *New Oxford History of Music III: Ars nova and the Renaissance* (London: Oxford University Press, 1960), 187 and 192–3. He includes *Specialis virgo*, and *Ascendit Christus*.

20 The antiphon *Regali ex progenie* is found in modern chant books for the feast of the Nativity of the Virgin; the chant melody is not used in the motet. *Sancta Maria virgo intercede* is an English antiphon found in the Sarum Antiphoner. The chant is quoted in part in Harrison, *Medieval Britain*, 296, ex. 76, and in full in Hughes, EECM 8, 180.

21 On English three-voice isorhythmic motets, see Allsen, "Style," 144–86. He discusses these two Dunstaple motets (which he considers experimental works) and *Hac clara die*: see 159–61, 168–71, 181–2, 341–2, 497–9, 500–2.

22 See Bent, *Dunstaple*, 34–5: "in these duets, which occur as changes of texture within three- or four-part pieces, the lower part is as active as the top, with highly developed interplay between them"; and Allsen, "Style," 161–2.

23 Each half of the tenor (not counting the final long) has 40 measures. This is equivalent to 40 perfect breves in the upper parts; for the tenor it is 20 breves in the first half under ₵ (120 minims), and 30 breves in the second half under C (120 minims). The upper parts, however, each have one additional semibreve at the beginning of the final duet (m. 61). This would result in the cadence on C in m. 66 arriving on the beat, but the end of the piece would not land on the beginning of a perfection (unless one added a four-beat measure during the duet). I have thus emended the upper voices, changing the Gs in m. 61 from breves (whole note in the modern notation) to semibreves (half notes in the transcription).

24 The Ct. goes below the T only in mm. 14–15, 36–7, 53, 74, and 77.

25 In m. 76 the contratenor moves to the octave with the tenor, and the discantus moves to the twelfth, as in an "Italian" cadence – here the middle voice comes close to being contra-puntally essential.

26 See Bent, EECM 22, x, and Critical commentary, 169, 180–1, 183–4.

27 See Trent 92–1, fols. 136′, 137′ and Trent 92–2, fol. 193. In *Regali ex progenie* and *O sanctissime presul*, only the tenor is labeled; in Merques's *Castrum/Virgo* the contratenor label is in the correct location, under the music before the beginning of the text. See also Bent, EECM 22, x, and *Dunstaple*, 27, n. 4.

28 See Allsen, "Style," 151–9 and 194–6; in *O sacrum manna* (the isorhythmic motet in Trent 89), the tenor rests for the first half of each talea.

29 Strohm, *REM*, 250–2.

30 I owe the identification of these texts to Alejandro Planchart, in a communication on the AMS listserve of 21 September 1994 entitled "Garden variety motets."

31 See Allsen, "Style," 233; on *Magnanime*, 463–5.

32 For an early cyclic Mass that apparently lacks a pre-existent tenor, see the *Missa Sine nomine* attributed variously to Benet, Power, and Dunstaple (edited by Bukofzer in *Dunstable*, 56–9, 71). See also Strohm, *REM*, 232, and Gareth Curtis, "Jean Pullois and the Cyclic Mass – Or a Case of Mistaken Identity?" *Music and Letters* 62 (1981): 41–59. He thinks that this Mass's tenor is pre-existent, but paraphrased differently in each movement.

33 See Gareth Curtis, "Stylistic Layers in the English Mass Repertory c. 1400–1450," *Proceedings of the Royal Musical Association* 109 (1982–3): 23–38. The usual texture for the three-voice cantus firmus Masses is "two active parts – the discantus and the contra – around a slower-moving tenor" (p. 26). See also Strohm, *REM*, 229–34.

34 See the edition by Gareth Curtis (Newton Abbot: Antico Edition, 1982), 16, for a table showing the mensuration signs for each movement in all sources. The proportions in the Power Mass are 28 ₵ breves (= 168 minims) in the first half to 42 C breves (= 168 minims) in the second half.

35 On proportional relationships in the Mass repertory, see Gareth Curtis, "Musical Design," 160–4. For the relative lengths of the two halves of the tenors of *Regali ex progenie* and *Missa Alma redemptoris mater*, see notes 23 and 34 in this chapter.

36 See Curtis, "Stylistic Layers," 24, and "Musical Design," 155–6; Hamm, *Chronology*, 123–30.

37 See Strohm, *REM*, 403–4.

38 Strohm, *REM*, 234–7, 240, 242; Wegman, "Petrus de Domarto," 296 and 302, where he proposes that "four-voice Mass writing on the Continent started in the Southern Netherlands in the late 1440s, in response to the recent transmission of the anonymous English *Missa Caput*."

39 On the complex source situation and the misattribution to Du Fay, see Strohm, "Quellenkritische Untersuchungen an der Missa 'Caput'," in *Quellenstudien zur Musik der Renaissance II: Datierung und Filiation von Musikhandschriften der Josquin-Zeit*, ed. Ludwig Finscher (Wiesbaden: Harrasowitz, 1982), 153–76. On dating see Bent, "Trent 93," 88–90; Strohm, *REM*, 242, and review of Lockwood, *Ferrara*, *Music and Letters* 67 (1986): 285; and Wegman, "Petrus de Domarto," 299–300.

40 See below, chapter 11, n. 37.

41 On the style of *Caput* see Manfred Bukofzer, "*Caput*: A Liturgico-Musical Study," in *Studies in Medieval and Renaissance Music* (New York: Norton, 1950), 217–310; Wegman, "Petrus de Domarto," 296, and Strohm, *REM*, 234–6.

42 See, for example, Bukofzer, "*Caput*": "it is, in other words, an isorhythmic tenor the *taleae* of

which have grown to gigantic proportions, namely an entire movement" (p. 263); see also Howard Mayer Brown, *Music in the Renaissance* (Englewood Cliffs: Prentice Hall, 1976), 43. Brothers finds that real isorhythmic techniques are used only in a limited number of cyclic Masses ("Vestiges," 2–3).

43 See Bukofzer, "*Caput*," ex. 4, 260; he comments that the two *cursus* "differ radically in their rhythmic arrangement" (p. 261).

44 Unlike *Caput*, fifteenth-century isorhythmic motets usually repeat the color more than once; English motets almost invariably present the color three times, with two taleae each (see Allsen, "Style," 183–5).

45 See Bukofzer, "*Caput*," 264, for a table that presents the length of the tenor rests (and thus duets) for each movement of the Mass. On English "talea introductions," see Allsen, "Style," 152, 154, 183–6.

46 See Bukofzer, "*Caput*," 272: "The melodic interest of the composition rests squarely in the highest voice ... This is true not only of the extended duets ... but also of the four-part sections."

47 See Strohm, *REM*, 234–5.

48 Dunstaple's *Veni/Veni* has a "5–1" cadence at the end, as a result of the cantus firmus; Bent (*Dunstaple*, 55) comments that the cadence "is unique in Dunstaple's entire output." There are quite a few "5–1" cadences in Sarto's *O Romanorum rex*, but they are not major cadences at the ends of sections.

49 See, for example, the cadences at the end of both halves of the Gloria; at the end of the Credo; and the final cadence of the Agnus.

11 FREELY COMPOSED FOUR-VOICE WRITING IN TRANSITION

1 There is one double-discantus motet in Trent 89: *Odas clangat* (89.577–78). The imitative duets and "Italian" cadences resemble earlier double-discantus motets, but the rhythmic language and approach to form belong to the motet after mid-century, so I will discuss it in chapter 12. There are three late double-discantus motets in Munich 3154 (*Ave salve gaude vale*, in which the upper voices have a canon at the unison, *En lectulum Salomonis*, and a textless motet, fols. 25′–27); these are discussed in Stephan, *Burgundisch-Niederländische Motette*, 63–5.

2 See Clement A. Miller, "Early Gaffuriana: New Answers to Old Questions," *Musical Quarterly* 56 (1970): 367–88.

3 There is not enough text in *Gaudeat ecclesia* to allow for syllabic declamation of the repeated minims, so Nosow suggests that the Trent 88 copy is a contrafactum ("Florid," 108–51, esp. 110–14).

4 On *Ibo michi* see Lockwood, *Ferrara*, 74–7 and Strohm, *REM*, 266. Dunstaple's *Descendi in ortum* also resembles a double-discantus motet, in that D2 begins the two-voice introitus on the same pitch as D1 and has the root in the final cadence. Nevertheless, the range of D2 is considerably lower than D1's, so I include it with the single-discantus motets (Table 11.2).

5 On *Mirandas parit* see Nosow, "Florid," 122, 126–31.

6 Alejandro Planchart has suggested that it may have been part of a Vespers service for St. Anthony of Padua composed by Du Fay for Bologna in 1436–7; see "Guillaume Dufay's Masses: A View of the Manuscript Traditions," *Papers read at the Dufay Quincentenary Conference,* ed. Allan Atlas (New York: Brooklyn College, 1976), 33–7; see also Nosow, "Florid," 280–6, 291–5.

7 See Besseler, *Bourdon,* 28, 48, 169–70, 176, 237. The clefs of *O proles/O sidus* resemble those of the English Mass, *Salve sancta parens* (C2 C4 C4 C4), found in Trent 93 and 90 (an incomplete Kyrie is found in an English fragment). Bent hypothesizes that one of the contratenors was added to this work (EECM 22, 181). Could Du Fay have known this Mass?

8 There is one exception: in mm. 37–8 Ct. 2 moves in contrary motion to a G octave with the discantus. The counterpoint is still complete without Ct. 2, however, since discantus and tenor move third to fifth. Ct. 2 thus turns a weak 3–5 progression into a 6/3–8/5 cadence, undercutting the 6–8 cadence between discantus and tenor on the same pitch one measure later.

9 The transformation of duets into trios also occurs when a voice is added to *O pulcherrima,* discussed below (Ex. 11.3).

10 This is the texting in Modena X.1.11, the most completely texted source. In the two Trent sources the "O sidus" text is lacking altogether.

11 See Stephen Self, *The 'Si Placet' Repertoire of 1480–1530* (Madison: A-R Editions, 1996), 91.

12 On *Cantemus domino* see Bukofzer, *Studies in Medieval and Renaissance Music,* 126–7, 145–8. I have included it here, rather than in chapter 10, because it seems more similar to the freely composed works than to the isorhythmic motets and the three-voice tenor motets.

13 There is an anonymous *Regina celi* in Trent 89 (583–4) with the tenor on the bottom, similar ranges, and peculiar voice labels:

Ct. 1	[Disc.]	Ct. 2	T
C2/C1	C2	C4	F4
d–ee	G–aa	C–e	GG–b.

The voice labeled Ct. 1 functions as the discantus at major cadences, but is copied on the top right. The confused voice labels and the low tenor make it likely that this is an English work, although no one has yet suggested it.

14 See Hughes, EECM 8, 173: "Iste triplex potest cantari vel dimitti ad placitum"; and Brian Trowell, ed., *John Plummer: Four Motets* (Banbury: Plainsong and Medieval Music Society, 1968), 34.

15 On *O pulcherrima* see chapter 9, n. 9 (p. 341). In the three-voice version of *Anima mea* in Trent 90 there is an indecipherable word, probably a composer attribution, followed by the words "in agone composuit," perhaps a reference to some kind of competition (see Gozzi, *Trent 93,* 114). Feininger read the name as Forest, and this was accepted by Bukofzer in "Forest," *MGG,* vol. IV, cols. 509–13. This reading is now generally rejected (see Strohm, *REM,* 220–1, and Curtis and Wathey, "List," 54). All agree, however, that both pieces are English.

16 While the clef of *Anima mea*'s upper contratenor is C2, it fits just as well in C3. On the standard ranges of sixteenth-century vocal polyphony, see Bernhard Meier, *The Modes of Classical Vocal Polyphony, Described According to the Sources,* with revisions by the author, trans.

Ellen S. Beebe (New York: Broude Brothers, 1988), 47–88, esp. 84–8; and Harold Powers, "Tonal Types and Modal Categories in Renaissance Polyphony," *Journal of the American Musicological Society* 34 (1981): 436, where he refers to the "standard SATB combination" (C1, C3, C4, F4) and the higher "chiavette" (G2, C2, C3, F3).

17 Curtis comments "Still more obviously advanced, and undoubtedly Pullois's masterpiece, is the motet 'Flos de spina', which glories in a complexity of texture reminiscent of Regis"; "'Flos de spina' . . . is highly unusual in the context of its earliest surviving source, Trent 90," "Jean Pullois," 49 and 50. Strohm comments that "Ockeghem (and Regis?) seem anticipated rather than emulated in the florid and varied motet 'Flos de spina'" (*REM*, 443–4).

18 See Pamela F. Starr, "Music and Music Patronage at the Papal Court, 1447–1474" (Ph.D. dissertation, Yale University, 1987), 167–75, for biography, and "Rome as the Center of the Universe: Papal Grace and Musical Patronage," *Early Music History* 11 (1992): 228–34, for an account of how Puyllois obtained a benefice for Ockeghem. See also Montagna, "Johannes Pullois," 109–14.

19 Starr, "Music Patronage," 162, n. 178, 168–9, and "Rome," 231.

20 "Petrus de Domarto," 293–4, 297, 300–1.

21 On the sale of the Masses in Ferrara, see Lockwood, *Ferrara*, 52; Strohm, *REM*, 242, and his review of Lockwood, *Ferrara*, 284. This theory is also reported by Bent, "Johannes Wiser," 89–90, and Starr, "Music Patronage," 163. Bent reports that Strohm hypothesizes that the Masses may have reached Trent from Ferrara in 1452, when Emperor Frederick III stopped in Ferrara on his way to Rome for his coronation, and then presumably stopped in Trent on the way back home to his court in Austria.

22 Saunders, *The Dating*, 188; "Trent 93 and Trent 90," 70. On SP B80, see Christopher Reynolds, "The Origins of San Pietro B 80 and the Development of a Roman Sacred Repertory," *Early Music History* 1 (1981): 280–6.

23 Bent (*Dunstaple*, 37) comments that Dunstaple's use of imitation is virtually limited to "long pedal notes."

24 For an example by Regis, see *Clangat plebs*, mm. 13–15. Ludwig Finscher calls imitation at half a beat *fuga ad minimam*, and notes that it can be found "seasoning most of the duets in the first part" of *Omnium bonorum plena* (*Loyset Compère*, 136).

25 The tenor's range is from A to c, the second contratenor's from A to d.

26 The final cadence is rather clumsy: the low contratenor leaps up a seventh from A to G to move in unison with the high contratenor to the fifth above the tenor.

27 There are duets for the two contratenors, mm. 18–22 and 89–91; for first contratenor and tenor, mm. 35–9, and for discantus and first contratenor in mm. 59–79.

28 For other works including clef combinations a seventh apart (C2, F3, F3, or C1, C4, C4) see Peter Gülke, ed., *Johannes Pullois: Opera omnia* (Rome: American Institute of Musicology, 1967): the canonic/double-discantus Gloria (24), *Les larmes* (36), *Pour prison* (37), *Puisque fortune* (40), *So lanc so meer* (43), *Sum bien peu* (44), and *Op eenen tijd* (50).

29 Gareth Curtis ("Stylistic Layers," 36) found a four-voice English Gloria/Credo pair in Trent 90 with the *Flos de spina* texture. He suggests that it is a transitional texture on the way to the *Caput* texture, but my work suggests that the two textures coexisted for some time.

30 Stephan lists the motet "T?" which means it may be a tenor motet (*Burgundisch-Niederländischer Motette*, 107); he discusses the work in a section called "Analogien der Tenormottete" (pp. 65, 67), and finds that the tenor melody looks pre-existent. He also proposes that *Flos de spina* uses chant paraphrase in the discantus (p. 67, n. 37).

31 *REM*, 242 (motto), 428–9.

32 Strohm, *REM*, 404–5, 232. He finds that the Bedyngham cycle is especially close to Puyllois's Mass, while Curtis ("Jean Pullois," 48) calls the Benet/Dunstaple/Power "a reasonably plausible brother."

33 See Curtis, "Jean Pullois," 42–8, and Strohm, *REM*, 405, n. 109.

34 Reynolds, *Papal Patronage*, 158–62.

35 Curtis, "Jean Pullois," 50–9. Montagna ("Johannes Pullois," 110, n. 72), Bent ("Johannes Wiser," 92), Strohm (*REM*, 242), and Reynolds (*Papal Patronage*, 150, n. 12) all think the Mass is by Puyllois, and is not English.

36 "Petrus de Domarto," 301; Wegman also points out Puyllois's Mass is copied in the group of six mostly English Masses (including *Caput*) copied in Trent 93 and 90.

37 See Strohm, *REM*, 415–24; also Wegman, "Petrus de Domarto," 282–97, 301–2. Domarto's *Spiritus almus* uses the *Caput* texture down a third, uses a final melisma of a "highly symbolic" chant, and begins all sections with a duet and a common motto. Ockeghem's *Caput* adopts the original *Caput* tenor literally, then transposes it down an octave. The style of de Insula's *O admirabile commercium* is very similar to *Caput*. *Se la face* uses the *Caput* texture, has strict cantus firmus treatment, and makes reference to the opening motto; but see Brothers, "*Contenance angloise*," 34–5, who finds more connections to Du Fay's own earlier works. All these works are copied in Trent 88.

38 Puyllois's second section is in cut-C ($\mathcal{C}$); *Caput*'s second section is in cut-C in some sources (Lucca, Trent 93, and 90) and C in others (Coventry, Trent 88 and 89). See Strohm, "Quellenkritische Untersuchungen," 162–4.

The number of perfect breves under O in the first half of *Flos de spina* is almost the same as the number of imperfect longs under $\mathcal{C}$ in the second half (57 in the first half, 57½ in the second, plus the final long in each case; the temporal length of the two halves of course depends on one's interpretation of the mensural relationship between O and $\mathcal{C}$). In Power's *Missa Alma redemptoris* and in *Regali ex progenie* we saw similar relationships of equality between the two halves; there, however, the relationship was at the level of the tenor's minims or semibreves. The two halves of *Caput* do not have such an equivalency, and the insertion of differing numbers of rests means that the section lengths are different from movement to movement.

39 On the mensural plan of the Mass, see Curtis, "Jean Pullois," 52.

40 See Table 9.1.3 for the mensurations of English cantilenas; for the mensurations of the earliest Mass cycles, see Strohm, *REM*, 230. Nos. 4–8 on his list use OCO, nos. 2, 3, 9 (*Caput*) and 10 (*Veterem hominem*, an imitation of *Caput*) use OC.

41 Strohm, *REM*, 422.

42 *AH*, vol. XX, 122, no. 155. The volume is entitled *Cantiones natalitiae*, and the sources for the text go back to the thirteenth century. One source is Florentine, another Franciscan.

43 Elisha is in Kings III and IV; Jesus refers to him in Luke 4.27.

44 See, for example, Hans Heinrich Eggebrecht, "Machauts Motette Nr. 9," *Archiv für Musikwissenschaft* 19–20 (1962–3): 281–93, and 25 (1968): 173–95, and Cumming, "Concord," 187–204, for typology in *Rex Karole*.

12 THE FOUR-VOICE MOTET *C.* 1450–1475

1 On Martini's Mass and its model see Burkholder, "Johannes Martini," 486–9; ex. 2 shows the beginning of the model and the Gloria.

2 On Habsburg patronage of musical settings of classical poetry see Strohm, *REM*, 537–9; on the broader European cultivation of this genre see Kate van Orden, "*Les Vers lascifs d'Horace*: Arcadelt's Latin Chansons," *Journal of Musicology* 14 (1996): 338–69, and her bibliography. *Tu ne quesieris* is the earliest Horace setting known; its rhythms are not derived from those of the classical meter. The text warns against trying to predict the future, and says to enjoy life, drink wine, and "carpe diem."

3 See Snow, "The Manuscript Strahov D.G.IV.47" (Ph.D. dissertation, University of Illinois, 1968), 379 and 474, n. 60, for transcription and variant readings; see *DTÖ* 53, 56 for the Trent 89 reading.

4 Strohm describes the "formula for the late-fifteenth-century [tenor] motet: two sections, each introduced by a long duet and provided with its own climax, and a cantus firmus in double cursus or interrupted in the middle" (*REM*, 429).

5 For Masses with secular tenors, see Strohm, *REM*, 403–5, 416, 423–35, especially tables 4 and 5.

6 See Planchart, "Parts with Words," and Gareth Curtis, "Brussels, Bibliothèque Royale MS 5557, and the Texting of Dufay's 'Ecce ancilla domini' and 'Ave regina caelorum' Masses," *Acta musicologica* 51 (1979): 73–86.

7 See Margaret Bent, "New and Little-known Fragments of English Medieval Polyphony," *Journal of the American Musicological Society* 21 (1968): 147–8, n. 15. Margaret Bent informed me (personal communication, 6 November 1995) that *Stella celi* replaces an earlier text in Trent 88, but the earlier text is impossible to read. Although there is a *So ys emprentid* Kyrie by Walter Frye in the Lucca Codex (see Strohm, *Bruges*, 125 and 194), it treats the chanson's rhythms strictly; our motet's treatment is isomelic, like that of Le Rouge's Mass, so I think that it belongs with Le Rouge's cycle.

8 Only two – *Salve virgo* and *O pater eterne* – have single cursus; both are associated with Masses, in which double cursus is less common. The other exceptions all have multiple cursus: the second cursus is incomplete in *Stella celi* and *Salve regina/T: Le serviteur, Advenisti* and *Perpulchra* have triple cursus; *In hydraulis* has quadruple cursus.

9 See Tom Brothers, "Vestiges," 3, n. 6. In the case of chant paraphrases the tenor may be paraphrased differently, with different added pitches; in the case of chanson tenors, rhythms are varied in a new way.

10 Gareth Curtis comments ("Stylistic Layers," 38, n. 45) that double cursus is "a rare occurrence among the stricter English cantus firmus masses." In Strohm's table of "Four-part Mass cycles with strict cantus firmus treatment," seven of the seventeen Masses have double cursus (*REM*, 423–4).

11 The pieces without opening duets for both *partes* are anomalous in other ways, as well: *Advenisti* is a peculiar dedicatory motet from Trent; *Stella celi* has both *partes* in the same mensuration; and *Perpulchra Sion filia* is fully texted and reverses the normal order of mensurations.

12 For a translation see Spilsted, "Toward the Genesis," 64. See also Adler and Koller, *DTÖ* 14, XVII, and Gerber, "Trent 88," 12–13, 244–5.

13 See Adler and Koller, *DTÖ* 14, XVIII; *DTÖ* 76, 77–9, 105; Sparks, *Cantus firmus*, 191–2; Finscher and Laubenthal, "Cantiones," 309–12, and Strohm, *REM*, 412: he hints (n. 122) that the piece might be by Ockeghem, who entered the King of France's service shortly before the occasion celebrated in the motet.

14 For text and translation see Isabel Pope and Masakata Kanazawa, *The Music Manuscript Montecassino 871: A Neapolitan Repertory of Sacred and Secular Music of the Late Fifteenth Century* (Oxford: Clarendon Press, 1978), 629–30. See also Fallows, *Dufay*, 71 and 130; and Strohm, *REM*, 413.

15 *O tres piteulx* can be seen in connection with a long tradition of French poetic laments set to music (Strohm, *REM*, 53, 193, and 413–14), almost all of which make reference to the motet: Andrieu uses polytextuality in *Armes, amours/O flour des flours*; Ockeghem quotes a fragment of *Dies irae* in the lower voices of *Mort tu as navré*, which has four voices, more common in the motet than the chanson (as does one version of Binchois's *Dueil angoisseux*); and Josquin uses a cantus firmus from the Requiem and five voices in *Nymphes des bois*. The greater formality of Du Fay's motet may be appropriate for a lament on the fall of a city, rather than on the death of a friend or teacher.

16 See David Howlett, "Busnois' Motet *In hydraulis*: An Exercise in Textual Reconstruction and Analysis," *Plainsong and Medieval Music* 4 (1995): 185–91.

17 Some of the possible descendants of this work are Ockeghem's *Ut heremita solus*; Josquin's *Ut Phebi radiis* and *Illibata Dei virgo nutrix*; and Isaac's *O decus ecclesie virgo, Rogamus te* (*La mi la sol*), and *Palle, palle*. See Stephan, *Burgundisch-Niederländische Mottete*, 50; Strohm, *REM*, 480, 638–40; and Taruskin, *Busnoys*, Commentary, 74–80.

18 Strohm, *REM*, 479; Sparks, *Cantus firmus*, 208, and Finscher, *Loyset Compère*, 131–40.

19 "The Mass-Motet Cycle."

20 See Geoffrey Chew, "The Early Cyclic Mass as an Expression of Royal and Papal Supremacy," *Music and Letters* 53 (1972): 254–79, and Strohm, *REM*, 229.

21 See Strohm, "Messzyklen," and *REM*, 428–9. See also above, chapter 8, notes 30 and 31.

22 The three-voice Masses are discussed in Gerber, "Trent 88," 101–8, and Strohm, *REM*, 424–32. Other possible fifteenth-century Mass-motet cycles include the following: Arnold de Lantins's *O pulcherrima mulierum* and his three-voice Mass discussed above in chapter 5 (Strohm, *REM*, 176–7); *Flos de spina* and the three-voice Puyllois *Missa sine nomine* discussed in chapter 11; Standley, the canonic motet *Quae est ista* (89.576) and canonic Mass "Ad fugam reservatam" (88.436–40; see Strohm, *REM*, 428, n. 163); and Du Fay's *Ave regina celorum III* and the *Missa Ave regina celorum* (Strohm, *REM*, 432).

23 Strohm, *REM*, 431–2. *Missa O rosa bella I* is discussed in Sparks, *Cantus firmus*, 136–8. All three *O rosa bella* Masses are published in *DTÖ* 22.

24 Strohm finds evidence of motets performed "after Mass" in Cambrai and Bruges, and

suggests that the Mass-motet cycle "initiated the resurrection of the great cantus firmus motet after the end of isorhythm" (*REM*, 429).

25 *Papal Patronage*, 303; Le Rouge's dates in Orléans are from Paula Higgins, "Antoine Busnois and Musical Culture in Late Fifteenth-Century France and Burgundy" (Ph.D. dissertation, Princeton University, 1987), 251, n. 521.

26 Reynolds, *Papal Patronage*, 150–63 and Tables 15–16.

27 *Ibid.*, 305–7: he identifies Compère with one Ludovicus Gregori. Both *Missa So ys emprentid* and *Omnium bonorum plena* were copied in San Pietro B80; Reynolds finds that "had Compère been a recent alumnus of the St. Peter's choir, Ausquier's inclusion of the motet *Omnium bonorum plena* in SP B80 would be easier to understand; for of all the pieces he copied, this motet is the least fitting" (p. 307).

28 Both Masses are listed as English by Curtis and Wathey, "List," 51 (M36 and M37); *Meditatio cordis* is listed as English by Hamm, "A Catalogue," 72. See Strohm, "Messzyklen," 87–91; Kirkman, "The Transmission of English Mass Cycles," 195–6; Snow, "Strahov," 89–92, 98–9. Of the three texts to the *Hilf und gib rat* motet I find the *Gaude rosa* text the best suited to the motet; the original text was however probably a lengthy Kyrie trope.

29 None of the three surviving Masses based on the chanson makes a good match with the motet: they treat the cantus firmus differently, and all present it at the original pitch (with a C final), while the motet presents it a step up on D. All three Masses are transcribed by Franz Schegar in *DTÖ* 38.

30 For discussion of several of these motets see Sparks, *Cantus firmus*, 192–3, and Stephan's perceptive chapter: "Die Motettische Choralbearbeitung," *Burgundisch-Niederländische Motette*, 71–86.

31 Karl Dèzes rejects the attribution in "Das Dufay zugeschribene Salve Regina eine deutsche Komposition: stilkritische Studie," *Zeitschrift für Musikwissenschaft* 10 (1927–8): 327–62. More recently David Fallows (*Dufay*, 299) and Alejandro Planchart ("Du Fay's Benefices," 168) have suggested that the attribution be reconsidered.

32 There is one brief trio (mm. 84–9) in which the discantus rests and the chant paraphrase is given to the high contratenor. The passage ("illos tuos") contains the only high d in the chant, and there are no high dd's in the discantus part; the trio was devised to avoid high dd's.

33 On *O beata infantia* see Stephan, *Burgundisch-Niederländische Mottette*, 83–4. Du Fay's (?) *Salve regina*, *O beata infantia*, and Puyllois's *Flos de spina* are among the most widely disseminated four-voice works of mid-century.

	90	89	Mu3154	SPB80	CS15	Mil 1	Strah
Salve regina		x	x			x	
O beata infantia		x	x	x	x		
Flos de spina	x			x	x	x	x

O beata and *Flos* turn up in the two Roman manuscripts in the same order, and very close to one another (see Reynolds, *Papal patronage*, 84). Do these connections have implications for provenance?

34 This passage is transcribed incorrectly by Christian Väterlein in his edition of the Glogauer Liederbuch, EDM 86, 34.

35 "List," 65.

36 I located the chant in the *Cantus* database (CAO H238): it is a fourth-mode antiphon for the Nativity of the Virgin found in the Salzburg Sanctorale (MS A-Vorau Stiftsbibliothek 287 (29), fol. 172′), a secular antiphoner of the first half of the fourteenth century. The provenance of the chant may suggest that the piece was associated in some way with the Imperial court.

37 When B moves to C in the bass (as in mm. 4, 13, and 103), resulting in a diminished fifth in the bass moving to a third, this is just believable without added accidentals, although the augmented fourth between the tenor and the high contratenor is hard to take. In some cases flats have been added to the high contratenor Bs (mm. 18 and 37 have flats, but the almost identical cadences at mm. 4 and 18 lack them). Should we flat the low Bs as well? In all such cadences, or just those with the signed B-flats in the high contratenor?

38 The sharps (natural signs) in the contratenors may have been added later, and it is difficult to be certain about what note(s) they apply to. In the low contratenor the sharp appears in the b space above the low B with the fermata, and next to the high b, implying that both Bs should be natural. In the high contratenor the sharp appears directly after the fermata on the line, and thus could apply to the previous B, or to the following G or b (meaning G-sharp or b-natural).

39 Du Fay wrote only two pieces with E finals, both among his late chansons: they are discussed in William Mahrt, "Guillaume Dufay's Chansons in the Phrygian Mode," *Studies in Music from the University of Western Ontario* 5 (1980): 89–98. Ockeghem also wrote two chansons with E finals: *Presque transi* and *Malheur me bat*; and of course the *Missa Mi-Mi*.

40 According to Strohm, *Vidi speciosam* is based on a responsory for the Assumption of the Virgin (*Bruges*, 133). The melody is not found in modern chant books, but Stephan points out that the chant is the same as that used as a long-note foreign tenor of Gaspar von Weerbecke's *Stabat mater dolorosa* (Chigi 245′–249: *Burgundisch-Niederländische Motette*, 115 and 114). I have used this tenor melody to determine which notes are derived from the chant.

41 In *Burgundisch-Niederländische Motette* Stephan comments that "aus der Choralbearbeitung wurde die durchimitierte Motette" (p. 85).

42 On *Ave Maria* see Stephan, *Burgundisch-Niederländische Mottette*, 82.

43 See Daniel E. Freeman, "On the Origins of the *Pater noster-Ave Maria* of Josquin Des Prez," *Musica Disciplina* 45 (1991): 169–219, for the history of the *Ave Maria* as a motet text. Freeman lists the Trent 91 motet, but misidentifies it as a setting without additional text after the standard salutation (p. 200).

44 On this motet see Patrick Macey, "Josquin's 'Little' *Ave Maria*: A Misplaced Motet from the *Vultum tuum* Cycle?" *Tijdschrift van de Vereniging voor Nederlandse Muziekgeschiedenis* 39 (1989): 38–53; and Warren Kirkendale, "*Circulatio*-Tradition, *Maria lactans*, and Josquin as Musical Orator," *Acta musicologica* 56 (1984): 69–92. Josquin paraphrased the antiphon in two other works; see Mattfeld, "Some Relationships," 163, 166, 180, and Willem Elders, "Plainchant in the Motets, Hymns, and *Magnificat* of Josquin des Prez," in *Josquin des Prez: Proceedings of the*

International Josquin Festival-Conference, New York, 1971, ed. Edward E. Lowinsky with Bonnie J. Blackburn (London: Oxford University Press, 1976), 530 and 537.

45 On *Ave regina celorum III* see Stephan, *Burgundisch-Niederländische Motette*, 14–16; Fallows, *Dufay*, 134, 211–12; Alejandro Planchart, "Notes on Guillaume Du Fay's Last Works," *Journal of Musicology* 13 (1995): 55–63. See also Brothers, "Contenance Angloise," 28, and *Chromatic Beauty*, 185–7.

46 "Last Works," 57–8. Planchart refers to the division of the opening duet into two parts (combined in Du Fay's case with a change of scoring) and to the sudden change of harmony at the entrance of the tenor. He goes on to suggest that Du Fay also models his mensural usage on *Caput*, in his use of imperfect tempus (C) with breve–semibreve movement.

47 In "Last Works," Planchart comments: "Du Fay ties this work . . . to the older tradition of the polytextual motet, by having the strophes sung over phrases of the liturgical text sung by the tenor, thus creating essentially a polytextual texture" (p. 58).

48 This point was made by Strohm, *REM*, 432.

49 Sparks calls this anticipation of the cantus firmus in the other voices "alternating statement": see *Cantus firmus*, 194–5. Aside from the opening duet, however, the references in the other voices to the chant are brief.

50 Stephan admits that no cantus firmus has been found for these pieces, but calls them "Analogien der Tenormotette" and lists them in his appendix with a T (for tenor motet) followed by a question mark. He does spend a few fascinating pages on them (*Burgundisch-Niederländischer Motette*, 63–7) – but that is in contrast to his forty-page chapter on the tenor motet (pp. 11–50).

51 Of the thirteen tenor motets listed in Table 12.2 the tenor is not labeled in only four cases, all of which can be explained. There is no text associated with the constructed tenor of *In hydraulis*. The "Stella celi" incipit in the tenor of *Stella celi/[T: So ys emprentid]* may be a reference to a *Stella celi* melody (see above, note 7). Both *Stella celi* and *Salve virgo/[T: Summe trinitati]* are separated from their Masses; as independent motets the identities of their tenors are less important. *Perpulchra Sion filia*'s tenor is fully texted, as are the other voices, so there is no room for a tenor label.

52 In *Burgundisch-Niederländischer Motette*, 104–15, Stephan lists motets from many of the mid- to late fifteenth-century sources. Among his 171 motets are all but five of the thirty-three motets listed in Tables 12.2–5. He gives the number of cursus for forty-five tenor motets. Of those, nine have a single cursus, four have 1&1/2 cursus, twenty-two have double cursus, and ten have three or more repetitions of the tenor melody. Since cantus firmus treatment became more varied toward the end of the century, these data confirm my sense that multiple cursus and pre-existent tenors go together.

53 Pseudo-double cursus also seems to argue against a pre-existent tenor, since it demands either a single cursus, with a tenor that can be divided into two sections that begin the same but go on very differently, or two different tenors that begin the same but go on differently.

54 For *Meditatio cordis* see Snow, "Mass-Motet Cycle," 311; for *Salve virgo* see the edition by Gareth Curtis, EECM 34: the chant is found on p. 200, and the motet on pp. 69–74. Or compare the chant to the tenor voice in Trent 88, 70'–71, where its melodic contour is more visible.

55 See the beginning of both chanson and motet in Snow, "Mass-Motet Cycle," 310; he also shows the beginnings of *O rosa bella* (p. 304) and *Esclave puist* (p. 308), as well as the other putative Mass-motet cycles.

56 See the discussion of *Regina celi* in chapter 11, note 13.

57 See Strohm, *REM*, 238, 399.

58 For settings of the text see Curtis and Wathey, "List," 57. For the story of its origin see *AH*, vol. XXXI, 199, and Christopher Page, "Marian Texts and Themes in an English Manuscript: A Miscellany in Two Parts," *Plainsong and Medieval Music* 5 (1996): 33–4.

59 See mm. 41–3 and 46–8.

60 See Stephan, *Burgundisch-Niederländische Motette*, 65–7, on the texture of *Gregatim grex*.

61 *Ibid.,* 63–7.

62 Lockwood calls *Perfunde celi rore* "a four-voice tenor motet with absorption of the cantus firmus into the active texture" (*Ferrara*, 258); see also Benevenuto Disertori, ed., *Johannes Martini: Magnificat e Messe*, AMMM 12 (Milan, 1964), i–iv (this last includes a transcription and commentary on the text of the motet).

63 See mm. 3, 4, 14, 21 (2x), 28, 31 (2 voices), 34, 47, 48. There is a similar figure using twice the values (semibreves and minims) in the *secunda pars*: mm. 9–10, 11–12 (2 voices), 11–13, 14–15, 16–17, 23–5, 29–30, 43–5, 52–3, 62–3, 63–5, 66–7, 75–6, 79–80.

64 On Martini's secular works, see Howard Mayer Brown, *Florentine Chansonnier*, Text Volume, 87–95.

65 See mm. 35–40, 95–9.

66 In *Chromatic Beauty*, Thomas Brothers comes to a similar conclusion about this motet: "By mixing paraphrased plainchant with the melodic lyricism of courtly love, the motet may be read as a universal statement. In terms of polyphonic texture it also represents a stylistic synthesis, for it blends old elements (polytextuality, true tenor foundation) with new (the pacing and integration of the voices). It is as if Du Fay offers up to Mary his entire life's work" (p. 187).

CONCLUSION

1 See Fallows, "Contenance angloise," 189, who comments that fifteenth-century composers, like birds, are "constantly on the move, migrating from north to south with the seasons, rarely laying down permanent roots."

2 "The Contenance Angloise," 192–5, 205.

3 Brothers, "*Contenance angloise.*"

4 See Brothers, "Vestiges."

5 On the later history of the occasional motet see Albert Dunning, *Die Staatsmotette, 1480–1555* (Utrecht: A. Ostheok, 1970).

6 Don Randel comments that "the most important development in the history of music in this period (or perhaps in any period thereafter until the demise of tonality) is still the most obviously musical one – the adoption of four-part texture as a norm." See "Dufay the Reader," in *Music and Language*, Studies in the History of Music 1 (New York: Broude Brothers, 1983), 78.

7 On the "Milan" motet, see Joshua Rifkin, "Josquin in Context: Toward a Chronology of the Motets," unpublished paper (I am grateful to Professor Rifkin for sending me a copy). On imitation and text treatment see Ludwig Finscher, "Zum Verhältnis von Imitationstechnik und Textbehandlung im Zeitalter Josquins," in *Renaissance-Studien. Helmuth Osthoff zum 80. Geburtstag*, ed. Ludwig Finscher, Frankfurter Beiträge zur Musikwissenschaft Bd. 11 (Tutzing: Schneider, 1979), 57–73.

8 For a recent statement of the view that Josquin was involved in the creation of the "Milan motet" in the early 1470s, see Patrick Macey, "Galeazzo Maria Sforza and Musical Patronage in Milan: Compère, Weerbeke and Josquin," *Early Music History* 15 (1996): 147–212. Just as my book was going to press, however, Lora Matthews and Paul Merkley published new findings that prove there were two Josquins in Milan; the famous composer (Desprez) first arrived there only in 1484. See "Iudochus de Picardia and Jossequin Lebloitte dit Deprez: The Names of the Singer(s)," *Journal of Musicology* 16 (1998): 200–26, esp. 223–6. This confirms the suspicions of David Fallows, who puts the creation of the "Milan motet" in the 1480s, and removes Josquin from Milan altogether; see "Josquin and Milan," *Plainsong and Medieval Music* 5 (1996): 69–80. Nevertheless, it is still possible that the "Milan motet" was created in the 1470s without Josquin's help.

9 The link between the Trent repertory and the "Milan" motet is found in the earlier sections of Munich 3154, in which we find four of the Trent motets, along with two anonymous *motetti missales* cycles and Josquin's *Ave Maria*; see Thomas Lee Noblitt, "Das Chorbuch des Nikolaus Leopold (München, Staatsbibliothek, Mus. Ms. 3154): Repertorium," *Archiv für Musikwissenschaft* 26 (1969): 169–208. In "Die Datierung der Handschrift Mus. Ms. 3154 der Staatsbibliothek München," *Musikforschung* 27 (1974): 36–56, Noblitt proposed copying dates for the various fascicles of Munich 3154 by means of watermark evidence; while some scholars are sceptical about the dates, no one has disproved them. According to Noblitt ("Datierung," 41–2, 48–50), *Anima mea* (89.640) and *O beata infantia* (89.639) are found in fascicle 1, copied in 1466–9; *In hydraulis* (91.1162) and the eight-voice Leise-motet *Ave mundi/Gottes namen* (89.667) are copied next to each other in fascicle 4, copied in 1471–4. Du Fay's (?) *Salve regina* (89.727), in fascicle 9, the *motetti missales*, in fascicle 5, and *Ave Maria*, in fascicle 15, are all on paper with watermark 6, apparently copied in 1476. Merkley's and Matthews' discovery ("Iudochus di Picardia") have made this last date much more problematic.

Bibliography of books and articles

Abrams, M. H. *The Mirror and the Lamp: Romantic Theory and the Critical Tradition.* New York and London: Oxford University Press, 1953.

Allsen, J. Michael. "Intertextuality and Compositional Process in Two Cantilena Motets by Hugo de Lantins." *Journal of Musicology* 11 (1993): 174–202.

"Style and Intertextuality in the Isorhythmic Motet 1400–1440." Ph.D. dissertation, University of Wisconsin, Madison, 1992.

"Two New Motets by Du Fay?" Unpublished paper presented at the American Musicological Society Meeting, New York, 1995.

Armstrong, Sharon Lee, Lila Gleitman, and Henry Gleitman. "What Some Concepts Might Not Be." *Cognition* 13 (1983): 263–308.

Atlas, Allan W. "Dufay's *Mon chier amy*: Another Piece for the Malatesta." In *Music in Renaissance Cities and Courts: Studies in Honor of Lewis Lockwood,* ed. Jessie Ann Owens and Anthony M. Cummings, 3–20. Detroit Monographs in Musicology/Studies in Music 18. Warren, Mich.: Harmonie Park Press, 1997.

Bent, Margaret. "A Contemporary Perception of Early Fifteenth-Century Style: Bologna Q15 as a Document of Scribal Editorial Initiative." *Musica Disciplina* 41 (1987): 183–201.

"Contexts for the Repertory Formation of Bologna Q15." Unpublished paper presented at the American Musicological Society Meeting, Austin, Texas, 1989.

Dunstaple. Oxford Studies of Composers 17. London: Oxford University Press, 1981.

"The Early Use of the Sign Ø." *Early Music* 24 (1996): 199–225.

"Forest." *NG,* vol VI: 705–6.

"The Fourteenth-Century Italian Motet." In *L'Ars nova italiana del trecento* VI, Atti del Congresso internazionale "L'Europa e la musica del trecento," Certaldo, 1984, ed. Giulio Cattin and Patrizia Dalla Vecchia, 85–125. Certaldo: Edizioni Polis, 1992.

"The Late-Medieval Motet." In *Companion to Medieval and Renaissance Music,* ed. Tess Knighton and David Fallows, 114–19. London: Dent, 1992.

"Manuscripts as Répertoires, Scribal Performance and the Performing Scribe." In Angelo Pompilio, *et al.,* eds. *Trasmissione e recezione delle forme di cultura musicale. Atti del XIV Congresso della Società Internazionale di Musicologia,* vol. I, 138–52 (including discussion). Turin: EDT, 1990.

357

Bibliography of books and articles

"New and Little-known Fragments of English Medieval Polyphony." *Journal of the American Musicological Society* 21 (1968): 137–56.

"Pietro Emiliani's Chaplain Bartolomeo Rossi da Carpi and the Lamentations of Johannes de Quadris in Vicenza." *Il Saggiatore Musicale: Rivista semestrale di musicologia* 2 (1995): 5–16.

"Power, Leonel." *NG*, vol. XV: 174–9.

"The Progeny of Old Hall: More Leaves from a Royal English Choirbook." In *Gordon Athol Anderson (1929–1981): In Memoriam*, 1–54. Musicological Studies 39/1. Henryville, Penn.: Institute of Mediaeval Music, 1984.

"Some Factors in the Control of Consonance and Sonority: Successive Composition and the Solus Tenor." In *Report of the Twelfth Congress, Berkeley 1977*, ed. Daniel Heartz and Bonnie Wade, 625–34. Kassel: Bärenreiter, 1981.

"Text Setting in Sacred Music of the Early 15th Century: Evidence and Implications." In *Musik und Text in der Mehrstimmigkeit des 14. und 15. Jahrhunderts*, ed. Ursula Günther and Ludwig Finscher, 291–326. Göttinger musikwissenschaftliche Arbeiten 10. Kassel: Bärenreiter, 1984.

"Trent 93 and Trent 90: Johannes Wiser at Work." In *I codici musicali trentini a cento anni dalla loro riscoperta: Atti del Convegno Laurence Feininger, la musicologia come missione*, Trent, 6–7 September 1985, ed. Nino Pirrotta and Danilo Curti, 84–111. Trent: Provincia Autonoma di Trento, Servizio Beni Culturali, 1986.

"The Yoxford Credo." In Lewis Lockwood and Edward Roesner, eds., *Essays in Musicology: A Tribute to Alvin Johnson*, 26–51. N.p.: American Musicological Society, 1990.

Bent, Margaret, ed. *Fifteenth-Century Liturgical Music II: Four Anonymous Masses*. Early English Church Music 22. London: Stainer & Bell, 1979. [EECM 22]

Bent, Margaret, with David Howlett. "*Subtiliter alternare*: The Yoxford motet *O amicus / Precursoris*." In *Studies in Medieval Music: Festschrift for Ernest H. Sanders*, ed. Peter M. Lefferts and Brian Seirup. *Current Musicology* 45–7 (1990): 43–84.

Bent, Margaret, and Andrew Hughes. "The Old Hall Manuscript: An Inventory." *Musica Disciplina* 21 (1967): 130–47.

Bent, Margaret, and Anne Hallmark, eds. *The Works of Johannes Ciconia*. Polyphonic Music of the Fourteenth Century 24. Monaco: L'Oiseau-Lyre, 1985. [*Ciconia*]

Berger, Anna Maria Busse. "Cut Signs in Fifteenth-Century Musical Practice." In *Music in Renaissance Cities and Courts: Studies in Honor of Lewis Lockwood*, ed. Jessie Ann Owens and Anthony M. Cummings, 101–12. Detroit Monographs in Musicology/Studies in Music 18. Warren, Mich.: Harmonie Park Press, 1997.

Mensuration and Proportion Signs: Origins and Evolution. Oxford: Clarendon Press, 1993.

"The Myth of *diminutio per tertiam partem*." *Journal of Musicology* 8 (1990): 398–426.

Besseler, Heinrich. *Bourdon und Fauxbourdon: Studien zum Ursprung der Niederländischen Musik*. Leipzig: Breitkopf und Härtel, 1950.

Besseler, Heinrich, ed. *Guillaume Dufay, Opera Omnia*. 6 vols. Corpus Mensurabilis Musicae 1. Rome: American Institute of Musicology, 1951–66. [DufayB]

Blackburn, Bonnie J. "On Compositional Process in the Fifteenth Century." *Journal of the American Musicological Society* 40 (1987): 210–84.

Blackburn, Bonnie J., Edward Lowinsky, and Clement Miller, eds. *A Correspondence of Renaissance Musicians*. Oxford: Oxford University Press, 1991.

Boone, Graeme. "Dufay's Early Chansons: Chronology and Style in the Manuscript Oxford, Bodleian Library, Canonici misc. 213." Ph.D. dissertation, Harvard University, 1987.

Bowen, José A. "The History of Remembered Innovation: Tradition and its Role in the Relationship between Musical Works and their Performances." *Journal of Musicology* 11 (1993): 139–73.

Bowers, Roger D. "Choral Institutions Within the English Church: Their Constitution and Development, 1340–1500." Ph.D. dissertation, University of East Anglia, Norwich, 1975.

"Fixed Points in the Chronology of English Fourteenth-Century Polyphony." *Music and Letters* 71 (1990): 313–35.

"Some Observations on the Life and Career of Lionel Power." *Proceedings of the Royal Musical Association* 102 (1975–6): 103–27.

Brewer, Charles. "The Introduction of the Ars nova into East-Central Europe: A Study of the Late Medieval Polish Sources." Ph.D. dissertation, City University of New York, 1984.

Brothers, Thomas. *Chromatic Beauty in the Late Medieval Chanson: An Interpretation of Manuscript Accidentals.* Cambridge: Cambridge University Press, 1997.

"*Contenance angloise* and Accidentals in Some Motets by Du Fay." *Plainsong and Medieval Music* 6 (1997): 21–51.

"Vestiges of the Isorhythmic Tradition in Mass and Motet, ca. 1450–1475." *Journal of the American Musicological Society* 45 (1991): 1–56.

Brown, Howard Mayer, ed. *A Florentine Chansonnier from the Time of Lorenzo the Magnificent: Florence, Biblioteca Nazionale Centrale, MS Banco Rari 229.* Text Volume; Music Volume. Monuments of Renaissance Music 7. Chicago: University of Chicago Press, 1983.

Music in the Renaissance. Englewood Cliffs: Prentice Hall, 1976.

Brown, Samuel Emmons, Jr. "The Motets of Ciconia, Dunstable, and Dufay." Ph.D. dissertation, Indiana University, 1962.

Bukofzer, Manfred. "The Beginnings of Choral Polyphony." In *Studies in Medieval and Renaissance Music,* 176–89. New York: Norton, 1950.

"*Caput*: A Liturgico-Musical Study." In *Studies in Medieval and Renaissance Music,* 217–310. New York: Norton, 1950.

"English Church Music of the Fifteenth Century." In *New Oxford History of Music III: Ars nova and the Renaissance,* ed. Dom Anselm Hughes and Gerald Abraham, 165–213. London: Oxford University Press, 1960.

"Forest." *MGG,* vol. IV, cols. 509–13.

"Frye." *MGG,* vol. IV, col. 1070.

"John Dunstable and the Music of his Time." *Proceedings of the Royal Musical Association* 65 (1938–9): 19–36.

"John Dunstable: A Quincentenary Report." *Musical Quarterly* 40 (1954): 29–49.

Burkholder, J. Peter. "Johannes Martini and the Imitation Mass of the Late Fifteenth Century." *Journal of the American Musicological Society* 38 (1985): 470–523. See also the correspondence in the same journal, 40 (1987): 130–9 and 576–9.

Burstyn, Shai. "Fifteenth-Century Polyphonic Settings of Verses from the Song of Songs." Ph.D. dissertation, Columbia University, New York, 1972.

Carapezza, Paolo Emilio. "Regina angelorum in musica picta: Walter Frye e il 'Maître au feuillage brodé'." *Rivista italiana di musicologia* 10 (1975): 134–54.

Bibliography of books and articles

Cattin, Giulio. "Formazione e attività delle cappelle polifoniche nelle cattedrali. La Musica nelle città." In *Storia della cultura veneta III: Dal Primo Quattrocento al Concilio di Trento*, pt. 3, 267–96. Vicenza, 1981.

"Testi tropati nei codici trentini." In *I codici musicali trentini a cento anni dalla loro riscoperta: Atti del Convegno Laurence Feininger, la musicologia come missione*, Trent, 6–7 September 1985, ed. Nino Pirrotta and Danilo Curti, 130–7. Trent: Provincia Autonoma di Trento, Servizio Beni Culturali, 1986.

"Virgo Mater Ecclesiae: Un tropo alla Salve regina nelle fonti monodiche e polifoniche dei sec. XIV-XV." In *L'Ars nova italiana del trecento* IV: 149–76. Certaldo: Comune di Certaldo, 1978.

Chew, Geoffrey. "The Early Cyclic Mass as an Expression of Royal and Papal Supremacy." *Music and Letters* 53 (1972): 254–79.

Churchland, Paul M. *The Engine of Reason, the Seat of the Soul: A Philosophical Journey into the Brain.* Cambridge, Mass.: MIT Press, 1995.

Clercx, Suzanne. *Johannes Ciconia: un musicien liégeois et son temps (vers 1335–1411).* 2 vols. Brussels: Palais des Academies, 1960.

Cox, Bobby Wayne. "The Motets of MS Bologna, Civico Museo Bibliografico Musicale, Q15." Ph.D. dissertation, North Texas State University, 1977. ["Q15"]

"'Pseudo-Augmentation' in the Manuscript Bologna, Civico Museo Bibliografico Musicale, Q 15 (BL)." *Journal of Musicology* 1 (1982): 420–3.

Crocker, Richard. "French Polyphony in the Thirteenth Century," "Polyphony in England in the Thirteenth Century." In *The New Oxford History of Music*, II: *The Early Middle Ages to 1300*, 2nd ed., ed. Richard Crocker and David Hiley, 636–720. Oxford and New York: Oxford University Press, 1990.

Cronon, William. *Changes in the Land: Indians, Colonists, and the Ecology of New England.* New York: Hill and Wang, 1983.

Cumming, Julie E. "The Aesthetics of the Medieval Motet and Cantilena." *Historical Performance* 7 (1994): 71–83.

"Concord out of Discord: Occasional Motets of the Early Quattrocento." Ph.D. dissertation, University of California, Berkeley, 1987.

"Music for the Doge in Early Renaissance Venice." *Speculum* 67 (1992): 324–64.

Cummings, Anthony M. "Toward an Interpretation of the Sixteenth-Century Motet." *Journal of the American Musicological Society* 34 (1981): 43–59.

Curtis, Gareth R. K. "Brussels, Bibliothèque Royale MS 5557, and the Texting of Dufay's 'Ecce ancilla domini' and 'Ave regina caelorum' Masses." *Acta musicologica* 51 (1979): 73–86.

"Jean Pullois and the Cyclic Mass – Or a Case of Mistaken Identity?" *Music and Letters* 62 (1981): 41–59.

"Musical Design and the Rise of the Cyclic Mass." In *Companion to Medieval and Renaissance Music*, ed. Tess Knighton and David Fallows, 154–64. London: Dent, 1992.

"Stylistic Layers in the English Mass Repertory, c. 1400–1450." *Proceedings of the Royal Musical Association* 109 (1982–83): 23–38.

Curtis, Gareth R. K. and Andrew Wathey. "Fifteenth-Century English Liturgical Music: A List of the Surviving Repertory." *RMA Research Chronicle* 27 (1994): 1–69. ["List"]

Curtius, Ernst Robert. *European Literature and the Latin Middle Ages.* Trans. Willard R. Trask. Bollingen Series 36. Princeton: Princeton University Press, 1953.

D'Accone, Frank A. "The Performance of Sacred Music in Italy During Josquin's Time, c. 1474–1525." In *Josquin des Prez: Proceedings of the International Josquin Festival-Conference, New York, 1971,* ed. Edward E. Lowinsky with Bonnie J. Blackburn, 601–18. London: Oxford University Press, 1976.

Dahlhaus, Carl. "Gattung." Brockhaus Riemann Musiklexikon, ed. Carl Dahlhaus and Hans Heinrich Eggebrecht. Wiesbaden: Brockhaus; Mainz: Schott, 1978, vol. I, 452.

Dammann, Rolf. "Geschichte der Begriffsbestimmung Motette." *Archiv für Musikwissenschaft* 16 (1959): 337–77.

Dangel-Hoffmann, Frohmut. *Der Mehrstimmige Introitus in Quellen des 15. Jahrhunderts.* Würzburger Musikhistorische Beiträge 3. Tutzing: Schneider, 1975.

Dannemann, Erna. *Die Spätgotische Musiktradition in Frankreich und Burgund vor dem Auftreten Guillaume Dufays.* Sammlung Musikwissenschaftlicher Abhandlungen 17 (22). Strasbourg: Heitz & Co., 1936.

Darwin, Charles. *The Origin of Species by Means of Natural Selection, or the Preservation of Favoured Races in the Struggle for Life.* [First ed.] London: John Murray, 1859. Ed. J. W. Burrow. London: Penguin, 1968.

Dawkins, Richard. *The Blind Watchmaker: Why the Evidence of Evolution Reveals a Universe without Design.* New York: Norton, 1987.

Debenedetti, Santorre. "Un trattatello del secolo XIV sopra la poesia musicale." *Studi medievali* 2 (1906–7): 79–80.

Dèzes, Karl. "Das Dufay zugeschriebene Salve Regina eine deutsche Komposition: stilkritische Studie." *Zeitschrift für Musikwissenschaft* 10 (1927–8): 327–62.

Diederichs, Elisabeth. *Die Anfänge der mehrstimmigen Lauda vom Ende des 14. bis zur Mitte des 15. Jahrhunderts.* Tutzing: Schneider, 1986.

Dreves, Guido Maria, and Clemens Blume, eds. *Analecta Hymnica Medii Aevi.* 52 vols. Leipzig, 1886–1909. *Register*, ed. Max Lütolf. 2 vols. Berne and Munich: Francke, 1978. [*AH*]

Dreyfus, Laurence. *Bach and the Patterns of Invention.* Cambridge, Mass.: Harvard University Press, 1996.

Dubrow, Heather. *Genre.* The Critical Idiom 42. London and New York: Methuen, 1982.

Duesen, Nancy van. "Sequence Repertories: A Reappraisal." *Musica Disciplina* 48 (1994): 99–123.

Dunning, Albert. *Die Staatsmotette, 1480–1555.* Utrecht: A. Osthoek, 1970.

Eggebrecht, Hans Heinrich. *Studien zur Musikalischen Terminologie.* Akademie der Wissenschaften und der Literatur, Abhandlungen der geistes- und sozialwissenschaftlichen Klasse, Jhg. 1955, no. 10. Wiesbaden: F. Steiner, 1955.

"Machauts Motette Nr. 9." *Archiv für Musikwissenschaft* 19–20 (1962–3): 281–93, and 25 (1968): 173–95.

Elders, Willem. "Guillaume Dufay as Musical Orator." *Tijdschrift van de Vereniging voor Nederlandse Muziekgeschiedenis* 31 (1981): 1–15.

"Guillaume Dufay's Concept of *Faux-Bourdon*." *Revue Belge de Musicologie* 43 (1989): 173–95.

"Humanism and Early Renaissance Music: A Study of the Ceremonial Music by Ciconia and Dufay." *Tijdschrift van de Vereniging voor Nederlandse Muziekgeschiedenis* 27 (1977): 65–101.

"Humanism and Music in the Early Renaissance." In International Musicological Society, *Report of the Twelfth Congress, Berkeley, 1977*, ed. Daniel Heartz and Bonnie Wade, 883–7, with responses 888–93. Kassel: Bärenreiter, 1981.

"Plainchant in the Motets, Hymns, and Magnificat of Josquin des Prez." In *Josquin des Prez: Proceedings of the International Josquin Festival-Conference, New York, 1971*, ed. Edward E. Lowinsky with Bonnie J. Blackburn, 522–42. London: Oxford University Press, 1976.

Etheridge, Jerry Haller. "The Works of Johannes de Limburgia." Ph.D. dissertation, Indiana University, 1972.

Fallows, David. "Binchois, Gilles de Bins dit." *NG*, vol. II, 709–22.

"The Contenance Angloise: English Influence on Continental Composers of the Fifteenth Century." *Renaissance Studies* 1 (1987): 189–208.

Dufay. London: Dent, 1982; rev. ed., 1987.

"Dufay and the Mass Proper Cycles of Trent 88." In *I codici musicali trentini a cento anni dalla loro riscoperta: Atti del Convegno Laurence Feininger, la musicologia come missione*, Trent, 6–7 September 1985, ed. Nino Pirrotta and Danilo Curti, 46–59. Trent: Provincia Autonoma di Trento, Servizio Beni Culturali, 1986.

"English Song Repertories of the Mid-Fifteenth Century." *Proceedings of the Royal Musical Association* 103 (1976–7): 61–79.

"Josquin and Milan." *Plainsong and Medieval Music* 5 (1996): 69–80.

Review of Lewis Lockwood, *Music in Renaissance Ferrara, 1400–1505* and Reinhard Strohm, *Music in Late Medieval Bruges. Early Music History* 6 (1986): 279–303.

"Songs in the Trent Codices: An Optimistic Handlist." In *I codici musicali trentini a cento anni dalla loro riscoperta: Atti del Convegno Laurence Feininger, la musicologia come missione*, Trent, 6–7 September 1985, ed. Nino Pirrotta and Danilo Curti, 170–9. Trent: Provincia Autonoma di Trento, Servizio Beni Culturali, 1986.

"Specific Information on the Ensembles for Composed Polyphony, 1400–1474." In *Studies in the Performance of Late Medieval Music*, ed. Stanley Boorman, 109–59. Cambridge: Cambridge University Press, 1983.

"Two Equal Voices: A French Song Repertory with Music for Two More Works of Oswald von Wolkenstein." *Early Music History* 7 (1987): 227–41.

Fallows, David, ed. *Oxford, Bodleian Library, MS Canonici Misc. 213*. Late Medieval and Early Renaissance Music in Facsimile 1. Chicago: University of Chicago Press, 1995.

Fellin, Eugene. "The Notation Types of Trecento Music." *L'Ars nova italiana del Trecento* IV: 213–20. Certaldo: Comune di Certaldo, 1978.

Finscher, Ludwig. *Loyset Compère*. Musicological Studies and Documents 12. N.p.: American Institute of Musicology, 1964.

"Motette, II, Von Dufay bis Lasso." *MGG*, vol. IX, cols. 646–56.

"Zum Verhältnis von Imitationstechnik und Textbehandlung im Zeitalter Josquins." In *Renaissance-Studien. Helmuth Osthoff zum 80. Geburtstag*, ed. Ludwig Finscher, 57–73. Frankfurter Beiträge zur Musikwissenschaft Bd. 11. Tutzing: Schneider, 1979.

Finscher, Ludwig, and Annegrit Laubenthal. "'Cantiones quae vulgo motectae vocantur': Arten der Motette im 15. und 16. Jahrhundert." In *Die Musik des 15. und 16. Jahrhunderts*, ed. Ludwig Finscher, Teil 2, ch. 4, 277–370. *Neues Handbuch der Musikwissenschaft*, vol. III. Laaber: Laaber-Verlag, 1990.

Fischer, Kurt von. "Die Lauda 'Ave Mater' und ihre verschiedenen Fassungen." In *Colloquium Amicorum: Joseph Schmidt-Görg zum 70. Geburtstag*, ed. Siegfried Kross and Hans Schmidt, 93–9. Bonn: Beethovenhaus, 1967.

  "Zur Entwicklung der italienischen Trecento-Notation." *Archiv für Musikwissenschaft* 16 (1959): 87–99.

Fishelov, David. *Metaphors of Genre: The Role of Analogies in Genre Theory*. University Park, Penn.: The Pennsylvania State University Press, 1993.

Fowler, Alastair. *Kinds of Literature: An Introduction to the Theory of Genres and Modes*. Cambridge, Mass.: Harvard University Press, 1982.

Freeman, Daniel E. "On the Origins of the *Pater noster–Ave Maria* of Josquin Des Prez." *Musica disciplina* 45 (1991): 169–219.

Fuller, Sarah. "Modal Tenors and Tonal Orientation in Motets of Guillaume de Machaut." In *Studies in Medieval Music: Festschrift for Ernest H. Sanders*, ed. Peter M. Lefferts and Brian Seirup. *Current Musicology* 45–7 (1990): 199–245.

  "On Sonority in Fourteenth-Century Polyphony: Some Preliminary Reflections." *Journal of Music Theory* 30 (1986): 35–70.

Gallo, F. Alberto, ed. *Il codice musicale 2216 della Biblioteca Universitaria di Bologna*, 2 parts. Monumenta lyrica medii aevi italica III: Mensurabilia, III. Vol. I, facsimile; vol. II, discussion and inventory. Bologna: Forni, Editore 1966–71.

Gallo, F. Alberto, and Giovanni Mantese. *Richerche sulle origini della cappella musicale del duomo di Vicenza*. Civiltà veneziana saggi 15. Venice: Istituto per la collaborazione culturale Venezia – Roma, 1964.

Ganser, Hans and Rainer Herpichböhm, eds. *Oswald von Wolkenstein-Liederbuch: Eine Auswahl von Melodien*. Göppinger Arbeiten zur Germanistik 240. Göppingen: Kümmerle Verlag, 1978.

Gerber, Rebecca Lynn. "The Manuscript Trent, Castello del Buonconsiglio, 88: A Study of Fifteenth-Century Manuscript Transmission and Repertory." Ph.D. dissertation, University of California, Santa Barbara, 1985. [Gerber]

Gómez Muntané, Maria Carmen. *La música en la Casa Real Catalano-Aragonesa durante los años 1336–1437*. 2 vols. Barcelona: Bosch, 1979.

Gossett, Philip. "Techniques of Unification in Early Cyclic Masses and Mass Pairs." *Journal of the American Musicological Society* 19 (1966): 205–31.

Gottlieb, Louis. "The Cyclic Masses of Trent Codex 89." Ph.D. dissertation, University of California, Berkeley, 1958.

Gozzi, Marco. *Il manoscritto Trento Museo Provinciale d'Arte, cod. 1377 (Tr 90) con un'analisi del repertorio non derivato da Tr 93*, 2 vols. Cremona: Studi e testi musicali 1. Cremona: Centro di Musicologia "Walter Stauffer," 1992. [Gozzi]

Gülke, Peter, ed. *Johannes Pullois: Opera omnia*. Corpus Mensurabilis Musicae 41. Rome: American Institute of Musicology, 1967.

Günther, Ursula. "Die Anwendung der Diminution in der Handschrift Chantilly." *Archiv für Musikwissenschaft* 17 (1960): 1–21.

"Critical Years in European Musical History, 1400–1430." Round Table in *International Musicological Society, Report of the Tenth Congress, Ljubljana 1967*, ed. Dragotin Cvetko, 43–60. Kassel: Bärenreiter, 1970.

"The Fourteenth-Century Motet and its Development." *Musica Disciplina* 12 (1958): 27–59.

"Der Gebrauch des *tempus perfectum diminutum* in der Handschrift Chantilly." *Archiv für Musikwissenschaft* 17 (1960): 277–97.

Haagh, Barbara. "The Meeting of Sacred Ritual and Secular Piety: Endowments for Music." In *Companion to Medieval and Renaissance Music*, ed. Tess Knighton and David Fallows, 60–8. London: Dent, 1992.

"Crispijne and Abertijne: Two Tenors at the Church of St Niklaas, Brussels." *Music and Letters* 76 (1995): 325–44.

Haberl, Franz X. "Die römische 'schola cantorum' und die päpstlichen Kapellsänger bis zur Mitte des 16. Jahrhunderts." *Bausteine für Musikgeschichte* 3. Leipzig: Breitkopf und Härtel, 1888. Also in *Vierteljahrschrift für Musikwissenschaft* 3 (1887): 189–296.

Hallmark, Anne. "Gratiosus, Ciconia, and other Musicians at Padua Cathedral: Some Footnotes to Present Knowledge." In *L'Ars nova italiana del trecento* VI, Atti del Congresso internazionale "L'Europa e la musica del trecento," Certaldo, 1984, ed. Giulio Cattin and Patrizia Dalla Vecchia, 69–84. Certaldo: Edizioni Polis, 1992.

"*Protector, imo verus pater*. Francesco Zabarella's Patronage of Johannes Ciconia." In *Music in Renaissance Cities and Courts: Studies in Honor of Lewis Lockwood*, ed. Jessie Ann Owens and Anthony M. Cummings, 153–68. Detroit Monographs in Musicology/Studies in Music 18. Warren, Mich.: Harmonie Park Press, 1997.

Hamm, Charles. "A Catalogue of Anonymous English Music in Fifteenth-Century Continental Manuscripts." *Musica Disciplina* 22 (1968): 47–76.

A Chronology of the Works of Guillaume Dufay, Based on a Study of Mensural Practice. Princeton Studies in Music 1. Princeton: Princeton University Press, 1964.

"A Group of Anonymous English Pieces in Trent 87," *Music and Letters* 41 (1960): 211–15.

"Manuscript Structure in the Dufay Era." *Acta Musicologica* 34 (1962): 166–84.

"The Motets of Lionel Power." In *Studies in Music History: Essays for Oliver Strunk*, ed. Harold Powers, 127–36. Princeton: Princeton University Press, 1968.

"The Reson Mass." *Journal of the American Musicological Society* 18 (1965): 5–21.

Hamm, Charles, ed. *Leonel Power: Complete Works*, I, *The Motets*. Corpus Mensurabilis Musicae 50. Rome: American Institute of Musicology, 1969.

Hamm, Charles, and Herbert Kellman, eds. *Census-Catalogue of Manuscript Sources of Polyphonic Music, 1400–1550*. 5 vols. Renaissance Manuscript Studies 1. Neuhausen-Stuttgart: American Institute of Musicology, 1979–88.

Hamm, Charles, Jerry Call, and Herbert Kellman. "Sources, MS, IX: Renaissance Polyphony," *NG*, vol. XVII, 674–701.

Hamm, Charles, and Ann Besser Scott. "A Study and Inventory of the Manuscript Modena, Biblioteca Estense, αX.1.11 (ModB)." *Musica Disciplina* 26 (1972): 101–43.

Harrison, Frank Llewellyn. *Music in Medieval Britain*. New York: Praeger, 1958.

"Tradition and Innovation in Instrumental Usage 1100–1450." In *Aspects of Medieval and Renaissance Music: A Birthday Offering to Gustave Reese*, ed. Jan LaRue, 319–35. New York: Norton, 1966.

Higgins, Paula. "Antoine Busnois and Musical Culture in Late Fifteenth-Century France and Burgundy." Ph.D. dissertation, Princeton University, 1987.

"*In Hydraulis* Revisited: New Light on the Career of Antoine Busnois." *Journal of the American Musicological Society* 39 (1986): 36–86.

"Love and Death in the Fifteenth-Century Motet: A Reading of Busnoys's *Anima mea lique-facta est/Stirps Jesse.*" In *Hearing the Motet: Essays on the Motet of the Middle Ages and Renaissance*, ed. Dolores Pesce, 142–68. Oxford: Oxford University Press, 1997.

"Music and Musicians at the Sainte-Chapelle of the Bourges Palace, 1415–1515." In Angelo Pompilio, *et al.*, eds. *Trasmissione e recezione delle forme di cultura musicale. Atti del XIV Congresso della Società Internazionale di Musicologia.* vol. III, 689–701. Turin: EDT, 1990.

Hiley, David. *Western Plainchant: A Handbook.* Oxford: Clarendon Press, 1993.

Holford-Strevens, Leofranc. "Du Fay the Poet? Problems in the Texts of his Motets." *Early Music History* 16 (1997): 97–165.

The Holy Bible: Douay Rheims Version. Baltimore: John Murphy Company, 1899; repr. Tan Books and Publishers, 1971.

Howlett, David. "Busnois' Motet *In hydraulis:* An Exercise in Textual Reconstruction and Analysis." *Plainsong and Medieval Music* 4 (1995): 185–91.

Hughes, Andrew. "The Old Hall Manuscript: A Re-Appraisal." *Musica Disciplina* 21 (1967): 97–129.

"Some Notes on the Early Fifteenth-Century Contratenor." *Music and Letters* 50 (1969): 376–87.

Hughes, Andrew, ed. *Fifteenth-Century Liturgical Music I: Antiphons and Music for Holy Week and Easter.* Early English Church Music 8. London: Stainer and Bell, 1964. [EECM 8]

Huglo, Michel. "Antiphon." *NG,* vol. I, 471–81.

Jauss, Hans Robert. *Toward an Aesthetic of Reception.* Trans. Timothy Bahti. Introduction by Paul de Man. Theory and History of Literature, Volume II. Minneapolis, University of Minnesota Press, 1982. See especially ch. 1, "Literary History as a Challenge to Literary Theory," 3–45, which originally appeared in German in 1970 (Suhrkamp Verlag); and ch. 3, "Theory of Genres and Medieval Literature," 76–109, which originally appeared in German in *Grundriss der Romanischen Literaturen des Mittelalters* vol. IV, Carl Winter Universitäts Verlag, 1972.

Just, Martin. *Der Mensuralkodex Mus. ms. 40021 der Staatsbibliothek Preussischer Kulturbesitz Berlin: Untersuchungen zum Repertoire einer deutschen Quelle des 15. Jahrhunderts.* 2 vols. Würzburger Musikhistorische Beiträge, Bd. 1. Tutzing: Schneider, 1975.

Kallberg, Jeffrey. "The Rhetoric of Genre: Chopin's Nocturne in G Minor." *Nineteenth-Century Music* 11 (1988): 238–61.

Kanazawa, Masakata. "Polyphonic Music for Vespers during the Fifteenth Century." Ph.D. dissertation, Harvard University, 1966.

Kempton, Willet. *The Folk Classification of Ceramics: A Study of Cognitive Prototypes.* New York: Academic Press, 1981.

Kenney, Sylvia W. "Contrafacta in the Works of Walter Frye." *Journal of the American Musicological Society* 8 (1955): 181–202.

"In Praise of the Lauda." In *Aspects of Medieval and Renaissance Music: A Birthday Offering to Gustave Reese*, ed. Jan LaRue, 489–99. New York: Norton, 1966.

Walter Frye and the Contenance Angloise. Yale Studies in the History of Music 3. New Haven: Yale University Press, 1964.

Kirkendale, Warren. "Circulatio-Tradition, *Maria Lactans*, and Josquin as Musical Orator." *Acta Musicologica* 56 (1984): 69–92.

Kirkman, Andrew. "The Transmission of English Mass Cycles in the Mid to Late Fifteenth Century: A Case Study in Context." *Music and Letters* 75 (1994): 180–99.

    The Three-Voice Mass in the Later Fifteenth and Early Sixteenth Centuries: Style, Distribution, and Case Studies. New York: Garland, 1995.

Kivy, Peter. *Authenticities: Philosophical Reflections on Musical Performance.* Ithaca: Cornell University Press, 1995.

Lakoff, George. "Hedges: A Study in Meaning Criteria and the Logic of Fuzzy Concepts." *Proceedings of the Chicago Linguistics Society* 8 (1972): 183–228.

    Women, Fire, and Dangerous Things: What Categories Reveal About the Mind. Chicago: University of Chicago Press, 1987.

Lakoff, George, and Mark Johnson. *Metaphors We Live By.* Chicago: University of Chicago Press, 1980.

Lawler, Traugott, ed. & trans. *The Parisiana Poetria of John of Garland.* Yale Studies in English 182. New Haven and London: Yale University Press, 1974.

Leech-Wilkinson, Daniel. *Compositional Techniques in the Four-Part Isorhythmic Motets of Philippe de Vitry and his Contemporaries.* 2 vols. New York: Garland, 1989.

Lefferts, Peter M. "Cantilena and Antiphon: Music for Marian Services in Late Medieval England." In *Studies in Medieval Music: Festschrift for Ernest H. Sanders,* ed. Peter M. Lefferts and Brian Seirup. *Current Musicology* 45–7 (1990): 247–82.

    The Motet in England in the Fourteenth Century. Ann Arbor: UMI Research Press, 1986.

Leverett, Adelyn Peck. "A Paleographical and Repertorial Study of the Manuscript Trento, Castello del Buonconsiglio, 91 (1378)." 2 vols. Ph.D. dissertation, Princeton University, 1990.

Levy, Janet M. "Texture as a Sign in Classic and Early Romantic Music." *Journal of the American Musicological Society* 35 (1982): 482–531.

Lewis, Ann. "Anti-Semitism in an Early Fifteenth-Century Motet: *Tu, nephanda.*" *Plainsong and Medieval Music* 3 (1994): 45–55.

Lewis, Ann, ed. *Johannes de Lymburgia: Four Motets, The Song of Songs.* Antico Church Music RCM 3. Newton Abbot: Antico Edition, 1985.

Litterick, Louise. "Performing Franco-Netherlandish Secular Music of the Late Fifteenth Century: Texted and Untexted Parts in the Sources." *Early Music* 8 (1980): 474–85.

Lockwood, Lewis. *Music in Renaissance Ferrara, 1400–1505.* Cambridge, Mass.: Harvard University Press, 1984.

Lowinsky, Edward E., and Bonnie J. Blackburn, eds. *Josquin des Prez: Proceedings of the International Josquin Festival-Conference, New York, 1971.* London: Oxford University Press, 1976.

Macey, Patrick. "Galeazzo Maria Sforza and Musical Patronage in Milan: Compère, Weerbeke and Josquin." *Early Music History* 15 (1996): 147–212.

    "Josquin's 'Little' *Ave Maria*: A Misplaced Motet from the *Vultum tuum* cycle?" *Tijdschrift van de Vereniging voor Nederlandse Muziekgeschiedenis* 39 (1989): 38–53.

Mahrt, William. "Guillaume Dufay's Chansons in the Phrygian Mode." *Studies in Music from the University of Western Ontario* 5 (1980): 89–98.

Mandelbaum, Maurice. "Family Resemblances and Generalizations Concerning the Arts." *American Philosophical Quarterly* 2 (1965): 219–28.

Mattfeld, Jacquelyn A. "Some Relationships between Texts and Cantus Firmi in the Liturgical Motets of Josquin de Prez." *Journal of the American Musicological Society* 14 (1961): 159–83.

Matthews, Lora, and Merkley, Paul. "Iudochus de Picardia and Jossequin Lebloitte dit Deprez: The Names of the Singer(s)." *Journal of Musicology* 16 (1998): 200–26.

Mayr, Ernst. *Animal Species and Evolution.* Cambridge, Mass.: Belknap Press, 1963.

Meconi, Honey. "Art-Song Reworkings: An Overview." *Journal of the Royal Musicological Society* 119 (1994): 1–42.

Meier, Bernhard. *The Modes of Classical Vocal Polyphony, Described According to the Sources*, with revisions by the author, trans. Ellen S. Beebe. New York: Broude Brothers, 1988.

Mele, Giampaolo. "Una precisazione su un documento di Giovanni Duca di Gerona e promogenito d'Aragona, riguardante la sua cappella musicale." *Anuario Musical* 38 (1983): 255–60.

Miller, Clement A. "Early Gaffuriana: New Answers to Old Questions." *Musical Quarterly* 56 (1970): 367–88.

Mitchell, Robert. "The Paleography and Repertory of Trent Codices 89 and 91, together with Analyses and Editions of Six Mass Cycles by Franco-Flemish Composers from Trent Codex 89." 2 vols. Ph.D. dissertation, University of Exeter, 1989.

Mixter, Keith. "Brassart, Johannes." *NG,* vol. III, 208–9.

"Feragut, Beltrame." *NG,* vol. VI, 468.

"Johannes de Lymburgia." *NG,* vol. IX, 666–7.

"Johannes de Sarto." *NG,* vol. IX, 668.

Moll, Kevin N., ed. and trans. *Counterpoint and Compositional Process in the Time of Dufay: Perspectives from German Musicology.* Criticism and Analysis of Early Music. New York: Garland, 1997.

Montagna, Gerald. "Caron, Hayne, Compère: A Transmission Reassessment." *Early Music History* 7 (1987): 107–57.

"Johannes Pullois in the Context of his Era." *Revue Belge de Musicologie* 42 (1988): 83–117.

Morson, Gary Saul. *The Boundaries of Genre: Dostoevsky's Diary of a Writer and the Traditions of Literary Utopia.* Austin: University of Texas Press, 1981.

Noble, Jeremy. "The Function of Josquin's Motets." *Tijdschrift van de Vereniging voor Nederlandse Muziekgeschiedenis* 35 (1985): 9–31.

Noblitt, Thomas Lee. "Das Chorbuch des Nikolaus Leopold (München, Staatsbibliothek, Mus. Ms. 3154): Repertorium." *Archiv für Musikwissenschaft* 26 (1969): 169–208.

"Die Datierung der Handschrift Mus. Ms. 3154 der Staatsbibliothek München." *Musikforschung* 27 (1974): 36–56.

Nosow, Robert. "Du Fay and the Cultures of Renaissance Florence." In *Hearing the Motet: Essays on the Motet of the Middle Ages and Renaissance*, ed. Dolores Pesce, 104–21. Oxford: Oxford University Press, 1997.

"The Equal-Discantus Motet Style After Ciconia." *Musica Disciplina* 45 (1991): 221–75.

Bibliography of books and articles

"The Florid and Equal-Discantus Motet Styles of Fifteenth-Century Italy." Ph.D. dissertation, University of North Carolina, Chapel Hill, 1992.

Olson, Gary M., Robert L. Mack, and Susan A. Duffy. "Cognitive Aspects of Genre." *Poetics* 10 (1981): 283–315.

Orden, Kate van. "*Les Vers lascifs d'Horace*: Arcadelt's Latin Chansons." *Journal of Musicology* 14 (1996): 338–69.

Owens, Jessie Ann, ed. Introduction to *Kraków, Biblioteka Jagiellońska, Glogauer Liederbuch*. 3 vols. Renaissance Music in Facsimile 6. New York: Garland, 1986.

Page, Christopher. "Marian Texts and Themes in an English Manuscript: A Miscellany in Two Parts." *Plainsong and Medieval Music* 5 (1996): 23–44.

Perkins, Leeman. "Motet, II, Renaissance." *NG*, vol. XII, 628–37.

Pietzsch, Gerhard. *Zur Pflege der Musik an den deutschen Universitäten bis zur Mitte des 16. Jahrhunderts*. Repr. Hildesheim and New York: Olms, 1971.

Pinker, Steven. *How the Mind Works*. New York: Norton, 1997.

Pirrotta, Nino. "Music and Cultural Tendencies in Fifteenth-Century Italy." *Journal of the American Musicological Society* 19 (1966): 127–61.

Pirrotta, Nino, and Danilo Curti, eds. *I codici musicali trentini a cento anni dall loro riscoperta: Atti del Convegno Laurence Feininger, la musicologia come missione*, Trent, 6–7 September 1985. Trent: Provincia Autonoma di Trento, Servizio Beni Culturali, 1986. [*I codici*]

Plamenac, Dragan. "Another Paduan Fragment of Trecento Music." *Journal of the American Musicological Society* 8 (1955): 165–81.

Planchart, Alejandro Enrique. "The Early Career of Guillaume Du Fay." *Journal of the American Musicological Society* 46 (1993): 341–68.

"Guillaume Du Fay's Benefices and his Relationship to the Court of Burgundy." *Early Music History* 8 (1988): 117–71.

"Guillaume Du Fay's Second Style." In *Music in Renaissance Cities and Courts: Studies in Honor of Lewis Lockwood*, ed. Jessie Ann Owens and Anthony M. Cummings, 307–40. Detroit Monographs in Musicology/Studies in Music 18. Warren, Mich.: Harmonie Park Press, 1997.

"Guillaume Dufay's Masses: A View of the Manuscript Traditions." In *Dufay Quincentenary Conference. Brooklyn College 1974*, ed. Allan Atlas, 26–60. New York: Brooklyn College, 1976.

"Notes on Guillaume Du Fay's Last Works." *Journal of Musicology* 13 (1995): 55–72.

"Parts with Words and without Words: The Evidence for Multiple Texts in Fifteenth-Century Masses." In *Studies in the Performance of Late Medieval Music*, ed. Stanley Boorman, 227–51. Cambridge: Cambridge University Press, 1983.

"The Relative Speed of *Tempora* in the Dufay Period." *RMA Research Chronicle* 17 (1981): 33–51.

"Tempo and Proportions." In *Performance Practice: Music Before 1600*, ed. Howard M. Brown and Stanley Sadie, 126–44. The Norton/Grove Handbooks in Music. New York: Norton, 1990.

"What's in a Name? Reflections on Some Works of Guillaume Du Fay." *Early Music* 16 (1988): 165–75.

Polk, Keith. *German Instrumental Music of the Late Middle Ages*. Cambridge: Cambridge University Press, 1992.

"Innovation in Instrumental Music 1450–1510: The Role of German Performers within

European Culture." In *Music in the German Renaissance: Sources, Styles, and Contexts*, ed. John Kmetz, 202–14. Cambridge: Cambridge University Press, 1994.

Pompilio, Angelo, *et al.*, eds. *Trasmissione e recezione delle forme di cultura musicale. Atti del XIV Congresso della Società Internazionale di Musicologia*. 3 vols. Turin: EDT, 1990. I: Round Tables. III: Free Papers.

Pope, Isabel, and Masakata Kanazawa. *The Music Manuscript Montecassino 871: A Neapolitan Repertory of Sacred and Secular Music of the Late Fifteenth Century*. Oxford: Clarendon Press, 1978.

Powers, Harold. "Tonal Types and Modal Categories in Renaissance Polyphony." *Journal of the American Musicological Society* 34 (1981): 428–70.

Prosdocimus de Beldemandis. *Expositiones tractatus pratice cantus mensurabilis magistri Johannis de Muris*. Ed. F. Alberto Gallo, *Antiquae musicae italicae scriptores* III, pt. 1. Bologna: Università degli Studi de Bologna, Istituto di Studi Musicali e Teatrali, 1966.

Rabinowitz, Peter J. *Before Reading: Narrative Conventions and the Politics of Interpretation*. Ithaca: Cornell University Press, 1987.

"Circumstantial Evidence: Music Analysis and Theories of Reading." *Mosaic* 18 (1985): 159–73.

Randel, Don Michael. "Dufay the Reader." In *Music and Language*, 38–78. Studies in the History of Music 1. New York: Broude Brothers, 1983.

Reaney, Gilbert. "The Isorhythmic Motet and its Social Background." In *Internationale musik- wissenschaftlichen Kongress, Kassel 1962*, ed. Georg Reichert and Martin Just, 25–7. Gesellschaft für Musikforschung, Berichte. Kassel: Bärenreiter, 1963.

"Text Underlay in Early Fifteenth-Century Music Manuscripts." In *Essays in Musicology in Honor of Dragan Plamenac on his 70th Birthday*, ed. Gustave Reese and Robert J. Snow, 245–51. Pittsburgh: University of Pittsburgh Press, 1969.

Reaney, Gilbert, ed. *Early Fifteenth-Century Music*, 7 vols. Corpus Mensurabilis Musicae 11. N.p.: American Institute of Musicology, 1955–83. [Reaney]

Reynolds, Christopher. "The Origins of San Pietro B 80 and the Development of a Roman Sacred Repertory." *Early Music History* 1 (1981): 257–304.

Papal Patronage and the Music of St. Peter's 1380–1513. Berkeley: University of California Press, 1995.

"Sacred Polyphony." In *Performance Practice: Music before 1600*, ed. Howard Mayer Brown and Stanley Sadie, 185–200. Norton/Grove Handbooks in Music. New York: Norton, 1989.

Reynolds, Robert Davis Jr. "Evolution of Notational Practices in Manuscripts between 1400 and 1450." Ph.D. dissertation, Ohio State University, 1974.

Rifkin, Joshua. "Josquin in Context: Toward a Chronology of the Motets," unpublished paper.

Rosch, Eleanor. "Cognitive Representations of Semantic Categories." *Journal of Experimental Psychology: General* 104 (1975): 192–233.

Rosch, Eleanor, and Carolyn Mervis. "Family Resemblances: Studies in the Internal Structure of Categories." *Cognitive Psychology* 7 (1975): 573–605.

Rumbold, Ian. "The Compilation and Ownership of the 'St Emmeram' Codex (Munich, Bayerische Staatsbibliothek, Clm 14274)." *Early Music History* 2 (1982): 161–235.

Ryan, Marie-Laure. "Introduction: On the Why, What, and How of Generic Taxonomy." *Poetics* 10 (1981): 109–26.

Bibliography of books and articles

Salokar, Douglas. "*Ad augmentationem divini cultus*: Pious Foundations and Vespers Motets in the Church of Our Lady in Bruges." In *Musicology and Archival Research: Colloquium Proceedings Brussels 22–23.4.1993*, ed. Barbara Haagh, Frank Daelemans, and André Vanrie, 306–25. Archives et Bibliothèques de Belgique, Numéro spécial 46. Brussels: Algemeen Rijksarchief, 1994.

Sanders, Ernest H. "Cantilena (i)." *NG*, vol. III, 729–31.

    "Cantilena and Discant in 14th-Century England." *Musica Disciplina* 19 (1965): 7–52.

    "Discant, II: English." *NG*, vol. V, 492–4.

    "The Medieval Motet." In *Gattungen der Musik in Einzeldarstellung: Gedenkschrift Leo Schrade*, ed. Wulf Arlt and Ernst Lichtenhahn, 497–573. Bern: Francke Verlag, 1973.

    "Motet: I: Medieval." *NG*, vol. XII, 617–28.

Saunders, Suparmi Elizabeth. *The Dating of the Trent Codices from their Watermarks, with a Study of the Local Liturgy of Trent in the Fifteenth Century*. New York and London: Garland, 1989.

    "The Dating of Trent 93 and Trent 90." In *I codici musicali trentini a cento anni dalla loro riscoperta: Atti del Convegno Laurence Feininger, la musicologia come missione*, Trent, 6–7 September 1985, ed. Nino Pirrotta and Danilo Curti, 60–82. Trent: Provincia Autonoma di Trento, Servizio Beni Culturali, 1986.

Saville-Troike, Muriel. *The Ethnography of Communication*. Oxford: Basil Blackwell, 1982.

Schoop, Hans. "Lantins, de (4) Arnold; (5) Hugo." *NG*, vol. X, 457–8.

Schrade, Leo. "Political Compositions in French Music of the Twelfth and Thirteenth Centuries: The Coronation of French Kings." In Leo Schrade, *De Scientia Musicae Studia atque Orationes*, ed. Ernst Lichtenhahn, 152–211. Bern and Stuttgart: Paul Haupt, 1967. Originally published in *Annales Musicologiques* 1 (1953): 9–63.

Schroeder, Eunice. "The Stroke Comes Full Circle: Ø and ₵ in Writings on Music, ca. 1450–1540." *Musica Disciplina* 36 (1982): 119–66.

Schuler, Manfred. "Die Musik in Konstanz während des Konzils, 1414–1418." *Acta Musicologica* 38 (1966): 150–68.

    "Zur Geschichte der Kapelle Papst Eugens IV." *Acta musicologica* 60 (1968): 220–7.

    "Zur Geschichte der Kapelle Papst Martins V." *Archiv für Musikwissenschaft* 25 (1968): 30–45.

Self, Stephen. *The 'Si Placet' Repertoire of 1480–1530*. Recent Researches in the Music of the Renaissance 106. Madison: A-R Editions, 1996.

Snow, Robert. "The Mass-Motet Cycle: A Mid-Fifteenth-Century Experiment." In *Essays in Musicology in Honor of Dragan Plamenac on his 70th Birthday*, ed. Gustave Reese and Robert J. Snow, 301–20. Pittsburgh: University of Pittsburgh Press, 1969.

    "The Manuscript Strahov D.G.IV.47." Ph.D. dissertation, University of Illinois, 1968.

Sober, Elliott, ed. *Conceptual Issues in Evolutionary Biology*. Cambridge, Mass.: MIT Press, 1984.

Sparks, Edgar H. *Cantus Firmus in Mass and Motet, 1420–1520*. Berkeley and Los Angeles: University of California Press, 1963.

Spilsted, Gary. "The Paleography and Musical Repertory of Codex Tridentinus 93." Ph.D. dissertation, Harvard University, 1982.

    "Toward the Genesis of the Trent Codices: New Directions and New Findings." *Studies in Music from the University of Western Ontario* 1 (1976): 54–70.

Stäblein-Harder, Hannah. *Fourteenth-Century Mass Music in France*. Musicological Studies and Documents 7. N.p.: American Institute of Musicology, 1962.

Staehelin, Martin. "Mehrstimmige Repertoires im 14. und 15. Jahrhundert: Das Problem der verlorenen Quellen." In Angelo Pompilio, *et al.*, eds. *Trasmissione e recezione delle forme di cultura musicale. Atti del XIV Congresso della Società Internazionale di Musicologia*, vol. I, 153–9. Turin: EDT, 1990.

Starr, Pamela F. "The 'Ferrara Connection': A Case Study of Musical Recruitment in the Renaissance," *Studi Musicali* 18 (1989): 3–17.

"Letter to the Editors." *Plainsong and Medieval Music* 1 (1992): 215–16. [On Brassart and Sarto.]

"Music and Music Patronage at the Papal Court, 1447–1464." Ph.D. dissertation, Yale University, 1987.

"Rome as the Centre of the Universe: Papal Grace and Music Patronage." *Early Music History* 11 (1992): 223–62.

Steiner, Ruth. "Marian Antiphons at Cluny and Lewes." In *Music in the Medieval English Liturgy: Plainsong and Mediaeval Music Society Centennial Essays*, ed. Susan Rankin and David Hiley, 175–204. Oxford: Clarendon Press, 1993.

"Some Monophonic Latin Songs Composed around 1200." *Musical Quarterly* 52 (1966): 56–70.

Stephan, Wolfgang. *Die Burgundisch-Niederländische Motette zur Zeit Ockeghems*. Kassel: Bärenreiter, 1937; repr. 1973.

Stevens, John. *Music and Poetry in the Early Tudor Court*. London: Methuen, 1961; rev. ed., 1979.

Strohm, Reinhard. "Einheit und Funktion früher Messzyklen." In *Festschrift Rudolf Bockholdt zum 60. Geburtstag*, ed. N. Dubowy and S. Meyer-Eller, 141–60. Pfaffenhofen: Ludwig, 1990.

"European Politics and the Distribution of Music in the Early Fifteenth Century." *Early Music History* 1 (1981): 305–23.

"Introduction" to the Round Table "Costituzione e conservazione dei repertorii polifonici nei secoli XIV e XV." In Angelo Pompilio, *et al.*, eds. *Trasmissione e recezione delle forme di cultura musicale. Atti del XIV Congresso della Società Internazionale di Musicologia*, vol. I, 93–6. Turin: EDT, 1990. The whole session (pp. 97–184) has contributions by Wulf Arlt, John Nádas, Margaret Bent, Martin Staehelin, Jaromír Cerný, Kurt von Fischer, and Miroslaw Perz.

"Messzyklen über deutsche Lieder in den Trienter Codices." In *Liedstudien: Festschrift für Wolfgang Osthoff zum 60. Geburtstag*, ed. Martin Just and Reinhard Wiesend, 77–106. Tutzing: Schneider, 1989.

Music in Late Medieval Bruges. Oxford: Clarendon Press, 1985; rev. ed., 1990.

"Quellenkritische Untersuchungen und der Missa 'Caput'." In *Quellenstudien zur Musik der Renaissance II: Datierung und Filiation von Musikhandschriften der Josquin-Zeit*, ed. Ludwig Finscher, 153–76. Wölfenbütteler Forschungen 26. Wiesbaden: Harrasowitz, 1982.

Review of Lewis Lockwood, *Music in Renaissance Ferrara, 1400–1505. Music and Letters* 67 (1986): 283–6.

The Rise of European Music, 1380–1500. Cambridge: Cambridge University Press, 1993. [*REM*]

Summers, William J. "The Effect of Monasticism on Fourteenth-Century English Music." In *Actes du XIIIe congrès de la Société Internationale de Musicologie: La musique et le rite sacré et profane*, ed. Marc Honneger and Paul Prevost, vol. II, 104–42. Strasbourg: Association des Publications près les Universités de Strasbourg, 1986.

"Fourteenth-Century English Music: A Review of Three Recent Publications." *Journal of Musicology* 8 (1990): 118–41.

Swales, John M. *Genre Analysis: English in Academic and Research Settings.* Cambridge Applied Linguistics. Cambridge: Cambridge University Press, 1990.

Taruskin, Richard, ed. *Antoine Busnoys: Collected Works,* Parts 2 & 3: *The Latin Texted Works.* Masters and Monuments of the Renaissance 5. New York: The Broude Trust, 1990.

Taylor, John R. *Linguistic Categorization: Prototypes in Linguistic Theory.* Oxford: Clarendon Press, 1989.

Tees, Miriam. "Chronology and Style in the Laborde Chansonnier." Unpublished M.A. thesis, McGill University, 1995.

Tinctoris, Johannes. *Dictionary of Musical Terms (Terminorum Musicae Diffinitorium).* Edited and translated by Carl Parrish. London: The Free Press of Glencoe, 1963.

    Liber de arte Contrapuncti. Trans. Albert Seay. Musicological Studies and Documents 5. N.p.: American Institute of Musicology, 1961.

    Theoretical Works. 2 vols. Corpus Scriptorum de Musica 22. N.p.: American Institute of Musicology, 1975.

Tischler, Hans. "A Three-Part Rondellus in Trent MS 87." *Journal of the American Musicological Society* 24 (1971): 449–57.

Trent Codices, facsimile ed. *Codex Tridentinus* 87–93. 7 vols. Rome: Bibliopola, Vivarelli & Gullà, 1970.

Trowell, Brian. "Frye, Walter." *NG,* vol. VI, 876–9.

    "Proportion in the Music of Dunstable," *Proceedings of the Royal Musical Association* 105 (1978–9): 100–41.

Trowell, Brian, ed. *John Plummer: Four Motets.* Banbury: Plainsong and Medieval Society, 1968.

Trumble, Ernest. *Fauxbourdon: An Historical Survey.* Musicological Studies 3. Brooklyn: Institute of Medieval Music, 1959.

Turner, Charles. "Proportion and Form in the Continental Isorhythmic Motet c. 1385–1450." *Music Analysis* 10 (1991): 89–124.

Ugolinus Urbevetanus. *Declaratio musicae disciplinae,* 3 vols. Ed. Albert Seay. Corpus Scriptorum de Musica 7. Rome: American Institute of Musicology, 1959–62.

Van, Guillaume de. "Inventory of Manuscript Bologna Liceo Musicale, Q15 (olim 37)." *Musica Disciplina* 2 (1948): 231–57.

Wackernagel, Bettina, ed. *Das Liederbuch des Dr. Hartmann Schedel* [facsimile]. Das Erbe deutsche Musik 84. Kassel: Bärenreiter, 1978.

Ward, Tom R. *The Polyphonic Office Hymn, 1400–1520: A Descriptive Catalogue.* Renaissance Manuscript Studies, no. 3. American Institute of Musicology: Hänssler-Verlag, 1980.

    "A Central European Repertory in Munich, Bayerische Staatsbibliothek, MS Clm 14274." *Early Music History* 1 (1981): 325–43.

    "The Office Hymns of the Trent Manuscripts." In *I codici musicali trentini a cento anni dalla loro riscoperta: Atti del Convegno Laurence Feininger, la musicologia come missione,* Trent, 6–7 September 1985, ed. Nino Pirrotta and Danilo Curti, 112–29. Trent: Provincia Autonoma di Trento, Servizio Beni Culturali, 1986.

    "The Structure of the Manuscript Trent 92–I." *Musica Disciplina* 29 (1975): 127–47.

    "Touront [Tauranth], Johannes." *NG,* vol. XIX, 99.

Warren, Charles W. "Punctus Organi and Cantus Coronatus in the Music of Dufay." In *Papers Read at the Dufay Quincentenary Conference, Brooklyn College, December 6–7, 1974*, ed. Alan W. Atlas, 128–43. Brooklyn: Brooklyn College, 1976.

Wathey, Andrew. "Dunstable in France." *Music and Letters* 67 (1986): 1–36.

"The Peace of 1360–1369 and Anglo-French Musical Relations." *Early Music History* 9 (1990): 129–74.

"The Motets of Philippe de Vitry and the Fourteenth-Century Renaissance." *Early Music History* 12 (1993): 119–50.

Wegman, Rob C. "An Anonymous Twin of Johannes Ockegem's Missa Quinti Toni in San Pietro B 80." *Tijdschrift van de Vereniging voor Nederlandse Muziekgeschiedenis* 37 (1987): 25–48.

"Petrus de Domarto's *Missa Spiritus almus* and the Early History of the Four-Voice Mass in the Fifteenth Century." *Early Music History* 10 (1991): 235–303.

"What is 'acceleratio mensurae'?" *Music and Letters* 73 (1992): 515–24.

Weiner, Jonathan. *The Beak of the Finch: A Story of Evolution in our Time.* New York: Alfred A. Knopf, Inc., 1994.

Weiss, Susan Forscher. "Bologna Q18: Some Reflections on Content and Context." *Journal of the American Musicological Society* 41 (1988): 63–101.

Welker, Lorenz. "New Light on Oswald von Wolkenstein: Central European Traditions and Burgundian Polyphony." *Early Music History* 7 (1989): 187–226.

Wellek, René. "The Concept of Evolution in Literary History." In Wellek, *Concepts of Criticism*, 37–53. New Haven: Yale University Press, 1973.

White, Richard James. "The Battre Section of Trent Codex 87." 2 vols. Ph.D. dissertation, Indiana University, 1975.

Widaman, Jean. "The Mass Ordinary Settings of Arnold de Lantins: A Case Study in the Transmission of Early Fifteenth-Century Music." 2 vols. Ph.D. dissertation, Brandeis University, 1987.

Wittgenstein, Ludwig. *Philosophical Investigations.* Translated by G. E. M. Anscombe. Oxford: Blackwell, 1953.

Wright, Craig. "Dufay at Cambrai: Discoveries and Revisions." *Journal of the American Musicological Society* 28 (1975): 175–229.

Music and Ceremony at Notre Dame of Paris, 500–1550. Cambridge: Cambridge University Press, 1989.

Wright, Peter. "The Aosta-Trent Relationship Reconsidered." In *I codici musicali trentini a cento anni dalla loro riscoperta: Atti del Convegno Laurence Feininger, la musicologia come missione*, Trent, 6–7 September 1985, ed. Nino Pirrotta and Danilo Curti, 138–57. Trent: Provincia Autonoma di Trento, Servizio Beni Culturali, 1986.

"The Compilation of Trent 87–I and 92–II." *Early Music History* 2 (1982): 237–71.

"Johannes Brassart and Johannes de Sarto." *Plainsong and Medieval Music* 1 (1992): 46–61.

"On the Origins of Trent 87–I and 92–II." *Early Music History* 6 (1986): 245–70.

The Related Parts of Trent, Museo Provinciale d'Arte, MSS 87 (1374) and 92 (1379): A Paleographical and Text-Critical Study. New York and London: Garland, 1989.

"Paper Evidence and the Dating of Trent 91." *Music and Letters* 76 (1995): 487–508, plates I–VI.

Modern editions of music

Abbreviations correspond to those in the Index of works and in the musical examples.

Allsen = J. Michael Allsen. "Style and Intertextuality in the Isorhythmic Motet 1400–1440." Ph.D. dissertation, University of Wisconsin, Madison, 1992.

AllsenInt = J. Michael Allsen. "Intertextuality and Compositional Process in Two Cantilena Motets by Hugo de Lantins." *Journal of Musicology* 11 (1993): 174–202.

AMMM 12 = Benvenuto Disertori, ed. *Johannes Martini: Magnificat e Messe.* Archivium Musices Metropolitanum Mediolanense 12. Milan: Veneranda fabbrica del duomo di Milano, 1964.

Binchois = Philip Kaye, ed. *The Sacred Music of Gilles Binchois.* Oxford: Oxford University Press, 1992.

Brassart = Keith Mixter, ed. *Johannes Brassart: Opera Omnia.* Vol. II, Motets. Corpus Mensurabilis Musicae 35. N.p.: American Institute of Musicology, 1971.

Burstyn = Shai Burstyn. "Fifteenth-Century Polyphonic Settings of Verses from the Song of Songs." Ph.D. dissertation, Columbia University, 1972.

Busnoys = Richard Taruskin, ed. *Antoine Busnoys: Collected Works*, Parts 2 & 3: *The Latin Texted Works.* Masters and Monuments of the Renaissance 5. New York: The Broude Trust, 1990.

Cantilupe = Brian Trowell and Andrew Wathey. "John Benet's 'Lux fulget ex Anglia – O pater pietatis – Salve Thoma': The Reconstruction of a Fragmentary Fifteenth-Century Motet in Honour of St. Thomas Cantilupe." In *St. Thomas Cantilupe, Bishop of Hereford: Essays in his Honour*, ed. Meryl Jancey, 159–80. Hereford, 1982.

Cattin = Giulio Cattin. "Virgo Mater Ecclesiae: Un tropo alla Salve regina nelle fonti mono-diche e polifoniche dei sec. XIV-XV." In *L'Ars nova italiana del trecento*, vol. IV: 149–76. Certaldo: Comune di Certaldo, 1978.

Ciconia = Margaret Bent and Anne Hallmark, eds. *The Works of Johannes Ciconia.* Polyphonic Music of the Fourteenth Century 24. Monaco: L'Oiseau-Lyre, 1985.

Clercx = Suzanne Clercx. *Johannes Ciconia: un musicien liégeois et son temps (vers 1335–1411).* 2 vols. Brussels: Palais des Academies, 1960.

Compère = Ludwig Finscher, ed. *Loyset Compère: Opera Omnia*, vol. IV. Corpus Mensurabilis Musicae 15. Rome: American Institute of Musicology, 1961.

374

Cox = Bobby Wayne Cox. "The Motets of MS Bologna, Civico Museo Bibliografico Musicale, Q15." 2 vols. Ph.D. dissertation, North Texas State University, 1977.

CoxPseudo = Bobby Wayne Cox. "'Pseudo-Augmentation' in the Manuscript Bologna, Civico Museo Bibliografico Musicale, Q 15 (BL)." *Journal of Musicology* 1 (1982): 419–48.

Disertori = B. Disertori. "L'epistola all'Italia del Petrarca musicata nei codici tridentini." *Rivista Musicale Italiana* 46 (1942): 65–78.

DPLSER I = Laurence K. J. Feininger, ed. Documenta polyphoniae liturgicae sanctae ecclesiae romanae, Ser. I.A (Ordinarium missae), no. 2. Lionel Power, *Missa super Alma redemptoris mater*. Rome: Societas Universalis Sanctae Ceciliae, 1950.

DPLSER IV = Laurence K. J. Feininger, ed. Documenta polyphoniae liturgicae sanctae ecclesiae romanae, Ser. IV (Motecta), no. 1. Standley, *Quae est ista (Fuga reservata)*. Rome: Societas Universalis Sanctae Ceciliae, 1947.

DTÖ 14 = Guido Adler and Oswald Koller, eds. *Sechs Trienter Codices. Geistliche und Weltliche Compositionen des XV. Jahrhunderts*. Erste Auswahl. Denkmäler der Tonkunst in Österreich Jg. 7, vols. 14–15. Vienna: Artaria, 1900. Repr. Graz: Akademische Druck- und Verlaganstalt, 1959. Includes inventory of Trent 87–92.

DTÖ 22 = Guido Adler and Oswald Koller, eds. *Sechs Trienter Codices. Geistliche und Weltliche Compositionen des XV. Jahrhunderts*. Zweite Auswahl. Denkmäler der Tonkunst in Österreich Jg. 11, vol. 22. Vienna: Artaria, 1904. Repr. Graz: Akademische Druck- und Verlaganstalt, 1959.

DTÖ 53 = Rudolf Ficker and Alfred Orel, eds. *Sechs Trienter Codices. Geistliche und weltliche Compositionen des XV. Jahrhunderts*. Vierte Auswahl. Denkmäler der Tonkunst in Österreich, Jg. 27, vol. 53. Vienna: Universal Edition, 1920. Repr. Graz: Akademische Druck- und Verlaganstalt, 1959.

DTÖ 61 = Rudolf von Ficker, ed. *Sieben Trienter Codices. Geistliche und weltliche Compositionen des XIV. und XV. Jahrhunderts*. Fünfte Auswahl. Denkmäler der Tonkunst in Österreich, Jg. 31, vol. 61. Vienna: Universal Edition, 1933. Includes inventory of Trent 93.

DTÖ 76 = Rudolf von Ficker, ed. *Sieben Trienter Codices. Geistliche und weltliche Compositionen des XIV. und XV. Jahrhunderts*. Sechste Auswahl. Denkmäler der Tonkunst in Österreich, Jg. 40, vol. 76. Vienna: Universal Edition, 1933.

DufayB = Heinrich Besseler, ed. *Guillaume Dufay, Opera Omnia*. 6 vols. Corpus Mensurabilis Musicae 1. Rome: American Institute of Musicology, 1951–66.

DufayV = Guillaume de Van, ed. *Guglielmi Dufay: Opera Omnia*. 4 fascicles. Corpus Mensurabilis Musicae 1. Rome: American Institute of Musicology, 1947–9.

Dunstable = Manfred Bukofzer, ed. *John Dunstable, Complete Works*. 2nd ed., revised by Margaret Bent, Ian Bent and Brian Trowell. Musica Britannica 8. London: Stainer and Bell, 1970.

EDM 33 = Rudolf Gerber, Ludwig Finscher, and Wolfgang Dömling, eds. *Der Mensuralkodex des Nikolaus Apel (Ms. 1494 der Universitätsbibliothek Leipzig)*. 3 vols. Das Erbe deutscher Musik 32–4. Kassel: Bärenreiter, 1956–75.

EDM 37–9 = Bertha Antonia Wallner, ed. *Das Buxheimer Orgelbuch*. 3 vols. Das Erbe deutscher Musik 37–9. Kassel: Bärenreiter, 1959.

EDM 80–3 = Thomas Noblitt, ed. *Munich, Staatsbibliothek, Mus. Ms. 3154*. Das Erbe deutscher Musik 80–3. Kassel: Bärenreiter, 1987–96.

Modern editions of music

EDM 85–6 = Christian Väterlein, ed. *Das Glogauer Liederbuch.* Das Erbe deutscher Musik 85–6. Kassel: Bärenreiter, 1981.

EECM 8 = Andrew Hughes, ed. *Fifteenth-Century Liturgical Music I: Antiphons and Music for Holy Week and Easter.* Early English Church Music 8. London: Stainer and Bell, 1964.

EECM 34 = Gareth Curtis, ed. *Fifteenth-Century Liturgical Music III: The Brussels Masses.* Early English Church Music 34. London: Stainer and Bell, 1989.

Etheridge = Jerry Haller Etheridge. "The Works of Johannes de Limburgia." Ph.D. dissertation, Indiana University, 1972.

Ex. = Complete pieces found as musical examples in this book. Long but incomplete excerpts are marked with an asterisk ("Ex. 12.5*").

Frye = Sylvia Kenney, ed. *Collected Works of Walter Frye.* Corpus Mensurabilis Musicae 19. Rome: American Institute of Musicology, 1960.

Gerber = Rebecca Lynn Gerber. "The Manuscript Trent, Castello del Buonconsiglio, 88: A Study of Fifteenth-Century Manuscript Transmission and Repertory." Ph.D. dissertation, University of California, Santa Barbara, 1985.

Gozzi = Marco Gozzi. *Il manoscritto Trento Museo Provinciale d'Arte, cod. 1377 (Tr 90) con un'analisi del repertorio non derivato da Tr 93.* 2 vols. Cremona Studi e testi musicali 1. Cremona: Centro di Musicologia "Walter Stauffer," 1992.

Günther = Ursula Günther, ed. *The Motets of the Manuscripts Chantilly, Musée Condé, 564 (olim 1047) and Modena, Biblioteca Estense, αM.5,24 (olim lat. 568).* Corpus Mensurabilis Musicae 39. N.p.: American Institute of Musicology, 1965.

Hüschen = Heinrich Hüschen, ed. *The Motet.* Anthology of Music 47. Cologne: Arno Volk, 1937.

Igoe = James T. Igoe. "Johannes Franchois de Gembloux." *Nuova rivista musicale italiana* 4 (1970): 3–50.

IMM 3 = Brian Trowell, ed. *Music of the Mid-Fifteenth Century (i).* Invitation to Medieval Music 3. London: Stainer and Bell, 1976.

Lewis = Ann Lewis, ed. *Johannes de Lymburgia: Four Motets, The Song of Songs.* Antico Church Music RCM 3. Newton Abbot: Antico Edition, 1985.

Loyan = Richard Loyan, ed. *Canons in the Trent Codices.* Corpus Mensurabilis Musicae 38. N.p.: American Institute of Musicology, 1967.

Marix = Jeanne Marix, ed. *Les musiciens de la cour de Bourgogne au XVe siècle.* Paris: L'Oiseau Lyre, 1937.

Marrocco = W. Thomas Marrocco and Nicholas Sandon, eds. *The Oxford Anthology of Music: Medieval Music.* London: Oxford University Press, 1977.

MC = Isabel Pope and Masakata Kanazawa. *The Music Manuscript Montecassino 871: A Neapolitan Repertory of Sacred and Secular Music of the Late Fifteenth Century.* Oxford: Clarendon Press, 1978.

MPLSER = Laurence K. J. Feininger, ed. *Missae auctore Gulielmo Dufay cum missis anonimis.* Monumenta polyphoniae liturgicae sanctae ecclesiae romanae, Ser. 1, Tome II. Rome: Societas Universalis Sanctae Ceciliae, 1951–63.

Nosow = Robert Nosow. "The Florid and Equal-Discantus Motet Styles of Fifteenth-Century Italy." Ph.D. dissertation, University of North Carolina, Chapel Hill, 1992.

NosowEqual = Robert Nosow. "The Equal-Discantus Motet Style After Ciconia." *Musica Disciplina* 45 (1991): 221–75.

OH = Margaret Bent and Andrew Hughes, eds. *The Old Hall Manuscript.* 3 vols. Corpus Mensurabilis Musicae 46. Rome: American Institute of Musicology, 1969–73.

Plamenac = Dragan Plamenac. "Another Paduan Fragment of Trecento Music." *Journal of the American Musicological Society* 8 (1955): 165–81.

Planchart = Alejandro Enrique Planchart, ed. *Missae Caput.* Collegium Musicum 5. New Haven and London: Yale University Press, 1964.

Plummer = Brian Trowell, ed. *Four Motets by John Plummer.* Banbury: Plainsong and Mediaeval Music Society, The Piers Press, 1968.

PMFC 5 = Frank Llewellyn Harrison, ed. *Motets of French Provenance.* Texts, with commentary by A. G. Rigg, in a supplementary pamphlet. Polyphonic Music of the Fourteenth Century 5. Monaco: L'Oiseau Lyre, 1968.

Power = Charles Hamm, ed. *Leonel Power: Complete Works*, I, *The Motets.* Corpus Mensurabilis Musicae 50. Rome: American Institute of Musicology, 1969.

PowerMass = Gareth Curtis, ed. *Lionel Power: Mass, Alma redemptoris mater.* Newton Abbot: Antico, 1982.

PS = Charles van den Borren, ed. *Polyphonia Sacra.* London: The Plainsong and Mediaeval Music Society, 1932.

Pullois = Peter Gülke, ed., *Johannes Pullois: Opera omnia.* Corpus Mensurabilis Musicae 41. Rome: American Institute of Musicology, 1967.

Quadris = Giulio Cattin, ed. *Johannes de Quadris: Opera.* Antiquae Musicae Italicae Monumenta Veneta. Bologna: A.M.I.S., 1972.

Reaney = Gilbert Reaney, ed. *Early Fifteenth-Century Music.* 7 vols. Corpus Mensurabilis Musicae 11. N.p.: American Institute of Musicology, 1955–83.

REM = Reinhard Strohm. *The Rise of European Music, 1380–1500.* Cambridge: Cambridge University Press, 1993.

Romano = F. Alberto Gallo, ed. *Antonii Romani Opera.* Antiquae Musicae Italicae: Monumenta Veneta Sacra 1. Bologna: Università degli studi di Bologna, 1965.

Schering = Arnold Schering, ed. *Geschichte der Musik in Beispielen.* Leipzig: Breitkopf und Härtel, 1931; repr. New York: Broude Brothers, 1959.

Scott = Ann Besser Scott. "Ibo michi ad montem mirre – A New Motet by Plummer?" *Musical Quarterly* 58 (1972): 543–56.

Self = Stephen Self, ed. *The 'Si placet' Repertoire of 1480–1530.* Recent Researches in the Music of the Renaissance 106. Madison: A-R Editions, 1996.

Smijers = Albert A. Smijers, ed. *Van Ockeghem tot Sweelinck.* Nederlandse Muziekgeschiedenis in Voorbeelden, fasc. 1. Amsterdam: G. Alsbach, 1939; 2nd ed., 1952.

Snow = Robert Snow. "The Manuscript Strahov D.G.IV.47." Ph.D. dissertation, University of Illinois, 1968.

SnowCycle = Robert Snow. "The Mass-Motet Cycle: A Mid-Fifteenth-Century Experiment." In *Essays in Musicology in Honor of Dragan Plamenac on his 70th Birthday*, ed. Gustave Reese and Robert J. Snow, 301–20. Pittsburgh: University of Pittsburgh Press, 1969.

Stevens = Denis Stevens. "Petrarch's Greeting to Italy." *Musical Times* 115 (1974): 834–6. Musical supplement.

StrohmB = Reinhard Strohm. *Music in Late Medieval Bruges.* Oxford: Clarendon Press, 1985; revised ed., 1990.

Modern editions of music

Vicenza = F. Alberto Gallo and Giovanni Mantese. *Richerche sulle origini della cappella musicale del duomo di Vicenza.* Civiltà veneziana saggi, 15. Venice: Istituto per la collaborazione culturale Venezia–Roma, 1964.

Vincenet = Bertran E. Davis, ed. *The Collected Works of Vincenet.* Recent Researches in the Music of the Middle Ages and Early Renaissance 9–10. Madison: A-R Editions, 1978.

Widaman = Jean Widaman. "The Mass Ordinary Settings of Arnold de Lantins: A Case Study in the Transmission of Early Fifteenth-Century Music." Ph.D. dissertation, Brandeis University, 1987.

Sources and sigla

87–92, or Trent 87–92 = Trent, Castello del Buon Consiglio, Monumenti e Collezioni Provinciali (olim Museo Provinciale d'Arte) MSS 1374–79 (olim MSS 87–92).

93, or Trent 93 = Trent, Archivio Capitolare, MS 93

87–1 = the first part of Trent 87 (fols. 1–218, including 87.1–162)

87–2 = the second part (Battre section) of Trent 87 (fols. 219–65, including 87.163–98)

92–1 (simply 92 in the Index) = the first part of Trent 92 (fols. 1–143, including 92.1365–1509)

922 or 92–2 = the second part of 92 (fols. 144–62, including 922.1510–85)

TR+ = 87–1, 92–1 and 92–2.

  When followed by a period and another number ("87.100") the number after the period is the one assigned to the piece in the inventory of the Trent Codices published in *DTÖ* 14 (for 87–92) and 61 (for 93).

Antwerp = Antwerp, Museum Plantin-Moretus, MS M6

Aosta, or Ao = Aosta, Biblioteca del Seminario maggiore, A¹ D19

Apel, or Apel Codex = Leipzig, Universitätsbibliothek, MS 1494

B2216, or Bologna 2216 = Bologna, Biblioteca Universitaria, MS 2216

BerK = Berlin, Staatliche Museen, Kupferstichkabinett, MS 78.C.28 (olim Hamilton 451)

Berlin 40021 = Berlin, Deutsche Staatsbibliothek (formerly Staatsbibliothek Preussischer Kulturbesitz), MS mus. 40021 (olim Z21)

Bol Q16 = Bologna, Civico Museo Bibliografico Musicale, MS Q16 (olim 143)

Bologna Q15 = *see* Q15, below

Br 5557 = Brussels, Bibliothèque Royale de Belgique, MS 5557

Brat 33 = Bratislava, Miestne Pracovisko Matice Slovenskej MS Inc. 33

Bux, or Buxheim = Munich, Bayerische Staatsbibliothek, Mus. MS 3192 (olim Cod. gall. 902; Buxheim Orgelbuch)

Breslau 2016 = Warsaw, Biblioteka Uniwersytecka, Oddzial Zbiorów Myzychniych, MS Mf. 2016 (olim Rps. mus. 58)

Brussels 9126 = Brussels, Bibliothèque Royale de Belgique, MS 9126

Cant 128 = Canterbury Cathedral Library, MS Add. 128

Canti C = *Canti C no. cento cinquanta*. Venice: Ottaviano dei Petrucci, 1504 (RISM 1504³)

Sources and sigla

Cas = Rome, Biblioteca Casanatense, MS 2856 (Casanatense Chansonnier)

Chantilly = Chantilly, Musée Condé, MS 564 (olim 1047)

Chigi = Rome, Biblioteca Vaticana, Chigiana C.VIII.234

Columbia = New York, Columbia University, Smith Western MS Add. 21

Cop 17 = Copenhagen, Det Kongelige Bibliotek, MS fragment 17 a (olim Musikhistorisk Museum 598)

Coventry = Coventry, City Record Office, MS A3

CS 15, 35, 44, 63 = Vatican City, Biblioteca Apostolica Vaticana, Archivio della Capella Sistina MSS 15, 35, 44, 63

Del Lago = Letter by Giovanni del Lago to Giovanni Spataro, Venice, 15 August 1533. Ed. and trans. in Bonnie J. Blackburn, Edward E. Lowinsky, and Clement Miller, eds., *A Correspondence of Renaissance Musicians* (Oxford: Oxford University Press, 1991), 653–64.

Dijon 2837 = Dijon, Bibliothèque publique, MS 2837

Eg = London, British Library, Egerton MS 3307

F112bis = Florence, Biblioteca Nazionale Centrale, MS Magliabechi XIX, 112bis

F2211 = Florence, Archivio Capitolare San Lorenzo, MS 2211

F2356 = Florence, Biblioteca Riccardiana, MS 2356

F2794 = Florence, Biblioteca Riccardiana, MS 2794

FPanc = Florence, Biblioteca Nazionale Centrale, MS Panc. 26

Gaffurius = Gaffurius, *Tractatus practicabilium proportionum* (*c.* 1482). See Clement A. Miller, "Early Gaffuriana: New Answers to Old Questions," *Musical Quarterly* 56 (1970): 367–88.

Glog, or Glogauer = Berlin, Deutsche Staatsbibliothek, Mus. MS 40098 (Glogauer Liederbuch)

Ithaca = Ithaca, Cornell University Library, MSS Rare BX C30 O635 (Ferrara fragments)

Krakow 8a = Kraków, Biblioteka Jagiellońska, MS 8a

Lab = Washington (D.C.), Library of Congress, MS M 2.1.L 25 (Case) (Laborde Chansonnier)

Lausanne = Lausanne, Bibliothèque Cantonale et Universitaire, MS A e 15

Lo 54324 = London, British Library, MS Add. 54324

Lo 5665 = London, British Library, MS Add. 5665

Lucca = Lucca, Archivio di Stato, MS 238

Maidstone = Maidstone, Kent Archives Office, PRC 50/5 (olim 49)

MC, or Montecassino = Montecassino, Biblioteca dell' Abbazia, MS 871

Milan 1, 2, 3, and 4 = Milan, Archivo della Veneranda Fabbrica del Duomo, Sezione Musicale, Librone 1 (olim 2269), Librone 2 (olim 2268), Librone 3 (olim 2267), Librone 4 (olim 2266) (Gaffurius Codices)

Milan 49 = Milan, Biblioteca Nazionale Braidense, MS AD.XIV.49

Mod, or Modena X.1.11 = Modena, Biblioteca estense, MS α. X.1.11 (olim lat. 471)

ModD = Modena, Biblioteca estense, MS α. M.1.13 (olim lat. 456)

Motetti A = *Motetti A numero trentatre A.* Venice: Ottaviano dei Petrucci, 1502 (RISM 1502[1])

Mu 3154, or Munich 3154 = Munich, Bayerische Staatsbibliothek, Mus. MS 3154 (Leopold Codex)

Mu 3224 = Munich, Bayerische Staatsbibliothek, Mus. MS 3224

Mu 5023 = Munich, Bayerische Staatsbibliothek, Clm 5023

MuEm = Munich, Bayerische Staatsbibliothek, Clm 14274 (olim Mus. 3232a)

Ob26 = Oxford, Bodleian Library, MS Archivum Seldenianum B.26

Oc87 = Oxford, Bodleian Library, MS Add. C 87

OH, or Old Hall = London, British Library MS Add. 57950 (olim Old Hall Green, St. Edmunds College Library, MS without shelf no.)

Olc89 = Oxford, Lincoln College, Latin 89

Olc124 = Oxford, Lincoln College, Latin 124

Ouc16 = Oxford, Bodleian Library, MS University College 16

Ox 213, or Oxford 213 = Oxford, Bodleian Library, MS Canonici Misc. 213

PadB = Padua, Biblioteca Universitaria, MS 1115

PadD = Padua, Biblioteca Universitaria, MS 1106

Par 4379 = Paris, Bibliothèque Nationale, Département des Manuscrits, Nouvelles Acquisitions Françaises, MS 4379, part III

Paris 676 = Paris, Bibliothèque Nationale, Département de Musique, Réserve Vm7, MS 676

Pemb = Cambridge, University Library, MS Pembroke 314 (olim Incunab. C 47)

Per 431 = Perugia, Biblioteca comunale augusta, MS 431 (olim G. 20)

Pix = Paris, Bibliothèque nationale, fonds français, MS 15123 (Pixérécourt chansonnier)

Poz7022 = Poznań, Biblioteka Uniwersytecka, MS 7022 (Lwów fragments)

Q15, or Bologna Q15 = Bologna, Civico Museo Bibliografico Musicale, MS Q15
When followed by a period and a number (Q15.274) the reference is to the number in the second column of Guillaume de Van's "Inventory of Manuscript Bologna Liceo Musicale, Q15 (olim 37)," *Musica Disciplina* 2 (1948): 231–57. This is also the numbering system used by Cox.

Sched, or Schedel = Munich, Bayerisches Staatsbibliothek, Cgm 810 (olim Mus. MS 3232; Cim. 351a; Schedelsches Liederbuch)

SevP = Seville, Biblioteca Capitular y Colombina, MS 5–1–43 and Paris, Bibliothèque nationale, nouv. acq. fr., MS 4379, part I

Siena = Siena, Biblioteca Comunale degli Intronati, MS K.I.2.

Siena 36 = Siena, Biblioteca Comunale degli Intronati, MS L.V.36

SP B80, or San Pietro B80 = Vatican City, Biblioteca Apostolica Vaticana, MS San Pietro B 80

Spec, or Speciálník = Hradec Králové, Krajske Muzeum, MS II A 7 (Speciálník)

Str = Strasbourg, former Bibliothèque Municipale, MS 222 C. 22 (destroyed in 1870)

Strah, or Strahov = Prague, Památník Národního Písemnictví, MS D.G.IV.47 (Strahov Codex)

Trent 87–93 = see above, 87–92, 93

TR+ or TRplus = 87–1, 92–1 and 92–2

Ven = Venice, Biblioteca Nazionale Marciana, MS 7554 (olim Italiani IX, 145)

Verona 755, 757, 758 = Verona, Biblioteca Capitolare, MSS DCCLV, DCCLVII, DCCLVIII

Wolf = Wolfenbüttel, Herzog-August-Bibliothek, MS Guelf. 287 extravag. (Wolfenbüttel chansonnier)

Yox = Yoxford, private possession

Notes on the index of works

This index lists subgenre assignments, sources, and modern editions of the following (often overlapping) categories of pieces:

- All the motets listed by name in tables or text.
- All the pieces I have identified as motets in Bologna Q15, Modena X.1.11, and the Trent Codices (except for Trent 87–2).
- Selected works from other sources, if mentioned in the book.
- Masses related in some way to motets discussed in the book (all listed as "Missa . . .")
- Two Du Fay chansons discussed in chapter 5.

Works are listed in alphabetical order by title, *not* composer. I chose to sort by title because of the number of anonymous works and works with conflicting attributions; this sorting method also allows one to locate easily all the settings of a single text. For page references to individual works see the General index, where works are listed by composer, then title.

Abbreviations for subgenre identifications in the index of works

3-v T	Three-voice tenor motet
4-v ch par	Four-voice chant-paraphrase motet
4-v free	Four-voice freely composed motet
4-v song	Four-voice song motet

4-v T	Four-voice tenor motet
4-v T/chpar	Four-voice hybrid of the tenor and chant-paraphrase motet
5-v free	Five-voice freely composed motet
5-v T	Five-voice tenor motet
8-v T	Eight-voice tenor motet
Ballade	Ballade
Border 2v	Borderline motet with two voices
Borderline	Borderline motet with more than two voices
Canon Mass	Canonic Mass
Canon 3v (5v, 6v)	Canonic motet for three voices (five voices, six voices)
Ch ctfact?	Possible chanson contrafact
Cont cant	Continental cantilena
Ctfact Ag.	Contrafact Agnus Dei
Ctfact Gl.	Contrafact Gloria
Ctfact K?	Possible contrafact Kyrie
Cut-circle	Cut-circle motet
Declamation	Declamation motet
Dev D-D	Devotional double-discantus motet
Eng cant I	English cantilena, Band I (Dunstaple's generation)
Eng cant II	English cantilena, Band II (Plummer's generation)
Eng Iso	English isorhythmic motet, four voices
Eng Iso 3v	English isorhythmic motet, three voices
Iso	"French" (continental) isorhythmic motet, four voices
Iso 1D	Isorhythmic motet, continental, one discantus (i.e. the triplum is higher than the motetus)
Iso 3v	Isorhythmic motet, continental, three voices
Iso 5v	Isorhythmic motet, continental, five voices
Italian	Italian motet
Leise	Leise (German devotional song)
Mass	Cyclic Mass
Other D-D	Other double-discantus motet
Retro D-D	Retrospective double-discantus motet
Song motet	Song motet
Tenor Mass	Tenor Mass
Trans 4-v	Transitional four-voice motet
Trans 5-v	Transitional five-voice motet
Unus–chorus	Unus–chorus motet

Index of works

Title	Composer	Subgenre(s)	Sources	Editions
Ad honorem sancte	Grenon	Iso	Ox213 Q15.209	Cox PS Reaney VII
Adoretur beata	Anon.	5-v T	89.585	DTÖ 76
Advenisti/Advenit	Anon.	Cont cant	88.394	DTÖ 14
Advenisti: Venisti	Anon.	4-v T	88.452	DTÖ 14
Albane misse celitus	Ciconia	Italian	Q15.273	Ciconia Clercx Cox
Albanus/Quoque	Dunstaple	Eng Iso 3v	Mod 88′	Dunstable
Alma redemptoris	Dunstaple/Power/Binchois	Eng cant I	93.1828 Aosta Milan 49 Mod 134′ Q15.192	DTÖ 76 Dunstable Power
Alma redemptoris	Forest	Eng cant I	90.1052 Aosta Mod 94′ Q15.164	Burstyn DTÖ 53 Ex. 4.3
Alma redemptoris	Power/Dunstaple	Eng cant I	922.1524 Aosta Mod 100B	DTÖ 53 Dunstable Power
Alma redemptoris (I)	Du Fay	Cont cant	B2216 Q15.224	DufayB V
Alma redemptoris (II)	Du Fay	Cont cant Cut-circle	922.1532 Mod 57′	DufayB V
Alma redemptoris/ T: Et genitorem	Anon.	3-v T	91.1319 Apel Canti C	DTÖ 53 EDM 33
Altissimi Dei filio	Anon.	Ch ctfact?	90.989	Gozzi
Anima mea	Anon.	4-v free	89.640	Burstyn

Title	Composer	Subgenre(s)	Sources	Editions
Anima mea (*cont.*)		Eng cant II	90.1046–47	DTÖ 76
		Trans 4-v	Mu 3154	EDM 80
Anima mea	Du Fay	Cont cant	87.142	DTÖ 53
		Dev D-D	Ox 213	DufayB V
			Q15.235	
Anima mea (B)	Power	Eng cant I	Mod 110′	Power
Anima mea (A)	Power	Eng cant I	B2216	Power
			F112bis	
			Mod 117′	
			MuEm	
Anima mea/	Busnoys	3-v T	Br 5557	Busnoys
T: Stirps Jesse			CS 15	Smijers
Anna mater	Plummer	Eng cant II	Oc87	EECM 8
		Trans 4-v		Plummer
Apostolo glorioso	Du Fay	Iso 5v	Q15.237	Cox
				DTÖ 76
				DufayB I
				DufayV II
Ascendit Christus/	Forest/Dunstaple	3-v T	Mod 96′	DTÖ 76
T: Alma			OH	Dunstaple
				OH
Assit herus rex	Anon.	Ch ctfact?	89.601	—
Aurea flamigeri	Romanus	Italian	Q15.219	Cox
				Reaney VI
				Romano
Ave beatissima	Anon.	4-v T/chpar	89.728	—
				Ex. 12.5*
Ave gemma	Lantins, H. de	Dev D-D	Q15.207	Cox
				NosowEqual
Ave Maria/O Maria	Brassart	Iso	87.29	Brassart
			Q15.229	Cox
				DTÖ 14
Ave Maria gratia plena	Anon.	4-v T/chpar	91.1318	—
Ave mater nostri	Lymburgia	Cut-circle	Q15.265	Etheridge
Ave mater O Maria	Sarto, Johannes de	Cut-circle	922.1529	Cox
			Q15.182	Ex. 5.1
Ave mater pietatis	Anon.	Cut-circle	Q15.233	Cox
				Nosow
Ave mundi/Gottes namen	Anon.	8-v T	89.667	DTÖ 14
		Leise	Mu 3154	EDM 80
Ave regina celorum	Anon.	5-v free	89.567	—
			Lausanne	
Ave regina celorum	Dunstaple	Eng cant I	92.1449	DTÖ 76
			F112bis	Dunstable
			Mod 102′	
Ave regina celorum	Forest	Eng cant I	87.102	—
			Mod 118′	

Title	Composer	Subgenre(s)	Sources	Editions
Beata dei genitrix	Dunstaple/Binchois	Eng cant I	90.1048 Aosta Mod 133' MuEm Q15.289	DTÖ 76 Dunstable
Beata mater	Dunstaple/Binchois	Eng cant I	87.131 Aosta Mod 91 MuEm Ob26 Olc89	Binchois DTÖ 14 Dunstable EECM 8
Bene ad te coclea	Anon.	Ch ctfact?	93.1844	—
Benedicta es	De Anglia	Eng cant I	922.1531 B2216 Olc124 Q15.185	DTÖ 76 Power
Benedicta sit sancta	Anon.	Canon 6v	89.586	Loyan
Cantemus Domino/ T: Gaudent	Anon.	5-v T Trans 5-v	Eg	EECM 8
Carminibus festos	Romanus	Italian	Q15.206	Cox Reaney VI Romano
Caro mea vere est cibus	Rubeus	Italian	Q15.262	Reaney V
Castrum/Virgo/ T: Benedicamus	Merques	3-v T Cont cant	922.1539 Aosta	DTÖ 76
Christe sanctorum/ Tibi Christe	Dunstaple	Eng Iso 3v	Mod 95'	Dunstable
Christi nutu sublimato	Brassart	Other D-D	87.48 Aosta (2x) MuEm	Brassart
Christus Deus noster	Anon.	Ch ctfact?	93.1836	—
Compangant or O generosa	Touront	Song motet	89.579 91.1336 Bol Q16 Spec Strah	Ex. 9.2
Congruit mortalibus	Lymburgia	Cut-circle	Q15.187	Cox Etheridge
Crux fidelis	Dunstaple	Eng cant I	92.1504 Mod 97'	DTÖ 14 Dunstable
Cuius fructus ventris	Anon.	Iso	Aosta Dijon 2837 Q15.231	Cox
Descendi in ortum	Anon.	Dev D-D	Q15.191	Burstyn Nosow
Descendi in ortum	Dunstaple	Eng cant II Trans 4-v	Lo 54324 Maidstone	Dunstable

Index of works

Title	Composer	Subgenre(s)	Sources	Editions
Descendi in ortum	Lymburgia	Cont cant Cut-circle	Q15.183	Burstyn Etheridge Lewis
Descendi in ortum	Plummer	Eng cant II	90.1030 90.995 Bux Mod 105′ Olc89	EDM 38 Plummer
Deus decorum inclite	Anon.	Ch ctfact?	89.603	—
Dies dignus/Demon dolens	Dunstaple	Eng Iso 3v	Mod 92′	Dunstable
Doctorum principem	Ciconia	Italian	Q15.272	Ciconia Clercx Cox
Dominicus a dono	Monte, Cristoforus de	Italian	Q15.220	Cox Ex. 4.1
Ducalis sedes	Romanus	Italian	B2216 Q15.243	Cox Reaney VI Romano Schering
Ecclesie militantis	Du Fay	Iso 5v	87.53&70	DufayB I DufayV II
Ego dormio	Anon.	Eng cant II	88.211	—
Elizabet Zacharie	Du Fay?	Iso	87.143	DTÖ 76
Excelsa civitas Vincencia	Feragut	Cut-circle	Ox 213 Q15.271	Cox *PS* Reaney VII Vicenza
Flos de spina	Puyllois	4-v free	90.1122 CS 15 Milan 1 SP B80 Strah	Ex. 11.5 Pullois
Flos florum	Du Fay	Cut-circle	Mod 56′ Ox 213 Q15.234	Cox DufayB I DufayV I Hüschen Nosow
Flos virginum/M. Coda di Pavon	Martini	4-v song Ctfact Gl.	91.1288	AMMM 12
Fortis cum quaevis actio	Brassart	Other D-D	87.50 Ox 213	Brassart
Fulgens iubar	Du Fay	Iso 1D	Mod 121′	DufayB I DufayV II
Gaude Dei genitrix	Anon.	Other D-D	922.1527 Ox 213	PS

Title	Composer	Subgenre(s)	Sources	Editions
Gaude felix Anna/ Gaude mater	Dunstaple	Eng Iso 3v	Mod 129'	Dunstable
Gaude felix Padua	Lymburgia	Cut-circle	Q15.288	Illegible
Gaude flore virginali	Anon.	4-v free	89.617–18	—
Gaude Maria/T: Meditatio	Anon.	4-v T Ctfact k?	88.416–17	—
Gaude Maria/T: Esclave puist	Anon.	4-v T	88.496	Gerber
Gaude martyr/Collaudemus	Forest	Eng Iso 3v	Mod 126'	—
Gaude regina	Anon.	4-v free	89.582	—
Gaude tu baptista	Benoit	Iso	Q15.195	Cox Reaney III
Gaude virgo Katerina	Dunstaple	Eng cant I	Mod 84'	Dunstable
Gaude virgo mater	Du Fay	Dev D-D	MuEm Q15.193	DufayB V
Gaude virgo	Anon.	Eng cant I	87.97	—
Gaude virgo/Gaude virgo	Dunstaple	Eng Iso	Mod 113'	Dunstable
Gaudeat ecclesia	Quadris, Johannes de	Other D-D	88.207 Gaffurius	DTÖ 76 Quadris
Gloria sanctorum	Dunstaple	Eng cant I	Mod 112'	Dunstable
Gloriose virginis	Power	Other D-D	F112bis Mod 74	Power
Gregatim grex	Anon.	4-v free	89.580–1	DTÖ 76
Hac clara die	Anon.	3-v T Eng Iso 3v	92.1498	DTÖ 76
Hec dies	Anon.	Borderline	Q15.190	—
Ibo michi ad montem	Anon.	Eng cant II	90.991–2	Burstyn Scott
Ibo michi ad montem	Anon.	Other D-D	Ithaca MuEm	—
Ibo michi ad montem	Power	Eng cant I	Mod 98'	Power
Ibo michi ad montem	Stone	Eng cant II	Mod 104'	Burstyn
Ihesu salvator	Salinis	Retro D-D	F2211 Ox 213 Q15.213 Str	Cox Ex. 6.2 *PS* Reaney VII
Imera dat hodierno	Grossin	Cut-circle Declamation	92.1481 B2216 MuEm Ox 213 Par 4379 Q15.203	Cox DTÖ 14 Reaney III
In hac die celebri	Lymburgia	Cut-circle	Q15.189	Cox Etheridge

Title	Composer	Subgenre(s)	Sources	Editions
In hydraulis	Busnoys	4-v T	91.1162 Mu 3154	Busnoys DTÖ 14 EDM 80
In Pharaonis atrio	Anon.	Declamation	MuEm Q15.249	Cox
Inclita stella maris	Du Fay	Other D-D	Q15.173	Cox DufayB I DufayV I
Jhesu Christe/M. Coda di pavon	Martini	4-v song Ctfact Ag.	91.1289	AMMM 12
Jhesus postquam	Brixia, Matheus de	Italian	Q15.221	Cox NosowEqual Vicenza
Lamberte vir inclite	Brassart?	Other D-D	87.47 Aosta	Brassart DTÖ 76
Levavi oculos	Anon.	4-v free	89.656	—
Lux fulget ex Anglia/ O pater	Benet	Eng Iso 3v	Mod 135'	Cantilupe
Magnanime/Nexus	Du Fay	3-v T Iso 3v	Mod 63'	DufayB I DufayV II
Magne decus potencie	Brassart	Iso	Q15.252	Brassart Cox
Martires dei incliti	Lymburgia	Cut-circle	Q15.186	Cox Etheridge Vicenza
Mater dulcis mater pia	Grossin	Iso	Mod 69'	Reaney III
Mater ora filium	Power	Eng cant I	92.1505 922.1536 Mod 110	DTÖ 14 Power
Mirandas parit or Imperatrix	Du Fay	Other D-D	88.212 Mod 62'	DufayB I DufayV I
Missa Ad fugam reservatam	Standley	Canon Mass	88	DPLSER I Loyan
Missa Alma redemptoris mater	Power	Tenor Mass	87 90 93 Aosta	DPLSER I PowerMass
Missa Ave regina celorum	Du Fay	Tenor Mass	Br 5557 ModD Poz7022 SP B80	DufayB III MPLSER
Missa Caput	Anon.	Tenor Mass	88 89 90 93 Coventry	DufayB II MPLSER Planchart

Title	Composer	Subgenre(s)	Sources	Editions
Missa Caput (*cont.*)			Lo 54324	
			Lucca	
Missa Coda di pavon	Martini	Tenor Mass	Milan 2	AMMM 12
			ModD	
			Siena	
Missa Esclave puist	Anon.	Tenor Mass	88	Gerber
Missa Hilf und gib rat	Philipus	Tenor Mass	Strah	Snow
Missa Meditatio cordis	Anon.	Tenor Mass	Strah	Snow
Missa O rosa bella (I)	Anon.	Tenor Mass	88	DTÖ 22
			Lucca	
Missa O rosa bella (III)	Anon.	Tenor Mass	89	DTÖ 22
			Strah	
Missa sine nomine	Puyllois	Mass	87	Pullois
			90	
			93	
			Mu 3154	
			Strah	
Missa So ys emprentid	Le Rouge	Tenor Mass	90	—
			SP B80	
Missa Summe trinitati	Frye	Tenor Mass	Br 5557	EECM 34
				Frye
Missa Verbum or O pulcherrima	Lantins, A. de	Mass	B2216	*PS*
			MuEm	Widaman
			Ox 213	
			Q15	
Missus est Gabriel	Rubeus	Italian	Q15.200	Reaney V
Mon chier amy	Du Fay	Ballade	Ox 213	DufayB VI
Moribus et genere	Du Fay	Iso 1D	Mod 74'	DufayB I
				DufayV II
Nesciens mater	Anon.	Eng cant II	90.1143–4	Gozzi
Nova vobis gaudia	Grenon	Iso	Q15.176	Cox
				Marix
Nove cantum melodie	Binchois	Iso 1D	Mod 71	Binchois
				Marix
Nuper rosarum	Du Fay	Iso 1D	92.1381	DufayB I
			Mod 67'	DufayV II
O admirabile commercium	Anon.	Eng cant I	92.1492	—
O baptista mirabilis	Lymburgia	Cut-circle	Q15.286	Illegible
O beata infantia	Anon.	4-v ch par	89.639	EDM 80
			CS 15	
			CS 44	
			Mu 3154	
			SP B80	
O beate Sebastiane	Anon.	Ch ctfact?	90.1078	Gozzi

Index of works

Title	Composer	Subgenre(s)	Sources	Editions
O beate Sebastiane	Du Fay	Cut-circle	Mod 58′ Q15.292	DufayB I DufayV I
O beatum incendium	Ciconia	Border 2v	PadB Q15.255	Ciconia Clercx Cox
O castitatis lilium or Advocata	Touront	Song motet	89.599 Glog Spec	EDM 85
O crux gloriosa	Dunstaple	Eng cant I	922.1523 Mod 119′	DTÖ 14 Dunstable
O domina gloriosa	Verben	Cut-circle	87.150	DTÖ 76
O dulcis Jhesu memoria	Anon.	Song motet	89.777	—
O felix flos Florentia	Civitato, Antonius de	Italian	Q15.208	Cox Reaney V
O felix templum	Ciconia	Italian	Ox 213 Q15.216	Ciconia Clercx Cox Hüschen PS
O florens rosa	Anon.	4-v song	89.654	—
O florens rosa	Touront	Song motet	88.426 Sched Strah	DTÖ 14
O florens rosa or Ave regina	Frye	Eng cant II	90.1087 Sched Strah (2x)	Frye
O flos fragrans	Brassart	Cut-circle	87.129 Ox 213 Q15.264	Brassart Cox DTÖ 14
O flos in divo	Loqueville	Iso	Q15.253	Cox Reaney III
O gemma lux	Du Fay	Iso	Ox 213 Q15.263	Cox DufayB I DufayV II
O gloriosa et laudabilis	Anon.	Ch ctfact?	89.661	—
O gloriosa regina	Touront	Song motet	91.1298 Bol Q16 Cas F2356 FPanc Paris 676 Per 431 Pix SevP Strah Verona 757	DTÖ 14 Vincenet
O gloriose tiro	Du Fay?	Iso 1D	Mod 65′	DufayB I DufayV II
O lux et decus	Lantins, H. de	Cut-circle	Q15.181	Allsenlnt

392

Title	Composer	Subgenre(s)	Sources	Editions
O Maria maris stella	Lymburgia	Cut-circle	Q15.284	Cox Etheridge
O Maria virgo davitica	Anon.	Italian	MuEm PadD Q15.227	Cox Plamenac
O Padua sidus	Ciconia	Italian	Q15.256	Ciconia Clercx Cox
O pater eterne/ T: O rosa bella	Anon.	4-v T	Milan 1 Strah	SnowCycle
O Petre Christi discipule	Ciconia	Border 2v	Q15.258	Ciconia Clercx Cox
O pia virgo Fides	Anon.	Iso	Mod 72′	Allsen
O proles/O sidus	Du Fay	Cut-circle Trans 4-v	87.88 88.347 Mod 60′	DufayB I DufayV I
O pulcherrima	Anon.	Eng cant II Trans 4-v	88.239 93.1838 BerK Columbia F2356 Krakow 8a Lucca Pix Sched SevP (ind)	Burstyn StrohmB
O pulcherrima	Lantins, A. de	Cut-circle	B2216 Ox 213 Q15.178	*PS*
O quam luce glorifica	Anon.	4-v free	88.238	Gerber
O quam mirabilis	Sarto, Johannes de	Cut-circle	922.1528 Ox 213 Q15.276	Cox DTÖ 14
O sacrum convivium	Anon.	Cont cant	88.489	—
O sacrum manna	Anon.	Iso	89.590	DTÖ 76
O sancte Sebastiane	Du Fay	Iso	Ox 213 Q15.211	Cox DufayB I DufayV II
O sanctissime presul	Anon.	3-v T	92.1506	DTÖ 76 StrohmB
O sidus Hispanie	Anon.	Other D-D Trans 5-v	88.346	DTÖ 76
O tres piteulx or Lamentatio	Du Fay	4-v T	F2794 MC	DufayB VI MC
O virum omnimoda	Ciconia	Italian	B2216 Q15.254 Siena 36	Ciconia Clercx Cox
Odas clangat	Anon.	4-v free	89.577–8	—

Index of works

Title	Composer	Subgenre(s)	Sources	Editions
Omnium bonorum plena	Compère	4-v T	91.1161 SP B80	Compère DTÖ 14
Ostendit mihi	Lymburgia	Cut-circle	Q15.167	Etheridge
Perfunde celi rore	Martini	4-v free	91.1169	AMMM 12
Perpulchra Sion filia	Anon.	4-v T	89.615	—
Petrum Marcello venetum	Ciconia	Italian	Q15.245	Ciconia Clercx Cox
Pie pater Dominice	Civitato, Antonius de	Italian	Q15.242	Cox Reaney V
Plasmatoris humani	Grenon	Iso	Q15.223	Cox
Plaude decus	Monte, Cristoforus de	Italian	Q15.215	Cox DTÖ 76
Preco/Precursor	Dunstaple	Eng Iso	922.1538 Cant 128 Mod 127'	DTÖ 76 Dunstable
Prevalet simplicitas	Ruttis	Retro D-D	Ox 213 Q15.261	Cox PS
Primi pulchri	Arimino, Ludovicus de	Ch ctfact?	87.141	—
Protegat nos divina maiestas	Anon.	Ch ctfact?	87.111	—
Psallat chorus	Salinis	Retro D-D	F2211 Q15.247	Cox Reaney VII
Puer natus	Lymburgia	Dev D-D	Q15.205	Etheridge
Pulchra es amica mea	Lymburgia	Cut-circle	Q15.177	Burstyn Etheridge Lewis
Quae est ista	Standley?	Canon 3v	89.576	DPLSER IV Loyan
Qualis est dilectus	Anon.	Eng cant II	88.445	Burstyn
Qualis est dilectus	Forest/Plummer	Eng cant I	90.1049 93.1829 Mod 108' OH	OH
Quam pulchra es	Anon.	Eng cant II	90.1053	Burstyn
Quam pulchra es	Anon.	Eng cant II	88.444	Burstyn
Quam pulchra es	Anon.	Eng cant II	89.655	Burstyn
Quam pulchra es	Dunstaple	Declamation Eng cant I	92.1465 Aosta B2216 Mod 81' MuEm Pemb Q15.291	Dunstable Schering
Quam pulchra es	Piamor	Eng cant I	922.1526 Mod 93'	Burstyn Marrocco

Title	Composer	Subgenre(s)	Sources	Editions
Quam pulchra es	Power	Eng cant I	Mod 111′	Power
Recordare virgo	Lymburgia	Borderline	Q15.270	Etheridge
Recordare virgo	Touront	4-v ch par	89.591–2 Glog Spec Strah	EDM 85
Regali ex progenie	Anon.	3-v T	92.1494	Ex. 10.4
Regina celi	Anglicanus	Eng cant I	922.1576	—
Regina celi	Anon.	Eng cant I	Q15.238	Power
Regina celi	Anon.	Cont cant	88.363	—
Regina celi	Anon.	4-v free	89.583–4	—
Regina celi	Anon.	4-v ch par	89.637	—
Regina celi	Brassart	Cont cant	87.158–9	Brassart
Regina celi	Dunstaple	Eng cant I	Aosta F112bis Mu 3224 Q15.280	DTÖ 76 Dunstable
Regina celi	Lymburgia	Cont cant	Q15.199	Etheridge
Regina celi	Power	Eng cant I	90.1136 92.1507	Power
Regis celorum	Anon.	Canon 5v	89.587–9	Loyan
Resvellies vous	Du Fay	Ballade	Ox 213	DufayB VI
Rite maiorem	Du Fay	Iso	Q15.174	Cox DufayB I DufayV II
Romanorum rex	Sarto, Johannes de	Iso 1D	Aosta Del Lago	Brassart
Salve cara Deo tellus	Arimino, Ludovicus de	Cut-circle	87.144	DTÖ 76 Disertori Nosow Stevens
Salve flos Tuscae gentes	Du Fay	Iso 1D	Mod 64′	DufayB I DufayV II
Salve mater misericordie	Dupont	Cont cant	92.1495	—
Salve mater salvatoris	Power/Dunstaple	Eng cant I	922.1544 922.1562 Mod 116′	DTÖ 76 Dunstable Power
Salve pater creator	Carmen	Iso	Q15.246	Cox Reaney I
Salve regina	Anon.	Eng cant II	90.1025–6 Antwerp F112bis	DTÖ 53
Salve regina	Anon.	Eng cant II	90.1038 Antwerp	DTÖ 53
Salve regina	Anon.	Eng cant I	922.1575	DTÖ 53

Index of works

Title	Composer	Subgenre(s)	Sources	Editions
Salve regina	Anon.	Cont cant	93.1653	—
Salve regina	Anon.	4-v ch par	88.235	DTÖ 53
Salve regina	Anon.	Eng cant II	88.343	DTÖ 53
Salve regina	Anon.	Canon 3v	89.566	Loyan
Salve regina	Anon.	Cont cant	89.730	DTÖ 53
Salve regina	Du Fay[?]	4-v ch par	89.727 Milan 1 Mu 3154	DTÖ 14 EDM 81
Salve regina	Dunstaple	Eng cant I	87.24 Mod 82′	DTÖ 53 Dunstable
Salve regina	Power	Eng cant I	Q15.240	Power
Salve regina	Power/Dunstaple	Eng cant I	90.1081 922.1577 Aosta Columbia Lo 5665 Mod 86′	DTÖ 14 Dunstable Power
Salve regina	Reson	Cont cant	B2216 Q15.179	CoxPseudo Reaney II
Salve regina	Salinis	Unus-chorus	Q15.232	Reaney VII
Salve regina mater mire	Dunstaple	3-v T Eng cant I	Mod 91′	DTÖ 76 Dunstable
Salve regina peccatorum	Anon.	Cont cant	Mod 69	—
Salve regina/ T: Hilf und gib	Philipus	4-v T Ctfact K?	89.729 Strah	DTÖ 53 Snow
Salve regina/ T: Le serviteur	Anon.	4-v T	89.638	DTÖ 53
Salve scema	Dunstaple	Eng Iso	Mod 123′	DTÖ 76 Dunstable
Salve vere gracialis	Anon.	Cut-circle	Q15.188	Cox
Salve virgo mater/ T: Summe	Frye?	3-v T Ctfact K?	88.240	EECM 34 Frye Gerber
Sancta dei genitrix	Dunstaple	Eng cant I	Mod 89′	Dunstable
Sancta Maria non est tibi	Anon.	Eng cant I	87.130 922.1574	—
Sancta Maria non est tibi	Dunstaple	Eng cant I	922.1542 Mod 115	DTÖ 14 Dunstable
Sancta Maria succurre	Dunstaple	Eng cant I	87.104 90.1051 92.1502 Aosta Mod 136′	DTÖ 76 Dunstable
Sanctus itaque patriarcha	Civitato, Antonius de	Italian	Q15.274	Cox Reaney V
Si nichil actuleris	Salinis	Retro D-D	F2211 Q15.278	Cox Reaney VII

Title	Composer	Subgenre(s)	Sources	Editions
Specialis virgo	Dunstaple	3-v T Eng Iso 3v	92.1500 Mod 81	DTÖ 76 Dunstable
Speciosa facta es	Dunstaple	Eng cant I	922.1535 Mod 100A'	DTÖ 76 Dunstable
Spes nostra	Anon.	Eng cant I	Q15.184	Power
Stella celi/T: So ys	Le Rouge?	4-v T	88.204	—
Sub Arturo plebs	Alanus	Eng Iso 3v	Chantilly Q15.218 Yox	Cox DTÖ 76 Günther PMFC 5
Sub tuam protectionem	Dunstaple	Eng cant I	92.1463 Aosta Bux (2x) Mod 115' Q15.290	DTÖ 14 Dunstable EDM 37 EDM 38
Sub tuum presidium	Anon.	Eng cant II	90.1135	Gozzi
Summe summy	Velut	Retro D-D	87.33 Q15.260	Cox DTÖ 14 Reaney II
Summus secretarius	Brassart	Other D-D	Ox 213 Q15.275	Brassart Cox *PS*
Supremum est	Du Fay	3-v T Iso 3v	92.1391 B2216 Cop 17 Mod 66' MuEm Q15.168	Cox DTÖ 76 DufayB I DufayV II
Surge propera	Lymburgia	Cut-circle Dev D-D	Q15.204	Burstyn Etheridge Lewis
Surrexit Christus	Lymburgia	Unus-chorus	Q15.175	Etheridge
Te dignitas presularis	Brassart	Cut-circle	87.49 Q15.267	Brassart Cox DTÖ 76
Tellus/Splendida	Benet	Eng Iso 3v	Mod 125'	IMM3
Tota pulchra	Anon.	Eng cant II	88.446–7	Burstyn
Tota pulchra	Anon.	Eng cant II	88.448–9	Burstyn
Tota pulchra	Forest	Eng cant I	92.1459 Mod 99'	Burstyn DTÖ 76
Tota pulchra	Lantins, A. de	Cut-circle Declamation Dev D-D	B2216 MuEm Ox 213 Par 4379 Q15.202 Str	Ex. 6.1 *PS*

Index of works

Title	Composer	Subgenre(s)	Sources	Editions
Tota pulchra	Lymburgia	Dev D-D	Q15.197	Burstyn Etheridge Lewis
Tota pulchra	Plummer	Eng cant II	90.1050 Mod 120' Ob26	EECM 8 Plummer
Tota pulchra	Plummer	Eng cant II	Lucca Mod 101' Spec	Plummer
Tota pulchra	Stone	Eng cant II	Mod 103'	Burstyn
Tu ne quesieris	Anon.	4-v song	89.616	DTÖ 14
Tu nephanda prodigio	Lymburgia	Retro D-D	Q15.171	Cox Etheridge
Ut te per omnes	Ciconia	Italian	Ox 213 Q15.259	Ciconia Clercx Cox *PS*
Vassilissa ergo gaude	Du Fay	Iso	87.37 Ox 213 Q15.244	Cox DTÖ 53 DufayB I DufayV II
Venecie mundi splendor	Ciconia	Italian	Q15.257	Ciconia Clercx Cox
Veni dilecte my	Lymburgia/Du Fay	Declamation	87.100 Aosta Q15.279	DufayB I DufayV I Etheridge
Veni sancte/Consolator	Dunstaple	3-v T Eng Iso 3v	922.1543 Mod 131'	DTÖ 14 Dunstable
Veni sancte/Veni creator	Dunstaple	Eng Iso	922.1537 Aosta Mod 106' Mu 3224 OH	DTÖ 14 Dunstable OH
Venite adoremus	Carmen	Iso	Ox 213 Q15.217	Cox *PS* Reaney I
Verbum tuum	Rondelly	Iso	Q15.251	Cox
Vergene bella	Du Fay	Cut-circle	B2216 Ox 213 Q15.201	DufayB VI
Vidi speciosam	Anon.	4-v T/chpar	CS 15 Lucca	Ex. 12.6*
Virgo Maria non est tibi	Anon.	Ch ctfact?	93.1840	—
Virgo mater ecclesie	Anon.	Eng cant II	90.1061–2	Cattin Gozzi

Title	Composer	Subgenre(s)	Sources	Editions
Virgo prefulgens	Sandley/Binchois	3-v T Eng cant I	92.1545 Mod 132'	Binchois Marix
Virgo prudentissima or Salve	Power	Eng cant I	92.1456 Mod 109'	Power

Index

A slash between composers' names indicates conflicting attribution; a question mark indicates uncertainty of attribution or identification.

Frye/Bedingham
 So ys emprentid/Sancta Maria, 178, 258, 260
Frye, Walter, 185, 192–3, 201, 205, 255, 256,
  264–5, 265, 294
 Ave regina celorum mater, 177, 189, 192, 202,
  238, 292, 305 (Appendix)
  added voices, 232, 233, 235–6, 239, 256
 Missa So ys emprentid, 350 n.7
 Missa Summe trinitati, 180, 258, 264–5
 O florens rosa/Ave regina, 180, 181, 189, 193,
  342 n.25
 Salve virgo/T. Summe trinitati, 180, 216, 223,
  258, 265, 350 n.8, 354 n.51

Gaffurius, Franchinus, 229
Gayus
 Dyana, lux serena, 179
genealogy setting, 173
genre
 generic mixture, 156, 157, 158–9
 generic repertory, 27–40, 67
 hierarchy, 26, 40, 42–3, 121, 284, 285, 286
 identification or recognition, *see*
  classification
 as species, 18
 theory, 7, 9, 11
 see also categories; evolution, analogies
  with; family resemblance
Gerber, Rebecca, 173
Gerona, Duke of, 45
Gonzaga, Francesco, 73
Grenon, Nicholas, 65
 Ad honorem/Celorum regnum, 83
 Nova vobis gaudia, 83
 Plamatoris/Verbigine mater, 83
Grossin, Etienne, 330 n.20
 Imera dat hodierno, 110, 118, 121–2, 126,
  196, 305 (Appendix)

Habsburgs, 58, 290
Hack, Georg, Bishop of Trent, 200, 258,
 261
Hamm, Charles, 90, 186, 189

Hayne van Ghizeghem
 De tous biens pleine, 258, 262
hedges, 14
Hinderbach, Johannes, Provost of Trent
 Cathedral, 170
Horace
 Tu ne quesieris, 255, 256, 350 n.2
horizon of expectation, 24–25, 27, 39, 154,
 155
Horlay
 Puisque je suis infortunee, 248
Hundred Years War, 184
hymn settings, 48–9, 51–4, 59, 65, 67, 87, 132,
 159, 167
 by Du Fay, 317 n.37
 in the Trent Codices, 172–3

imitation, 80, 140–1, 202, 204, 230, 245, 250,
 268–70, 273, 276, 286, 296
 see also echo imitation
improvised polyphony, 26, 31, 127, 289
instrumental music, 176, 201, 255–6, 265,
 284, 294
Insula, Simon de
 Missa O admirabile commercium, 249, 349 n.37
introits, 172–3
introitus, 80, 140, 225, 283, 323 n.36
Isaac, Heinrich, 44, 202
 O decus ecclesie virgo, 351 n.17
 Palle, palle, 351 n.17
 Rogamus te (La mi la sol), 351 n.17
isorhythm, 15, 26, 34, 213–14, 314 n.24, 323
 n.34
 definition, 82
isorhythmic motet, 257, 266, 285
 with double-discantus texture, 207–8, 208
  (Table 10.1)
 features, 15
 with a single discantus, **208–15**, 209
  (Table 10.2), 294
 see also English isorhythmic motet; French
  isorhythmic motet; motet,
  fourteenth-century

Lymburgia, Johannes de (*cont.*)
 Descendi in ortum, 110, 116 (Ex. 5.4a), 131,
  145, 331 n.34
 Gaude felix Padua (St. Anthony of Padua),
  109, 111
 In hac die celebri (St. George), 110, 330 n.24
 Imnizabo regi meo, 321 n.12
 Magne dies leticie, 321 n.11
 Martires dei incliti (Sts. Leontius and
  Carpophorus), 111
 Mass, 118–19
 O baptista mirabilis (St. John the Baptist),
  109, 111
 O Maria maris stella, 110, 115, 118, 314 n.27
 Ostendit mihi angelus, 110, 320 n.8
 Puer natus in Bethleem, 139, 334–5 n.21
 Pulchra es amica mea, 110, 118, 145
 Recordare virgo mater, 143
 Regina celi, 131
 Surge propera, 110, 112 (Ex.5.2d), 117, 139,
  141, 145
 Surrexit Christus hodie, 132, 133
 Tota pulchra, 139, 140 (Ex. 6.3), 141, 145,
  225, 256
 Tu nephanda/Si inimicus, 135, 136, 334 n.18

Magnificat settings, 45–7, 48, 52, 55, 59, 65,
  167, 171
 in the Trent Codices, 173
Malatesta family, 109, 120
 Carlo (da Pesaro), 119
 Cleofe, 83
 Pandolfo (da Rimini), 83, 120
Malipiero, Francesco (bishop of Vicenza),
  111 (Feragut, *Excelsa civitas Vincencia*)
manuscripts containing motets, 56–7 (Table
  3.2)
 all-purpose collections, 55–8
 Central and Eastern European, 55–8, 60
 chapel manuscripts, 58, 59
 and Masses, 58–9
 presentation manuscripts, 58
 and secular music, 59

and Vespers music, 59
manuscripts of music, *see* 379–81 for
  complete shelf numbers and sigla
Aosta, 56, 58, 126, 148, 149 (Table 7.1),
  153, 169, 208, 215
Apel Codex, 57, 170
Berlin 40021, 48, 52–3, 57, 170
Bologna 2216, 55, 56, 126, 127, 148, 149
  (Table 7.1), 289
 organization, 65
Bologna Q15, 3, 45, 55, 56, **65–7**, 149
  (Table 7.1), 169, 207, 288
 compared to contemporary
  manuscripts, 148–54, 181–3
 copying, 66–7
 date, 65
 double-discantus texture in, 228
 English music in, 96, 153
 organization, 65, 66
 provenance, 66
 scribe, 65, 66, 146, 147, 151, 152, 154
Bologna Q18, 319 n.59
Breslau 2016, 57
Brussels 5557, 56, 58, 319 n.56
Brussels 9126, 57, 58
Chantilly, 45, 55
Chigi, 57, 58
CS 15, 57, 59, 183, 254
CS 35, 57, 58, 319 n.56
CS 63, 57
Cypriot, 45
Escorial IV.a.24, 248
Eton choirbook, 281
F112bis, 56, 59, 319 n.59
F2211 (San Lorenzo 2211), 134, 136
Glogauer, 56, 176, 201, 202
Leipzig 1494, *see* Apel Codex
Leopold Codex, *see* Munich 3154
Lucca, 56, 58, 276
MC, 57
Milan 1, 57, 59
Milan 1-4 (Gaffurius Codices), 183, 254
Milan 2, 57, 58, 319 n.56